NEEDLEWORK
BY
LADY M. ALFORD

DEDICATED BY PERMISSION

TO

THE QUEEN.

TO
THE QUEEN.

Your Majesty's most gracious acceptance of the Dedication of my book on "Needlework as Art" casts a light upon the subject that shows its worthiness, and my inability to do it justice. Still, I hope I may fill a gap in the artistic literature of our day, and I venture to lay my work at your Majesty's feet with loyal devotion.

MARIAN M. ALFORD.

[vii]

PREFACE.

In the Preface to the "Handbook of Art Needlework," which I edited for the Royal School at South Kensington in 1880, I undertook to write a second part, to be devoted to design, colour, and the common-sense modes of treating decorative art, as applied especially to embroidered hangings, furniture, dress, and the smaller objects of luxury.

Circumstances have, since then, obliged me to reconsider this intention; and I have found it more practicable to cast the information which I have collected from Eastern and Western sources into the form of a separate work, which in no way supersedes or interferes with the technical instruction supposed to be conveyed in a handbook. I have found so much amusement in learning for myself the history of the art of embroidery, and in tracing the beginnings and the interchanges of national schools, that I cannot but hope that I may excite a similar interest in some of my readers, and so induce those who are capable, to help and lift it to a higher place than it has been allowed in these latter days to occupy. If I have given too important a position to the art of needlework, I would observe that while I have been writing, decorative embroidery has come to the front, and is at this moment one of the hobbies of the day; and I would point out that it contains in itself all the [viii]necessary elements of art; it may exercise the imagination and the fancy; it needs education in form, colour, and composition, as well as the craft of a practised hand, to express its language and perfect its beauty.

I confess that when I undertook this task, I did not anticipate the time I have had to spend in collecting and epitomizing the many notices to be found in German, French, and English authors, on what has been considered among us, at least in this century, as merely a secondary art, and therefore, as such, of little importance. Cursory notices of needlework are scattered through almost every book on art; and under the head of textiles it is usual to find embroidery acknowledged as being worthy of notice, though not to be named in company with sculpture, architecture, or painting, however beautifully or thoughtfully its works may be carried out. I have tried to show that it deserves higher estimation.

My first intention was simply to consider STYLE, good or bad, as it influences our embroidery of to-day, and to find some rules by which to guide that of the future in its next phase. But when we search into the fluctuations of style, and their causes, we find they have an historical succession, and that we must begin at the beginning and trace them through the life of mankind.

This led me to attempt a sketch of consecutive styles, their overlap and variations.

I then found that DESIGN, PATTERNS, STITCHES, MATERIALS, each require a separate study.

COLOUR, as applied to dyes, claims to be regarded as differing from pigments on the painter's palette.

HANGINGS, DRESS, and ECCLESIASTICAL EMBROIDERIES each require different rules, and the study of the best examples of past centuries. Finally, it seems natural to dwell on our own proficiency in decorative work. ENGLISH EMBROIDERY has always excelled;

and, as we [ix]have again returned to this occupation, it is worth while to recollect what we have done of old.

In writing chapters on these subjects, I have found it most convenient to separate the historical and æsthetic questions from the technical rules, and the instruction which naturally belongs to a handbook, of which the purpose should be to teach the easiest and most orthodox manner of executing the simplest, and elaborating the finest works. Such questions ought not to be overlaid with archæological inquiries, or with the information which only profits the designer; though of course it is best that the knowledge of design should be part of the education of the craft.

Perhaps I may be found to have written a book too shallow for the learned, too deep for the frivolous, too technical for the general public, and too diffuse for the specialist of the craft.[1]

I must deprecate these criticisms by saying that I have written it for the benefit of those who know nothing of the art, and are too much engaged to seek information here and there; who yet, being women, have to select and to execute ornamental needlework; or, being artists, are vexed at the incongruities and want of intention in the decorations in daily domestic use; I have also sought to help the designer, that he or she may know something of the history of patterns and stitches.

[x]If my readers should be aware of repetitions, they must forgive them; remembering that the same idea has to be looked at sometimes from a different point of view, according to the use to which it is to be fitted. The same material may be employed for wall-hangings and dress, and then the principles which have been formulated have to be varied. I do not shrink from repetitions if they make my meaning clear, remembering the Duke of Wellington's direction to his private secretary, "Never mind repetitions; and *dot* your i's."

Portions of these chapters have been already published in No. 49 of the *Nineteenth Century*,[2] in 1881; and more was delivered in three unpublished lectures the same year.

I have acknowledged and noted on each page my authorities for the facts I have quoted. The illustrations that are not original, have been copied from other works by permission of authors and publishers. To all of these I wish to express my obligations and thanks, especially to Mr. Villiers Stuart, Dr. Anderson, Sir G. Birdwood, and Sir H. Layard, for their courtesy in allowing me the use of their plates. To my old and valued friend, Mr. Newton, I wish to express my gratitude for his unstinted gifts of time and trouble, bestowed in criticizing and correcting my book, encouraging me to give it to the public, and making it more worthy of publication.

I have largely quoted Charles Blanc ("Ornament in Dress," English translation), Von Bock ("Liturgische Gewänder"), Dr. Rock ("The Church of our Fathers" and "Introduction to Textiles"), Semper ("Der Stil"), Yates ("Textrinum Antiquorum"), and Yule ("Marco Polo"), besides many others. But these authorities often differ, and, after weighing their arguments, I have ventured to select for my use the facts and theories [xi]which accord with my own views. Facts are often so interdependent and closely linked, that it requires great care to distinguish where they have been shaped or coloured (however unintentionally) to fit each other or the writer's preconceived ideas. Certain it is that facts are but useless heaps till the thread of a theory is found on which to hang them. This process, like that of stringing pearls, has to be often repeated, till each occupies its right place. Only those who have adopted and cherished a theory can appreciate the pain of cutting the thread, to displace what appeared to be a pearl, but which, from its false position as to date or place, or its doubtful origin, has proved only an empty manufactured glass bead of error.

This has happened to me more than once; and since I read my lectures I have had to change my opinions in several instances. If, therefore, any of my readers should observe such changes, I hope they will give me credit for trying to convey *now* what appears to me on each subject a correct impression.

FOOTNOTES:

[1]Besides the art, I have sought to give something of the archæology of needlework. Now the qualifications for being a teacher on such subjects are rarely to be met with, all combined. Mr. Newton, in his "Essays on Art and Archæology," p. 37, says that "the archæologist should combine with the æsthetic culture of the artist, and the trained judgment

2

of the historian and the philologist, that critical acumen, required for classification and interpretation; nor should that habitual suspicion which must ever attend the scrutiny and precede the warranty of evidence, give too sceptical a bias to his mind." Such authorities have been interrogated on each part of my subject.

[2]Quoted by permission of the Editor.

NEEDLEWORK AS ART.
INTRODUCTION.

The book of the Science of Art has yet to be written. Art has been called the Flower of Life, and also the Consoler;—adorning the existence of the strong and bright,—sheltering and comforting the sad and solitary ones of the earth. But, rather, it resembles a wide-spreading tree, covered with varied blossoms—bearing many fruits.

To point out the history and the possibilities in the future of each branch that shades, refreshes, and gives wholesome fruit to the world, would be a task worthy of a master-hand and a pen of gold. But less ambitious labourers in the field of investigation which is only as yet partly cultivated, may each assist, by carefully collecting a little heap of ascertained facts; and it is, indeed, the duty of each as he passes to add his pebble to the slowly accumulating cairn of recorded human knowledge.

Some one has said, "Build your house of little bricks of facts, and you will soon find it inhabited by a body of truth; and that truth will ally itself with other houses of facts, and in time a well-ordered, cosmical city will arise."

My pebble is not yet polished. It is neither a diamond nor a ruby, but I think there are a few streaks of golden light in it, which I may venture to add to the daily [2]accumulating treasure in the house of human artistic knowledge.

My object in writing this volume is to fill up an empty space in the English library of art.

The great exponents of poetic thought—verse, sculpture, painting, and architecture—have long since been well interpreted and appreciated. Men and women have written much and well on these large subjects, and we may hope for more ere long. The secondary or smaller arts have been hitherto neglected by us,—either treated merely as crafts, to which artistic education may give help, or as the natural or inferior outcome of the primal arts, having no claim to the possession of special laws and history. And yet, when Moses wrote and Homer sang, needlework was no new thing. It was already consecrated by legendary and traditionary custom to the highest uses. The gods themselves were honoured by its service, and it preceded written history in recording heroic deeds and national triumphs.

It may be said that ivory carving is sculpture, and illuminated manuscripts and coloured glass windows are painting. But for metal work, whether in iron or gold, a place must be kept apart; and the same privileges are due to embroidery and to metallurgy. All arts must of necessity have their own laws and rules, which ensure their beauty of execution and their special forms of design; these two last, from the nature of their materials, and the modes of working them, must be studied independently of any connection with painting, architecture, or sculpture.

Yet, if the unity of nature is an accepted fact,[3] then the acceptance of the unity of art must follow. Art must be considered as the selection of natural phenomena by individual minds capable of assimilating and reproducing them in certain forms and with certain materials [3]adapted to the national taste, needs, and power of appreciation. If man cannot originate materials, he can invent combinations;—and this is Art.

If proportion, colour, and sound alike depend on certain mathematical measurements, and on rhythmical vibrations, there must be a real and tangible relation between these elements, though applied to obtain different results. In music, as in all art, harmony is, or ought to be, a first consideration. We have seen by experiment how a note of our scale can by touch form geometrical figures with sand on a sheet of glass,—here form obeys the force of harmony. But what is harmony?

By analogy we may argue from the art of music. We who believe that we have acquired the knowledge of music as a science, beyond all preceding knowledge of the subject, have in Europe been able to enjoy only our own musical scales; whereas throughout the East, those accepted by the human ear are very various, and appear to depart from what to our senses is harmony. Those Oriental musics have either been adapted to the Oriental ear, or the ear has been adapted to appreciate the forms and laws of harmony with which it came in contact.

The same questions occur to us while examining into the different forms of decorative art; and we are constantly reminded that the laws which should govern them, are perhaps, infinitely larger and wider than we with our limited human capacities and experience, have hitherto been able to appreciate.

"Ars longa—vita brevis" has been so often said, that from a proverb it has become a truism; but it must continue to be the refrain of those who write upon art. The subject is so long, and its ramifications are so intricate, that it is difficult to include them all under one category.

[4]My furthest aim here is to trace back the art of needlework to its beginning, without turning my eyes to the right or the left, though I cannot help feeling myself drawn aside almost irresistibly by casual glimpses of architecture, sculpture, and painting, which here and there touch very nearly the history of needlework.

Except where they visibly influence each other, I avoid dealing with the greater arts, leaving them to the study of the learned in each special branch.

All art, however, throws reflected lights, and gleaning in the track of those authors who have preceded us, we often pick up valuable hints which we accept, and make use of them gladly.

Some writers have thought it incumbent on them to give a local habitation and an abiding place to needlework, and they have regarded it as a branch of painting. But I cannot endorse this classification. According to Semper, indeed, it is the mother-art of sculpture and painting, instead of being the offspring of either or both, as others have maintained.[4] They have, indeed, such distinct functions that each may justly boast its own original sources. Painting is the art of colour; sculpture is that of form; embroidery is the art of clothing forms. They are all so ancient, that in seeking to ascertain [5]their beginnings and dates. It is difficult to fix the precedence of one over another. We may compare, distinguish, and yet again change our opinions as fresh facts come under our observation.

The art of needlework reached its climax long ago, and is now very old. History and faded rags are the only witnesses to its fabulous glories, in Classical, Oriental, and early Mediæval days. It would appear that nothing new remains to be invented. Copies of past styles, and selections from the scraps we retain and value as models, are all that we can boast of now.

Dr. Rock truly says that few persons of the present day have the faintest idea of the labour, the money, the time, often bestowed of old upon embroideries which had been designed as well as wrought by the hands of men and women, each in their own craft the best and ablest of their day.

Time is too short, our life too densely crowded, to allow leisure for the extravagance of what is, after all, only a luxury of art—no longer a civilizer, as of old, but just an efflorescence of our culture.

Embroidery is now essentially "decoration," and nothing more. It is intended to appeal to the sense of beauty of the eye, rather than to the imagination. The designer for needlework should be an artist, but he need not be a poet. You may omit this art altogether, and you need be none the less sumptuously clothed and lodged. Yet it is worthy of careful study as historical evidence, and that in the present and future, as in the past, it may be an *art*, and not merely a *craft*.

For the great web of history is composed of many threads of divers colours, and the warp and the woof are often exchanged, yet so connected and knotted together that the continuity is never broken. On this web, Time has drawn the picture of the past—sometimes faintly, [6]sometimes with indelible tints and pronounced forms. By poetry; by architecture and its decorations; by dress, which represents and distinguishes nationalities; by customs, such as the different forms of burial; or even by such details as painting the eyes; also by the tradition and outcome of the laws of the tribes that flowed consecutively over Europe from the East; by the institutions which remained immutably fixed on their native soil, such as those of the Code of Manu, and those of Babylon, inscribed on bricks or clay; or by the words, their form and lettering, in which these are handed down to us;—out of all these the history of man is being reconstructed.

How valuable is every witness to the ancient records, which were fading into myths in the memories of men. How joyfully is each little fact hailed as a landmark, in the general fog of doubt!

Now embroidery may boast that it is a source of landmarks for all time.

Without presuming to fix a date for its first beginning, that which I wish to impress on the mind of the reader is the long continuity of the art of needlework.

The sense of antiquity induces reverence, and I claim for the needle an older and more illustrious age than can be accorded to the brush. While the great pendulum of Time has swung art in sculpture, painting, and architecture, from its cradle as in Mycenæ, to its throne in Athens in the days of Pericles, and then back again to the basest poverty of decaying Rome—needle work, continually refreshed from Eastern inspiration, never has fallen so low, though it had never aspired as high as its greater sister arts.

The stuffs and fabrics of various materials of the Egyptians, Chinese, Assyrians, and Chaldeans are named in the earliest records of the human race. How much these decorations depended on weaving, and how much [7]on embroidery with the needle, may in each case be disputed. The products of the Babylonian looms are alluded to in the Book of Joshua. Their beauty tempted Achan to rescue them when Jericho fell;[5] and Ezekiel speaks of the embroideries of Canneh, Haran, and Eden, as well as of their cloths of purple and blue, and their chests of garments of divers colours[6].

All these fabrics are named as merchandise, and were carried to the sea-coast, and thence over the ancient world, by the Phœnicians, the great shipowners and dealers of the East.

Indian needlework and design is 4000 years old; and the long perspective of Egyptian art, while leading us still further back into unlimited periods, shows it changing so slowly, that we feel as if it had been all but stationary from the beginning.

The Chinese claim 5000 years as the life of their history; but if, as is now suggested, their civilization is Accadian or Proto-Babylonian, their wonderful artistic and scientific knowledge may have been fragments of the great dispersal, secreted and preserved behind the wonderful wall[7] of stone, silence, and law, where it has lain fossilized ever since. One cannot but wonder at the perfection of the textile manufactures of the Chinese, their marvellous embroideries, and the peculiar modes of construction and design throughout their arts, which have shown but few moments of change in growth—scarcely a sign of evolution. And we may fairly surmise that this Accadian culture (if such it be) is reflected from antediluvian tradition.

The archæology of Oriental art is most interesting. [8]We contemplate with awe the vast splendours of the consecutive civilizations of the East; the ancient richness and fertility of the whole of the Asiatic continent; the genius for empire and for commerce; the creative power which seemed to pour itself forth, unchecked by wars and conquests; the great dynasties which rose and fell, leaving behind them gigantic works, and the records of fabulous luxury in the empires of China, Assyria, India, and Persia, of which the remains have been of late years excavated, deciphered, and confronted with the historical texts which we have inherited, and had only partly believed. And studying these new aspects of history, we are saddened, thinking that the sunrise comes to us from shining over desert sands or the mounds of empty cities, where the lion and the jackal "reassert their primeval possession," or where the European and the Tartar, from the West and from the East, dispute their rights to suzerainty. We are dazzled and confused when we look back to those great days when the over-peopled kingdoms sent forth whole tribes, eastward to the confines of Asia, southward over India, and westward over Europe; and we bow reverently before the mighty Power that led the Jews, by a promise and a hope, across the seething nationalities, through the long passage of time from Abraham to Solomon; and which is again giving into the hands of those Oriental-looking men, so much power in shaping the destiny of mankind through their great riches.

Moses commanded the Hebrew people to lend and never to borrow. They have obeyed his precept, except in art; to that they have lent or given nothing. There is no national Jewish art. For music only do they show artistic genius, and that is European and not Oriental. As illustrating their lack of intuitive decorative art, one need only refer to the architecture of the first, second, and third Temple buildings, which apparently reflected [9]Babylonian and Semitic influences on an early Chaldean type. The embroideries mentioned by different writers, from Moses to Josephus, appear to have had always a Babylonian, or later a Persian inspiration.

This absence of artistic genius is very remarkable in a people that had its origin in the Eastern centre from whence all art has radiated.

The reason that so little survives of ancient embroidery is evident. Woollen stuffs and threads decay quickly—the moth and rust do corrupt them—and the very few ancient bits that remain, have been preserved by the embalming process, which has kept the contents of tombs from becoming dust.

As to more modern embroideries, we ought to be thankful that the art has had its fashions; otherwise, the world would be overwhelmed with shabby rags. Human nature has a tendency to dislike the "old-fashioned"—i.e. the fashion of the last generation. That which our mothers worked or wore, is an object for affectionate sentiment, and the best specimens alone are preserved. That which belonged to our grandfathers and grandmothers has receded into the rococo; and a few more generations take us back to the antique, of which so little survives, from wear and tear, carelessness and theft, that we put away and preserve it as being curious and precious. We may hope that the general law of the survival of the fittest has guarded what is most remarkable.

Certain works have been consecrated by the hands that executed them, or by that of the donor, or by the purpose for which they were bestowed, and are mostly preserved in churches or national museums. Of these there are vestments and altar decorations worked by royal and noble ladies; and coronation garments given by Queens and Empresses, such as Queen Gisela's and the Empress Kunigunda's at Prague and Bamberg, and [10]Charlemagne's dalmatic at the Vatican, described in the chapter on ecclesiastical embroideries. Sculptured effigies help us as to embroidered patterns; for our forefathers often actually copied in bronze or stone the patterns of the garments in which the body was buried, or at any rate, those the man had worn in his life. Of these, King John's monument at Worcester, and the surcoat of the Black Prince at Canterbury, are remarkable examples.[8]

The succeeding chapters will contain sketches of the history of the different stitches, and of the best examples of stitch and style remaining to us; and I shall try to extract from both the best suggestions for guidance in design and handicraft.

Embroidery from its nature is essentially the woman's art.[9] It needs a sedentary life, industry and patience. It does not require a room to itself, and the worker may leave it at any moment between two stitches when called to other duties. Nunneries produced the finest work of the dark and middle ages; and their teaching inaugurated the workrooms in the palaces and castles, where young girls, whether royal, noble, or gentle, were trained in embroidery as an accomplishment and a household duty.

The history of domestic embroidery ought to be looked upon as that of an important factor in the humanizing effect of æsthetic culture.

The woman of the house has always been strong to fulfil her part in this civilizing influence with the implement which custom has awarded to her. Every man in the ancient East began his life under the tent or in the palace adorned by the hands of his mother and her [11]maidens, and his home was made beautiful by his wife and his sisters and their slaves. There, as in mediæval homes, lessons of morality and religion, and the love and fame of noble deeds, were taught by the painting of the needle to the minds of the young men, who would have scorned more direct teaching; and the children felt the influence, as the women wove what the bards sang.

Alas! we have but few specimens of embroideries of which we know the history, earlier than the tenth and eleventh centuries.[10] Yet from the days of the books of the Old Testament and the song of the siege of Troy, down to the present time, the woman of the house has adorned not only herself and her dear lord, but she has hung the walls, the seats, the bed, and the tables with her beautiful creations.

Homer's women were all artists with the needle. Venus seeking Helen,—

"Like fair Laodice in form and face,The loveliest nymph of Priam's royal race,Here in the palace at her loom she found:The golden web her own sad story crown'd.The Trojan wars she weaved (herself the prize),And the dire triumph of her fatal eyes."[11]

This must have been intended for hangings.

Hecuba's wardrobe is thus described:—

"The Phrygian queen to her rich wardrobe went,Where treasured odours breathed a costly scent;There lay the vestures of no vulgar art,Sidonian maids embroider'd every part.Here, as the queen revolved with careful eyesThe various textures and the various dyesShe chose a web that shone superior far,And glow'd refulgent as the morning star."[12]

The women of the Middle Ages were great at the [12]loom and frame. From the Kleine Heldenbuch of the thirteenth century, Rock quotes these lines:—

"Who taught me to embroider in a frame with silk,And to sketch and design the wild and tameBeasts of the forest and field?Also to picture on plain surfaces;Round about to place golden borders—narrow and a broad one—With stags and hinds, lifelike."

Gudrun, like the women of Homer, embroidered history—that of the ancestors of Siegfried.

But in the Middle Ages the embroiderers were ambitious artists. The deeds of Roland and the siege of Troy, all romantic and classical lore, provided subjects for the needle.

Shakespeare gives a pretty picture of the graceful weaver and embroiderer:—

* * * "Would ever with Marina be:—Be't when she weaves the sleided silk,With fingers long, small, white as milk;Or when she would with sharp neeld woundThe cambric, which she makes more soundBy hurting it....Deep clerks she dumbs; and with her neeld composesNature's own shape, of bud, bird, branch, or berry,That even her art sisters the natural roses."[13]

Before closing this Introduction, I will take the opportunity to protest against the abuse of the phrase "High Art." It is generally appropriated by that which is the lowest and most feeble.

An old design for a chair or table, by no means remarkable originally, but cheaply copied, and covered with a quaint and dismal cretonne or poorly worked pattern, of which the design is neither new nor artistic, is introduced by the upholsterer as belonging to "High Art furniture." The epithet has succeeded to what was once [13]"fashionable" and "elegant." To get rid of carpets, and put down rugs, to hang up rows of plates instead of family portraits—this also is "high art." Likewise gowns lumped upon the shoulders, with all the folds drawn across, instead of hanging draperies. The term is never used when we speak of the great arts—painting, sculpture, and architecture. It is, in fact, only the slang of the cabinet-maker, the upholsterer, and milliner.

All true Art is very high indeed and apparent; and needs not to be introduced with a puff. It sits enthroned between Poetry and History. Even those who are ignorant of its laws feel its influence, and the soothing grace which it sheds, falling like the rain, equally upon the just and the unjust. Man's nature always responds to the truly high and beautiful; only the most degraded are deprived of this source of happiness. And there are but few women, till debased by cruelty, misery, or drink, that do not try in some humble way (but especially with their needle) to adorn their own persons, their children, and their homes; and if their art is not high, it yet has the power to elevate them.[14] While the most ambitious women try a higher flight, into the regions of poetry, literature, painting, and even sculpture (why has no woman ever been an architect?), millions have enjoyed the art of the needle for thousands of years, and it will continue to be a solace and a delight as long as the world lasts, for, like all art, it gives the ever new joy of creation.

FOOTNOTES:

[3]See Duke of Argyll's "Unity of Nature."

[4]Walls, pillars, and roofs were certainly hung with textile ornament before they were carved or painted. This is Semper's theory, and though Woltmann and Woermann ("History of Painting," Eng. Trans., Sidney Colvin, p. 38) hardly accept this view, they do not gainsay

it. The women who wove hangings for the grove, or more literally, "coverings for the houses" of the grove, were probably the priestesses of Astarte, and wove and worked the hangings of various colours. 2 Kings xxii.; Ezek. xvi. 16-18.

"It is probable that the earliest kind of pictures were either woven or embroidered upon figured stuffs of various colours; and that in these decorations the Greeks in the first instance imitated the Semitic races, who had practised them from time immemorial." See Woltmann and Woermann's "History of Painting" (Eng. Trans.), p. 38.

[5]Joshua vii.

[6]Ezek. xxvii. 23.

[7]The wall of China, which, both figuratively and literally, enclosed its civilization, and fenced off that of the outer world, for thousands of years.

[8]When the tomb of King John was opened, the body was found wrapped in the same dress as that sculptured on his effigy. The surcoat of the Black Prince, of embroidered velvet, still hangs above his monument, on which it is exactly reproduced.

[9]Yet men, too, have wielded the embroidering needle.

[10]These remnants are not, like the straws in amber, only precious because they are curious; they are most suggestive as works of art.

[11]Pope's Homer, Iliad, book iii.

[12]Ibid. book vi.

[13]Shakespeare, "Pericles, Prince of Tyre," act iv. 20; v. 5.

[14]Surely it is a humanizing and Christian principle which in Italy permits artistic work to be done in the prisons where criminals are confined for life. Sisters of Mercy teach lace-making to the wretched women who, having committed great crimes, may never be seen again. The produce of the work helps to pay the expense of the prison, and at the same time a very small percentage is given to the prisoners to send to their friends, or to spend on little comforts, thus encouraging the poor human creatures to exercise their best powers. We believe this is sometimes allowed also in England and France.

[14]

CHAPTER I.
STYLE.

In venturing to approach so great a subject as the history of style, I would beg my readers to believe how well I am aware that on each point much more has been already carefully treated by previous writers, than will fall within the limits of a chapter that is intended only to throw light on textile art, and especially on embroidery.

I suppose it is the same in all subjects of human speculation which are worthy of serious study; and therefore I ought not to have been surprised to find how much has already been written on needlework and embroidery, and how unconsciously I, at least, have passed by and ignored these notices, till it struck me that I ought to know something of the history and principles of the art which with others, I was striving to revive and improve.

Then new and old facts crowded round me, and became significant and interesting. I longed to know something of the first worker and the first needle; and behold the needle has been found!—among the débris of the life of the Neolithic cave-man, made of bone and very neatly fashioned.

Alas! the workwoman and her work are gone to dust; but *there* is the needle!—proof positive that the craft existed before the last glacial period in Britain.[15]How long ago this was, we may conjecture, but can never finally ascertain. Then I find embroidery named by the earliest historians, by every poet of antiquity, and by the first travellers in the East; and it has been the subject [15]of laws and enactments from the date of the Code of Manu in India, to the present century. One becomes eager to systematize all this information, and to share with the workers and thinkers of the craft, the pleasure found in its study.

Perhaps what is here collected may appear somewhat bald and disjointed; but antiquity, both human and historical, is apt to be bald; and its dislocation and disjointed condition are owing to the frequent cataclysms, physical, political, and social, which needlework has survived, bringing down to us the same stitches which served the same purposes for decoration under the Code of Manu, and adorned the Sanctuary in the wilderness; and those stitches probably were not new then.

I propose to give a slight sketch of the origin of the styles[16] that have followed each other, noting the national influences that have displaced or altered them, and the overlap of style caused by outside events.

First, I would define what "STYLE" means.

Style is the mark impressed on art by a national period, short or long. It fades, it wanes, and then some historical element enters on the scene, which carries with it new materials, needs, and tastes (either imported or springing up under the new conditions). The style of the day in art and literature alters so perceptibly, that all who have had any artistic training are at once aware of the difference.

Of late years, the science of history has been greatly assisted by the science of language. When the mute language of art shall have been patiently deciphered, the historian will be furnished with new powers in his researches after truth.

The first "ineffaceable" is a *word*; the second a *pattern*. This is proved by the history of needlework.

[16]As the world grows old, its youth becomes more interesting. Alas! the childhood of mankind is so distant, and it was so long before it learned its letters, that but few facts have come down to us, on which we may firmly build our theories; yet we must acknowledge the great stride that has been made in the last few years, in the scientific mode of extracting history from the ruins and tombs, and even the dust-heaps, of the past. Whole epochs, which fifty years ago were as blank as the then maps of Central Africa, are being now gradually covered with landmarks.

Layard, Rawlinson, C. T. Newton, Botta, Rassam, Schliemann, Birch, G. Smith, and a crowd of archæologists, and even unscientific explorers, are collecting the materials from which the history of mankind is being reconstructed.

From them I have sought information about the art of embroidery, and I find that Semper gives it a high pre-eminence as to its antiquity, making it the foundation and starting-point of all art. He clothes not only man, but architecture, with the products of the loom and the needle; and derives from them in succession, painting, bas-relief, and sculpture.[17]

Style has to be considered in two different aspects, from two different standpoints. First, historically and archæologically, distinguishing and dating the forms which follow upon each other; and tracing them back in the order of their natural sequence; so as to guide us to the root, nay, to the seed[18] of each and all art.

[17]The subsidiary art of embroidery, in its highest form the handmaid of architecture, is full of suggestion, and may assist us greatly in the search which culminates in the text of "In the beginning."

The other point of view from which style should be considered is the æsthetic. This enables us to criticize the works of different periods; extracting, as far as we may, rules for the beautiful and the commendable, and seeking to find the "why?" also observing the operation of the law by which decay follows too soon after the best and highest efforts of genius, thought, and invention in art.

My present object is the history of consecutive styles, in so far as they concern needlework.

Alas! nothing endures. This law is acknowledged by Goethe, when he makes Jove answer Venus, who bewailed that all that is beautiful must die,—that he had only bestowed beauty on the evanescent.

It seems as if the moment the best is attained, men, ceasing to struggle for the better, fall back at once hopelessly and become mere imitators. They no longer follow a type, but copy a model, and then copy the copy. Imitation is a precipice, a swift descent through poverty of thought into the chaos of mannerism, in the place of style.

The imitative tendency, as existing in all human minds, cannot be ignored or despised. In individuals it accompanies enthusiasm for the beautiful, and the graceful charm of sympathy. It maintains continuity between specimen and specimen, between artist and artist, between century and century; and it is this which enables an adept to say with certainty of consecutive styles, "This is Spanish work of the sixteenth century; that is Flemish or German work of the seventeenth century."

[18]The theory of development and of the survival of the fittest has been worked so hard, that it sometimes breaks down under the task imposed upon it. It would need to include Death in its procedure. In our creed, Death, means the moment of entrance into a higher existence; but in art it means extinction, leaving behind neither a history nor an artisan—only, perhaps, an infinitely small tradition, like the grain of corn preserved in the wrappings of a mummy, from which at first accident, and then care and culture, may evoke a future life.

The various ways in which art has appeared at the beginning cannot here be discussed; nor how the Chinese and Hindu may have leapt into a perfection which has stood still for thousands of years, protected alike from expansion as from destruction, by the swaddling bands of codified custom; while Greek art rose like the sun, shone over the civilized world, and set—never again to see another epoch of glory. These subjects must be left for the study of the anthropological philosopher, who is working for the assistance and guidance of the future historian of art.

Style in needlework has passed through many phases since the aboriginal, prehistoric woman, with the bone needle, drew together the edges of the skins of the animals she had prepared for food.

For absolute necessity, in forming the garments and covering the tent, needlework need go no further than the seam. This, however, in the woven or plaited material, must fray where it is shaped, and become fringed at the edges. Every long seam is a suggestion, and every shaped edge a snare.

The fringe lends itself to the tassel, and the shaped seam suggests a pattern; up-stitches are needed for binding the web, and before she is aware of it, the worker finds herself adorning, *embroidering*; and the craft enters the outskirts of the region of art.

[19]The humble early efforts at decoration, called by the French "primitif," are the first we know and class, and are found in all savage attempts at ornament. This style consists mainly of straight lines, zigzags, wavy lines, dots, and little discs.[19]

Gold discs of many sizes, and worked with a variety of patterns, are found equally in the tomb of the warrior at Mycenæ, and in Ashantee, accompanied in both cases with gold masks covering the faces of the dead. The discs or buttons remind us of those found in Etruscan tombs, though the execution of these last is more advanced. They appear to be the origin of the "clavus" or nail-headed pattern woven into silks in the Palace of the Cæsars. The last recorded survival of this pattern is in woven materials for ecclesiastical purposes in the Middle Ages.

Of very early needlework we only find here and there a fragment, illustrated occasionally by passing allusions in poetry and history.

The ornamental art of Hissarlik[20] is so primitive that we cannot feel that it has any resemblance to that described as Trojan by Homer, who probably adorned his song with the art he had known elsewhere.[21]

We know not what the actual heroes of the Iliad and Odyssey wore; but we do know that what Homer describes, he must have seen. Was Homer, therefore, the contemporary of the siege of Troy?—or does he not rather speak of the customs and costumes of his own time, and apply them to the traditions of the heroic ages of Greece? Whatever be the date of Homer himself, we can, with the help of contemporary survivals, reconstruct the house and the hall, and even furnish them, [20]and clothe the women and the princes, the beggars and the herdsmen.

From the remains of Egyptian, Babylonian, and Assyrian art we can perceive their differences and their affinities. It is from textile fragments, found mostly in tombs, that we obtain dates, and can suggest them for other specimens.

The funeral tent of Shishak's mother-in-law, at Boulac, is most valuable as showing what was the textile art of that early period.[22]

Fig. 1.
Egyptian corselet. (Wilkinson's "Ancient Egyptians.")

The corselet which, according to Herodotus, was given by Amasis, King of Egypt, to the Temple of Minerva at Lindos, in Rhodes, was possibly worked in this style; for Babylonian embroidery was greatly prized in Egypt, and imitated.

The second corselet given by Amasis to the Lacædemonians was worked in gold and colours, with animals and other decorations. This was of the seventh century B.C.[23]

Amongst the arms painted on the wall of the tomb of Rameses, at Thebes (in Egypt), is a corselet, apparently of rich stuff,[24]embroidered with lions and other devices. (Fig. 1.)

[21]The Phœnicians imbibed and reproduced the styles they met with in their voyages. The bowls found in Cyprus described and engraved in the September number of the "Magazine of Art" (1883), are most interesting illustrations of the meeting of two national styles, the Assyrian and the Egyptian.[25]

Homer's "Shield of Achilles"[26] must, in general design, have resembled these bowls (see Pl. 5). They also recall the description by Josephus of the Temple veils at Jerusalem, which were Babylonian.[27]

Phœnicia, which was the carrier of all art, dropped specimens here and there, for many hundred years, along the borders of the Mediterranean and the coasts of Spain. We fancy we can trace her ocean-path by the western shores of Africa, and even to America; otherwise, how could it happen that a mummy-wrapping in Peru should so nearly resemble some of those wrappings found at Saccarah,[28] in Egypt, woven in precisely the same tapestry fashion?

Among the puzzling phenomena due probably to Phœnician commerce, is the complete suite of the sacerdotal ornaments of a High Priest, found in his tomb,[29] now in the Vatican Museum. This reminds us of other specimens of archaic art from distant sources, that our [22]attention is forcibly arrested, and we wonder whence they came, and whether they were collected from alien civilizations by the Phœnicians before they dispersed them.[30]

Certain Egyptian sculptures of deformed and repulsive divinities—idols of the baser sort—are most interesting and puzzling by their affinity in style to the Indo-Dravidian and the art of Mexico, while they are entirely unlike that of Egypt. If Atlantis and its arts never existed, it may be suggested that it was the eastern coast of America that was spoken of under that name by the Egyptian priest with whom Herodotus conversed.

The Babylonian and Ninevite embroideries, carefully executed on their bas-reliefs, have a masculine look, which suggests the design of an artist and the work of slaves. There is no following out of graceful fancies; one set of selected forms (each probably with a symbolical intention) following another. The effect, as seen on the sculptures in the British Museum, is royally gorgeous; and one feels that creatures inferior to monarchs or satraps could never have aspired to such splendours. Probably the embroidery on their corselets was executed in gold wire, treated as thread, and taken through the material; and the same system was carried out in adorning the trappings of the horses and the chariots. The solid masses of embroidery may have been afterwards subjected to the action of the hammer, which would account for their appearing like jeweller's work in the bas-reliefs (Pl. 1 and 2).

Pl. 1.

See larger image
Assurbanipal fighting lions.
British Museum.

Pl. 2.

See larger image
Portion of a Babylonian Royal Mantle. Layard's "Monuments," series i., pl. 9.

The style of the Babylonian embroideries appears to have been naturalistic though conventionalized. We may judge of their styles for different purposes by the reliefs in the British Museum. From their veils and [23]curtains at a later date, when they had crossed their art with that of India, we may imagine the mystical design of the Temple curtain as described by Josephus; in fact, as much as possible embracing all things on the earth and above it, excepting the images of the heavenly bodies.[31]

Small carpets from Persia of the Middle Ages, as well as those woven and embroidered even to the present day, are echoes of the ancient Babylonian style, and most interesting as historical records of the traditions of human taste. Our artistic interests are stirred when we read in Ezekiel lists of the fabrics and materials of which Tyre had become the central depôt, and we enjoy tracing them to the various looms, named in verse and history, where they were adorned with embroidery, and then either became articles of commerce, or were stored away to be kept religiously as heirlooms, or presented as gifts to the temples or to honoured guests.

Mr. G. Smith, after saying that the Babylonian is without doubt the oldest of civilizations, continues thus:—"To us the history of Babylonia has an interest beyond that of Egypt, on account of its more intimate connection [24]with our own civilization.[32] Babylon was the centre from which it spread into Assyria, thence to Asia Minor and Phœnicia, then to Greece and Rome, and so to all Europe. The Jews brought the traditions of the creation and of early religion from Ur of the Chaldees,[33] and thus preserved they became the heritage of all mankind; while the science and civilization of that wonderful people (the Babylonians) became the basis of modern research and advancement."[34]

The hangings of the Tabernacle are so carefully described in the book of Exodus, that we can see in fancy the linen curtains, blue or white, embroidered in scarlet, purple, blue, and gold; the cherubim in the woven material; the fringes enriched with flowers, buds, fruit, and golden bells: and we can appreciate how little of Egyptian art and style the children of Israel brought back from their long captivity, and how soon they reverted to their ancient Chaldean proclivities, after returning to their wandering life of the tent.

On the bronze gates from the mound of Balawat, near Nimroud, set up by Shalmaneser to celebrate his conquest of Tyre and Sidon,[35] we find a portable tabernacle, evidently meant to accompany the army on a march. It is not much larger than a four-post bed, with transverse poles for drawing the curtains, all fringed with bells and fruit. This is an illustration of the motive for the Tabernacle of the forty years' wandering in the desert. (Fig. 2.)

[25]

Fig. 2.
Tabernacle on gates of Balawat, time of Shalmaneser II. (British Museum).

Egyptian textile art is, perhaps, that of which we have the most early specimens. These are to be seen at Boulac, at Vienna, Turin, and the British Museum.[36]The Hieroglyphic, the Archaic, and the Græco-Egyptian are all unmistakably the consecutive outcome of the national original style, which had totally disappeared in the beginning of our era. Few of the embroideries are more than two thousand five hundred years old. But the great piece of patchwork in leather, "the funeral tent of an Egyptian queen," as it covered the remains of a contemporary of Solomon,[37] absolutely [26]exhibits the proficiency of the designer and the needlework of the eleventh century B.C. (Pl. 44.)

The connection between Indian and Egyptian early art appears to have existed only in their use of the lotus as an emblem and a constant decoration; but their manner of employing it was characteristically different. (Pl. 12 and 13.)

The Phœnicians carried with them the seeds of the Egyptian style over the ancient world; but these seeds only took root and flourished on the soil of Greece. The imitations of Egyptian style reappeared in Rome, and again in France "under the two Empires." In both cases they were only imitations, and neither had any permanent influence on the art of their day.

I shall have to allude very often to our Eastern sources of artistic culture.

Our own Aryan ancestors were so impregnated with beautiful ideas, that we must believe that we inherit from them all our graceful appreciation of naturalistic ornament. But even Aryan art met with reverses on its Eastern soil, from which it constantly rose again and renewed itself.

The Mongols crushed for a time the element of beauty in India. They introduced a barbarous and hideous style which has its only counterpart in that of Central America. It was the produce of a religion, superstitious, cruel, and devilish.

The Aryan art of India, which was elegant and spiritual, was revived by the kindred influence of Persia, and by the Renaissance in Europe. Italian and other artists were employed in India, and "the spirit of aerial grace, and the delicate sense of beauty in natural forms, blossomed afresh and flourished for 300 years. Birds, [27]flowers, fruit, butterflies, became once more the legitimate ornament of every material."[38]

I continue to quote from Sir G. Birdwood's "Arts of India." "The Code of Manu, from 900 to 300 B.C., has secured to the village system of India a permanent class of hereditary artistic workmen and artisans, who have through these 2500 years, at least, been trained to the same manipulations, and who therefore translate any foreign work which is placed before them to copy, into something characteristically Indian."[39] Indian art has borrowed freely from all sources without losing its own individuality. It has been said, "There is nothing newer in it than of the sixteenth century; and even then nothing was original, especially in the minor arts." But this is owing to the Hindu being equally endowed with assimilative and receptive capacity,[40] so that in the hands of the Indian craftsman everything assumes the distinctive expression of ancient Indian art.

In India everything is hand-wrought; but as the spirit of its decorative art "is that of a crystallized tradition, its type has remained almost unaltered since the Aryan genius culminated in the Ramâyana and Mahabhârata—and yet each artisan in India is a true artist."[41] In art, unfortunately, "the letter killeth;" and true artists as they [28]are, the ancient traditions bind and cramp them, while the ancient materials, the dyes, and the absolute command of time are failing: so that the beauty of Indian embroideries and other decorations is gradually reducing itself to mannerism, which is more dangerous to art than even had been the vicissitudes of war; for when peaceful days returned, and the waves of conquest had subsided, the ancient arts were found again deeply embedded in the traditions of the people. They gradually returned to their old ways, which are so indelible in the Hindu mind, that they will perhaps survive even the fashions of to-day.[42]

From Yates' account it would appear that Europe had been fertilized with taste in art and manufactures from the East by three different routes.

The Egyptian civilization, with all its Eastern antecedents and traditions, came to us by the Mediterranean and the Adriatic; the Phœnicians being the merchants who brought it through those channels. The Etruscans, who were the pedlars of Europe, travelled north, conveying golden ornaments and coral, and bringing back jet and amber. Their commercial track is to be traced by the contents of tombs on their path.[43]

Pl. 3.

See larger image
St. John. From King Alfred's Celtic Book of the Gospels.
Lambeth Palace Library.

Secondly, there was also a Slavonian route from Eastern Asia, which conveyed Oriental art to the north [29]of Europe. Celtic art, which certainly has something of the Indo-Chinese style, came to us probably by this route. Another branch of the Celtic family was settled on the north-eastern shores of the Adriatic. Celtic ideas and forms in art probably crossed Europe from this point,[44] and came to us meeting a cognate influence,[45] arriving from the north.[46] (Pl. 3.)

Thirdly, Oriental taste and textiles came from the Byzantine Empire in the early days of Christianity, spreading to Sicily, Italy, Spain, and finally to France, Germany, and Britain.

Runic art, whether Scandinavian or our own purer Celtic, is so remarkable for its independence of all other European national and traditional design, that I cannot omit a brief notice of it, though we have no ascertained relics of any of its embroideries.[47] It appears to have received, in addition to its own universal stamp—evidently derived from one original source—certain influences impressed on it like a seal by each country through which it flowed.[48] Wherever the Runes are [30]carved in stone, or worked on bronze, gold, silver, ivory, or wood, or painted in their splendid illuminations (pl. 4), the involved serpent, which was the sign of their faith, appears, sometimes covered with Runic inscriptions; and this inscribed serpent, later, is twined round or heaped at the foot of the peculiar Scandinavian-shaped cross, the type of conversion. The serpent was sometimes altered into the partial semblance of a four-footed animal, the body and tail being lengthened and twined, and sometimes split, to give a new turn to the pattern. (Fig. 3.) All these zoomorphic patterns, as well as the human figures seen in the Book of Kells, the missal at Lambeth, and the Lindisfarne Book (which is, however, more English in its style), are yet of an Indo-Chinese type; the wicker-work motives often replacing the involved serpent design.

Fig. 3.
Celtic Zoomorphic pattern.

The Paganism of our own Celtic art, when it appears, is an interpolation between our first and second Christian conversions, and was brought to us in the incursions of the Vikings over Scotland and into England.

See larger image
Page from the Lindisfarne MSS. British Museum

Pl. 5.

See larger image
Silver bowl from Palestrina. Ganneau. "Journal Asiatique, Coupe de Palestrina." 1880.

Our knowledge of their advanced and most singular art [31]comes out of their tombs, in which the warrior was laid with all his arms and his horse and his precious possessions, splendidly clothed according to his degree—in the belief that he would need them again in a future world.

This northern tradition was so long-lived, that Frederick Casimir, a knight of the Teutonic Order, was buried with his sword and his horse at Treves, in 1781.[49]

Greek embroideries we can perfectly appreciate, by studying Hope's "Costumes of the Ancients," and the works of Millingen and others; also the fictile vases in the British Museum and elsewhere. On these are depicted the Hellenic gods, the wars, and the home life of the Greeks. The worked or woven patterns on their draperies are infinitely varied, and range over many centuries of design, and they are almost always beautiful. It is melancholy to have to confess that in this, as in all their art, the Greek taste is inimitable; yet we may profit by the lessons it teaches us. These are: variety without redundancy; grace without affectation; simplicity without poverty; the appropriate, the harmonious, and the serene, rather than that which is astonishing, painful, or awe-inspiring. These principles were carried into the smallest arts, and we can trace them in the shaping of a cup or the decoration of a mantle, as in the frieze of the Parthenon.

Homer makes constant mention of the women's work. Penelope's web is oftenest quoted. This was a shroud for her Father-in-law. Ulysses brought home a large collection of fine embroidered garments, contributed by his fair hostesses during his travels.

Pallas Athene patronized the craft of the embroiderers; and the sacred peplos which robed her statue, and was renewed every year, was embroidered by noble maidens, [32]under the superintendence of a priestess of her temple. It represented the battles of the gods and the giants (fig. 4), till the portraits of living men were profanely introduced into the design. The new peplos was carried to the temple, floating like a flag, in procession through the city.

The goddess to whom the Greeks gave the protection of this art was wise as well as accomplished, and knew that it was good for women reverently to approach art by painting with their needles. She always was seen in embroidered garments, and worked as well as wove them herself. She appeared to Ulysses in the steading of Eumœus, the swineherd, as a "woman tall and fair, and skilful in splendid handiwork."[50]

Fig. 4.
Pallas Athene attired in the sacred peplos.
(Panathenaic Vase, British Museum.)

[33]Homer never tires of praising the women's work, and the chests of splendid garments laid up in the treasure-houses.[51] Helen gave of her work to Telemachus: "Helen, the fair lady, stood by the coffer wherein were her robes of curious needlework which she herself had wrought. Then Helen, the fair lady, lifted it out, the widest and most beautifully embroidered of all—and it shone like a star; and this she sent as a gift to his future wife."[52]

Semper's theory is, that the one chief import of Oriental style being embroideries, therefore the hangings and dresses arriving from Asia gave the poetic Greek the motives for his art, his civilization, his legends, and his gods.[53] This may or may not be; there is no doubt that they influenced them.[54]

Böttiger accordingly believes that Homer's descriptions of beautiful dress and furnishings are derived from, or at least influenced by, what he had learnt of the Babylonian and Chaldean embroideries. This is very probable, and would account for his poetical design on the shield of Achilles, in which his own inspiration dictated the possibilities of the then practised arts of Asia, of which the fame and occasional glimpses were already drifting westward. (Plate 5.)

The description of the shield of Achilles is as follows: Hephaistos, "the lame god," "threw bronze that weareth not, into the fire; and tin, and precious gold and silver." "He fashioned the shield great and strong, with five folds [34](or circles) in the shield itself." "Then wrought he the earth and the sea, and the unwearying sun, and the moon waxing to its full, and the signs, every one wherewith the heavens are crowned." "Also he fashioned therein two cities of mortal men; and here were marriage feasts, and brides led home by the blaze of torches—young men whirling in the dance, and the women standing each at her door marvelling." Then a street fight, and the elders sitting in judgment. The other city was being besieged; and there is a wonderful description of the battle fought on the river banks, and "Strife, Tumult, and Death" personified, and mingling in the fight. Then he set in the shield the labours of the husbandman. This is so exquisitely beautiful that with difficulty I refrain from quoting it all. "He wrought thereon a herd of kine with upright horns, and the kine were fashioned of gold and tin," "and herdsmen of gold were following after them." "Also did the glorious lame god devise a dancing-place like unto that which once, in wide Knosos, Daidalos wrought for Ariadne of the lovely tresses. There were youths dancing and maidens of costly wooing, their hands upon their waists." "And now would they run round with deft feet exceedingly lightly"—"and now would they run in lines to meet each other." "And a great company stood round the lovely dance in joy; and among them a divine minstrel was making music on his lyre; and through the midst of them, as he began his strain, two tumblers whirled. Also he set therein the great might of the River of Ocean, around the utmost rim of the cunningly-fashioned shield."[55]

There is, indeed, every proof that Greek art was the joint product of the Egyptian and Assyrian civilizations. Their amalgamation gave birth to the archaic style, struggling to express the strength and the beauty of [35]man—half heroic, half divine. Gradually, all the surrounding decorations of life assumed as a governing principle and motive, the worth of noble beauty.

The Greeks were the first artists. They broke away from the ancient trammels of customary forms, and replaced law with liberty of thought, and tradition with poetry.

They destroyed no old ideas, but they selected, appropriated, and evoked beauty from every source. From the great days of Athens we may date the moment when materials became entirely subservient to art, and the minds of individual men were stamped on their works and dated them. Phases indeed followed each other, showing the links of tradition which still bound men's minds together to a certain extent, and formed the general style of the day. Yet there was in art from that time—life, sometimes death,—but then a resurrection.

It appears from classical writers that about 300 B.C. Greek art had thrown itself into many new forms. Painting, for example, had tried all themes excepting landscapes. We are told that within the space of 150 years the art had passed through every technical stage; from the tinted profile system of Polygnotus to the proper pictorial system of natural scenes, composed with natural backgrounds; and Peiraiïkos is named as an artist of genre—a painter of barbers and cobblers, booths, asses, eatables, and such-like realistic subjects.[56]

I suppose there is no doubt that all the Romans knew or felt of art was borrowed directly or indirectly from Greece,[57] first through Phœnician and perhaps Etruscan sources, and finally by conquest. Everything we have of their [36]art shows their imitation of Grecian models. Their embroideries would certainly have shown the same impress.

Greece—herself crushed and demoralized—even as late as the Eastern Empire gave to Rome the fashion of the Byzantine taste, which she at once adopted, and it was called the Romanesque. This style, which was partly Arab, still prevails in Eastern Europe, having clung to the Greek Church. In her best days, Roman poetry, architecture, and decorative arts were Greek of Greece, imitating its highest types, but never creating.

It is surely allowable to quote here one of Virgil's Homeric echoes, which touches upon our especial subject,—

"Mournful at heart at that supreme farewell,Andromache brings robes of border'd gold;A Phrygian cloak, too, for Ascanius.And yielding not the palm in courtesy,Loads him with woven treasures, and thus speaks:'Take these gifts, too, to serve as monumentsOf my hand-labour, boy; so may they bearTheir witness to Andromache's long love,The wife of Hector:—take them, these last giftsThy kindred can bestow; in this sad worldSole image left of my Astyanax!'"[58]

It is sad to mark how not only the refinements of taste, but even the guiding principles of art, were gradually lost in the humiliation of a conquered people, the dulness and discouragement which followed on the expatriation or destruction of their accumulated treasures, and the deterioration of the Greek artist and artisan, carried prisoners to Rome, and settled there because it was the seat of luxury and empire. As the captive Jews hung their harps on the willow-trees by the waters of Babylon, and refused to sing, so Greek [37]genius succumbed, weighed down by Roman chains. It sickened and died in exile.

Late Roman art reminds us of the art of Etruria in its archaic days, except that the freshness and promise are wanting, and that the one was in its first, the other its second childhood.

Before entering on the subject of Christian art, I must again refer, however briefly, to the Eastern origin of all art. It is evident that this had always flowed in streams of many types from that high watershed of Central Asia, where our human race is said to have been created, and whence all wisdom and knowledge have emanated. In the image of the Creator, man issued from thence, endowed with the gift of the creative power. Wave after wave of fresh and apparently differing nationalities followed each other; partially submerging those that had gone before, and spreading till it had reached the furthest shores of the Northern seas and the Atlantic, and encircled the Mediterranean. They all followed the same course from east to west. The Greek civilization was indeed so dazzling and strong, that it lighted the world all around; and India, Persia, and Assyria felt its influence reflected back on its old Asian cradle.

But from the same high watershed[59] flowed other tribal types towards China, Java, and Japan, that had no affinity with any western civilization; and while the Assyrian, Persian, Indian, and Mongolian styles mixed and overlapped so near their sources, that it is sometimes hardly possible to reason out and classify their resemblances and their differences, the tribes flowing Eastward turned aside and went their own way, and have remained till now perfectly distinct.[60]

[38]In spite of their matchless dexterity in the manipulation of their materials, the infinite variety of their stitches, and exquisite finish in execution, carrying out to the utmost point the intended effect, yet Chinese and Japanese textile art differs in its inner principles from all our accepted canons of taste; so that their want of harmony, and sometimes their absurdity, is a puzzle of which we cannot find the key. This I have already alluded to (p. 3).

I purposely avoid the questions suggested by Chinese art. The immense antiquity it claims cannot be allowed without hesitation. M. Terrien de la Couperie, however, believes that he has found the actual point of departure of Chinese civilization, and he considers it to be an early offshoot from Babylon.[61] He supports his theory on linguistic grounds, and we must anxiously wait to see if it is corroborated by further researches into the earliest records of the archaic Chinese literature. But immobility in art is a Chinese characteristic, and no national cataclysms seem to have disturbed it. The oldest specimens known are very like the most modern. Yet an adept, learned in Chinese art, can detect the signs which mark its different epochs.

In this they differ from the Japanese, who, added to their inherited exquisite appreciation of natural beauty, have a power of assimilation that might lead in time to their possessing a school of art which, being really original, might become the style of the future. The civilization of Japan is not older than the fifth century A.D., and was probably then imported from Corea. Some of the earliest [39]specimens we know of their art are embroidered religious pictures by the son of a Mikado Sholokutaiski, who was in the seventh century the great apostle of Buddhism in Japan; and the next earliest works are by the first nun, Honi, in the eighth century. We have European work as old, and it is most interesting to compare the differences of their styles and stitches.

We must now return to the beginning of our era, when we find Greek taste, such as it was, still influencing and colouring art in Italy, and throughout Europe, Asia, and Africa, wherever Roman colonies were founded, till the eighth century. It died hard; but by that time the barbarians had poured from the east and north in successive waves, and conquered and suppressed the classical civilization.

Nothing is so puzzling in textile art as the mixture of styles during the first 1000 years A.D. The Græco-Roman, the Byzantine, and the Egyptian, crossed by the Arabian, Persian, and Indian styles, were reproduced in the Sicilian looms. Certain stock patterns, such as the reclining hares or fawns, as we find them on the Shishak pall, or that of the Tree of Life, approached by worshipping men or animals, originating in Assyrian art, are employed as borders, and fill up vacant spaces. The information collected from the tombs in the Crimea immediately preceding our era, is supplemented by the variety in style and materials from the Fayoum, now placed by Herr Graf'schen in the Museum at Vienna.

Christian art, which began in Byzantium, gradually grew, and formed itself into the Gothic,[62] which in time overcame the general chaos of style.

[40]Eastern art continued to flow westward, modifying and suggesting. When the Phœnicians and Carthaginians had laid down their ancient commercial sceptre, it was taken up by the Greeks, and later by the Venetians and Genoese, always trading with Asiatic goods. Then the arts of the Scandinavians[63] and of the Celts (who were the weavers), though barbaric, still retained and spread certain Oriental traditions. Luxury was born in Babylon, and Persia became its nurse, whence all its glories and refinements spread over the world. But if luxury was Babylonian, art was Greek. Alas! the love of luxury survived in Rome the taste for art.

Pl. 6.

See larger image
The Empress Theodora. Mosaic at Ravenna. Church of San. Vitale.

At Ravenna we learn much of the early Christian period from the mosaics in the churches. The Empress Theodora and her ladies appear to be clothed in Indian shawl stuffs. (Plate 6.) These, of course, had drifted [41]into Rome, as they had long done into the Greek islands, by the Red Sea or by land through Tyre. Ezekiel (590 B.C.) mentions the Indian trade through Aden. Theodora's dress has a deep border of gold, embroidered with classical warriors pursuing each other with swords.[64] Works enriched with precious stones and pearls now appear for the first time in European art, and testify to its Oriental impress.

The Byzantine Christian style was essentially the art of mosaic. Its patterns for architecture or dress, easily square themselves into little compartments, suggesting the stitches of "counted" embroideries ("opus pulvinarium").

In the beginning of the fourth century, when Greek influence was still languishing, we may date the commencement of ecclesiastical art. It was a new birth, and had to struggle through an infancy of nearly 800 years, ignoring, or unconscious of all rules of drawing, colouring, and design. Outlines filled in with flat surfaces of colours represented again the art of painting, which had returned to archaic types, and in no way differed from the essential properties of the art of "acu pingere" or needlework, which was in the same phase—being, fortunately for it, that to which it was best suited.

Therefore fine works of art were then executed by the needle, of which a very few survive, either in description or copied into more lasting materials; and showing that, with the minor arts of mosaic and illumination, it was in a state of higher perfection than the greater arts, which till the twelfth century were all but in abeyance.

In discussing textile art, I am obliged to pass over a part of the dark ages, and to approach the period when it must be studied chiefly in Sicily, which became the half-way house on the high road to the East, and later [42]the resting-place of the Crusaders to and from the Holy Land.

Sicily, which had succeeded to Constantinople as being the great manufacturing mart during the Middle Ages, was in the hands of the Moors, the origin and source of all European Gothic textile art. Yet even at Palermo and Messina this art was long controlled by the traditions of Greece, ancient and modern, while fertilized by Persian and Indian forms and traditional symbolisms.

The next European phase was the Gothic.[65] This was Arab and Moresque steeped in northern ideas; and finding its congenial soil, it grew into the most splendid, thoughtful, and finished style, far transcending anything that it had borrowed from eastern or southern sources.

All its traditions were carried out in the smaller decorative arts—mosaics, ivories, and metal works; and, last and not least, beautiful embroideries, to adorn the altars and the dresses of monarchs and nobles. (Plate 7.)

When taste was imperfect or declined, then the decorations were all rude, and the embroideries shared in the general rudeness or poverty; but as these crafts rose again, adding to themselves grace and beauty by study and experience, then needlework in England, Germany, France, Italy, and Spain grew and flourished.[66]

See larger image
Italian embroidery XV. Century
Kensington Museum
See larger image
Italian orphreys XVI. Century
South Kensington Museum
See larger image
Orphreys French and Spanish
XVI. Century

[43]Then came the Reformation, which, in Germany and England especially, gave a blow to the arts which had reserved their best efforts for the Church; and the change of style effected by the Renaissance was not suited to the solemnity of ecclesiastical decoration.

The styles of the fifteenth and sixteenth century embroideries are better adapted for secular purposes; though their extreme beauty as architectural ornament in Italy, reconciles one to their want of religious character, on the principle that it was allowable to dedicate to the Church all that in its day was brightest and best. (Plate 8.)

We possess much domestic embroidery of the Renaissance which is exceedingly beautiful—Italian, Spanish, and German. English needlework had lost its prestige from the time of the Reformation.[67]

The best efforts of the German schools of embroidery preceded the Reformation, while those of Belgium never lost their excellence,[68] and still hold their high position among the workers of golden orphreys. In Italy they always retained much of the classical element. Probably the ancient frescoes which served as models were originally painted by Greek artists and their Roman imitators. This style flourished for a hundred years. The French adopted and modified it.

The decorative style of that period is sometimes called the Arabesque, and sometimes the Grotesque. [44]The fashion was really copied from the excavated palaces and tombs of the best Roman era. Raphael admired, and caused his pupils to imitate and copy them; and they influenced all decorative art for a considerable period. As long as beautiful forms of flowers, fruit, birds, and animals were adhered to, the Arabesque was a charming decoration, gay and brilliant; but when the beautiful was set aside, and the ugly ideas were reproduced, the style became the Grotesque, which word only means the grotto, cave, or tomb style, and is as undescriptive to us as the word Arabesque, which has nothing to do with the Arabs or their arts.

It would appear that if the beautiful only is permissible in decorative art, and that if without beauty there is no reason that it should exist at all, then the Grotesque should not be allowed, except as a scherzo of the pencil; to be relegated, like all other caricatures, to the portfolio.

A grotesque is something startling, laughable, perhaps ridiculous. A woman with the head of a goose and a flowery tail may be a symbolical, but it never can be an agreeable object. When the idea conveyed is a great one, then it is excusable. The Ninevite bull, with a human head and five legs, is a grotesque, but it is also a symbol of majesty and might. A Satyr is a grotesque, but he has been so long recorded and accepted that he has ceased to surprise us; and the Greeks spent so much genius in making him a graceful creature, that he has become picturesque, if not beautiful.

Arabesques and Grotesques have now so long prevailed in decoration, that we have ceased to criticize them on principle, and accept them gratefully, in proportion to the gay fancy and reticent genius of the designer. Most Arabesques are, in fact, only graceful nonsense.

Pl. 9.

See larger image

Spanish Coverlet, from Goa. Velvet and gold, Plâteresque style, seventeenth century.

Vitruvius (writing first century B.C.) says, that "in his time, on the covering of the walls were painted rather [45]monstrosities than images of known things. Thus, instead of columns you will see reeds with crisp foliage, and candlesticks supporting temples; and on the top of these there are rods and twisted ornaments, and in the volutes senseless little figures sitting there; likewise flowers with figures growing out of their calyxes. Here a human head, there an animal's."[69]Evidently Vitruvius did not approve of grotesques, and his contemporary criticism is most valuable and amusing.

In the Louis Quatorze period, a species of vegetable grotesque was the fashion, from which we suffer even now, and it deserves censure. Leaves and flowers of different plants were made to grow from the same stem, as only artificial flowers could do. The Greeks introduced into their decorations sprays and wreaths of bay, olive, oak, ivy, and vine, with their fruits; which are exquisitely composed and carefully studied from nature. It is true that they sometimes invented flowers of different shapes, following each other on the same stem, and untrammelled by any natural laws. These classical freaks of fancy are so graceful that their want of truth does not shock us, but they are more safely copied than imitated.

The Renaissance was particularly marked in Spain and Portugal by the embroideries which the latter drew from their Indian possessions in Goa, whilst we in England were sedulously thrusting from our shores any beautiful Indian textiles that we imagined could injure our own home manufactures. It was, consequently, the worst phase of needlework with us, while Spanish and Portuguese embroideries of the sixteenth and seventeenth centuries are especially fine, their designs being European, and their needlework Oriental. Their Renaissance, which went by the name of the Plâteresque, is a style apart. (Pl. 9.) [46]The reason of its name is that it seems to have been originally intended for, and is best suited to, the shapes and decorations of gold and silver plate. It is extremely rich and ornate; not so appropriate to architecture as to the smaller arts, and wanting, perhaps, the simplicity which gives dignity. The style called Louis Quatorze following on the Renaissance in Germany, England, Spain, Italy, and France, assumed in each of these countries distinguishing characteristics, into which we have not time to enter now. In this style France took the lead and appropriated it, and rightly named it after the magnificent monarch who fostered it. This was a splendid era; and its furniture and wall decorations, dress, plate, and books shine in all the fertile richness and grace of French artistic ingenuity.[70] The new style asserted itself everywhere, and remodelled every art; but the long reign of Louis Quatorze gave the fashion time to wane and change. Under Louis XV. the defects increased and the beauties diminished. The fine heavy borders were broken up into fragmentary forms; all flow and strength were eliminated; and what remained of the Louis Quatorze style became, under its next phase, only remarkable for the sparkling prettiness which is inherent in all French art.

In Italy this very ornate style was distinguished as the "Sette-cento," and was a chastened imitation or appropriation of the Spanish Plâteresque and the French Louis Quatorze. In Germany it was a decided heavy copy of both, of which there are splendid examples in the adornment of the German palaces, royal and episcopal. In England the Continental taste was faintly reflected during the reign of Queen Anne and the first [47]Georges; but except in the characteristic upholstery of the Chippendales, and one or two palaces, such as Blenheim and Castle Howard, we did not produce much that was original in the style of that day.

Under Louis XV., Boucher and Watteau, in France, produced designs that were well suited to tapestries and embroideries. All the heathen gods, with Cupids, garlands, floating ribbons, crowns, and cyphers were everywhere carved, gilded, and worked. It was the visible tide of the frivolity in which poor Marie Antoinette was drowned; though before the Revolution she had somewhat simplified the forms of decoration, and straight lines instead of curves, and delicacy rather than splendour, had superseded, at least at court, the extravagant richness of palatial furniture.

This was followed by the Revolution; and then came the attempt at classical severity (so contrary to the French nature) which the Republic affected.[71] Dress was adorned with embroidered spots and Etruscan borders, and the ladies wore diadems, and tried to be as like as possible to the Greek women painted in fictile art. Napoleon attempted a dress which was supposed to be Roman at his coronation. Trophies were woven and embroidered, and the "honeysuckle," "key," and "egg and anchor" patterns were everywhere. With the fall of the Empire the classical taste collapsed, and the Egyptian, Greek, and Roman furniture were handed over to hotels and lodging-houses. In most of the palaces on the Continent an apartment is still to be seen, furnished in this style. It was the necessary tribute of flattery to the great conqueror, who in that character inhabited so many [48]of them for a short time. But there was no sign of the style being taken up enthusiastically anywhere out of France.

After the fall of the Empire, all pretence of style was in abeyance, and it was then gradually replaced by a general craving for the "antique," the "rococo," and finally the "baroc," as the outcome of that part of a gentleman's education called the "grand tour." Every one bought up old furniture; Italy and Spain were ransacked; and foreign works of all ages were added to the hereditary house furnishings. Every wealthy home became a museum. Now the numerous exhibitions of the last few years, bringing together the works of all Europe and other continents, have enabled us to continue to collect and compare and furnish, without any reference to a particular style.

Meantime "Young England" had become æsthetic. Bohemianism was the fashion, and the studio had to be furnished as a picturesque lounge:—ragged tapestries for backgrounds; antique chairs and bits of colour as cushions and draperies; shiny earthenware pots to hold a flower and to catch a high light. All these bridged the space between the new æstheticism and the old family museums; and from their combination arose the style called by courtesy the "Queen Anne"—a style which can be brought within the reach of the most moderate fortunes. In humble mansions you will be aware of the grouping of the old pieces of furniture, culminating perhaps in "my grandmother's cabinet," and her portrait by Hogarth; or "my great-grandfather's sword and pistols, which he carried at Culloden;" and his father's clock, a relic perhaps of the Scotch Dutch.

The English style of to-day is really a conglomerate of the preceding two hundred years, and it is formed from the débris of our family life. It belongs mostly to [49]the period of the pigtail; but it stretches back, and includes all that followed the Protectorate, and is therefore coeval with the wig. The name of "Queen Anne" would really do as well as any other, only that the style of her reign, which was heavy Louis Quatorze, is looked upon with suspicion, and never admitted for imitation. The "Nineteenth Century" would be a better name, for it has formed itself only within the last thirty years, in the very heart of the century, and is, in fact, a fortunate result of preceding conditions. It owes its existence, as I have said, partly to the archæological tendencies of the day.

The maimed tables and chairs, which had painfully ascended from saloon to bedroom, nursery, and attic, till they reposed in the garret (the Bedlam of crazy furniture), now have descended in all the prestige of antiquarian and family interest. Their history is recorded; the old embroideries are restored, named, and honoured. What is not beautiful, is credited with being "quaint"—the "quaint" is more easily imitated than the beautiful; and we have elected this for the characteristic of our new decorations. To be quaint, is really to be funny without intending it, and its claim to prettiness is its *naïveté*, which is sometimes touching as well as amusing: this was the special characteristic of the revival in the Middle

Ages. To imitate quaintness must be a mistake in art; as in life it is absurd to imitate innocence.

The nineteenth century "Queen Anne" has its merits. [50][72] It combines simplicity, roominess and comfort, colour, light and shade. Soft colouring to harmonize the new furniture with the tender tints of the faded quaintnesses just restored to society; care in grouping even the commonest objects, so as to give pleasure to the eye; a revived taste for embroidered instead of woven materials, giving scope to the talents of the women of the house;—all these are so much gained in every-day domestic decoration. The poorest and most trivial arrangements are striving to attain to a something artistic and agreeable. This is still confined to the educated classes; but as good and bad alike have to begin on the surface, and gradually filter through to the dregs of society, we may hope that the women who wore the last chignon and the last crinoline may yet solace their sordid lives in flowing or tight woollen garments, adorned with their own needlework; and that the dark-stained floor of the cottage or humble lodging will set off the shining brass kettle, and the flower in a brown or blue pot, consciously selected with a view to the picturesque, and enjoyed accordingly.

From what we know, it would seem that a vital change in a national style is never produced by the inspiration of one individual genius or great original inventor. It invariably evolves itself slowly, by the patient, persistent efforts of generations, polishing and touching up the same motive, and at last reaching human perfection.

The annihilation of a style is oftenest caused by war passing over the land, or revolution breaking up the fountains of social life, and swamping the art and the artist.

But another cause of such an extinction—perhaps the [51]saddest—is that having reached perfection as far as it may, it deteriorates, sickens, corrupts, and finally is thrown aside—superseded, hidden, and overlapped by a newer fashion; and the worst and latest effort discredits in the eyes of men, the splendid successes that preceded its fall. Though the next succeeding phase may be less worthy to live than the last, yet, carrying with it the freshness of a new spring, it is acceptable for the time being.

The moral I should draw from this is, that you cannot force style; you may prune, direct, and polish it, but you must accept that of your day, and only in accordance with that taste can your work be useful. Not accepting it idly or wearily, but cheerfully, on principle, seeking to raise it; refusing by word or deed to truckle to the false, the base, or the lawless in your art, or to act against the acknowledged canons of good taste. Not for a moment should ambition be checked, but it should always be accompanied by the grace of modesty.

To the young decorator or artist who feels the glow of original design prompting him to reject old lines, and follow his own new and perhaps crude ideas, a few words of warning, and encouragement also, may be of use.

In art, as in poetry, we may recognize the Psalmist's experience: "My heart burned within me, and at the last I spake with my tongue."

In small as in great things, crude ideas should not be brought to the front. No one should give his thoughts to the world till his heart has *burned* within him, and he has been *forced* to express himself.

Another wise saying, "Read yourself full, and then write yourself empty," also applies to art. Knowledge must first be accumulated before you can originate.

[52]Wait till your experience and your thoughts insist on expression; then subject the expressed idea to cultivated criticism, and profit by the opinion you would respect if another's work, and not your own, were under discussion.

It is true that taste is surprisingly various. Some will dislike your design, because its style is a reflection of the Gothic; another may be objected to as being frivolously Oriental-looking and brilliant, whereas the critic likes only the sober and the dull. Few are sufficiently educated to appreciate style: and we cannot rule our own by anybody's opinion; but we can generalize and find something that shall be agreeable to all—something approaching to a golden mean. The artist for decoration should be sensitively alive to any suggestion from the style of that which he is to adorn, remembering the antecedent motives of its form, its history, and its date. He should try to make his new work harmonize with the old; but of one thing he may be certain—unless he absolutely copies an old design, his own will carry the visible and unmistakable stamp of his day.

Even while suggesting copies this difficulty arises—how can a perfect facsimile be obtained? No reproduction is ever really exact, unless cast off by the hundred, stamped or printed by a machine.

It has been said that the translator of a poem adds to, or takes from the original, that which he has or has not of the same poetical power; and in art the copy requires the same qualities to guide the hand that transmits the original motive to another material. An artist usually carries out his own ideas from the first sketch blocked out on the canvas, or scribbled on the bit of waste paper, to the last finishing touch. It is, as far as it can be in human art, the visible transcript of his own thought. In needlework [53]this can hardly ever be. The designer, whether he be St. Dunstan, Pollaiolo, Torrigiano, or Walter Crane, only executes a drawing which leaves his hands for good, and is translated into embroidery by the patient needlewoman who simply fills in an outline, ignorant of art, unappreciative of its subtleties, and incapable of giving life and expression, even when she is aware that they are indicated in the original design. This is almost always the case; but there are exceptions. Charlemagne's dalmatic, for instance, shows signs of having been either the work of the artist himself, or else carried out under his immediate supervision.

FOOTNOTES:

[15]Boyd Dawkins' "Early Man in Britain," p. 285. See also chapter on stitches (*post*), p. 195.

[16]Some of these styles survive; some are still perceptible as traditions or echoes; some have totally disappeared in our modern art, such as the Primitive or the Egyptian.

[17]See Semper, "Der Stil."

[18]The history of Gaul begins in the 7th, and that of Britain in the 1st century B.C., while the civilization of Egypt dates back to more than 4000 B.C.; therefore the historical overlap is very great. It is probable that a large portion of Europe was in its neolithic age, while the scribes were composing their records of war and commerce in the great cities on the Nile, and that the neolithic civilization lingered in remote regions while the voice of Pericles was heard in Athens, and the name of Hannibal was a terror in Italy.—See Boyd Dawkins' "Early Man in Britain," p. 481.

[19]See chapter on patterns.

[20]In the Troad.

[21]Some of the Egyptian arts we know are pre-Homeric (if Homer really sang 800 B.C.), and Asiatic art was then in its highest development.

[22]See chapter on stitches, cut work (*post*). This funeral tent is a monumental work, inasmuch as the inscription inwrought on it gives us the name and title of her in whose honour it was made, and whose remains it covered. See Villiers Stewart's "Funeral Tent of an Egyptian Queen."

[23]Herodotus, book ii. c. 182; book iii. c. 47 (Rawlinson's Trans.). See Rock's Introduction, p. xiv.

[24]Homer mentions "Sidonian stuffs and Phœnician skill" (Iliad, v. 170); also "Sidonian Embroidery." Ibid. vi. 287-295.

[25]The Assyrian designs are such as are now still worked at Benares, and being full of animals, they are called Shikurgah, or "happy hunting-grounds." See Sir G. Birdwood's "Industrial Arts of India," p. 236. See also Plate 4.

[26]See Perrot and Chipiez (pp. 737-757); also Clermont Ganneau's Histoire de l'Art, "L'Imagerie Phénicienne," Plate 1, pt. 1. Coupe de Palestrina. He says that certain scenes from the "Shield of Achilles" are literally to be found on Phœnician vases that have come down to us—vases of which Homer himself must have seen some of analogous design.

[27]Homer speaks of Sidonian embroideries, "Iliad," vi., 287-295.

[28]See Egyptian fragments in the British Museum, and the specimens of Peruvian textiles; and Reiss and Stübel's "Necropolis of Ancon in Peru."

[29]At Cervetri, Dennis' "Etruria," ed. 1878, i. p. 268.

[30]The restless activity of the Phœnicians has often helped to confuse our æsthetic knowledge, and has caused the waste of much speculation in ascertaining how certain objects of luxury, belonging to distant civilizations, can possibly have arrived at the places where we find them.

[31]"The Beautiful Gate of the Temple was covered all over with gold. It had also golden vines above it, from which hung clusters of grapes as tall as a man's height.... It had golden doors of 55 cubits altitude, and 16 in breadth: but before these doors there was a veil of equal largeness with the doors. It was a Babylonian curtain of blue, fine linen, and scarlet and purple; of an admixture that was truly wonderful. Nor was the mixture without its mystical interpretation; but was a kind of image of the universe. For by the scarlet was to be enigmatically signified fire; by the fine flax, the earth; by the blue, the air, and by the purple, the sea;—two of them having their colours for the foundation of this resemblance; but the fine flax and the purple have their own origin for this foundation, the earth producing the one, and the sea the other. This curtain had also embroidered upon it all that was mystical in the heavens excepting the twelve signs of the zodiac, representing living creatures." Josephus (Trans. by Whiston), p. 895.

[32]See also M. E. Harkness and Stuart Poole, "Assyrian Life and History," p. 66.

[33]The visions of Ezekiel and St. John remind us of the composite figures and animals in Ninevite sculptures, and the prophetic poetry helps us to interpret their symbolism.

[34]G. Smith's "Ancient History of the Monuments," Babylonia, p. 33. Edited by Sayce.

[35]In the British Museum. See "Bronze Ornaments of Palace Gates, Balawat," pl. E 5.

[36]See Auberville's "Ornement des Tissus," pl. 1.

[37]The Egyptian queen in question was mother-in-law to Shishak, whose daughter married Solomon. After his son-in-law's death, Shishak plundered the "King's House," and carried to Egypt the golden shields or panels (1 Kings xiv. 26). The golden vessels went to Babylon later, and the golden candlesticks to Rome.

[38]Sir G. Birdwood repeatedly points out that the Vedic was the art that worshipped and served nature. The Puranic is the ideal and distorted. The Moguls, about 700 B.C., introduced their ugly Dravidian art. Through the Sassanian art of Persia, that of India was influenced. Possibly the very forms which in India are copied from Assyrian temples and palaces, may have travelled first to Assyria upon Indian stuffs and jewellery (Sir G. Birdwood's "Industrial Arts of India," i. p. 236).

[39]Ibid., p. 130 (ed. 1884).

[40]Nearchus (Strabo, XV. i. 67) says that the people of India had such a genius for imitation that they counterfeited sponges, which they saw used by the Macedonians, and produced perfect imitations of the real object. See Sir G. Birdwood's "Industrial Arts of India," ii. p. 133 (ed. 1884).

[41]Ibid., ii. p. 131 (ed. 1884).

[42]See Sir G. Birdwood, p. 129 (ed. 1884). If Fergusson is right in suggesting that the art of Central America was planted there in the third or fourth century of our era, it would, perhaps, appear to have taken refuge in America when it was driven out of India by the Sassanians, and was really Dravidian. He gives to the Turanian races all the mound buildings, as well as the fylfot or mystic cross, and he looks in Central India for the discovery of some remains that will give us the secret of the origin of the Indo-Aryan style. He thinks the Archaic Dravidian is allied with the Chinese. See Fergusson's "Architecture."

[43]Etruscan and Indian golden ornaments, including the "Bolla" and the "Trichinopoly" chains and coral, are to be found throughout Scandinavia and in Ireland. See "Atlas de l'Archéologie du Nord," par la Société Royale des Antiquaires du Nord. Copenhagen, 1857.

[44]Arrian tells us of the Celts, "a people near the Great Ionian Bay," who sent an embassy to Alexander before the battle of the Granicus—"a people strong and of a haughty spirit." Alexander asked them if they feared anything. They answered that they feared the "sky might fall upon their heads." He dismissed them, observing that the Celts were an arrogant nation (Arrian, i. 4, 10).

[45]According to Yates, the merchandise of Eastern Asia passed through Slavonia to the north of Europe in the Middle Ages, without the intervention of Greece or Italy. This

may account for certain terms of nomenclature which evidently came with goods transported straight to the north. Yates' "Textrinum Antiquorum," vol. i. p. 225-246.

[46]These northern ideas, spreading over Germany, England, and France, flourished especially on German soil; and Oriental-patterned embroideries for hangings and dress were worked in every stitch, on every material, as may be seen in the museums and printed catalogues of Vienna, Berlin, Munich, &c.

[47]Except, perhaps, the Serpent and Tree cope in Bock's Kleinodien.

[48]The different Celtic nationalities are always recognizable. There was found in a grave-mound at Hof, in Norway, a brooch, showing at a glance that it was Christian and Celtic, though taken from the grave of a pagan Viking. Another at Berdal, in Norway, was at once recognized by M. Lorange as being undoubtedly Irish. There are many other instances of evident Celtic Christian art found on the west coast of Norway under similar conditions—probably spoil from the British Islands, which were subject to the descents of the pagan Vikings for centuries after the time of St. Columba's preaching of Christianity in Scotland. For information on the subject, see G. Stephen's "Monuments of Runic Art," and F. Anderson's "Pagan Art in Scotland."

[49]"Scotland in Pagan Times," by J. Anderson, pp. 3-7.

[50]On a vase in the British Museum, Minerva appears with her ægis on her breast, and clothed in a petticoat and upper tunic worked in sprays, and a border of kneeling lions. On another Panathenaic vase she has a gown bordered with fighting men, evidently the sacred peplos. (Fig. 4.)

[51]See the account of the veil of Herè in the Iliad, and that of the mantle of Ulysses in the Odyssey.

[52]See Butcher and Lang's Odyssey.

[53]"Der Stil."

[54]The Greeks collected into one focus all that they found of beauty in art from many distant sources—Egyptian, Indian, Assyrian—and thus fired their inborn genius, which thenceforth radiated its splendour over the whole civilized world.

[55]Homer's Iliad, xviii. 480-617 (Butcher and Lang).

[56]See "Woltmann and Woermann." Trans. Sidney Colvin, p. 64.

[57]Except, perhaps, the keystone arch.

[58]Virg. Æneid iii. Trans. G.L.G.

[59]The Indian Cush.

[60]Except in the art of the Celts, whose Indo-Chinese style shows evidence of Mongolian importation, and later we find traces of a similar influence: for instance, "Yarkand rugs are semi-Chinese, semi-Tartar, resembling also the works of India and Persia. It is easy to distinguish from what source each comes, as one perceives the influence of the neighbouring native art" ("On Japan," by Dresser, p. 322).

[61]See a paper by M. Terrien de la Couperie in the Journal of the Society of Arts, 1881.

[62]"Rome had to be overthrown that the new religion and the new civilization might be established. Christianity did its work in winning to it those Teutonic conquerors, but how vast was the cost to the world, occasioned by the necessity of casting into the boiling cauldron of barbarous warfare, that noble civilization and the treasures which Rome had gathered in the spoil of a conquered universe! Had any old Roman, or Christian father been gifted with Jeremiah's prescience, he might have seen the fire blazing amidst the forests of Germany, and the cauldron settling down with its mouth turned towards the south, and would have uttered his lamentation in plaintive tones, such as Jeremiah's, and in the same melancholy key" ("Holy Bible," with Commentary by Canon Cook, Introduction to Jeremiah, vol. i. p. 319).

[63]Scandinavian art became strongly tinctured with that of Byzantium. The Varangian Guards were, probably, answerable for this, by their intercourse between Greece and their native land, which lasted so many centuries. There have come down to us, as witnesses of this intercourse, many coins and much jewellery, in which all that is Oriental in its style has been leavened by its passage through Byzantine and Romanesque channels.

Gibbon, writing of this period, says: "The habits of pilgrimage and piracy had approximated the countries of the earth" (see Gibbon's "Decline and Fall," chap. lv.).

Greek embroidered patterns and Greek forms of dress still linger in Iceland. There was lately brought to England a bride's dress, which might have belonged to the Greek wife of a Varangian guardsman. It is embroidered with a border in gold of the classical honeysuckle pattern; and the bridal wreath of gilt metal flowers might, from its style, be supposed to have been taken from a Greek tomb.

[64] Evidently an imitation of the peplos of Minerva (see fig. 4, p. 32).

[65] The descent from the Persian of Arab or Moorish art, as we generally call it when speaking of its Spanish development, is to be accounted for by the presence of a considerable colony of Persians in Spain in the time of the Moors, as attested by numerous documents still in existence. See Col. Murdoch Smith's "Preface to Persian Art," Series of Art Handbooks of the Kensington Museum.

[66] Ronsard, poet, politician, and diplomatist, compares the Queen of Navarre to Pallas Athene:—

"Elle adonnait son courageA mainte bel ouvrageDessus la toile, et encorA joindre la soie et l'or.Vous d'un pareil exerciseMariez par artificeDessus la toile en mainte traitsL'or et la soie en pourtraict."

[67] Mary de Medici brought back with her from Italy Federigo Vinciolo as her designer for embroideries.

[68] See "Art Needlework," by E. Maxse, and "Manuel de la Broderie," by Madame E. F. Celnart.

[69] From the Italian translation by Signor Minghetti.

[70] Gaston, Duke of Orleans (died 1660), kept hothouses on purpose to supply models for floral textile designs. Le Brun often drew the embroideries for the hangings in rooms he had himself designed and decorated.

[71] We have all seen the dining-room wine-coolers modelled in imitation of Roman tombs; and there is a drawing-room in a splendid mansion still furnished with cinerary urns covering the walls, while curule chairs most uncomfortably furnish the seats.

[72] In his designs for papers and textiles, Mr. Morris' poetical and artistic feeling—his admiration and sensitiveness for all that is beautiful and graceful (as well as quaint)—his respect for precedent, added to his own fanciful originality,—have given a colour and seal to the whole decorative art of England of to-day. It is a step towards a new school. The sobriety and tenderness of his colouring gives a sense of harmony, and reconciles us to his repetitions of large vegetable forms, which remind us sometimes of a kitchen-garden in a tornado. For domestic decoration we should, as far as possible, adhere to reposing forms and colours. Our flowers should lie in their allotted spaces, quiet and undisturbed by elemental struggles, which have no business in our windowed and glass-protected rooms.

[54]

CHAPTER II.
DESIGN.

Gorgo. Behold these 'broideries! Finer saw you never.

Praxinoë. Ye gods! What artists work'd these pictures in?What kind of painter could these clear lines limn?How true they stand! nay, lifelike, moving ever;Not worked—*created!* Woman, thou art clever!

(Scene at a Festival)*Theocritus*, Idyll xv. line 78.

The word design, as applied to needlework, includes the principles and laws of the art: the motives and their hereditary outcome; the art creating the principles; the laws controlling the art.

Design means intention, motive, and should as such be applied to the smallest as to the greatest efforts of art. That which results from it, either as picture or pattern, is a record of the thoughts which produced it, and by its style fixes the date, of its production.

I will first consider the principles of design, and afterwards, in another chapter, inquire into the origin of patterns; investigating their motives, and using them as examples, and also as warnings.

The individual genius of the artist works first in design, though his work is for the use of the craftsman or artisan, his collaborator; for the two, head and hands, must work together, or else will render each other inoperative or ineffective.

The artisan, by right of his title, claims a part in the art itself; the craftsman, by his name, points out that he, too, has to work out the craft, the mystery, the inner meaning, of the design or intention.

The designer himself is subject to the prejudices called [55]the taste of his day. He is necessarily under the influence which that taste has imposed upon him, and from which no spontaneous efforts of genius can entirely emancipate him. Whether he is conceiving a temple for the worship of a national faith, or the edging for the robe of a fair votaress, or the pattern on the border of a cup of gold or brass, he cannot avoid the force of tradition and of custom, which comes from afar, weighted with the power of long descent, and which crushes individuality, unless it is of the most robust nature.

Of very early design we have most curious and mysterious glimpses. The cave man was an artist. The few scratches on a bone, cleverly showing the forms of a dog or a stag, a whale or a seal, nay, the figure of a man, have enabled us to ascertain and to classify the Palæolithic cave man; from whom his less civilized successor, the Neolithic man, may be distinguished by his absence of all animal design.[73]

These fragmentary scraps of information, pieced together only in these later years, teach us the value of very small facts which time and care are now accumulating, and which, being the remains of lives and nations passed away, still serve as the soil in which history can be fertilized.

We have no means of judging whether the cave man was an artist on a greater or more advanced scale than [56]is actually shown by the bone-scratchings; the only other relic of his handiwork is the needle.[74]

It is evident that a direct imitation of nature, such as is seen in these "graffiti," and at an immense distance in advance of them, in the earliest known Egyptian sculptures, preceded all conventional art. Some of the earliest portrait statues in the Museum at Boulac exhibit a high degree of naturalistic design before it became subservient to the expression of the faith of the people. As soon as art was found to be the fittest conveyance of symbolism, it became the consecrated medium for transmitting language, thought, and history, and was reduced to forms in which it was contented to remain petrified for many centuries, entirely foregoing the study or imitation of nature.[75] It recorded customs, historical events, and religious beliefs; receiving from the last the impress of the unchangeable and the absolute, which it gave to the other subjects on which it touched. It ceased to be a creative art (if it had ever aspired to such a function), and was never the embodiment of individual thought. This phase prevailed under different manifestations in Assyria and China. Pictorial art had, in fact, become merely the nursing mother of the alphabet, guiding its first steps—the hieroglyphic delineation or expression of thoughts and facts.[76]

[57]In Egypt, the change from the first period of actual imitation of nature was succeeded by many centuries of the very slowest progress. Renouf speaks,[77]however, of "the astonishing identity that is visible through all the periods of Egyptian art" (for you could never mistake anything Egyptian for the produce of any other country). "This identity and slow movement," he says, "are not inconsistent with an immense amount of change, which must exist if there is any real life." In fact, there were periods of relative progress, repose, and decay, and every age had its peculiar character. Birch, Lepsius, or Marriette could at once tell you the age of a statue, inscription, or manuscript, by the characteristic signs which actually fix[78] the date.

Design, unconsciously has a slowly altering and persistently onward movement, which but seldom repeats itself. It is one of the most remarkable instances of evolution. But it also has its cataclysms (however we may account for them), of which the Greek apotheosis of all art is a shining example, and the total disappearance of classical influence in Europe before the Renaissance is another.

I will instance one prevailing habit of Egyptian art.[79] In the long processional subjects, and in individual separate figures, it was usual to draw the head in perfect profile, the body facing you, but not completely—a sort [58]of compromise with a three-quarter view of it—and the feet following each other, on the same line as the profile. This mode of representing the human figure was only effaced gradually by the introduction of Greek art, and continued to be the conventional and decorative method even in the latest days of Egyptian art; and it is curious to observe, that in the Dark ages European design fell into the same habit. We cannot imagine that this distorted way of drawing the human figure could have any intentional meaning, and therefore may simply believe that it had become a custom; and that when art has so stiffened and consolidated itself by precedent and long tradition, as in Egypt and in India, certain errors as well as certain truths become, as it were, ingrained into it. Plato remarked of Egyptian art, that "the pictures and statues they made ten thousand years ago were in no particular better than those they make now."[80]

One day, however, the Greek broke away from the ancient bonds of custom. The body was made to accompany the head, and the feet followed suit. But the strange fact remains that for several thousand years men walked in profile, all out of drawing. Evidently originality was not in much estimation among the Egyptian patrons of art. Design seemed to have restricted itself to effective adaptations in a few permitted forms in architecture and painting, and the illumination of the papyrus MSS.

Egyptian elasticity of design found some scope in its domestic ornamentation, in jewellery and hangings, but especially in its embroideries for dress. Here much ingenuity was shown, and the patterns on walls and the ceilings of tombs give us the designs which Semper considers as having been originally intended for textile purposes. He strains to a point to which I can hardly [59]follow him, the theory that all decorations were originally textile (except such as proceeded in China from the lattice-work motive); though I willingly accept the idea that textile decoration was one of the first and most active promoters of design.

It is not possible for us to trace systematically the different points at which Egyptian and Asiatic art touch, but we can see that they were always acting and reacting on each other in the later centuries before our era, and that Greece profited by them. The first efforts of both to break through this chrysalis stage, resulted in the early Greek archaic style. Its strongly marked, muscular humanity reminds one of all the conflicting impressions struggling in the conception of the great artist who first embodied them. They appear to be breaking out from the trammels of Egyptian and Assyrian styles, which by meeting had engendered life; and Greek art was the child of their union. Then art, having shaken off symbolism as its only purpose, and seeking to represent the forms of men, yet possessed by a guiding spirit, first sought to convey the idea of expression. The worship of humanity, mingling with that of their gods, produced the Heroic ideal; and all the attributes of their heroes—majesty, beauty, grace, and passion—had to be depicted; as well as rage, sorrow, despair, and revenge. These were soon to be surrounded with all the splendours of the arts of decoration.

Greece had prepared for this outburst of excellence and the perfect science of art, by collecting the traditions, the symbols, the experience in colouring, and the knowledge of beautiful forms, human and ideal. All that was needed for the advent of the man who could design and create types of beauty for all ages was thus accumulated, and the man came, and his name was Pheidias. A crowd followed him, all steeped in the same flood of poetry [60]and art; and for several centuries they filled the world with the sense and science of beauty. Then the function of the designer—the artist—was changed and elevated, and he became, through the great days of Greek and Roman Pagan art, and afterwards through the rise of that of Christianity, the exponent of all that was poetical and ennobling in the life of man.

But though the Greek artist had broken the chains of prescribed form, he still adhered to the "motive"—the inner symbolical thought—and strove to express it as it had never been expressed before.[81] New principles were evoked, and the artist, while revelling in the "sweetness and light" of freedom, framed for himself standards of taste and refinement, which he left as a heritage to all succeeding generations.

I fear that I am repeating a platitude when insisting that freedom in all design, but especially that employed in decoration, must be kept within certain boundaries; otherwise it becomes lawless. Rules, like all other controlling circumstances, are of the greatest service to the artist, as they suggest what he can do, as well as decide what he ought not to attempt. All boundaries are highly suggestive; the size of a sheet of paper—the form of a panel—the colours in the box of pigments—even the touch of the brush which comes to hand,—all these help to shape the idea to our ends, and assist us in giving to the original motive the [61]form which is most suitable. These restrictions are often regarded as impediments by the impatient artist; whereas he ought to look on them as hints and suggestions, and claim their assistance, instead of struggling against them. Let us accept the principle that it is good for each of our efforts at decoration that we are controlled by the space allotted to its composition. The relative size (small, perhaps, for a table-cover, but large for that of a book) and the shape to which we are limited, alter all the conditions of a design. Whether it is square or oblong, or lengthened into a frieze; whether it must be divided into parts, including more than one motive, or be grouped round one centre; whether it is to be repeated more than once within the range of the eye, or whether it is to disappear into space upwards or horizontally; and whether it is to stand alone, or be framed with lines or a border,—all these restrictions must govern the design, or, in its highest phase, the composition.

The composition must consist of supporting lines well balanced, and "values" filling up the whole surface of the space, which is to contain it, and beyond which it must not seek to extend. As we have in embroidery no distances—only a foreground—the design must be placed all on one plane. The title of "composition" cannot be granted to a bouquet or a bird cast on one corner of a square of linen, however gracefully it may be drawn. It does not cover the space allotted to it.

If we carefully study the great and guiding principles that have been distinctly formulated by some of the Continental authorities on decorative art, we shall find much help in composing our designs. Nothing is more interesting than to search for the foundation of the structure which centuries have helped to raise, and to dig out, as it were, the original plan or thought of the [62]founder. So it is most instructive to learn the fundamental rules by which such results are secured.

M. Blanc[82] says of the general laws of ornamentation: "There can be no nobler satisfaction to the mind, than to be able to unravel what is beyond measure complicated, to diminish what is apparently immense, and to reduce to a few clear points what has been till now involved in a haze of obscurity. Just as the twenty-six letters of the alphabet have been, and always will be sufficient to form the expression of the words necessary for all human thought, so certain elements susceptible of combination among themselves have sufficed, and will suffice, to create ornament, whose variety may be indefinitely multiplied."

He reduces ornamental design to five principles, Repetition, Alternation, Symmetry, Progression, and Confusion.

Fig. 5.
Wave Pattern.

First, Repetition. "You may act on the mind, through sight, by the same means as those that will excite physical sensations. A single prick of a pin is nothing, but a hundred such will be intolerably painful. Repetition produces pleasurable sensations, as well as painful ones." An insignificant form can become interesting by repetition, and by the suggestion which, singly, it could not originate. For example, the rolling of the Greek scroll or wave pattern awakens in us the idea of one object following another. "It also suggests the waves of the ocean; or the poet may see in it a troop of maidens pursuing each other in space, not frivolously, but in cadence, as if executing a mystic [63]dance." Change the curves into angular forms, as making the key pattern, and it will no longer flow, but become as severe as the other was graceful. No principle gives greater pleasure than repetition, and next to it,*alternation.*

Fig. 6.
Key Pattern.

Variety is here added to the law of repetition. "There can be repetition without alternation, but no alternation without repetition." Alternation is, then, a succession of two objects recurring regularly in turn; and the cadence of appearance and disappearance gives pleasure to the senses, whether it be addressed to taste, hearing, or sight. Alternate rhymes, and even short and long lines, soothe the ear in verse. In form, the alternations are the more agreeable, the more they differ. Such are, in architecture, a succession of metopes and triglyphs on a Doric frieze, where the circle and the straight lines relieve each other.

Fig. 7.
Metopes and Triglyphs.

Symmetry. The correspondence of two parts opposite to each other is symmetrical. "A living being, man or animal, is composed of two parts, which appear to have been united down one central line. Without being identical, if you folded them down the line, they would overlap and perfectly cover each other. Man is born with the sense of symmetry, to match his outward form; and he appreciates its existence, and instinctively feels the want of it. Symmetry is another [64]word for justness of proportion. The Greeks understood by symmetry, the condition of a body of which the members have a common measure among themselves. We expect the two sides of a living being to correspond, and we look for these proportions in the living body to balance each other, which we do not expect to find in any other natural object. A large leaf at the end of a slender stem may be as appropriate, and give as much pleasure, as a small leaf in the same position; but a huge hand at the end of an arm is not so agreeable to our sense of symmetry as one of the size and outline which we naturally expect to see.

"The mind of man expects to find, outside of himself and his own proportions, something which he feels is proportionate and symmetrical; in fact, he at once detects the want of it. The Japanese, with delicacy and taste, often substitute for symmetry its corollary—balance. The Chinese or Japanese vase will often have an appreciable affinity and resemblance to a Greek one, each preserving a secret balance, even in the extremest whimsicality of its composition. Proportion is another corollary to symmetry, if it is not another word for some of its qualities."

"Progression. In this principle are included long perspectives, pyramidal forms in architecture, and certain processional compositions."

"For pyramidal surfaces, such as pediments, a progressive ornament is the fittest. All the buildings in the East, and in the ancient cities of Central America, which are raised on pyramids of steps, show the tendency to this species of effect in giving dignity to the buildings placed on such platforms."

"Perspectives are highly attractive specimens of progression, which, when made use of in the decorations of a theatre, produce delightful illusions."

[65]M. Blanc quotes Bernardin de St. Pierre, who says: "When the branches of a plant are disposed in a uniform plan of diminishing size, as in the pyramidal shape of a pine, there is progression; and if these trees be planted in long avenues, diminishing in height and colour, as each tree does in itself, our pleasure is redoubled, because progression here becomes infinite. It is owing to this feeling of infinity that we take pleasure in looking at anything that presents progression, such as nurseries in different stages of growth, the slopes of hills retreating to the horizon at different levels—interminable perspectives."

All floral compositions which give the effect or impression of growth may be included in the progressive principle. A composition which, beginning as it were with a stem, spreads and floreates equally on each side; thrusting outwards and upwards, and ending in a topmost twig or bud, is governed by this principle.

Confusion. Boileau is quoted by M. Blanc as saying, "A fine disorder is often the effect of art;" and he adds, "But before he said it, nature had shown it." Here we must observe that the confusions or disorders of nature are all subject to certain laws; and it is in adopting this idea, that an artistic confusion may give us the sense of its being ordered by, and subject to definite rules. These rules act as the frame affects the picture, circumscribing its irregularities, and restricting them to a certain area. "The artist-painter is, in a small space, permitted to employ confusion, because the art of the cabinet-maker will keep the geometrical effect in view." When the Japanese throw their ornaments, apparently without rule, here and there on the japanned box, they reckon on the square shape being sufficiently marked to the eye by its shining surface and sharp corners.

The confusion in a Japanese landscape is so beautiful [66]that one appreciates the innate sense of balance, which modifies the confusion—rules and orders it.

"In the hands of the designer, confusion is only a method of rendering order visible in a happy disorder. Here contraries meet and touch.... Admit these as the principles of all decoration, and you will find that, by following and combining them, you may produce varieties as numberless as the sands of the sea, and that a latent equilibrium will reduce nearly every complication and confusion to perfect harmony."

Each of the five principles we have discussed has its corollary, which adds to the resources of the decorative artist. These are as follows:—To Repetition belongs harmony, or consonance; to Alternation, contrast; to Symmetry, radiation; to Progression, gradation; to balanced Confusion, deliberate complication.[83]

Harmonies in form and in colour are produced in different ways—sometimes by repetition with variation; sometimes by the different parts being rather reflected on each than repeated. This explains the harmony that may be called consonance, if I rightly understand M. Blanc's theory.

Contrast is most generally understood as a common resource in the hands of the artist for producing strong effects; but M. Blanc cleverly expresses the reticence needed to ensure contrast being pleasurable, not painful. "To adorn persons or things," he says, "is not simply for the purpose of causing them to be conspicuous; it is that they may be admired. It is not simply to draw attention to them, but that they may be regarded with feelings of pleasure.... If contrast be needed, let it be used as the means of rendering the whole more powerful, brilliant, and striking. For instance, if orange is intended to predominate in a decoration, let blue be mingled with [67]it, but sparingly. Let the complementary colour be its auxiliary, and not its rival." Contrasts are always unpleasant, if the two forces struggle with each other for pre-eminence, whether it be in form or in colour. The rule to be observed in all ornamental design is this: "that contrasting objects, instead of disturbing unity, should assist it by giving most effect to that we wish to bring forward and display."

Radiation belongs to the principle of symmetry, starting from a centre from which all lines diverge, and to which all lines point. This is to be found throughout nature, from the rays of the sun to the petals of the daisy. All decorative art employs and illustrates it.

"*Gradation* in colour, as in form, is not quite synonymous with progression, but expresses a series of adroitly managed transitions. The English intermingle in their decoration, colours very finely blended; nor do they find any transition too delicate. This, as in all principles of ornament, has to be employed according to the feelings intended to be produced on the mind of the spectator—whether for absolute contrast or for imperceptible progression, when the tenderest colours are needed."

Complication is illustrated by M. Blanc, by a quotation from "Ziegler."[84]"Complication is another aspect of the art which owns the same sentiment as that expressed by Dædalus in his labyrinth, Solomon in his mysterious seal, the Greeks in their interlacing and winding ornaments, the Byzantines, the Moors, and the architects of our cathedrals in their finest works. Intertwined mosaics, and intersection of arches and ribs, all spring from complication."

To follow the interlacing line of an ornament, gives the mind the pleasure of untying the Gordian knot, without cutting it. It gives the excitement of curiosity, [68]pursuit, and discovery. "When we see these traceries so skilfully plaited, in which straight lines and curves intermingle, cross, branch out, disappear and recur, we experience a high pleasure in unravelling a puzzle which at first, perhaps, appeared to be undecipherable; and in acknowledging that a latent arrangement may be recognized in what at first, and at a distance, seems an inextricable confusion." The Celtic, Moorish, and Gothic styles illustrate and are explained by these remarks; and they are well worthy the attention of the designer.

Having so freely borrowed from M. Blanc's chapter on the general laws of ornamentation, I will finish my quotations with the words with which he concludes: "There is no decoration in the works of nature or the inventions of men which does not owe its birth to one of the original principles here enumerated, viz. Repetition, Alternation, Symmetry, Progression, and Balanced Confusion; or else to one of their secondary causes, consonance, contrast, radiation, gradation, and complication; or lastly, to a combination of these different elements, which all finally lose themselves in a primordial cause—the origin of the movements of the universe—ORDER."[85]

The extracts from M. Blanc's works I have carefully placed between commas, being most anxious to express my obligation to him for his carefully formulated epitome of the laws of design. But though I have largely quoted, there remains still much most interesting and suggestive matter, which I recommend the reader to seek in his book.

Though we should call to our aid the general laws of design for all art, we must select from them what is specially appropriate for the needs of our craft. From [69]the art of needlework we should eliminate as much as possible all ideas of *roundness*, all variety of surface and effects of light and shadow and contrasting colours. Unity, softness, grace, refinement, brightness, cheerfulness, pleasant suggestions,—these should be the objects in view when we design the panels for the drawing-room or boudoir, the hangings for the bed, or the cover for the table—harmony which will satisfy the eye, thoughts that shall please the mind.

The objects in nature that give us the most unalloyed pleasure—birds and flowers—are those that from all time have served as the materials for decorative design, and therefore have been moulded into the traditional patterns which have descended to us from the earliest times. Design must follow the scientific laws of art, and shape the variations of traditional forms from which we cannot escape. In our present search after these inner truths, I repeat that we have nothing to do with the rules of painting, sculpture, and architecture, or any other of the secondary arts, such as wood carving, metal work, &c.; these having each their own intrinsic principles, which must be worked out as corollaries from the general laws of composition which govern all Aryan art.[86]

It is curious that in drawing on the flat, in ancient [70]frescoes, there appear to be no acknowledged rules of perspective—hardly more in Pompeii, than on early Chinese screens and plates; or than later in the Bayeux tapestries. And yet the Greeks, with their unerring instinct, actually made use of false architectural perspectives to add to the effects of height and depth in their colonnaded buildings.[87] They sensibly diminished the circumference of the columns, and used other means in their designs for this purpose. They understood the principle, but they did not carry it into flat decorative art. They did not attempt, when they painted a landscape on the wall, to do more than recall the idea they were sketching; and never thought of vying in scientific or naturalistic imitation with the real landscape they saw through the window; they did not wish to interfere with the effect of the statue, or the human figures grouped in front of it, to which the wall served as a background. Those threw shadows and cast lights; but in the flat there were no shadows, no perspective—all was flat.[88] We must draw from this the deduction that the Greeks held that flatness was an essential quality of wall decoration (except in friezes) as well as of all textile ornament; and for every reason we must accept this flatness as a general law for designs in embroidery.

In hangings and dress materials, flatness is more agreeable than a complicated shaded design, especially when it is further confused by folds, disturbing and interrupting the flow of the lines of the pattern.

The reader will perceive that the laws of composition for textiles quoted from M. Blanc, apply perfectly to designs on the flat, and to outlined sketches in black and[71]white, as well as to the most elaborate compositions for pictures, either historical or "genre." They are rules which should be understood and employed by the man who draws for a wall-paper or an area railing; and certainly by him who makes patterns for our schools of design.

It may therefore be laid down as a general rule, that all designs for embroidery should be considered first as outlined drawings, covering a flat surface, and then filled in with colour. The outlines should as little as possible overlap one another, as flatness is one of the first objects to be remembered; and this, of course, will be disturbed by the parts passing over or under each other. Indian designs in flowers have invariably a wonderful flatness, in the absence of all light and shadow; joined to a naturalistic suggestion of detail, which is accounted for by their traditional mode of copying from nature. The branch or blossom to be copied, is laid on the ground and pegged down with care, to eliminate every variety of surface, and every branch and twig so arranged that they may not cross or touch each other. This conventional composition is then drawn, and every natural distinction in the form carefully copied. I would suggest that this idea should be accepted as useful for imitation among ourselves in certain conventional compositions of vegetable forms. Perhaps it is our

Aryan ancestry that has given us a prevailing taste for such decorations; and it is worth while to consider how best to manipulate them.[89]

Clinging as we do to these floral designs, we can see that they are the only ones that bear repetition, whether covering the surface of the material in the rich irregularity [72]of the flowers in a field, or conventionalized into a form or a pattern.

The eye is never shocked or fatigued by such repetitions in orderly confusion, or trained by the hand into artistic shapes or meanderings of tracery. But when embroidery or weaving attempts to represent animals or typical human figures, repetition immediately becomes tiresome. A Madonna surrounded by angels, comes in badly, repeated over and over again as a pattern, broken up by folds, cut up by a seam, dislocated in the joining, and repeated in tiers. Such a design is figured in Auberville's book.[90] The drawing is beautiful, but by repetition it becomes ridiculous. I therefore deprecate this kind of ornament in textile work. For this reason embroidery, which can be fitted to each space that is to be covered, is preferable to woven designs, however richly or perfectly they may be carried out.

Another class of design, which must be considered apart, is the conventional-geometrical, of which the special distinction appears to be that it consists of echoes or fragments of what we have seen elsewhere. These conventional patterns are often merely the *detritus* of past styles or motives crushed and placed by time in a sort of kaleidoscope. They remind one of the little wreaths of broken shells and coloured sea-weeds left on the sands by the retiring waves after a storm, and are sometimes full of beauty and suggestion. (Pl. 17.) We trace in these fragmentary patterns forgotten links with different civilizations; and we ponder on the historical events which have brought them into juxtaposition. These kaleidoscope patterns are to be seen in Persian and Turkish carpets of the present day, and we find, on examination, little bits which can only be the remnants of a broken-up motive, probably as much lost now to the [73]designer who inherits the traditional form, as to us who can only see the vague results.

I illustrate this remark by giving the border of a modern Persian carpet which has certainly had Egyptian ancestry. The boat, the beetle, and the prehistoric cross are to be found in it.

Fig. 8.
Persian Carpet.

Many conventional patterns of to-day are descendants of the lattice-work of Chinese art, and of the zigzags, lines, and discs of barbarous primitive ornamentation.

The traceries in Indian stone windows show some of the most charming geometrical forms, and are akin to the Persian and Russian modes of composing conventional patterns. They appear on very ancient metal work, and are the motives of all the embroideries in the Greek islands and the principalities, and of the linen embroideries of Russia. Their Byzantine origin gave its impress to the European schools of the Middle Ages, and the pattern-books of Germany and Venice of the sixteenth century are full of them. They are best suited for the mosaic stitches, and, kept in their places as decoration, they are useful for carpets and borders.

It should be impressed on our young artists, that, in composing their designs, they must be influenced by the [74]materials to be employed, and the purpose for which the decoration is intended. Thus in textile design for dress and hangings (excepting for tapestries) the fact must never be lost sight of that they will be subject to disturbance by crossing folds and crumplings, which will break up the lines of the pattern. It is therefore evident that a design fitted for a rigid material in a fixed place, such as an architectural decoration in wood, stone, or stucco, must be subject to a treatment different from that which befits an embroidered curtain or panel.

Stone and wood, being materials of uniform colour, require all the help of recessed shadows and projections to catch the light; whereas in textiles, form is assisted by colour, and smoothness of surface is a primary consideration. The strongly accentuated design for wood-carving becomes poor and lifeless when deprived of its essential conditions and *raison d'être*, and the pattern which looks charming, outlined and filled in with colour, could be hardly seen incised on a flat stone surface. This seems a truism, but the neglect of these plain axioms causes many mistakes in decorative art. Mr. Redgrave says: "A design must be bad which applies the same treatment to different materials." He further says: "The position of the ornament requires special consideration. The varied quantities, bolder relief, and coarser execution are not only allowable, but absolutely necessary, at heights considerably above the eye. Moreover, each fabric has its own peculiar lustre, texture, &c. Thus, in the use of hangings, curtains, &c., the design might be suitable in silk, and coarse or dull in woollen."[91]

Here I venture to differ from Mr. Redgrave. Perspective is as much to be respected in decoration as in pictures, near to the eye; and the gradation in size and [75]colour, as the ornament travels up into height or fades into distance, is a phase of pleasure which should not be checked by enlargement of form or reinforcement of colouring.

It is hardly necessary to warn our artists against a sort of design which is conventional, yet had its own meaning in the beginning. This is to be found in Indian carvings and embroideries of a certain date, or imitating the works of that distant period. It proceeded from a hideous worship of monstrous Dravidian divinities. Their statues are to be found, surrounded by coarsely designed patterns, in the temple architecture of the first and second centuries. Its characteristics are idols in niches or shrines, distorted in form or attitude; foliage of unnatural, twisted plants, added to the recurring of the lotus and tree of life; or animals destroying each other, or kneeling in worship to the idols. These ugly designs are purely conventional. Fergusson suggests that they were introduced into Mexico in the fourth or fifth centuries A.D. by Buddhism.[92]

Those many-armed, sometimes many-faced divinities drove out the beautiful Aryan types, which, however, resumed their sway when the wave of the Renaissance flowed back to India, and was remodelled by Oriental taste to the lovely designs we find in the Taj Mahal.

In M. Blanc's classification of ornament, he has placed Gothic design under the head of deliberate complication. The whole of the Gothic decorations, which are a gradual growth in one direction, arose from the study of interlacing boughs and stems, employed as the enrichment of the newly-grown forms of the vaulted roofs. The possibilities of great size and height covered these designs and [76]inspired all their decoration; and the effect of reiteration and long recurring lines in perspective was essentially the motive of these avenues in stone.[93]

Here enter the principles of repetition and progression, and you will find how carefully the designers of the twelfth, thirteenth, and fourteenth centuries worked up to these ideas. You will see in their embroideries, shining figures or pictures in gold, silver, and coloured silks, shimmering on dark velvet backgrounds, each design terminating a perspective of architectural forms which enhances their brilliancy. The most effective, probably, [77]were generally employed for the adornment of the high altar, so as to be seen from a great distance. The smaller and less distinct and more delicate ornaments were reserved for the side chapels or for smaller churches, where such distant effects were inappropriate. But the motives of ecclesiastical embroidery will be discussed in a future chapter.

All attempts at pictorial art are a mistake in textiles. It does not enter into such designs; and when by chance it is allowed to be so used, it is an error of judgment, and only exhibits a laborious and useless ingenuity. It is no longer an artistic delineation of a natural object, but becomes an imitation of another way of rendering such objects.

Mr. Redgrave says that pictorial art in our manufactures is one of our great mistakes. "The picture must be independent of the material, the thought alone should govern it; whereas in decoration the material must be one of the suggestors of the thought, its use must govern the design."

Perhaps it will appear to my readers that here I repeat, in different forms, what has been said in a previous chapter on the history of style. I think that it is better to do so, than to omit to show where style and design must accompany each other. Style, without any reference to design, would be but a barren subject; and design, without reference to style, would become lawless, and soon be lost in the mazes of bad taste and mannerism. Both subjects are of so large and important a nature that I do not attempt to do more than point out how, in their history and their influence, they belong to the craft of embroidery.

Such influences belong to all art; and though I am anxious to confine myself to only one section of it, I find it difficult to resist the temptation to generalize and [78]stray from the prescribed path, when large and important views are opened on every side, as I travel on from point to point.

In sketching the history of design, as well as I may in so short a space, it is only considered in the light in which it illustrates our craft.

I repeat that the design should be informed by the motive which suggested it, and by the need which has called it forth; and it must be moulded to the space it has to fill, and the position it will occupy. The design must be modified into different outward forms, according to whether it is to be fitted to the edge of a building against the sky; to a high panelled wall; to be applied as a frieze, or round the capital of a pillar; to the embroidered cover of an altar, or the silken hangings of a bed, or the framed flat spaces on the walls of a saloon. In fact, "intention," "place," and "shape" are necessary motives and limits to a flat design.

Leaving aside all architectural ornamentation, and adhering only to my own subject, embroidery, I will limit my observations to the three purposes here suggested. Firstly, as the central effect of the holiest part of a church; secondly, in the domestic and comfortable room, to be adorned and made cheerful; and thirdly, as decking the refined and gay saloon or banqueting-hall.

To the church we should devote the most splendid and effective contrasts, to blaze unframed against dark empty backgrounds, or amidst stone and marble decorations; something set apart from its surroundings, and asserting that separation, is the desirable effect to be attained.

A totally different set of rules come into play when we have to select the decorations of a bedroom. Here a background does not exist. We are surrounded by four walls very near to the eye, so that perspectives are a secondary interest, if indeed they can claim any [79]consideration; severe and magnificent ornamentation is out of place, except perhaps in that time-honoured institution—to be found in every great house possessing a suite of reception-rooms—the State bedroom, where the display of hangings and embroideries was the first motive of the decoration of the past, clothing and garnishing the bare spaces on the lofty walls. Space and separateness are not the object or aim of the bedroom of to-day; but lightness, snugness, and cheerful comfort, with which the design of the textile ornaments have much to do. This will in a later chapter come under the head of furniture.

For the saloon we may accept any splendour of rich and costly design, and the variously shaped panels assist in suggesting the form of the decoration. The plain or moulded panels, called in Italian "targhe," or shields, seem to be descended from the actual shields of gold which Solomon hung on the walls of the king's house in the Forest of Lebanon.[94] The motive was apparently Tyrian, and traces of it are also to be found in Assyrian sculpture.[95]

The practice of framing the design gives opportunities for change of materials, colour, and pattern, permitting the employment of different flat surfaces laid on each other, and scope for endless enrichment; the framed picture being, perhaps, the central culminating attraction, crowning, as it were, the textile ornamentation.

I merely give these instances as illustrating the rule that we have more than once laid down, that a design cannot fitly be employed except in the position for which the artist has composed it. I will, however, add that though it is right to give due consideration to the [80]preparation of each work for its intended use, yet we often have charming suggestions offered to us, by the chance acquisition of a beautiful artistic specimen, which finds its own place and accommodates itself to the surrounding colours and forms. These are the happy accidents of which the cultivated artistic eye takes advantage, adding them to the experience which may help those who are seeking for the rules of harmony and contrast in design.

Research into the mysteries and principles of design applies to woven arabesques and patterns, and must include machine-made textile ornament, and all decorative needlework. It is, in fact, the fabric for the million which most especially needs the careful study of guiding rules. When a plant sends forth hundreds of winged, wind-blown seeds, like the thistle, it spreads itself over wide fields, and is more mischievous than a more noxious growth, such as the deadly nightshade, which only drops an occasional berry into the earth. So a common cheap chintz or carpet, with a poor, gaudy, motiveless design, carries a bad style into thousands of homes wherever our commerce extends; disgracing us, while it corrupts the taste of other nations.

In addressing our young designers, I would remind them that in art the race is not always to the strong. Prudence and educated powers, thoughtfulness and study, often carry us where unassisted and uncultivated genius has signally failed. Even such facilities as are afforded by the acquirement of freehand drawing, as taught in our schools of art, are not to be despised. The workman should thoroughly master his tools, or they will hamper him. The first step towards design is that you should learn to draw. After this, appreciation and observation are necessary, and due balance in outline and colour should be studied; and all this is as much needed in [81]drawing a pattern as in composing a picture. The difference lies in our art being only decorative, wherein beauty and fitness are to be remembered, and nothing else; whereas the picture may have to record historical facts, or to inspire poetical thoughts—to awe or to touch the beholder. A decorative design is only asked to delight him. Intelligent delight, however, can only be evoked by intelligent art, and to this, decoration must be subjected.

FOOTNOTES:

[73]The earliest art we know (the bone-scratching) is naturalistic and imitative. We are unaware of any attempt at a pattern of the prehistoric period. The lake cities are of so vague a date that their ornaments on pottery are puzzling rather than instructive. The earliest Hellenic pottery was scratched or painted. Cuttle-fish, repeated over and over again, are among the earliest attempts at a pattern, by repetition of a natural object. Naturalism soon fell into symbolism, which appropriated it and all art, and the upheaval of a new culture was needed to lift it once more into the region of individual creation. See Boyd Dawkins' "Early Man in Britain;" also General Pitt Rivers's Museum of Prehistoric Art, lately presented to the University of Oxford.

[74]See Boyd Dawkins' "Early Man in Britain."

[75]"I hope, indeed, to enable them" (the members of his class) "to read, above all, the minds of semi-barbarous nations in the only language by which their feelings were capable of expression; and those whose temper inclines them to take a pleasure in mythic symbols, will not probably be induced to quit the profound fields of investigation which early art will open to them, and which belong to it alone. For this is a general law, that supposing the intellect of the workman the same, the more imitatively complete his art, the less he will mean by it, and the ruder the symbol, the deeper the intention."—Ruskin's "Oxford Lectures on Art," 1870, p. 19.

[76]See Isaac Taylor's "History of the Alphabet."

[77]Renouf's Hibbert Lectures, 1879, p. 67.

[78]Now there is a point of view in which we may regard the imitative art of all races, the most civilized as well as the most barbarous—in reference to the power of correctly representing animal and vegetable forms, such as they exist in nature. The perfection of such imitation depends not so much on the manual dexterity of the artist as on his intelligence and comprehension of the type of the essential qualities of the form he desires to represent. See Ch. T. Newton's "Essays on Art and Archæology," p. 17.

[79]See Wilkinson's "Ancient Egyptians."

[80]Plato's Second Book of Laws, p. 656.

[81]"The religion of the Greeks penetrated into their institutions and daily life. The myth was not only embodied in the sculptures of Pheidias on the Parthenon, and portrayed in the paintings of Polygnotus in the Stoa Poikile; it was repeated in a more compendious and abbreviated form on the fictile vase of the Athenian household, on the coin circulated in the market-place, on the mirror in which the Aspasia of the day beheld her charms. Every domestic implement was made the vehicle of figurative language, or fashioned into a symbol."—Newton's "Essays on Art and Archæology," p. 23.

[82]"Art in Ornament and Dress," by M. Charles Blanc, formerly Director of the French Institute. Eng. Trans., Chapman and Hall, London.

[83]See Charles Blanc's "Art in Ornament and Dress," p. 31.

[84]Charles Blanc's "Art in Ornament and Dress," p. 43.

[85]Charles Blanc's "Art in Ornament and Dress," pp. 43, 45, 46.

[86]Chinese design shows naturalistic art arrested and perpetuated on totally different principles. Their representations are all equally allied to their art of picture-painting, whether on china with the brush, or on textiles with the needle. The flatness of the picture is still preserved by their ignorance of perspective. When they attempted to express different distances, they did so by placing them one above another, so that in reading the composition the eye first takes in the distant horizon; next below it, the middle distance; and being thus prepared, it comes down to the actual living foreground, on which rests the dramatic action and interest addressed to the spectator. The Chinese understood many of the secrets of art, yet never achieved perspective.

[87]See Mr. Penrose's work on the measurements of the Parthenon at Athens. Published by the Society of the Dilettanti.

[88]Marked outlines in embroidery add to the flatness, and enable us to omit cast shadows. In this it differs entirely from pictorial art, where one of the great objects is to avoid flatness.

[89]Semper's theory, already mentioned, is that textile design was certainly flat; that it was the first form of decoration, and was followed by bas-relief, which could not at once rid itself of the original motive.

[90]Auberville's "Ornamentation des Tissus" (eleventh century).

[91]Redgrave's "Manual of Design," pp. 43-45.

[92]This idolatrous type was introduced into England by the Buccaneers, and reflected on our carvings and embroideries of the time of James I., slightly modified by the Italian Renaissance of that period. As this sort of vulgar ornamentation has once prevailed, let us protect ourselves against its possible recurrence.

[93]While making this passing allusion to the theory that the origin of all Gothic decoration is mainly founded on the motive of interlacing stems and foliage, I wish to guard myself against being supposed in any way to argue against other beginnings, whenever they can be proved. I have said before that most decorations have a mixed ancestry. But when I see single or clustered columns starting from the ground—spreading at the base like the gnarled root, and growing till they culminate in crowns of foliage, forming symmetrical capitals, like the first clusters of leaves on a strong young sapling—then the branches spreading and interlacing, only checked at equal intervals by a lovely leaf or burgeon, till they meet in blossoms on the highest point of the arch,—I cannot but adhere to the old idea that rows of trees meeting overhead suggested Gothic ornament as well as Gothic Architecture. The Spanish or Moresque Gothic was overloaded with leaves and flowers, and the German Gothic was enriched with fantastic trees and flowers, each according to its national taste and fashion. A Gothic tree is a very conventional plant; and generally carries only one leaf on each branch. I have given a specimen of archaic trees from the Bayeux tapestry. They are typical of the Gothic botanical idea and style down to the fourteenth century. (Fig.13.)

Nor is this interpretation of Gothic design other than a result of its descent from the Egyptian ancestral motive, where the temple columns represented the single stem of the lotus with one large blossom for its capital, or else a bundle of stems of the lotus, palm, and convolvulus flowering together into a beautiful cluster. Even the gigantic columns of the great hypæthral hall at Karnac are only a stupendous exaggeration of the same stalk and flower motive. From these were derived the forms of the early Greek column—soon enriched by substituting the Acanthus for the Lotus, but often retaining the convolvulus.

[94]1 Kings x.; Ezek. xxvii. 10, 11. See Stanley's "Lectures on the Jewish Church."

[95]Layard's "Nineveh and its Remains," vol. ii. p. 388; Rawlinson's "Ancient Monarchies," vol. ii. p. 2.

[82]

CHAPTER III.
PATTERNS.

In the last chapter on design I have described patterns as the examples or illustrations of the art of decoration, and as being the records of the motives which produced them in different eras. My present object is to class and define patterns as decorative art.

It is argued by some archæologists that the recurrence of a pattern, for instance the "wave," over the whole world, proves that it really came from many sources, under the same conditions of life and art; showing also that a pattern is a thing that, like a flower, must grow, if the culture of the race be equal. I do not believe this. We can nearly always trace the family history of a pattern to its original motive; and in the very few cases where we are unable to do so, it is hardly necessary to cover our ignorance by stretching the fashionable theory of development over the few instances that are as yet unaccountable.

I have been repeatedly asked to procure or to invent a new pattern. Such is my respect for the decorative achievement called a "pattern," that I cannot hope for the moment of inspiration in which I might create such a thing. If any one has in his lifetime invented a pattern, he has done something truly remarkable, and as rare as is a really original thought on any subject. Patterns are commonly, like men, the result of many centuries of long descent from ancestors of remote antiquity.

[83]Individuals differ from their ancestors through inherited and surrounding conditions, and through the modifying powers of evolution, climate, and education. So also a pattern has, besides its ancestry and descent, the unconscious mark or seal of its day; and it is easy to trace whence it comes, if we set ourselves to examine the style of it seriously.

The patterns of which we can nearly always name at once the nationality, are the Assyrian, the Chinese, the Egyptian, the Hindu (Aryan and Turanian), the Persian, the Archaic and the highly developed Grecian; the Roman, the Celtic, the Byzantine, the Arabian, the Gothic, the Renaissance, the Spanish Plâteresque, the Louis Quatorze, and those of the art of Central America.

The pattern cannot exist without design. Design means intention and motive. Many of the motives in Oriental textile decorations are suggestive of intention, as is shown by their names. Among Indian patterns we meet with "ripples of silver," "sunshine and shade," "pigeon's eye," "peacock's neck," &c.[96]

Patterns must be classed either by their dates, when ascertained, or according to their style, which must generally be allowed to cover vast areas and periods irregularly drifting down, overlapping, or being absorbed or effaced by the circumstances they have encountered.

Only when a national style has been obstinately fixed, as in China, and bound down by strict laws and religious formulas, suited exactly to the people for whom they were evolved out of the national life, and imprinted on it by their own lawgivers, philosophers, and priests; and neither imposed by conquerors, nor swept over by the waves of a new civilization;—only in such cases can [84]we find a continuity of decorative art which leads us far back on its traces. Then, on this long track, we learn how little, man, the decorating animal, has really advanced in his powers of creation. He has gone more than once to a certain point, and has then either been petrified by law and custom—turned into a pillar of salt, like Lot's wife, because he has looked back instead of striving to advance, or else through poverty or satiety has fallen into the last stage of the Seven Ages, "*sans* eyes, *sans* teeth—*sans* everything." When what is good is neither perceived nor desired, then the arts, small and great, dwindle and disappear, and nothing remains to show that they have been, but a name, and perhaps a pattern.

Chinese design is the most striking example of the first of these phases; and the extinction of all classical art with the fall of Paganism in Rome is an instance of the second.

In the chapter on style it is said that a pattern is as ineffaceable as a word. But one will occasionally disappear for a time, till the ruin that covers it is cleared away, and the lost design recovered and employed simply as a decoration, if it is beautiful; or perhaps fitted with a new meaning, and so it makes a fresh start.

The importance of patterns, when traceable to their origin, as a means of investigating historical influences cannot be too much insisted on, and their history is full of suggestion as a guide to the decorator. Much has been argued and much ascertained from the evidence of these fragments of national civilizations, showing how an idea or a myth has been, as it were, engrafted into the essence of another national idea, partly altering what it finds, and changing to fit itself to its new surroundings. Eastern patterns have travelled far, and lasted long; and continue still to hold the fancy, and exercise the ingenuity, of the artist and decorator. When we find a pattern [85]of which the nationality is strongly marked, it is worth our while to ascertain its date and history, which will help us to recognize cognate design wherever we may meet it. However, this is often not to be done; and then it is best to set these puzzling examples aside, and to await patiently the elucidation, which may come from some source of which we are as yet ignorant.

In very early art we have little remaining but patterns, on which we may found theories by tracing them home to their original source. The oldest patterns had each a meaning and an intention. When a pattern has been enduring and far spread, it is because it was originally the expression of an idea or a symbol.

In the earliest dawn of civilization, the arts were the repositories of the myths and mysteries of national faiths. Embroidery was one of these arts, and the border which edged the garment of a divinity, the veil which covered the grave of a loved one, or the flower-buds and fruit which fringed the hangings and curtains in the sanctuary, each had a meaning, and therefore a use. These symbolical designs and forms were constantly reproduced; and all human ingenuity was exercised in reforming, remodelling, and adding perfect grace to the expression of the same idea.

Patterns may be ranged under four heads—the Primitive, the Naturalistic, the Conventional, and the Geometrical.

The primitive are those of which we know not the ancestry, and rarely can guess the motive. To us they are, in general, simply rude decorations. The naturalistic are those which are borrowed from natural forms, and are either only imitative, or else convey some hidden meaning. The conventional are those which, by long descent, have [86]come to be accepted simply as ornamental art, with or without reference to an original motive, now lost. The geometrical or symmetrical are founded on form only, and in so far resemble our experience of the primitive; they express no meaning, and only serve to satisfy the eye by their balance and their ingenuity.

PRIMITIVE.

The first patterned forms with which we are acquainted are the primitive. They are found in all parts of the inhabited world. In our present ignorance as to the beginnings of the scattered tribes of men, we cannot judge if these are the remains of an earlier art or the first germs of a new one. Of one thing there is no doubt: this primitive decoration consists entirely of pattern; that is to say, of the repetition of certain (to us) inexpressive forms, which by reiteration assume importance and in some degree express beauty—the beauty of what Monsieur Blanc calls "cadence."

After these first unintelligible forms, which simply by repetition become accepted patterns, come those called the Prehistoric, of which we know or guess something as to their original meaning, and which, having been reduced from the hieroglyphic-symbolical to the conventional, have thus crystallized themselves, by constant use, into a pattern. Such, for instance, is the simplest form of the "wave" pattern, which in very early art was a representation of water.

The prehistoric water or wave patterns had other forms; for instance, zigzags, upright or horizontal, and undulating lines which are intelligible as expressing smooth or rough water. In general, however, the primitive and prehistoric patterns convey no idea, and consist, as we have said elsewhere, of lines, straight or wavy, [87]sometimes intersected; of angles, zigzags, groups of dots, rings and little discs, and crosses of the Swastika shape. (Plate 10.)

Pl. 10.

See larger image
WAVE PATTERNS.
1, 4, 9, 12, 13. Greek Wave Patterns. 2. Key or Mæander, Greek Wave. 3. Greek Broken Wave. 5, 6, 7. Egyptian Smooth and Rippling Water Patterns. 8. Mediæval

Wave. 10, 11, 14. Assyrian. 15. Persian or Greek (from Glass Bowl, British Museum). 16. English Waves (Durham Embroideries.)

Where shall the tartan be placed? It is certainly primitive, and apparently had no intention beyond that of employing as many coloured threads as there were dyes, so as to form the brightest contrasts, or else to be as invisible as possible either in the sunshine or in the shade. The Gauls brought this kind of weaving with them from the East, and probably invented the pattern, if such a motiveless design can be so called. It had its classical name, "Polymita," and was admired in Rome when newly imported, as being something original and barbaric. The Romans found it in Britain, and Boadicea wore a tartan dress on the day of her defeat. Perhaps even then fashions came from France, and it may have been her best tunic from across the Channel. This fabric may have been imported by the Belgic Gauls, and was so easily woven on house looms, that it became in time the feudal dress of the Scottish tribes and clans, and the colours were ingeniously arranged to show the most different effects. The tartan has always been a resource for the woollen trade, and the fashion constantly recurs in France, either from sentiment or the actually inherited Gallic taste; but it remains a primitive pattern, and nothing can make it artistic. No embroidery can soften the constantly recurring angles, and only fringes can be employed to decorate a tartan costume. Pliny tells us of the ingenuity of Zeuxis, who, to show his wealth, had his name embroidered in gold in the squared compartments of his outer garment.[97]

Primitive patterns still linger in many savage nations, but especially throughout uncivilized Africa. Curious to say, the very ancient fossilized early art of Egypt does [88]not assist us to trace it back to a prehistoric style, though it may lead us into prehistoric times.

NATURALISTIC.

The phases of the naturalistic patterns are constantly recurring. Art is always tending to realism, in the laudable effort to reach the motive without the shackles of rules. Each phase has fallen a prey to symbolism, to conventionalism, or to mannerism, which last symptom marks the decline and fall of art. We shall find these phases everywhere in the design of patterns.

Naturalism has always striven, by simple repetition, to reduce to patterns the forms of flowers, fruits, animals, birds, insects, reptiles, and other natural objects.

In flower patterns the simplest forms by repetition make sometimes the richest patterns, and the most effective. (Plate 11, Nos. 1 and 2.)

It is remarkable that one very beautiful class of natural objects is rarely employed in ancient decoration[98]—shells and corals. The barbarous tribes of the West Coast of Africa alone seem to have appreciated their forms, and added them to their small repertory of naturalistic patterns. They do not appear in any European or Asiatic textiles till the seventeenth century, when shells were much used in the decorations of the reigns of Queen Anne and Louis Quatorze.

The first change from naturalism into the conventional was through symbolism, and belonged to the time when unwritten thought was first recorded by pictured signs, which then ceased to be merely decoration. We find that the naturalism of the earliest Egyptians and Asiatics was soon entirely absorbed by the effort to express some hidden meaning or mystery, and then to fit the representation [89]to a special place and purpose, and to restore it, as it were, to decorative art.

Pl. 11.

See larger image

1. Persian Flower Border. 2. Egyptian Border, composed of Head-dress of the god Nile (Wilkinson's "Ancient Egyptians"). 3. Assyrian. 4. Assyrian.

The lotus and the patterns founded on its forms, and the many emblematic meanings attached to them, are notable examples of these transmutations in style and intention, and of the value given to their intention and use in Egypt and India, where each development was immediately crystallized into a recognized pattern, and given its place and language. It received its "*mot d'ordre*," and continued to act upon it long after the meaning was forgotten or out of date.

The rolling pattern which had so long represented only the "wave," was given to the really straight stem of the lotus, and its blossom, substituted for the wave's crest, now filled many a frieze in Indian temple architecture; whereas the lotus stems in Egypt were still bound in sheaves to form columns, and the flowers, buds, and leaves spread and blossomed into capitals. Here we have symbolism and conventionalized naturalism, all combined, showing how their principles, though quite distinct, can mix and unite. The conventional form often superseded and effaced the naturalistic, and became the sign of an idea, or the hieroglyphic picture of a thing; immovable and unalterable in Egypt, where every effort was made to secure eternity on earth, but continually returning to naturalism in India, where the Aryan tendency, with the assistance of the "Code of Manu," always recurred to the restoration of the ancient naturalistic motive.

In the India Museum we may see the "wave" motive converted into a lotus pattern by rolling the long stems, and filling up the spaces between with the full-faced blossom. Sometimes the pattern is started by the figure of an elephant, from whose mouth the stem of the flower of the sun proceeds. This occurs so often that it must [90]originally have had a meaning. Sometimes the sacred convolvulus takes the place of the lotus. (Plate 12.)

On an Egyptian mural painting are seen parties of men snaring ducks among papyrus and lotus plants. These are entirely conventional, and are, in fact, a sort of recognized hieroglyphic representing the idea of a lotus.[99]

The lotus was the accepted emblem of the sun, and reduced to a many-leaved radiating pattern may be found as an architectural ornament on the outside of the Buddhist "topes," of which the models are on the staircase of the British Museum.[100] (Plate 13.)

We have Sir G. Birdwood's authority for believing that, though the actual lotus was a native of India, and carried thence to Egypt, its decorative use as a pattern was Egyptian, and so returned to India. Both accepted it as their "sunflower."[101]

Pl. 12.
See larger image
1. Indian Rolling Lotus Pattern. 2, 3. Indian Lotus Patterns. 4, 5. Egyptian Lotus Patterns. 6. Sacred Convolvulus. Indian (seventeenth century).

Pl. 13.
See larger image
1, 2. Indian Designs of Assyrian Daisy and Egyptian Lotus. 3. Vitruvian Scroll. Vignola. Architecture.

Can it be our Aryan descent which induces in us the earnest adoration, in our art of to-day, of our northern prototype of the sun's emblem? I fear that we must acknowledge that our æsthetic worship of our sunflowers is somewhat false and affected. Æstheticism is not art. Sunflowers, painted or embroidered as decoration, do not "take" if they are ordered and ranged, and reduced to a pattern like those of Egypt. They must be naturalistic, and, if possible, remind us of a disorderly cottage garden; whereas in India they were adapted [91]from nature on fixed principles, which immediately reduced them to the conventional.

See larger image
Sunflower pattern, R. S. A. N.
XIX. Century

I give an illustration of a Gothic sunflower resembling a transfigured rose; and another of an ordered naturalistic sunflower pattern, from a design of the Royal School of Art Needlework. (Plate 14.)

Fig. 9.
Gothic Sunflower. From Christ's College Chapel, Cambridge.

I have given this account of the patterns founded on the lotus, as we can almost from this distance of time take a bird's-eye view of its rise in naturalism, its spread, dispersion, and its crystallization into conventional forms; also we can trace how the lotus patterns of Indian art have resulted, when accepted in Europe, in nothing but the rolling wave, carrying flower forms which no longer represent a lotus; and how the lotus bud and flower pattern has become in time the classical "egg and tongue;" which, however, may have resulted also from a combination of other motives.

Representations of animal forms are sometimes very remarkable in phases of naturalism. The few remains of Celtic art that have survived are entirely animal, or very nearly so. In their stone, gold, silver, and bronze work, and in illuminated MSS., we meet with only animal forms; never a flower or a leaf.

Besides the Indo-Chinese patterns in Celtic art, which [92]suggest the Chinese lattice-work (so strongly insisted on by Semper as a constant motive), we also find in all their decorations compartments containing involved patterns of cords or strings knitted or plaited, suggesting the entrails of animals, which by these hunting people were consulted as being mysteriously prophetic of approaching events, especially success or failure in the chase, and impending warlike raids.[102] There is no other way of accounting for these designs, which are peculiar to the race, unless we believe they always represent snakes. (Pl. 15.)

In England much that was characteristic of the style was lost as soon as the Saxons drove out the Celts, who carried it to Ireland, as may be seen in the Book of Kells, and the carving of the Harp of Tara, and the Celtic jewels in the Irish museums; but the interlacing patterns survived throughout Anglo-Saxon art, and were marvellously ingenious and beautiful; witness the Durham Book of St. Cuthbert.

We have no Celtic textiles remaining to us, unless some embroidery in the Marien-Kirche collection at Dantzic may be of that style and time. This is suggested by its altogether Indo-Chinese and very barbarous character;[103] and one of the coronation mantles in Bock's "Kleinodien" is Runic in its peculiar serpent design.

See larger image
Illumination from the Lindisfarne Gospels, about A.D. 700

Pl. 16.

See larger image
Demeter. From a Greek Vase in the British Museum.

"Judging from their illuminated MSS.," it is said, "the elements borrowed from textile art by the Celts are plaits, bows, zigzags, knots, geometrical figures in various symmetrically developed combinations, crosses, whorls, and lattice-work; next, those taken from metal work, such as spirals and nail-heads let into borders; thirdly, simple or composite zoomorphic forms, such as bodies of [93]snakes, birds' heads on long necks, lizards, dogs, dragons, and the like."[104]They well understood how to make a pattern by the repetition of objects of any class.

Pl. 17.

See larger image
1. Embroidery on a Greek Mantle, third century B.C., from the Tomb of the Seven Brothers, Crimea.
2. Egyptian Painted and Embroidered Linen. The cone, the bead, the daisy, the wave, the lotus under water, are all shown on this fragment.

Pl. 18.

See larger image
EGYPTIAN TAPESTRY.
1. Woven and embroidered on a Sleeve. 2. Woven and embroidered. 3. Painted and embroidered.

Representations of human figures in embroideries probably originated in hangings for the wall; but have been treated as decorative forms, both by the Indians and the Greeks, for wearing apparel. The peplos of Minerva was bordered with fighting gods and giants, and the Empress Theodora's dress in the Ravenna mosaic repeats exactly the same motive. (See Fig. 4, and Pl. 6.)

There are two other examples of such Greek patterns. The mantle of Demeter on a Greek vase in the British Museum, of the best period (Pl. 16), is embroidered with flying genii and victorious chariots; and the embroidered mantle lately found in a Crimean tomb, is of precisely the same style of design, and the one illustrates the other. These instances are so exceptional, that it is curious that here, as in the case of the peplos, in each case there should happen to be a duplicate. (Plates 16 and 17, No. 1.)

In Babylonian, Assyrian, and Chaldean art we constantly find animal forms in patterns. The lion and the hare, birds and insects, are the commonest; and there are some instances of human figures reduced to a pattern in these sculptured representations of textiles. (Plate 2.)

There are curiously woven little human figures finished with the needle on the sleeve of an Egyptian dress in the British Museum, from Saccarah (Pl. 18), and, of course, when such a design is small, it ceases to be very objectionable. On the whole, however, naturalistic designs for embroideries are more safely confined to floral decorations, excepting always flat tapestries for walls, which, representing pictures, may be as naturalistic as their purpose and style will admit.

Animal forms are often reduced to patterns by [94]repetition in Indian and Persian embroidery.[105] The drawing is naturalistic, but the colouring is fanciful. We may see any day, on Persian rugs, scarlet lions pursuing and capturing blue or yellow hares. The flatness and want of all shadows tends to the conventional. Lions, bulls, cats, beetles, and serpents abound especially in Egyptian design; insects, reptiles, and fish in Asiatic patterns, where animals are sometimes made to walk in pairs, with their heads and tails twisted into a pattern.

Though landscapes are so rarely worked that the subject is, perhaps, hardly worthy of notice, yet such mistaken specimens of ingenuity have occurred. An altar frontal was exhibited at Zurich, in 1883, containing some really exquisitely worked landscapes, which were quite out of place, both as art and as decoration, for an ecclesiastical purpose. This was of the beginning of the last century.[106]

While we appreciate and should take advantage of our national tendency to naturalistic design, we must beware of looking on fixed rules as bonds which cramp our liberty, and of thinking that nature should be our only guide to an otherwise unassisted and unfettered inspiration. Without the wholesome checks of experience and educated taste, and the knowledge which teaches us what to avoid, as well as what to imitate, founded on the successes and failures of others, we fall into weak imitations of natural objects.

[95]Mr. Redgrave points out how unpleasant and jarring to our sense of what is appropriate, and therefore how offensive to good taste and common sense, it is to tread on a carpet of water-lilies swimming in blue pools, or on fruits and flowers heaped up and casting shadows probably towards the light.[107] Woollen lions and tigers, as large as life, basking before the fire in a wreath of roses, are alarming rather than agreeable, and are of the nature of a practical joke in art. It is the search for novelty in naturalism that leads to such astonishing compositions; and these, being successively rejected in the heart of our civilization and culture, are drifted away to vulgarize our colonies, or to be sold cheap to furnish Continental hotels, and make the English traveller blush for his home manufactures.

SYMBOLICAL AND CONVENTIONAL.

Though it is true that the highest art, pictorial and sculptural, is always struggling towards naturalism, the art of decoration is, by its nature, constantly tending to conventionalism. Patterns, if not absolutely geometrical or naturalistic, must be classed under this principle. Let us examine what is meant by a conventional pattern.

It may be said that the conventional includes every form—the symbolic, the naturalistic, or even the hieroglyphic—that is selected and consecrated to convey a certain idea. The lily of Florence, which is something between a lily and an iris, but unlike either, is a conventional form; likewise the lily of France, which it is said was once a conventional frog. The rose of England, the shamrock, and the thistle have always been more naturalistic than is usual in such heraldic designs; but [96]the parti-coloured rose of York and Lancaster was decidedly conventional, and heraldic.

Conventional patterns now are those which, having been originally naturalistic in style, but perhaps emblematic as to their motive, have been repeated till the meaning and form have been lost; or else, as in the case of the lotus, the emblem is forgotten, and nothing remains but the recognized conventional form.

One conventional pattern which, having commenced by being a symbol, has been repeated and varied till it has allowed the original essential meaning to escape, is the "palm-leaf" or "cone" pattern on French or Paisley shawls, which, having been a sacred emblem—

the tree of life—in Persia, became in Europe, when the religious myth was lost, only a shawl pattern—merely a leaf, with plant painted within its outlines. (Plate 23, Nos. 10, 11.)

Decorative designs become conventional in spite of the intention of the designer. He is overruled by the spaces to be covered and the materials to be employed. His design must produce a flat pattern; he must repeat it again and again; he must give it a strong outline; he must distribute it regularly at certain intervals. Repetition at once conventionalizes the most naturalistic drawing, and the most sacred and mysterious emblem. Alternation is equally a source of conventionalism. There is no motive that cannot be conventionalized into a pattern by repetition. A Gothic crown and a true lily, repeated, will make an ecclesiastical conventional pattern. Then come all the Arabian and Moresque forms (which are mostly geometric), and also the Gothic (which are partly geometric and partly naturalistic, especially those in German and debased Spanish and Portuguese Gothic design).

Pl. 19.

See larger image
1. Key Pattern. 2. Broken-up Key. 3. Beads. 4. Key and sign of Land. 5. Wave and Babylonian Daisy. 6. Key and Fundata. 7. Wave and Bead. 8. Wave and Daisy. 9. Key and Sun Cross. These Key Patterns from Ceiling of a Tomb at Saccarah, in Egypt. (Wilkinson's "Ancient Egyptians.")

Then we must accept as conventional all those which may be called kaleidoscope patterns, which are broken [97]fragments of old motives, repeated or "radiated" so as to become partly geometrical, wholly conventional. (See Pl. 17, No. 2.)

Conventional patterns may be reduced into three kinds.

First, the naturalistic, which have by repetition been adapted for decorative art.

Secondly, the symbolical—Pagan or Christian, religious or historical, including the Heraldic.

Thirdly, those conventional forms which may never have had any inner meaning, or else, having originally had one, have lost it.

All these exist, sometimes apart and sometimes mingled; so that some thought must be expended in seeking the motive which has brought them together, and finding in each the internal evidence of its descent.

It is evident that patterns, conventionalized and brought from distant sources, sometimes meet and amalgamate. When the origin of a conventional pattern is disputed, it is worth while to examine if it has a double parentage. Let me give, as an instance, the key pattern. It may have been, as Semper believes, originally Chinese, and derived from wicker-work design. It represents also the broken or dislocated "wave," the symbol of the River Mæander,[108] and for water generally. We find it everywhere in company with the wave, which never could have had any connection with wicker-work, not only in China, but in Persia, India, Egypt, Arabia, Greece, Rome, and Central America. (Pl. 19.)

Can any invention of man show a more symbolical intention than the wave pattern? The airy leap drawn downwards by the force of gravitation; controlled, and [98]again made to return, but strong to insist on its own curve of predilection, rushing back under the same circle; strengthened by the downward movement to spring again from its original plane; beginning afresh its Sisyphus labour, and facing the next effort with the same grace and agility. Undying force, and eternal flowing unrest—these are the evident intention and symbol of the wave pattern. Though I believe the key pattern to be a modification of the wave form, yet the locking and unlocking movement suggests a repetition of the Tau, or key of life.

Fig. 10.

When we admire the friezes of garlands hung between the skulls of oxen and goats, we cannot for a moment doubt the sacrificial idea on which the design was founded. When the wreaths are carried by dancing children, we recognize the impersonation of the rejoicing of the dædal earth.

The Greeks, however strongly they exerted themselves to throw off the shackles of conventionality in sculpture, painting, and architecture, yet yielded to the traditional force of the symbolical pattern, and accepted most of the Oriental forms, merely remodelling them for their own use, and adding to their significance what their culture required; at the same time giving infinite variety, as their perfect taste dictated.

Pl. 20.

See larger image
TREES OF LIFE.
1, 2, 3, 5. Assyrian. 4. Sicilian Silk. (Birdwood's "Indian Arts," pp. 331, 335, 336, 337.)

Aristophanes, in "The Frogs," laughs at the Persian carpet patterns—their unnatural birds and beasts and flowers—whilst he claims for his own frogs, that they at least have the merit of being natural.[109] This little touch [99]of art throws a gleam of inner light on the struggle towards originality and truth which characterized the Greek principles of beauty and fitness in literature and art, in direct contrast to that which was always turning back to those fossil forms which were only respectable on account of their age and their mystery, but of which the tradition and intention were already lost.

Roman patterns were merely Greek adaptations with an Etruscan flavour, which was a survival of the earliest Italian art. Perhaps the indigenous element had been already modified by Phœnician influence.

In taking stock of Oriental symbolical patterns, we find that one of those of the widest ancestry and longest continuity is the "Sacred Hom."[110] (Pl. 20-24.) This is to be found in Babylonian, Persian,[111] Indian, Greek, and Roman art; and consequently it prevails in all European decoration (except the Gothic), where it was reduced to unrecognizable forms.

Sir George Birdwood says the Hom or Homa was the Sanskrit Soma, used as an intoxicating drink by the early Brahmins, and was extracted from the plant of that name, an almost leafless succulent Asclepiad. It appears to have changed its conventional form as other plants by fermentation came to the front, containing what appeared to be the "spirit of life"—the *aqua vitæ*.

[100]The palm, with its wonderful fruit, which is convertible into intoxicating drinks, and afterwards the vine itself, were each of them moulded into analogous conventional fruit forms, which keep as much as possible within the limits of the original cone shape. (Pl. 21.)

Pl. 21.

See larger image
1. Tree of Life and Lions. Gate of Mycenæ. 2. Persian or Sicilian Silk. Tree of Life and Leopards.

Pl. 22.

See larger image
1. Split Lotus Fruit on Chinese Bowl. 2. Split Lotus resembling Tree of Life. Frieze by Benozzo Gozzoli, Ricardi Palace, Florence. 3. Petal of Flower on Glass Bowl from Southern Italy. British Museum.

There is a palm-tree which absolutely carries a cone in the heart of its crown of fronds.[112] This may have helped to preserve the original motive of the sacred tree of life. The cone form in classical art was drawn from the pine cone and the artichoke; and in mediæval art these were sometimes replaced by the pomegranate, and in the late Renaissance by the pine-apple, newly arrived from the West Indies.[113] It is a good example of the blending of one vegetable form into another, making the sequence, of which each phase in the East had an historical cause or a symbolical meaning,[114] but which in Europe had gradually lost all motive, and was simply an [101]acknowledged decorative form.[115] In architectural ornament it is called the honeysuckle,[116] which it had grown to resemble in the days of Greece.

Pl. 23.

See larger image
Different forms of Tree of Life, from Sicilian Silks.

Pl. 24.

Modern Embroidery from the Principalities, in which the cone-shaped tree grows into a vine,
and the two animals at the foot have lost their shape and intention.

This sacred tree, the Homa of Zoroaster and of the later Persians, has so early a beginning that we find it on Assyrian monuments.[117] Rock says "that, perhaps, it stood for the tree of life, which grew in Paradise." It is represented as a subject of homage to men and animals, and it invariably stands between priests and kings, or beasts kneeling to it. It is figured on the small bucket for religious rites, carried in the hands, or embroidered in the upper sleeve of the monarch's tunic. It always represents a shrub, sometimes bearing a series of umbels of seven flowers each. (Pl. 2, 20.)

Sometimes the expression of the symbol is reduced to the cone-fruit of the homa alone; or even to a blossom, as in the two glass bowls in the Slade collection in the British Museum, from a tomb at Chiusi, in Etruria. Here the design is a flower, of which each petal contains the essential emblem—a plant within a plant. These bowls, pronounced to be Greek of the fourth century B.C., have yet to me a strong Oriental character. (Pl. 22, No. 3.)

[102]I have spoken of the lotus as a naturalistic pattern. One mode of drawing and embroidering its flower in India, is to cut it in two; half the blossom is then carefully and almost botanically copied, thus conveying the inner meaning of the sacred flower. (Pl. 22, No. 3.)

Another conventional pattern, common to all times of art and all nations, is that called in architecture the "egg and tongue" pattern. (Pl. 13.) This, as I have already said, is supposed to be derived directly from the lotus. The Egyptians formed it from the bud and blossom; and the pattern is found in India, Greece, and Rome, changing continually and yet retaining its identity. Vitruvius claimed to have given it the last touch and finish, so that in Italy it was called the Vitruvian scroll; and it is common to all decoration, even in textiles, though it is hardly suited for weaving or embroidery. This is one of the earliest patterns which, having ceased long ago to be a religious emblem or sign, still survives by its decorative fitness, and perpetuates the echoes of its origin.

Pl. 25.

See larger image
TYPICAL CROSSES.
1. Swastika. 2. From a Greek Vase, 765 B.C. 3. Indian Sectarial Mark of Sakti race. 4. Buddhist and Jainis mark. 5. Early Rhodian Pottery. 6. Egyptian prehistoric Cross. 7. Tau Cross. 8. Mark of land, Egyptian and Ninevite. 9. Ditto. 10. Clavus. 11, 12, 13. Scandinavian Sun and Moon Crosses. 14, 15, 16. Celtic. 17. Chrysoclavus. 18, 19. Stauracin patterns. 20. Scandinavian, from Norway. 21. Runic Cross. 22. Cross at Palenque, in Temple of the Sun. 23. Scotch Celtic Cross. 24. Cross from Iona. 25, 26. Runic Crosses. 27. Cross on the Dalmatic of Charlemagne. 28. From the Mantle of Henry II., Emperor of Germany.

Of the conventional symbolical forms of the early Christian Church I shall speak more fully in the chapter on ecclesiastical art, and therefore would only point out here, while touching on symbolical decoration, how that phase of Christian art is a great historical instance of the deep ancient meanings it illustrates; showing the motive to be often in accordance with the inherited pagan symbol, and yet differing from it. Pre-eminent among these is the emblem of the Cross, so early and universally used, full of mysterious secret allusions to the groping faiths of idolatrous nations, before the great fundamental idea of the "Word" was attached to it. This was one of the old signs used as a pattern, and transfigured into a fresh type, of which the radiance reflected back light upon all that preceded it, even as [103]Chinese ancestors are ennobled by the deeds of their descendants.

Pl. 26.

See larger image
1. Pallas Athene, from a vase in Lord Northampton's Collection. 2. Ajax in a cloak embroidered with swastika, sun cross, and prehistoric water patterns. Etruscan Museum. Vatican.

The cross (Pl. 25), was a sign and a pattern in prehistoric art. It was the double of the Tau, the Egyptian emblem of life; and while the Jews reject the Christian cross, they still claim to have warned off the destroying angel by this sign in blood over the lintels of their doors in the first Passover.

But the most ancient and universal form of the cross is that of the Swastika, or Fylfote. This "prehistoric cross" is said to be formed of two fire-sticks, belonging to the ancient worship of the sun, laid across each other ready for friction; but losing that meaning, from an emblem they fell into a pattern, and this you will still find, utterly meaningless, on Persian carpets of to-day.

Sir G. Birdwood gives the Swastika as the sectarial mark of the Sakti sects in India. Fergusson names it with the mound buildings, as belonging to all Buddhist art; and examples of the Swastika are to be found on Rhodian pottery from the Necropolis of Kamiros, where we find also the key pattern.

In early Greek art the Swastika and Gammadion are everywhere, especially as embroidery on dress. Minerva's petticoats are sometimes worked all over with the latter. On an early Greek vase in the Museo Gregoriano, are painted Ajax and Achilles playing at dice; and the mantle of Ajax is squared into an embroidered pattern that alternately represents a sun or star and a Gammadion (Pl. 26, No. 2). But it is unnecessary to multiply classical examples, which are endless.

The Christian Cross was often formed by converting the Tau into the Gamma, the sacred letter of the Greeks. It is said to have been the emblem of the corner-stone, and as a pattern, was called, down to the thirteenth century, the "Gammadion;" and though it had lost its [104]original motive, it continued to preserve the idea of a secret and mystical meaning.

The Gammadion, as well as the Swastika, enters largely into the illuminations of the Celtic Book of Kells and those of the Lindisfarne MSS.; also it is to be found on the Celtic shields in the British Museum, together with the Swastika. Both appear in the Persian carpets of to-day, and as patterns were, in ecclesiastical decoration, employed down to the fifteenth century, both for European and British textiles. The Swastika, as well as the wave pattern, is of mysterious and universal antiquity, and has certainly traversed four thousand years,—how much more we dare not say. It is to be found throughout Egyptian and Indian art—never in that of Assyria.

Of the time of Rameses the Second we have two figures in a mural painting, an ally and an enemy, a guest and a prisoner, both clothed in embroidered garments,*parsemés* with the prehistoric cross.

Fig. 11.
Egyptian Enemy and Ally.

In the chapter on ecclesiastical art I shall again refer to this immemorial symbolical and conventional pattern. I much regret that, in the absence of a translation, I am prevented from availing myself of the accumulated learning on the subject of "The Prehistoric Cross," by Baron Ernest de Bunsen.

Pl. 27.

Imitation of a Carpet carved in stone, from Nineveh, showing the Indian Lotus and the Assyrian Daisy. (In the British Museum.)

There was a pattern called the "crenelated" which apparently was derived from the Assyrian battlement, and is found throughout classic art, somewhat conventionalized.[118] [105]It is named as an embroidered pattern in the inscription recording votive offerings of dresses in the temple of Athene at Athens.[119]

Fig. 12.
Crenelated Pattern.

We know something of the conventional and symbolical embroideries of Nineveh, which are quite unlike those of India, except in the adoption of the lotus for decoration.[120]These are best understood by illustrations; and, therefore, I give one of the beautiful sculptured carpets from Nineveh, in the British Museum (Pl.27), showing the Assyrian use of the lotus and cone, and the embroidered garment of a king from one of the sculptures in low relief (Plate 1). These are very stately—perfectly conventional and decorative; and we feel that they have grown where we find them, and are not borrowed from another civilization. What strikes us most, is the constant repetition and the little variety of ornament in these patterns. The forms are strongly marked—wheels or whorls, or daisies, often repeated. (The daisy belongs to Assyria as the lotus to Egypt.) The flowers are simply leafless blossoms. Splendid embroideries of sacred emblematical designs are, however, occasionally found, such as those from Layard's "Monuments" (Plate 2).

Much has been written on the early symbolism of plants and flowers. The sun-myths have enlisted all floral legendary lore, and conventional ornament was largely drawn from them.

Many symbols are present to us when we name certain plants. The lily is the acknowledged sign of purity, the rose of love, the honeysuckle of enduring [106]faith, the laurel of poetry, and the palm of victory; the oak of strength, the olive of peace. Some plants have accumulated more than one meaning. The vine has many attributes. It is an emblem of the mysteries of the Christian Church. It symbolizes plenty, joy, the family. Ivy means friendship, conviviality, remembrance.

The symbolism of beasts (*bestiaria*),[121] of birds (*volucraria*), and of stones (*lapidaria*) filled many volumes in the mediæval ages, and are well worthy of the study of the decorative artist. The symbolism of animals and birds especially, constantly attracts our attention in the Oriental and Sicilian textiles of the early Christian times, and to the end of the thirteenth century. Later, in European textile decoration, most animals were accepted as emblematic in Christian art, beginning with the symbols of the four Evangelists. All the virtues and all the vices found their animal emblems conventionalized, and were thus woven, embroidered, and painted.[122]

Reptiles and insects are included under the head of "beasts," and perhaps fishes also. Each was dowered with a symbolical meaning; and thus admitted into art, they were conventionalized by being strongly outlined, coloured flat; and by repetition without variation, were converted into patterns.

Pl. 28.
See larger image
1, 2. Gothic Tiles. 3. Gothic Border of a Dress. 4. Gothic Vine. Westminster Abbey.

When the use of heraldic illustration was added to the already accepted symbolism, animal decoration became very common, and soon forgot its symbolical motives, which were succeeded by Renaissance fanciful patterns; and then the conventionalized beast and its symbolism [107]disappeared from European decoration, except when it was a direct copy of an Oriental design.

Certain symbolical forms have, however, survived. The eagle has always meant empire, and the double-headed eagle, a double royalty.[123] Ezekiel represents Babylon and Egypt, symbolically, as two eagles.[124] But here we approach the subject of heraldry, which became a science in mediæval days; and every man and woman in any way remarkable, every chivalrous action and national event, became a subject for textile art, and was woven or worked with the needle on banner, hanging, or dress. The altar decorations received a new stimulus as historical records, as well as religious symbols, and pride and piety were equally enlisted in these gifts to the Church.

Byzantine patterns have a barbaric stamp, and yet have much of the grandiose about them; but they are to the last degree conventional. In the early mosaics, both in Constantinople and Rome, every face and head, every flower and animal, represents a type and not an individual.

Fig. 13.
Gothic Trees, from Bayeux tapestry.

Gothic foliage patterns, in England and elsewhere, [108]are a struggle between the naturalistic and the conventional. The Norman style and the Romanesque, which preceded it, and from which it was modified and elevated, show their vegetable forms thick-stemmed and few-leaved, whereas the Gothic aspired to a developed gracefulness; and the

Renaissance, which succeeded it, assumed all the freedom of natural flowers and plants, floating in the breeze, on their delicate stems. (Pl.28.)

All the Renaissance patterns, which, as their name denotes, were born again, like butterflies to frolic for a day of gay enjoyment, are purely decorative. Their generally charming, graceful forms group together to cover empty spaces with every regard to the rules of design and composition, but without any inner meaning. If we take these arabesques to pieces, we generally find the parts come from various sources; and having served last in pagan Rome for pagan purposes, had been slightly refashioned for Christian decorative art,[125] before the Byzantine inartistic taste, and barbaric splendour of metal-work patterns, had extinguished all the gay fancy of the arts of Southern Europe.

The mediæval revival was a return to the light and fantastic, and a protest against the solemnity of all Gothic art, which had had its great day, had culminated, and died out. The patterns of the Renaissance are all guided by the principles of repetition and duplication, or that of doubling the pattern, which repeats itself to right and left, as if folded down the middle.

The principal lines thus echoed one another; but the artist was permitted to vary the conventionalism of the general forms of figures, flowers, fruit, or butterflies, so as to balance and yet differ in every detail.

Pl. 29.

See larger image
CLOUD PATTERNS.
1, 2, 3, 7. Japanese. 4. Chinese. 5, 8, 9. Mediæval. 6. Badge of Richard II.

Pl. 30.

See larger image
Indo-Chinese Coverlet, supposed to have belonged to Oliver Cromwell. Hatfield House.

Amongst the conventional patterns which have descended to us, and are in general use without any [109]particular symbolical meaning being attached to them, we must instance those derived from the Cloud pattern. This is to be found in early Chinese and Indian art, but I do not recognize it in Egyptian or Greek decoration. It came through Byzantium, and took its place amongst early Christian patterns. (Pl. 29.)

Pl. 31.

See larger image
THE FUNDATA OR NETTED PATTERN.
Portion of a Phœnician Bowl from Cyprus.
Egyptian. Egyptian. Egyptian.

The cloud pattern is also Japanese, and is supposed to have been originally derived from Central Asia. It varies in shape, and is found as an ornament on the head of the sceptre in the collection at Nara, in Japan, which is twelve or thirteen hundred years old. There is an example of the cloud pattern in Aelfled's embroidery at Durham; and it is often found under the feet of saints in painted glass and embroideries before the fourteenth century. A curious Indian example exists in a coverlet belonging to the Marquis of Salisbury, said to have been the property of Oliver Cromwell, on which the central medallion is filled with white horses careering amidst the cloud pattern.[126] (Pl. 30.)

The *netted* pattern called Fundata is extremely ancient. We find it in Egyptian mural paintings, as well as in the centre of a Phœnician bowl from Cyprus, now in the Louvre. The mediæval Fundata was a silk material, covered with what appeared to be a gold network covering the stuff. It is supposed to be the same as that worn by Constantine,[127] and is named in ecclesiastical inventories as late as the fifteenth century. (Pl. 31.)

[110]All the wheel patterns are very ancient, and appear to be simply conventional wheels. In France they were called *roés*. There is a fine instance of this wheel pattern in Auberville's "Tissus." The wheels sometime enclose triumphal cars and other pictorial subjects. (Pl. 34.)

The patterns which are apparently composed with the intention of avoiding all meaning, are the Moorish. They are neither animal, vegetable, nor anything else. They show no motive in their complicated domes, their honeycombing, and their ingenious conventional forms; but cover equally textile fabrics or stucco ceilings without suggesting any idea, religious or symbolical.

All the splendid Italian brocades and velvet damasks were of conventional patterns, and like their Arab and Sicilian models, and also like their Spanish contemporaries, represented, and sought to represent nothing on earth. It was all floreated and meandering design; the motive reminding one of the pine-apple and the acanthus, or of vine stems meeting or parting, but never anything naturalistic for a moment. When animals were introduced it was always as a pattern doubled face to face, as if folded down a straight line.

We may say the same of the succeeding Louis Quatorze and the Louis Quinze styles, which were of the culminating period of clever and fantastic conventional decoration.

Our modern designs have phases of imitation, and the patterns of rich brocades which our great-grandmothers [111]wore, came into fashion again about the third decade of this century. Now we have been trying to find our inspirations further back, and some of our copies of the simpler Sicilian patterns, with an occasional pair of birds, or a conventional plant, imitating the motive of the tree of life, have been very pretty. The only defect is the poverty which results from the absence of any active and informing motive. It is, however, easier to criticize than to create.

Fig. 14.
Radiated Pattern.

I would venture here to find fault with a very common method of converting a natural object into a conventional pattern, by radiation. Certain modes of repetition are very objectionable. A pattern, for instance, repeated four times round a centre, or a natural flower repeated exactly, but lying north, south, east, and west, are more or less inartistic, we may say vulgar. (Fig. 14.)

Fig. 15.
Radiated Sunflower.

A natural flower may be conventionalized and radiated by placing it in the centre of the composition facing you; and the leaves arranged surrounding it, so as to formalize the design, though there is nothing really unnatural in the way in which they are made to grow. The illustration of a radiated sunflower explains my meaning.

It has been already observed that by repetition almost any object may be reduced to a pattern, but taste must be exercised in the selection of what is appropriate and [112]beautiful. Radiation is also really a useful factor in conventional art, but common sense must guide the artist here as well as taste. In radiating the forms of a flower, nature gives endless hints of beauty; but a radiating pattern of human figures would be ridiculous, and even the branches of a tree cannot be so treated.

The awning of the classic hypæthral hall or court was often reproduced in Roman arabesques. Sometimes we find it in a classical tomb, painted over the ceiling, and recalling its original use. This was revived in the Cinque-cento Renaissance; and again in Adams' "Eighteenth Century Decorations," it became an accepted pattern, called "the shell," losing its original motive, and descending to fill up the panels of tea-caddies and surround keyholes. When thus reduced to the appearance of a little ruff, it needs some thought to recognize it, and give it credit for its first motive.

Fig. 16.

It is amusing to find how a form which it seems impossible to reduce to a pattern, will yet fall into one by a judicious arrangement of light and shadow, and by repetition. There is a little frieze in one of the Indian [113]cases on the staircase in the British Museum, which is extremely pretty and effective. It consists of a repetition of little balconies with recesses and pillars and figures in pairs. I give it as illustrating the way conventional patterns grow. This balcony pattern is of the sixth century, A.D.

Fig. 17.
Indian Balcony Pattern, from steps of tope of Jamal-Zartri, Afghanistan. British Museum.

The ancient palmated pattern called Chrysoclavus, from the beginning of our era to the thirteenth century was partly a nail-headed design, and had become a Christian symbol. It was, probably, originally the primitive spot pattern; afterwards promoted to being an ornament of discs in colour or metal: this was Assyrian, Etruscan, and Mycenæan.[128] (Pl. 70.)

Among the conventional patterns which have apparently no hidden meaning, but which clearly show their descent, are the Chinese and Japanese wicker and lattice-work designs. The beauty of these is wonderful.

Semper shows that wicker (including bamboo work) was the foundation of all Chinese civilized life, for constructing houses, bridges, utensils, and for decoration. He gives this wicker-work origin to the universal key [114]pattern, which may, however, have a double source—the wave, and the wicker-work.

We find the Key pattern in a tomb at Essiout, in Egypt, painted perhaps about 1600 B.C., in company with some other very old friends,[129] the Tuscan border, the Egg and Tongue, and the Bead, the Daisy, and the Wave. (Pl. 17, No. 2.) We meet it everywhere in ancient and modern decoration. There are several forms of it on a large terra-cotta vase in the British Museum from Kameiros in Rhodes, and on Chinese fictiles and embroideries. It is found also on garments in Iceland, whither the Greek patterns must have drifted through Norway, and, as they could go no further, there they remained.

I have often spoken of the extraordinary survival of a pattern. This is easy to account for when fashion, "the disturber," had not yet existed. Then the ancient motive told its own tale, and its great age was its claim to perpetual youth; but it is more remarkable where we meet with revivals at distant periods, and apparently without any connecting link of ancestry or style.

For instance, the women of Genoa wore large cotton veils, printed with the Indian conventional tree and beast pattern, down to thirty years ago, when the fashion changed, and winter bonnets and summer muslin veils displaced the old costume. These patterns are now being printed in England on scores of cotton curtains for beds and windows.

[115]

GEOMETRICAL.

Geometrical patterns may be reduced to a very few primitive elements.

Fig. 18.
Varied adjustments of Square and Circle.

1. The Line, including straight and wavy lines.
2. The Angular Forms, including squares, oblongs, cubes, &c.
[116]3. The Triangular, including zigzags, diamonds, &c.
4. The Circular, including all spots, discs, and radiations.

All these can be blended or mixed so as to form endless varieties. For instance, the square and the circle can intersect each other in different proportions, so as to give an entirely new effect to the pattern, each time the balance is altered or the phase of the repetition varied. The illustration will explain this. (Fig. 18.)

Right angles may intersect each other so as to produce the whole gamut of Chinese lattice-work decoration, and all the Celtic and Scandinavian entwined patterns, from which so many of the embroideries in the Italian pictures of the fourteenth and fifteenth centuries are probably descended.

The Moorish patterns are geometrical, and are created on the principle of avoiding in art the representation of any created thing. They show much ingenuity in keeping clear of any possible meaning. Most of these conventional patterns are founded on the ogee-arch and a kind of honeycomb pattern, involved and inverted. Their tiles, which nearest approach textile design, have, indeed, certain vegetable forms added to the others, but always geometrically arranged as no vegetables ever grew.

Geometrical patterns begin with primitive forms, and come down to the floor-cloth designs of to-day. They can be extracted in endless variety from the combinations of the kaleidoscope. This style is well suited for pavements in mosaic—either secular or ecclesiastical.

The Opus Alexandrinum furnishes us with most beautiful examples and adaptations for large or small spaces, so as to form the richest or the simplest floor decorations. How worthily a church may be thus adorned may be seen on the vast area of the floor of [117]Santa Maria Maggiore in Rome, or that of the Church of St. Mark in Venice.

The nearest approach to the Opus Alexandrinum in textiles has been in Patchwork, of which a more artistic use may yet be made. We might exercise ingenuity in this direction, giving really fine and effective designs to our workers in patches, whose productions are, in general, simply alarming.

The fine quilting patterns of the sixteenth and seventeenth centuries are almost always geometrical, and make the best background to more resplendent embroideries overlying them, which is partly owing to their being only forms, and conveying no idea or inherited meaning. These expressionless designs are well fitted for spaces and borders in which the centres are elaborated, and require enclosing or framing; likewise, they are suited for large areas, which must not be perfectly plain, and yet not too disturbing to the eye, so as to distract it from the more important ornaments on the wall or ceiling. They suit carpets in passages or on staircases much better than any other kind of design, and form the best figured backgrounds for pictures. Both eye and mind often need repose, and therefore the simpler the geometrical pattern is, the better. Complicated and too ingenious combinations are painfully fatiguing. Simplicity and flatness are the greatest merits in such forms, as in shadowless patterns for textiles, and especially for embroideries.

If we turn to nature to assist us with new geometrical patterns, we shall find the most exquisite forms in the crystals of every newly-fallen snowflake, and in the nodal-points on a plate of metal or glass, covered with sand, and struck by sound. We shall hardly ever find in these a repetition of exactly the same combination, and their variety is only equalled by their beauty.

FOOTNOTES:

[96]Sir G. Birdwood tells us of patterns of an Indian brocade called "Chundtara" (moon and stars), figured all over with representations of heavenly bodies.

[97]Pliny, "Natural History," lib. xxx. c. 8, § 34.

[98]There is a shell pattern in gold on a twelfth century fragment of a Bishop's garment at Worcester.

[99]See Wilkinson's "Ancient Egyptians," vol. iii. pp. 132, 133, 350, 553.

[100]Bötticher, in his "Tektonik," will allow of but one origin for the "egg and tongue" pattern. I cannot give up the evident descent from the lotus flower and bud; but I have said before that a pattern has sometimes a double parentage, and it may be so in this case.

[101]The lotus is almost entirely lost as a native growth in India, and is fast disappearing in Egypt. The lotus blossom in Egypt was not only a sacred emblem, but also an *objet de luxe*. At their feasts, the honoured guests were presented with the flowers, and as they faded, slaves carried round baskets of fresh blossoms. See Wilkinson's "Manners and Customs of the Ancient Egyptians."

[102]See the Book of Lindisfarne, and the two Celtic bronze shields in the British Museum. These last are very curious. The long involved lines show their origin, and the shields are enriched with enamel and corals, in repetitions of the prehistoric cross.

[103]See "Album of Photographs of the Marien-Kirche, Dantzic," Taf. 31.

[104]Woltmann and Woermann, Eng. Trans., p. 202.

[105]Charlemagne's dress, in his tomb, was covered with golden elephants. This must have been Indian. His mantle was "*parsemé*" with golden bees.

[106]Elsewhere there is a notice of Miss Morritt's really beautifully embroidered landscapes at Rokeby; and all who saw them will remember the extremely clever and effective pictures in crewels by an accomplished American lady, Mrs. Oliver Wendell Holmes, exhibited in London a few years ago. These exceptional cases do not, however, disprove the objections against employing the most unfit and unmanageable materials for producing subjects alien to the art of embroidery.

[107]See Redgrave's "Manual of Design," pp. 50-61.

[108]See Appendix 21, by Ch. T. Newton, to the first edition of Ruskin's "Stones of Venice." He gives, as instances of this pattern, certain coins from Prienè, where the River Mæander is symbolized by the angular key pattern. Appendix, No. 1.

[109]"(Euripides *loquitur*) Not horse-cocks, nor yet goat-stags, such as they depict on Persian carpets" (Aristophanes, "The Frogs," v. 939-944). The Persian carpets, which are the legitimate descendants of Babylonian art, are curiously fragmentary. In a modern design are to be seen birds, indicated by a head, bill, and eyes; little coffee-pots, and flowers broken off at the stalks, and small quadrupeds without any particular form; also the prehistoric cross, the Tau, and bits of broken-up wave and key patterns. All these, repeated into a pattern, remind us of scraps in a kaleidoscope, thrown together accidentally, or else taken up by chance where history and art have dropped them.

[110]"Soma" or "Homa" ("Sarcostemma Viminale vel Brevistigma"), from Cashmere and the Hindu Cush, still used by the Brahmins, and the juice of which was the first intoxicant of the human race. See Birdwood's "Indian Art," vol. ii. pp. 336, 337.

[111]"The Hom, the sacred Persian tree, is constantly placed between two animals, chained to it." See Pl. 23, Nos. 1, 2, 3, 4, 5, 6.

[112]The Hom or Homa, the sacred tree of Assyrian and Persian sculpture and textiles, is accounted for as a pattern by Dr. Rock, who says: "From the earliest antiquity a tradition came down through middle Asia, of some holy tree, perhaps the tree of life spoken of as growing in Paradise." It is always represented as something like a shrub, and is a conventional portrait of a palm; but Rock says it has every look of having belonged to the family of the Asclepiadeæ. For its last transformation into a vine, see Pl. 24.

[113]Rock's "Introduction," p. cxxxi.

[114]Sir George Birdwood says: "The intimate absorption of Hindu life in the unseen realities of man's spiritual consciousness is seldom sufficiently acknowledged by Europeans, and, indeed, cannot be fully comprehended by men whose belief in the supernatural has been destroyed by the prevailing material ideas of modern society. Every thought, wish, and deed of the Hindu belongs to the world of the unseen as well as the seen; and nothing shows this more strikingly than the traditional works of India. Everything that is made has a direct religious use, or some religious symbolism. The materials of which different articles are fashioned, their weight, and the colours with which they are painted, are fixed by religious rule. An obscured symbolism of material and colour is to be traced also in the forms of things, even for the most domestic uses. Every detail of Indian decoration, Aryan or Turanian, has a religious meaning, and the arts of India will never be rightly understood until there are brought to their study, a familiar acquaintance with the character and subjects of the religious poetry, national legends, and mythological scriptures that have always been their inspiration, and of which they are the perfected imagery." See Sir George Birdwood's "Indian Arts," part i. p. 2.

[115]The Persian tree of life was not alien to the worship of the Zoroastrian religion of the Sassanides, and is said to have been the origin of the worship of Bacchus. It was introduced by Oriental weavers into Sicilian and Spanish stuffs.

[116]Sir G. Birdwood suggests that the honeysuckle pattern is derived from the Tree of Life, cone, and palm, refashioned and combined with the graceful ingenuity of Greek art, and covering a mixture of sacred traditional emblems.

[117]Haug, in his "Essays on the Sacred Writings of the Parsees" (pp. 132, 239), tells us that these people still hold the homa to be sacred, and from it squeeze a juice used by them in their religious ceremonies.

[118]See Perrot et Chipiez, "Histoire de l'Art," vol. ii. pp. 260, 267, Pl. xiv.

[119]See Appendix, No. 1.

[120]India, in return, afterwards influenced Persia, the successor of Babylon.

[121]In India, the elephant is a very common element in a pattern; in Egypt, the serpent; in Persia, the lion. In animal patterns, certain emblems were grouped together. The lion and the goose represent strength and prudence; the lion and eagle, strength and dominion; the lion and dove, strength and gentleness. We may see these double emblems on Sicilian textiles.

[122]Chinese art is crowded with symbolisms.

[123]The double-headed eagle was the badge of Saladin, as well as that of the Holy Roman Empire.

[124]Ezekiel xvii.

[125]In the earliest days of Christianity.

[126]"A cloud pattern from which issue two clasped hands is the device of Guizot Marchand or Guido Mercator, printer, in 1498. He lived at the College of Navarre."—Dibdin's "Decameron," ii. pp. 33-36.

[127]See Gori (tom. iii. pp. 20, 84), as cited by Rock, Introduction, p. liii. The same netted pattern was found in the grave of an Archbishop of York of about the end of the thirteenth century. Its name, *fundata*, is derived from *funda*, the fisherman's net; also, in later times, it was called *laqueata*. See Rock's Introduction (p. liv.). See also M. Ch. Clermont Ganneau's "L'Imagerie Phénicienne," Coupe de Palestrina; and Chaldée et Assyrie, in Perrot and Chipiez, ii. p. 736. Another instance is shown here of the fundata occurring in the bronze flat bowl copied from Layard's "Monuments," 2nd series, plate 62. The whole design of the bowl is Babylonian, consisting of a rich border of repetitions of the tree of life; each has the peculiar ornament of little knobs often seen on their head-dresses.

[128]See Bock's "L. Gewänder," p. 129; Gori, "Thes. Dipt." ii. pp. 20, 275; Marquardt, "Handbuch Röm. Alt." vii. pp. 527-31 (Eng. Trans.). Authorities differ in describing the Chrysoclavus. Sir G. Birdwood calls it a button pattern ("Indian Arts," vol. ii. p. 241). The "Chrysoclavus" was the name given to the palmated or triumphal pattern with which the consular robes are invariably embroidered in the Roman Consular ivories at Zurich, Halberstadt, and in the South Kensington Museum. The tenacious life of this pattern is curiously shown in the way it appears in the fifteenth century on Italian playing-cards. (See "Cartes à Jouer," an anonymous French book in the print-room of the British Museum.) The kings and knaves wear the Byzantine humeral, and the Chrysoclavus pattern is carved on their chairs. Till lately English playing-cards showed the same dress-pattern. I shall discuss the Latin Clavus and the Chrysoclavus amongst ecclesiastical embroideries, pp. 308, 336 (*post*).

[129]See Wilkinson's "Ancient Egyptians," i. p. 125. The date of these mural paintings may, however, be even as late as the time of Alexander the Great.

[118]
CHAPTER IV.
MATERIALS.
1. RAW MATERIALS.

The history of an art must, more or less, include that of its raw material.

This is too true to be disputed, but in the art of embroidery it opens out such endless avenues, through such vast regions of technical study, that we must acknowledge the difficulty, or rather the impossibility, of including in one volume even a tithe of the information already collected.

I shall, therefore, only dedicate a few pages to the history of those fibres which have always been most important in the different phases of our civilization.

Among books on textile materials, I must again name the "Textrinum Antiquorum," by Yates. His premature death, and the loss that the world of art and manufacture has sustained by the chain of his invaluable researches being broken, cannot be appreciated but through the study of the first and only volume of this already rare book, from which I venture to quote largely.

Semper's "Der Stil" is a work of reference on this subject, so valuable that it should, by a good translation, be placed within the reach of non-German scholars.

From Colonel Yule's "Marco Polo," and his abundant notes, we learn much of Asiatic textile art in the thirteenth century, and its early traditions in the immutable East, and Sir G. Birdwood's books on this Indian art are most instructive.

Egyptian textiles are splendidly illustrated by Sir [119]Gardiner Wilkinson. All these modern writers quote Pliny and the Periplus;[130] and Pliny quotes all the classic authors, from Homer to his day. Here is a wide field for gathering information regarding the materials for embroidery in past ages.

When we use the phrase "raw material" so glibly, with an æsthetic contempt for that which the art of man has neither manipulated nor reorganized, we show our own coarse appreciation, if not ignorance, of the wonderful inherent beauty and microscopic delicacy of form, colour, and substance of those materials which we fashion for our own uses.

Few know the structure of the tender filaments of wool, flax, cotton, and silk; or that each has its peculiar form and attributes, and its individual capabilities for the purposes for which they appear to us to have been created, i.e. the clothing and adornment of man's dress and his home.

I should like to draw attention to these well-attested facts.

Seen through a microscope, the forms of these raw materials differ greatly.

Flax is difficult to describe, as it varies according to the soil and climate it comes from. Its fibre, however, has always a shiny outer surface, and is transparent, cylindrical, and pipe-like; apparently with breaks or joints like those of a cane.

Cotton also varies so much in its own kind, that every description is different and somewhat puzzling. Semper says that it approaches the ribbon form, with thickened edges, and is like a half-cylinder twisted spirally; but when wetted with oil, it swells into a complete cylinder.[131]

[120]Wool and hair are hollow pipes without joints. Woollen fibres look like cylindrical snakes with a scaly surface. This roughness gives wool a clinging power which exceeds that of any other material, except the hair of some few animals.[132]

Silk threads consist of twin pipes laid parallel, and held together by the varnish with which they are glazed. Silk is tough and elastic.

The qualities needed for textile materials may be thus enumerated: Pliability, toughness (i.e. tensile strength), and intrinsic durability.

Of course, the material must to a certain degree influence the style of the fabric, and its selection must be according to the effect intended to be produced.[133] The fashions of the day, and the needs of the special manufacture, must greatly modify the choice of materials, which fluctuate, often disappear, and sometimes revive again.

Certain materials which have been, at one period, much admired, have been entirely lost; and indeed we may say that the only permanently employed textiles are wool, flax, cotton, and silk, which apparently never can be superseded. With them, all domestic requirements can be satisfied, and all artistic and decorative fabrics produced, varied, and perfected; and these, from all time recorded in history, have been enriched and glorified with gold, either inwoven or embroidered.

The game of "animal, vegetable, or mineral" might [121]well be played with textiles only. Nothing has been alien to the crafts which from time immemorial have spun, woven, felted, netted, and embroidered.

The materials now in general use, and which, once known, have never been abandoned, I have already named, and shall discuss their history separately; they are wool, flax, cotton, and silk. To these I must add hemp, both wild and cultivated.

Hemp is a kind of nettle. It was grown in Colchis, and in those cool regions which did not produce flax. Hemp is hardly grown in India, except to extract from it the narcotic, Cannabis Indica. It was a northern production used throughout Scandinavia. Herodotus (iv. 14) says, "Hemp grows in the land of the Scythians, in a wild state, but it is now cultivated." From its Latin name, *cannabis*, comes our canvas, which has always been much used as a ground for counted stitches and backing for embroidery, its stiffness being its qualification for such purposes.[134]

Jute (a rough sort of hemp) has been long an article of commercial importance for the manufacture of coarse-figured fabrics, dyed and woven, sometimes embroidered.

The fibre of the Aloe has been used in the Riviera for laces and "macrami" (knotted fringes).

The fibres of grasses, such as the "Honduras silk grass" (Rhea or Ramie), valuable for beauty, fineness, and toughness, have been worked or woven into stuffs.[135] This material is now coming into notice.

[122]Spartum is often named for coarse weaving;[136] also the fibres of barks, especially those of palm branches.[137]

Another substance of classic use, and even now employed, though rather as a curiosity than as an article of commerce, is the silky filament produced by the shell-fish pinna; and also the fibres of certain sea-weeds.

Fur and hair, especially that of camels and goats, has always been much prized.[138] We have seen both African and Indian striped or primitively decorated rugs of wool, touched here and there with scraps of cotton or silk, or some other odd material; and amongst them, tufts of human hair. The sentiment that motived the use of human hair has been either love or hate—the votive or the triumphal. We know that Delilah was not a stranger to this art. She wove into her web Samson's seven locks of strength, and "fastened them with a pin" (Judges xvi.).

In the thirteenth century it was the custom for ladies to weave their own hair into their gifts to favoured knights. King Ris, if he had received any such token [123]from his lady-love, returned it with interest; for he sent her a mantle in which were inwoven the beards of nine conquered kings, a tenth space being left for that of King Arthur, which he promised to add in course of time.[139]

Leather has been from the remotest antiquity employed for the art of embroidery, either for the ground, as in the mantle of Boadicea, made of skins with the fur turned inwards and the leather outside, dressed, and embroidered on the seams;[140] or else as fine inlaid and onlaid application, as in the "funeral tent of an Egyptian queen" in the museum at Boulac, which is certainly the earliest specimen of needlework decoration that exists.[141] (Pl. 44.) The old Indian embroideries in leather are generally applied one on another. The North American Indians also embroider on leather.[142]

Feather work will be discussed under the heading of "Opus Plumarium."[143]

On the surface of textiles many substances have been fastened down, in order to give brilliancy to the general effect—skins of insects, beetles' wings, the claws and teeth of various animals.[144]

Asbestos linen is the only mineral substance, besides gold, silver, and tin,[145]that has been employed in [124]embroidery. It has the remarkable quality of indestructibility by fire. Asbestos linen can be cleansed by fire instead of water.[146] It is a soapy crystal, found in veins of serpentine and cipolino in Cyprus, and other Greek islands. Pliny says it was woven for the funeral obsequies of monarchs, as it preserved the ashes apart, being itself unharmed by the fires of cremation. There are several fragments existing, found in tombs. One of these is in the British Museum.[147]

Marco Polo speaks of a stone fibre found at Chinchin, which answers in description to asbestos. It was spun by mixing it with threads of flax soaked in oil; and when woven, was passed through the fire to remove the flax and the oil.[148]

A miraculous napkin of asbestos was long kept at Monte Casino.

Coral, pearls, and beads of many forms have been used for the enrichment of embroideries, and for decorating textiles. The whole surface of the original fabric has often been entirely covered with them, or the pattern itself has been worked in nothing else. Pearls are constantly seen worked on dress, coats-of-arms, and embroidered portraits. Seed pearls, large coarse pearls, and sometimes fine and precious ones, were surrounded with gold thread embroidery. Coral was so much used in Sicilian embroideries, and so little elsewhere, that one gives the name of "Sicilian" to all such work; but occasionally we find coral embroideries in Spain and elsewhere (Pl. 32).

Pl. 32.
See larger image
Portion of Dalmatic embroidered by Blanche, Queen of Charles IV. of Bohemia (fifteenth century).

The figures in pearls, on a background of beaten gold. Bock's "Liturgische Gewänder." Vol. i. taf. xi.

[125]Beads of glass were common in Egypt from the earliest times, strung together by threads so as to form breastplates rather than necklaces. Whence beads originally came we cannot tell, but it seems that the Phœnicians dropped them on all the shores of the world. Then, as now, savages had a passion for beads, and civilized men and women still admire them as trimmings. In the Middle Ages they were sometimes worked into pictures.[149]

In as far as materials are essential to the art of embroidery, I must restrict myself to the history of silk, wool, flax, cotton, and gold. With these all the finest works have been executed for the artistic adornment of dress and hangings. All other materials have been occasional experiments, or else were resorted to in the absence or ignorance of the above five most important factors in our domestic civilization. The history of wool must take precedence as being that of the original, if not the first, of textile materials.

2. WOOL.

The wool of sheep and the hair of goats were used very early in the world's history for clothing, and probably also for hangings. The earliest civilizations plaited, span,[150] wove, and felted them.

There is no reason to suppose that goats and sheep preceded the creation of man. No early fossils record them. Our sheep are supposed by zoologists to be [126]descended from the Argali or Ovis Ammon of Linnæus, inhabiting the central regions of Asia.[151]

It is possible that plaited grasses may have preceded wool. But though certain prehistoric specimens are supposed to have been found in Spain, yet of this there is but imperfect proof.

The pastoral tribes wandering over those fair regions that extend from Khotan to Arabia, following their flocks and herds, and studying where best to feed, increase, and multiply them, and obtain from them the finest texture of wool, are spoken of nowhere more than in the collected books of the Old Testament, open to us all; and there we learn how important a place these shepherds held in the world's civilization. "Watching their flocks by night," they watched the stars also, and they were astronomers; seeking the best pastures and fodder, they learned to be botanists, florists, and agriculturalists. They became also philosophers, poets, prophets, and kings.[152] Job and his country were enriched through the breeding of sheep. The seven daughters of Jethro, the High-priest, tended their father's flocks.

The Arabians were always great breeders of sheep. The Greeks and Romans, from Homer to Virgil, sang of the herdsman's life. Our Lord Himself did not disdain to be called "the Good Shepherd."[153]

The merchants who traded from the Arabian Gulf to Egypt, and across thence to the shores of the Mediterranean, and the Phœnicians of Sidon who brought overland their bales of raw material and manufactured Oriental fabrics, knew well where to find the best goods for their customers; and we hear frequently whence came this or [127]that coloured wool. Chemmis, the city of Pan, retained its celebrity in the woollen trade down to the conquest of Egypt by the Romans. Nineveh and Babylon encouraged the manufactures and commerce in woollen tents, wall-hangings, and carpets. Nowhere were they so richly embroidered.[154]

Solomon purchased woollens from Egypt. Damascus supplied the Tyrians with wool for their rugs. The stuffs and textile fabrics of wool, of the Chinese, Assyrians, and Chaldeans, are recorded in the earliest writings of the human race. How much their decoration depended on weaving, and how much on embroidery, we cannot tell. The products of the Babylonian looms are alluded to in the Book of Joshua,[155] and also by Ezekiel.[156]

Assyrian stuffs were always celebrated for their splendid colours and various designs; among which were hunting scenes, battles, and special emblematic adornments.[157]

From Miletus came the wool valued most highly by the Greeks. Spain produced the best black, and the north of Italy the best white wool. The Narbonensian and Egyptian wools were supposed to be the most durable, and when they became shabby, were dipped again and served another generation.

From Yates' account of the great variety of wools, remarkable for their fine texture, their whiteness,[158] their [128]blackness,[159] or their redness, their cool or their warm tints, it is evident that the ancients valued highly these different qualities.[160] The cloths that were of greatest account were of the finest or the warmest kinds. The sheep of Miletus, Attica, Megaris, and Tarentum were clothed in jackets, in order to preserve the fineness and whiteness of their own coats, and to protect them from being torn by the thorny bushes in their pastures. Columella calls them the "covered" and the "soft," and says they were often kept in the house.

We find notices of the peculiarities of the various national breeds, caused by the soil on which their pasture grew, and the rivers and streams at which they drank, and these peculiarities were, if possible, encouraged. There is evidence also that some improvement of the breeds by crossing was practised in early times.

As in all the life of the Greeks, the religious element had much influence in perfecting their flocks of sheep—only the most beautiful animals were considered worthy of sacrifice to the gods.

A few of the rare specimens of stuffs which have been [129]rescued from tombs, especially in the Crimea, and in the Fayoum, in Egypt, show a wool so fine and shining that it might be taken for silk, and the beauty of the weaving is marvellous, and much varied in style.

A warrior's tomb in the district of Kuban contained a funeral pall, covering the sarcophagus, measuring at least three metres and a half each way, woven of brown wool, in twelve narrow strips sewn together and afterwards painted. The ground is yellowish, the design brown. The figures repeat mythical subjects, and alternate with patterns, and there is a border. One strip contains a scene from the story of Peleus and Thetis. Apparently this is Attic design. The coloured dresses worn by women of rank, and hung on the statues of the gods, were sometimes painted, sometimes stamped, and often embroidered, and they were nearly all of woollen fabrics.

One of the great advantages of wool is its power of absorbing colour, as the pigment sinks into its very fibre, instead of clinging to the surface. It can be dyed of deeper colours than flax, cotton, or silk.

Pliny tells us that Tanaquil combed, span, and wove her wool, and she herself made the royal mantle which Servius Tullius used to wear, and it was covered with a wavy pattern (undulata). Thence came the custom that when a maiden became a bride, her attendants carried a distaff trimmed with combed wool, and a spindle with yarn upon it. The robes worked by Tanaquil were dedicated by Servius Tullius to the statue of Fortune in her temple at Rome, and were still hanging there in the days of Tiberius.[161] Pliny remarks that it was a wonder that it neither fell from the image, nor was eaten by the moths, during five hundred and sixty years.

[130]He gives us interesting details of the weaving of woollen cloths, and speaks of the thick coarse wool with "great thick hair," used for carpets from the time of Homer. The same passage mentions felt. He tells us of the cloths with a curly nap, used in the days of Augustus; of the "papaverata" woven with flowers resembling poppies; and we hear from him of the cloth of divers colours woven in Babylon, and called thence Babylonica; and the Alexandrian webs, with many-coloured threads (polymita)[162], comparing them with those made in Gaul; and those woven by the Parthians.[163]

We have already said that the wool of Miletus was a proverbial favourite with the Greeks. Eustathius speaks of the excellence of the Milesian carpets and hangings. Virgil represents the virgins of Cyrene spinning Milesian wool dyed of a deep sea-green.[164]

In the British Museum is a fragment of Egyptian woollen or worsted embroidery on white linen, discoloured by its use as mummy wrapping; but the stitches of worsted remain a perfectly clear bright crimson and indigo blue. This shows how wool absorbs the colour and retains it. Even when the surface is faded, it can be made to emit it again by chemical processes.

In tombs in the Crimea have been found variously woven and adorned woollen fabrics. There are fragments resembling in their texture a fine rep—a sort of corded stuff; another material resembling a woollen crêpe, or fine "nun's gauze." This veiled a golden wreath. Then there is a stuff like what is now called "atlas"—a kind of woollen satin. Some woollens are woven simply like linen; some are wide, some very narrow, sewn together in strips, woven in meandering designs. [131]One, like a piece of Gobelin tapestry, has a border of ducks with yellow wings and dark green heads and throats,[165] and then another with a pattern of stags' heads. This description recalls the specimens on plate 16 and plate 39.

From these tombs are collected stuffs of wool, woven and embroidered in gold with combinations of many colours; and, in fact, through this collection, now placed in the Museum at St. Petersburg, we become aware that 300 B.C. the Greeks had learned all the secrets of the art of weaving wool. They, however, lost it, and it is only in India that its continuity was never broken. Indian looms still weave, of the finest fleeces, such shawls of Babylonian design as repeat the texture of the ancient Greek garments. But were they Greek? or did those beautiful woven fabrics come from Persia or India?[166]

The first we know of Scandinavian wool for dress, is a fragment from a Celtic barrow in Yorkshire—a woollen plaited shroud. This fabric was an advance upon the original northern savage costume—a sheep-skin fashioned and sewn with a fish-bone for a needle, sinews for thread, and a thorn for a pin. But we must imagine that some use was made, besides plaiting, of the spun wool, of which the early northern women have left us evidence, in the whorls of their spindles, from prehistoric times.

Wool has always appeared to be a natural material for dress. It is warm in winter, light in summer, and is always beautiful as it hangs in lovely soft draperies, heavy enough to draw the fabric into graceful curved lines, and yet capable of yielding to each movement in [132]little rippling folds, covering, but not concealing the forms to which they cling. Classical draperies are explained by it. What the Italians call the "eyes of the folds," are particularly beautiful in woollens, and lend themselves to sculpturesque art.

The other natural use of wool is for carpets. We have the evidence of the imitations, in mosaic, of carpets from the stone floors in Nineveh (now in the British Museum), that the art of weaving large and small rugs, and the principles of composition for such purposes was at that date well understood. The carpet-weaving traditions of Babylon appear to have been inherited by the occupiers of the soil, as it is supposed that the Saracens learned from Persia the art of weaving pile carpets, and imported thence craftsmen into Spain. We can trace Persian carpet patterns in Indian floor coverings. The Greeks called them *tapetes*, and the Latins adopted the name; and hence the Italian *tapeti*, French *tapis*, and our word tapestry.

As artistic material, to which the world owes much beauty and comfort, woollens have always played a great part in the decorations of our houses, as of our garments. Fabrics have been made of them of every description, from the cheapest and commonest to the most refined; but if woollen stuffs are to be beautiful, they must be *fine*, and worked or embroidered by hand.

Woollens brocaded or figured are not so effective as silken hangings. Woollen velvets are without light, dull and heavy. Still, even amongst our English fabrics, there have always been varieties of texture[167] and adaptations to different effects, and some are beautiful.

[133]Worsted thread, so called from Worsted, in Norfolk, where the materials for weaving and embroidering are manufactured, has always been very important in embroidery. Worsteds after a time gave way to a very beautiful material, called "German wool," which again has yielded the supremacy to "crewels"[168](resembling the old worsteds). These crewels are nearly the same in substance and in their loose texture as the threads prepared from wool for tapestry weaving.

We may claim, in England, the superiority in this manufacture, though we are constantly receiving from France novelties which give us good hints, and urge us to keep pace with the science of the Gobelins in their woollen dyes. The French, in return, employ our wools, especially those of Lincolnshire, in their tapestry workshops.

The wool and hair of goats should be a study by itself. They have from the earliest times been used in India for the finest and softest fabrics, such as the lovely shawls of Cashmere and the neighbouring provinces. Cloth of Tars in the Middle Ages is supposed to be what is now called Cashmere.

3. FLAX.

Boyd Dawkins tells us that "The art of spinning and the manufacture of linen were introduced into Europe in the Neolithic age, and have been preserved with little variation from that period to the present day, in certain remote parts of Europe, having only been superseded in modern times by the complicated machinery so familiar to us. The spindle and distaff, or perforated spindle whorls, are of stone, pottery, or bone, such as are constantly found in Neolithic tombs and habitations. Thread from [134]the Swiss lake cities is proved to be of flax, and there is evidence of weaving in some sort of loom."[169]

The meaning of the word Byssus has been disputed; some authorities asserting that it includes both flax and cotton fabrics. Without the aid of the microscope, the dispute as to whether the material of the Egyptian mummy wrappings was cotton or flax, or a mixture of the two, would never have been settled; but now that the difference of the structure of each has been clearly ascertained, we know that cotton was never employed in Egypt, except for certain domestic uses. The mummy wrappings are entirely linen. Cotton was forbidden for the priests' dress in the temple, though they might wear it when not on duty.[170]

There are specimens of Egyptian painted or printed patterns on fine linen in the British Museum;[171] and it is curious to see in Egyptian mural paintings the same patterned chintzes on furniture that were common a hundred years ago in England. Both must have come from India, and therefore were certainly cotton fabrics.

Herodotus says the mummy cloths were of "byssine sindon," which may be translated "linen cloth."[172] Cotton he calls "tree wool."

Yates has carefully argued the whole question, and, we think, has proved that byssus was flax, and not cotton. [135][173] He quotes Philo, who certainly must have believed that it was made of flax, from the description he gives of its appearance and qualities, which in no way apply to cotton or hemp. He says that "The Jewish high priests wore a linen garment of the purest byssus—which was a symbol of firmness, incorruption, and of the clearest splendour, for fine linen is very difficult to tear. It is made of nothing mortal, and becomes brighter and more resembling light, the more it is cleansed by washing."[174]

Here is another quotation: "Cloth of byssus symbolizes firm faith. Its threads surpass even ropes of broom in firmness and strength."[175] Pliny says the flax grown in Egypt was superior to any other, and it was exported to Arabia and India.[176] The first known existing fragment of flax linen in Europe was taken from the tomb of the Seven Brothers in the Crimea. Its date is 300 B.C.

In Solomon's time the Jews evidently depended upon Egypt for their fine linen. Herodotus describes the corselet of Amasis, the fineness of the linen, and the embroidered decorations of men and animals, partly gold and partly tree wool (i.e. cotton).[177]

All the finest linen certainly came then from Egypt, and was much finer than any that is now made. That we call cambric, was woven there many centuries before it was made in Cambray.[178]

Through the Phœnicians the fine linen came to Rome, [136]as appears from the following notice of embroidery on linen by Flavius Vopiscus, in his "Life of the Emperor Carinus:" "Why should I mention the linen cloths brought from Tyre and Sidon, which are so thin as to be transparent, which glow with purple, or are prized on account of their laborious embroideries?"[179]

The history of a fine embroidered linen curtain for a Roman house might have been this:—Grown in Egypt; carried to Nomenticum (Artois), and there woven; taken to India to be embroidered, and thence as merchandise to Rome.

While flax was making its way northward, the Celts must also have taken it across Europe from their resting-place, after emigrating from the East. The word *linen*—*lin-white*—is a Celtic epithet, whereas *flax* is an Anglo-Saxon word.[180]

The Atrebates wove linen in Artois, 1800 years ago. Jerome speaks of their "indumenta," or shirts of fine linen; and the great weavers of to-day are still the Flemish descendants of the Atrebates. Their Celtic descent is witnessed in the Irish by their superiority in the crafts of the loom.

The fine laces of Venice, France, and Belgium are all of linen, i.e. flaxen thread. Clearness and strength in these delicate fabrics cannot be obtained with cotton, which, especially when it is washed, swells and fluffs, and never has the radiant appearance and purity of flax.

Embroidery is always a natural accompaniment of fine linen. Those that are still preserved to us from early [137]and Middle-Age times are nearly all on linen, if not on silk. The woollen fragments are very few and imperfect. They have been invariably "fretted" by the moth.

White needle embroidery is mostly worked in linen-thread, though cotton-thread has been used a great deal, and is very fit for the purpose.

4. COTTON.

Cotton was native to India,[181] as flax was to Egypt. It not only was grown, woven, and printed there from the remotest antiquity, but was cultivated nowhere else. The Egyptians do not appear to have grown it till the fourteenth century A.D., though they had long imported it as raw material, and as plain and printed webs.[182] It was called tree-wool.

It was first woven in Italy in the thirteenth century, and used for making paper; and in the sixteenth, the plant was grown in the south of Europe. From Italy it was carried into the Low Countries, and only reached England in the seventeenth century,[183] so lately has the great staple of our manufactures first belonged to us.

The fibre of cotton has neither the strength nor the durability of flax or silk, but it is the third in the group of the most universally qualified materials for all purposes of domestic textile art, ranging from carpets and sails, to fine chintzes for dress, and filmy muslins. The cloudy effect of these delicate fabrics is their own peculiar beauty. Muslins for hangings, printed or embroidered, [138]have always been a luxury from India; they were called "carbasa," and were much esteemed in Rome as a protection against the sun.[184]

But we have much earlier notice of them, as being the curtains described in the Book of Esther, hung with silver rings to the pillars of marble in the banqueting hall at Susa or Shushan: "blue and white muslin" (i.e. carpas,[185] mistranslated "green" in the Authorized Version), "fastened with cords of fine linen and purple."

The word "carbasina" occurs in a play by Statius, evidently translated from a writer of the new Greek comedy period. It may be inferred, therefore, that the Greeks used cotton 200 B.C.[186] A century before, Nearchus (one of Alexander's admirals) speaks of the cotton-trees in India as if they were a new discovery. Yates gives us many quotations from Latin classical authors, proving the common use of cotton. Its Latin name was *bambacinum*, from *bombax*, hence the Italian *bambagio, bambagino, bambasino*.

The variety of cotton fabrics in India is very numerous, each having its distinctive beauties and qualities inherited by tradition from early times. They are enumerated and described in Sir G. Birdwood's "Arts of India." Almost all of them have been made to carry embroideries—the transparent muslins, [139][187] as well as the fine cloths, and the stronger and thicker fabrics.[188]

Most old English houses contain some hangings of thickly woven cotton, probably Indian, worked in crewel or worsted, of the time of James I., or a little earlier; and beautiful patterns wrought in silk or thread, on fine cotton linen, reminding one of the arabesques of the Taj Mahal, succeeded those of the Jacobean style.

Transparent muslins were often embroidered in gold and silver, or spangled and embossed with beetles' wings; and gold, silver, and silk were lavished on Indian cotton grounds, as well as on silken stuffs. Linen was not much embroidered in India, but often printed like chintz.

Buckram, or plush of cotton, was certainly imported from the East to England, from the thirteenth century to the time of Elizabeth. There is at Ashridge, in Hertfordshire, a small jacket of very fine cotton-plush amongst the baby linen prepared by Elizabeth for the expected heir of Philip and Mary, and there are other small dresses of this material of the date of James I. A similar material called fustian is also named by Marco Polo as a cotton fabric; it is supposed to have been made in Egypt by the Arabs. This sort of cotton-plush, variously manipulated, is repeatedly mentioned by Herr Graf'schen in his "Catalogue of Egyptian Textiles from the Fayoum."

Plano Carpini says the tunics of the Tartars were "bacramo," or else of baudichin (cloth of gold). Falstaff's "men in buckram" may be thus explained.[189]

[140]I have already said that cotton is inferior in its qualities to silk and flax, except in the production of transparent muslins. Its peculiarity is its tendency to "crinkle" or crumple in wearing, therefore it does not present a smooth flat surface, except by means of dressing, which unfits it for clinging effects but suits printed patterns. Such stuffs as workhouse sheeting, imitating certain fabrics of the sixteenth century, and which it has been the fashion of late to cover with embroidery, do not repay, by effective beauty, the trouble bestowed upon them.

5. GOLD.

A somewhat profane French writer, giving his ideas on the Creation, says that gold, the latest metal, was expressly created for the demoralization of mankind. This is an ugly version of the fact that it is found on the surface of the earth's crust, and that its beauty and worth makes it a desirable possession for which men will ever contend.

Gold adorns every work of the artistic animal—man. It is the most becoming setting to all other beautiful things, the most gorgeous reflection of light and colour, the richest and softest background, the most harmonious medium for high lights. In all works of decoration it represents sunshine where it is not, and doubles it where it is. The word "illumination" in books belongs to the gilded illustrations of immortal thoughts.

In embroideries, as grounding or as pattern, gold gives the glory: "Her clothing is of wrought gold." The raiment of needlework is comparatively ineffective without golden lights or background. As colour, it never can offend the eye, except when used to accentuate aggressively [141]a vulgar pattern, or when it flashes and dazzles from over-polish and too lavish expenditure.

Silver follows gold as a splendid element in decoration,[190] but it is not of such universal application and use; and when employed together, the proportion of gold should preponderate. Golden tissues belong to the earliest civilizations.

Sir G. Birdwood says that "The art of gold brocades is older than the Code of Manu.... The excellence of the art passed in the long course of ages, from one place to another; and Babylon, Tarsus, Alexandria, Baghdad, Damascus, Antioch, Tabriz, Sicily, and Tripoli successively became celebrated for their gold and silver-wrought tissues, silks, and brocades.... Through every disguise (and mingling of style) it is not impossible to infer the essential identity of the brocades with the fabrics of blue, purple, and scarlet, worked in gold, of ancient Babylonian art."[191]

The Israelites wove gold with their coloured woollens for the use of the sanctuary, and probably brought the art from Egypt; though I am not aware of any gold-woven stuffs from Egyptian tombs.[192]

Indian and Chinese stuffs were from time immemorial woven with gold.

The historians of Alexander the Great continually name gold as a material in dress.[193] Arrian, Justin, and Quintus Curtius, all speak of golden tissues as part of the luxury of the East.

[142]We hear of Darius' dress woven with golden hawks; and of the golden spoils of Persepolis; the dresses worn by Alexander's generals, and all his attendants clothed in purple and gold. Then, perhaps, the Babylonian tradition was brought to Europe; and ever after, purple and gold became the state apparel for courtiers as well as kings.[194]

The hangings of scarlet, purple, and gold used at the nuptials of Alexander, and at his funeral, and his pall of the same material, point to the fact that gold was a recognized element in splendid textile weaving, as well as in the earliest ornamental embroideries.[195]

Attalus II., king of Pergamus, was credited with being the inventor of gold weaving, but this must have been a mistake, as it was practised long before his time; but he may have devised some splendid golden tissues, which were called "Attalic," in honour of the king's patronage.[196] As, however, the gold flat plate or wire was probably that woven before his time,[197] it is possible that he may have invented or patronized the making of thread of gold, by twining it round flax or cotton.[198]

[143]Pliny says gold may be woven or spun like wool without any admixture of wool or flax,[199] and he quotes as examples the golden garment of Agrippina, and that worn by Tarquinius Priscus, mentioned by Verrius.

It appears that the Egyptians knew the art of drawing gold wire, as some pieces have been found in their jewellery;[200] but we know not by what process it was worked, either then, or in the dark ages.

A mechanic of Nuremberg, in the fourteenth century, invented a machine for the purpose; and this art of drawing wire was introduced into England 200 years later, in 1560.

The pure cut gold was in use in Rome to a late date.[201] St. Cecilia, martyred 230 A.D., was buried with her golden mantle lying at her feet; and in 821, when Pope Pascal opened her grave, he found the evidence of her martyrdom in that splendid garment, showing that it had been soaked in blood.[202]

There were found under the foundations of the new Basilica of St. Peter's, the bodies of Probus Anicius and his wife, Proba Faltonia, in a wrapping of gold.

Dr. Rock gives us more examples,[203] but we will only add that of the wife of the Emperor Honorius, who in [144]the year 400 A.D. was buried in a golden dress, which in 1544 was removed from her grave, and being melted, weighed 36 lbs.[204]

The Anglo-Saxon tomb opened at Chessell Down, in the Isle of Wight, contained fragments of a garment or wrapping woven with flat gold "plate." These remains are now in the British Museum.

Childeric was buried at Tournai, 485 A.D., and his dress of strips of pure gold was discovered and melted in 1653. But gold *thread* also was then very generally used in weaving gold tissues.

Claudian describes a Christian lady, Proba, in the fourth century, preparing the consular robes for her two sons on their being raised to the consulate:[205]—

"The joyful mother plies her knowing hands,And works on all the trabea golden bands;Draws the thin strips to all the length of gold,*To make the metal meaner threads enfold.*"

Pure gold was woven in the dark ages in England. St. Cuthbert's maniple at Durham is of pure gold thread. John Garland says the ladies wove golden cingulæ in the thirteenth century; and Henry I., according to Hoveden, was clothed in a robe of state of woven gold and gems of almost "divine splendour."[206]

A wrapping of beautiful gold brocade covered the coffin of Henry III. when his tomb was opened in 1871.[207]

The cope of St. Andrew at Aix, in Switzerland, is embroidered in a very simple pattern, with large circles containing St. Andrew's crosses.[208] This is worked in silver wire gilt, and is Byzantine of the twelfth century.

[145]In the writings of the Middle Ages we find constant reference to different golden fabrics. Among them are "samit" or "examitur" (a six-thread silk stuff, preciously inwoven with gold threads);[209] and "ciclatoun,"[210] which was remarkable for the lightness of its texture, and was woven with shining gold threads—but though light, it was stiff enough to carry heavy embroidery. We hear also of "baudekin," "nak," and cloth of pall. "Camoca" is "kincob."

There appears to be a link between embroidery in gold and the jewellers' work which in the Dark and Middle Ages was so often applied to ecclesiastical and royal dress and hangings. This link was beaten gold work, "aurobacutos," "beaten work," or "batony."[211] Beauchamp, Earl of Warwick in the time of Henry VI., went over to France, having a "coat for my lord's body, beat with fine gold (probably heraldic designs). For his ship, a streamer forty yards long and eight broad, with a great bear and griffin, and 400 'pencils' with the 'ragged staff' in silver." This mode lasted some time; for in 1538, Barbara Mason bequeathed to a church a "vestment of green silk beaten with gold." Probably [146]this beaten gold was really very thick gold-leaf laid on the silk or linen ground, as we see still in some Sicilian and Arab tissues. The embroidered banners taken from Charles le Téméraire, at Grandson, are finished with broad borders of gilded inscriptions, such as might be called beaten gold work.[212]

But besides this thick gold-leaf, there was another mode of enriching embroideries. Laminæ of gold were cut into shapes, and finished the work by accentuating the design in Eastern embroideries; They are found also in Greek tombs, and in the Middle Ages they varied from the little golden spangle to many other forms—circular rings, stars, crescents, moons, leaves, and solid pendant wedges of gold, all which approached the art of the goldsmith.

Fig. 19.
Spangles.

Enamel was soon added to the enrichment of these golden spangles, plates, or discs, which were enlarged to receive a design.[213] Of this style of embellishment we know none so striking as the saddle in the Museum at Munich, said to have been taken from a Turkish general in the fifteenth century. This is Italian of the finest cinque-cento style: blue velvet, covered with beautiful [147]gold embroidery, and every vacant space filled with spangles of endless forms, and of precious goldsmiths' and enamellers' work. The Persian stirrups attached to it are of a totally different style of enamelling and jewellery, and speak for themselves, and for the school they came from.[214]

Pl. 33.

See larger image

Window Hanging, by Gentil Bellini, from a Portrait of Mahomet II., property of Sir H. Layard.

Dr. Rock describes part of a chasuble wrought by Isabella of Spain and her maids of honour, in which the flowing design is worked out in small moulded spangles of gold and silver, set so as to overlap each other and give the effect of scales.

To a late period, gold and silver embroideries, enriched with spangles, have been lavished on the head-dresses and stomachers of the peasantry throughout the north of Europe and Switzerland.[215]

Pearls and gems, either threaded like beads, or in golden settings, are to be studied in the early pictures of the German and French schools; and the Anglo-Saxons excelled in such enrichments.

Sir Henry Layard has a portrait of the fifteenth century, of the Sultan Mahomet II., by Gentil Bellini, from which has been copied the accompanying beautiful embroidered design of a window-hanging.[216] The grace of the lines, and the delicate taste with which the gems are set in the work, are a lesson in art (pl. 33).

[148]India sent to Europe more art in gold thread than has ever been produced amongst us from our own workshops.[217]

The people of Goa, mostly Arabs, embroidered for the Portuguese those wonderful fabrics, glittering with gold and radiant with colours, which cover the beds and hang the rooms throughout Portugal and Spain.[218] The precious metals (often forming the whole grounding) were employed without stint; the patterns being either embroidered in coloured silks and gold; or on velvets or satins, with gold alone or mixed with silver.

The fine gold threads for embroidery, which have preserved their brilliancy for so many centuries, such as we find worked in Charlemagne's dalmatic, in Aelfled's maniple, and in the mitres of Thomas à Becket, are certainly Oriental. To England they came in the bales of the merchants who brought us our silk, and even our needles, from India. Later we imported and copied the different ways of giving effect to inferior metals, and the Spaniard's gilt parchment thread reached us from their Moorish manufactories.[219]

Designs were sometimes, in the sixteenth century, worked in gold twisted with coloured silks, sometimes only stitched down with them. The badges of the Order of the Dragon, instituted by the Emperor Sigismund, were thus embroidered, and placed on the cloaks of the knights. The work was so perfect that it resembled jewels of enamelled gold. Two ancient ones are in the Museum at Munich.

[149]Gold or silver or base metal wire was, in the later Middle Ages and down to our own times, much employed in the form of what is called "purl," i.e. coiled wire cut into short lengths, threaded on silk, and sewn down. German, Italian, and English embroideries were often enriched with this fabric. Sometimes the wire was twisted with coloured silks before it was coiled. There are beautiful specimens of this work of the days of Queen Elizabeth.

Still, throughout Europe the best works were carried out with the best materials, and these always came from the East. But we sometimes find that the pressure of circumstances has for a time caused the employment of adulterated metals that have perished; and thus many fine works of art have been spoiled.[220]

The use of bad materials has therefore been as unfortunate for art as that of pure gold, which has tempted so many ignorant persons to burn golden embroideries and tapestries, and melt down the ore they contain. How little of all that human skill and invention have carefully elaborated is now preserved to us! To gold and silver textiles their materials have been often a fatal dower.

It has sometimes puzzled any but the most experienced embroiderers to distinguish between the stuffs woven [150]with the golden threads on the surface, and finely brocaded or patterned in the loom; and those other cloths, embroidered by hand, which have been so manipulated that hardly an atom of the gold can be detected at the back. This is done by a technical mode of treating the surface, which is more easily shown than described. The gold is really drawn into the spaces between the threads of the canvas or linen grounding, but never pulled through. For many reasons this is an advantage, and when executed cunningly, as it was in England in the twelfth century, it is rich, beautiful, lasting, and economical. It is a peculiar mark of the "opus Anglicanum," and it is to be seen in the mitre at Munich, where this stitch is employed on a white satin ground;[221] also in the working of the two pluvials at San Giovanni Laterano at Rome, and at the Museum at Bologna, as well as that at Madrid, which are all three English of the thirteenth century, by design as well as by stitches.

I cannot close this chapter without naming the many schools of gold embroidery in Belgium, France, Germany, Italy, and Spain. The King of Bavaria has an establishment for gold work, and this is very finely carried out, highly raised, and richly designed.[222] In Spain there is also a Royal School, where stately works are executed.

It is to be regretted that the modern designs are motiveless, and not so beautiful as the old ones, and it is very difficult to have any ancient piece of work copied exactly. [151]Little modernisms creep in wherever the pattern has to be fitted into a new shape; for the accomplished needlewoman is seldom an artist.

All honour is due to certain manufacturers at Lyons who are working in the spirit of the old masters, and have been seriously considering how best to reproduce the beautiful soft surface of the gold thread of which the secret was lost in the fifteenth century.[223]

The old Chinese flat gold was, about the sixteenth century, superseded by what was manufactured in Spain, and is no longer imported or, perhaps, even made.

6. SILK.

The origin and history of silk is learnedly and elaborately discussed in Yates' "Textrinum Antiquorum." He gives us his authorities, and literal translations for the benefit of the unlearned, who cannot read the original texts. I have availed myself without hesitation of his quotations, and of the carefully considered opinions he has drawn from them.

It has been already said that wool and flax preceded silk in Egyptian, Greek, and Roman manufactures. There is no certain mention of silk in the Books of the Old Testament.[224] Silk is, however, named in the Code of Manu.[225]

[152]No shred of silk has been found in any Egyptian tomb, nor till lately, and with one exception only, in those of the Greeks.

Auberville says, "La soie ne fit son apparition en Europe que 300 ans avant notre ère."[226]

Pamphile, daughter of Plates, of Cos, is said by Aristotle to have there first woven silk (300 B.C.). Probably raw silk was brought to Cos from the interior of Asia, and Pamphile is by some supposed to have "effilèd" the solid manufactured silks, and woven them again into gauzy webs. Yates suggests that it is possible that Pamphile obtained cocoons and unwound them, as the passage in Aristotle may be so interpreted.

The specimen of early silk-weaving which we have above alluded to, was taken out of the "Tomb of the Seven Brothers" at Kertch, in the Crimea, and is of the third century B.C. It consists of several bits of very transparent painted silk. These fragments are an actual and yet a contemporary witness to the truth of the tradition of Pamphile's Coan webs, which are of the same date: possibly they were her handiwork.

Pl. 34.

See larger image
1. Classical Silk. Greek. (Semper's "Der Stil," p. 192.) 2. Classical Silk. Roman. (Auberville, pl. 4.)

Whether Pamphile's silk gauzes were the only fine webs of Cos,[227] is a disputed question. She has the credit of being the first to clothe victorious generals in triumphal garments, and she has been immortalized by her cleverness and industry. Both Aristotle and Pliny assert that she first invented the Coan webs, and that some of them were of silk is undoubted. The question is, How came [153]it there? whence and by what route? and what country was its original home and birthplace?

After stating the *pros* and *cons* of the question, how and where did silk first make its appearance, Sir G. Birdwood concludes that both the worm and the cocoon were known to the Greeks and Romans, by report and rare specimens, from the time of Alexander's return from his Indian campaign.[228]

Of course the remains of these fabrics are extremely scarce; and, in fact, only two are at present known to me besides the Kertch specimen. The first is given in Semper's "Der Stil," and is evidently classical Greek or Roman; but the silk material might have been effilèd from an Oriental stuff (pl. 34, No. 1). The second must have been originally a Roman pattern, modified by the Persian loom in which it was woven. This may have been a Roman triumphal robe of the date of Julius Cæsar (pl. 34, No. 2).

It is clear that Chinese silken stuffs were not generally known in Southern Europe till the time of Julius Cæsar, who displayed a profusion of silks in some of his splendid theatrical representations.

How silk first arrived from the East is disputed; some say it came by the Red Sea, and other authorities believe it was brought from China, *viâ* Persia, by land.

But it is not necessary that it should have entered our civilization by only one gate. The Periplus Maris Erythræi makes frequent mention of the trade in silks, through India, by the Indus to the coasts of the Erythrean Sea. They were also brought through Bactria to Barygaza, near Surat, from a city called Thina (China?). The author of the Periplus, of course, refers to some place in the country vaguely called Serica.[229]

That the trade which brought it into Europe was [154]difficult and limited, is proved by the fact that silk continued, even as late as the third century of our era, to be an article of luxury, of which the manufacture and use continued to be the subject of legal enactments and restrictions, for 600 years after Pamphile's first essay in silk-weaving in Cos.

"The Seres" was the name given by the ancients to the nation which produced silk; and it was undoubtedly that accepted for the distant region now called China, including Corea, and later, the kingdom of Khotan. The first mention of these people as a distinct nation is by Mela (iii. 7), who speaks of them as an "honest people, who bring what they have to sell, and return for their payments."[230]

The prevailing idea amongst the Greeks was that silk was combed from the trees. Seneca says:—

"Nor with Mæonian needle mark the web,Gathered by Eastern Seres from the trees."
Seneca the Tragedian, "Herc. Ætæus," 644.[231]

This was, till lately, believed to be only a fiction, intended to hide the truth and enhance the value of the new Coan material. But it is now ascertained that some of the wild silk in China is carried by the silkworm round the trees, wrapping them up, as it were, in large, untidy cocoons; so that, as usual, tradition had truth for its foundation.

There was always much mysterious report about the new material. Dionysius Periegetes tells of a barbarous [155]people called the Seres, who "renounce the care of sheep and oxen, but who comb the coloured flowers of the desert, and with them produce woven precious stuffs, of which they make figured garments, resembling the flowers of the field in beauty, and in texture the web of the spider."[232]

There is no doubt that as Egypt was the first to weave linen, and India to produce cotton textiles, so in China originated the material of silk and its manufacture.

M. Terrien de la Couperie, who has deciphered the Archaic books of the Chinese Records, sees there excellent linguistic proofs that the Chinese nation was originally a fragment of the first Babylonian civilization. He there finds that when these Accadians arrived on the furthest eastern coast of Asia, they met with and enslaved an aboriginal race, who already cultivated the silkworm, and wove and worked its produce, and were called by them "the Embroiderers."[233]

This is supposed to have been an historical event contemporary with the life of Abraham, and, therefore, 5000 years old.

The Chinese say that Tekin or Sin, the son of Japhet, instructed his children in painting, sculpture, and embroidery, and in the art of preparing *silk* for different woven fabrics.[234]

Whether we are justified or not in believing in so very early a date, at any rate we must remember that it is now ascertained that silk was used in China 2600 years before our era.

Auberville says there is a legend that the Empress [156]Si-ling-chi[235] (2600 B.C.) had the happy inspiration to invent the unwinding of the cocoon before the insect cut the threads; and for this discovery she was placed among the divinities.

Before her time, they had certainly for more than 300 years used the precious material in its mutilated condition.[236]

Some centuries later the Emperor Chan received tribute in linens and silken stuffs. Tissues of many colours were painted or richly embroidered.[237]

In the second century A.D., a prince of Khotan,[238] Kiu-sa-tan-na, was desirous of obtaining from China the eggs of the silkworm, but his request was refused; and it was prohibited that either eggs of the silkworm or seed of mulberry-trees should cross the border.

Then the King of Khotan asked for a Chinese princess in marriage, and this favour being granted, he found means to inform the lady privately that in her future kingdom she would find no silk to weave or work. The dread of such an aimless life roused all her womanly instincts. Defiance of the law, love of smuggling, and the wish to please her husband and benefit her future people, gave her courage to conceal the eggs and seeds in the folds of her dress and the meshes of her beautiful hair, and so she carried a most precious dower into her adopted country.[239] Thus was broken the spell which for more [157]than 3000 years had confined the secret of China within the fence of its wonderful wall; and later on, A.D. 530, the eggs were brought to Byzantium.[240]

From China, therefore, comes our silk.[241] We may say it is traced to the beginning; but how far back had the archæologist to grope before he could find it!

I transcribe a few more quotations from Yates' translations and authorities.[242]

In the Hippolytus of Euripides, 383, Phædra *loquitur*:—

"Remove, ye maids, the vests whose tissue glaresWith purple and with gold; far be the redOf Syrian murex; this the shining threadWhich furthest Seres gathers from the boughs."

Lucan describes the transparent material which veiled Cleopatra's form:—

"Her snowy breast shines through Sidonian threads,First by the comb of distant Seres struck;Divided then by Egypt's skilful hand,And with embroidery transparent made."

Pliny's account of silk and its manufacture is mostly fanciful, though founded on half-known facts.

The Latin poets of the Augustan age speak of silk attire with other luxurious customs from the East.[243] The Roman senate, in the reign of Tiberius, decreed that only women should wear silk, on account of its effeminacy.

[158]Silk was accumulated for the wardrobes of the empresses till A.D. 176, when Marcus Aurelius, "the Philosopher," sold all the imperial ornaments and the silken robes of his empress by auction in the Forum of Trajan.[244]

We learn that silk was precious and fabulously esteemed to the end of the second century A.D.; but it is seldom mentioned in the third century.

Ælius Lampridius speaks of a silken cord with which to hang himself, as an imperial extravagance on the part of Heliogabalus (and of this only one strand was silk); and he mentions that Alexander Severus rarely allowed himself a dress of silk (holosericum), and only gave away robes of partly silken substance.

Flavius Vopiscus says that Aurelian had no dress wholly of silk (holosericum).[245] His wife begged him to allow her a shawl of purple silk, and he replied, "Far be it from me to permit thread to be reckoned worth its weight in gold!"—for a pound of gold was then worth a pound of silk.

Flavius Vopiscus further states that the Emperor Carinus, however, gave away silken garments, as well as dresses of gold and silver, to Greek artificers, players, wrestlers, and musicians.[246]

Yates gives us a translation of an edict of Diocletian, giving a maximum of prices for articles in common use [159]in the Roman empire. It reads like a tailor's or a dress-maker's bill of to-day:—

DE NARIL.

To the tailor, for lining a fine vest	6
To the same, for an opening of an edging of silk	50
To the same, for an opening and an edging of a mixed tissue of silk and flax	30
For an edging of a coarser vest	4|24|7|

A monument at Tivoli is erected to the memory of his estimable wife, Valeria Chrysis, by "M. N. Poculus, silk manufacturer." This was probably an imperial office in the fourth century.[248]

From the first to the sixth centuries, poets and historians continually speak of silk,[249] praising its beauty or blaming it as extravagance or luxury; but according to Yates, all the information we collect from these sources requires to be tested as to accuracy, and is often erroneous.

I have spoken of the first silk-weaving in Cos, 300 B.C. The first arrival of the silkworm in Europe was in the sixth century, 900 years later. Cosmas Indicopleustes and another monk brought eggs from China in the hollow staves they carried in their hands. This was a great event in European commerce. The eggs were solemnly presented to the Emperor Justinian, and the monopoly of their cultivation is to be found in his law-ordaining codex.[250]

The monopoly of the silk manufactures was confined [160]to the area of the imperial palace of Constantinople, but the cultivation of the worm gradually spread over Greece, Asia Minor, and India.

The first allusion to the use of silk in the Christian Church is by Gregory Nazianzen (A.D. 370), "Ad Hellenium pro Monarchis Carmen:" "Silver and gold some bring to God, or the fine thread by Seres spun."[251] Basil illustrates the idea of the resurrection by the birth of the butterfly from the cocoon.[252]

Paul the Silentiary (A.D. 562) alludes to the frequent use of silk in the priests' vestments at the Church of St. Sophia at Constantinople.

Bede relates that the first Abbot of Wearmouth went to Rome for the fifth time inA.D. 685, and brought back with him two scarves or palls of incomparable workmanship, and entirely of silk, with which he purchased land of three families at the mouth of the Wear. Bede's own remains were wrapped in silk.

Auberville gives us, in his "Tissus," specimens of Roman silks between the first and seventh centuries, but he cannot fix their exact date.[253]

The finest webs of Holosericum from the imperial looms were generally bestowed upon the Church, and thus consecrated, the earliest ascertained specimens that [161]have survived have been preserved; and of these, most have been found in the tombs of saints, bishops, and kings who were buried in priestly as well as in royal garments.[254]

Among the silk and satin fabrics, the tissue called "Imperial" is mentioned by several early English authors. Roger de Wendover and Matthew Paris describe the apparition of King John as clad in "royal robes of Imperial."[255] William de Magna Villa brought from Greece, in 1170, a stuff called Imperial, "marbled" or variegated, and covered with lions woven in gold.

In the Eastern Empire, this industry after a time fell into the hands of the Jews; and in 1161, Benjamin of Tudela says the city of Thebes contained about 2000 Jewish silk-weavers.

The breeding of the worm in Europe seems to have been confined to Greece from the time of Justinian to the twelfth century; but in 1148, Roger, King of Sicily, brought as prisoners of war, from Corinth, Thebes, and Athens, many silk-weavers, and settled them at Palermo. "Then might be seen Corinthians and Thebans of both sexes, employed in weaving velvet stoles interwoven with gold, and serving like the Eretrians of old among the Persians."[256]

Hugh Falcandus[257] has left a description of the Royal manufactory at Palermo, and the Hotel de Tiraz which absorbed all the smaller Saracenic factories already started. [162]The Hotel de Tiraz had four great workshops, in which were separately carried on the weaving of plain tissues, velvets, examits and satins, and flowered stuffs (damasks), and lastly, gold brocades and embroideries. It was from the last that proceeded the real works of art, and the embroideries with pearls and precious stones.[258] The highest efforts of the loom were apparently finished with the needle,[259] as in the figured textiles of Egypt.

The continuity of Sicilian textile designs from the sixth to the sixteenth centuries (a thousand years) is very remarkable. Owing to its originally strongly stamped Oriental character, great knowledge of the arts of weaving, spinning, and dyeing silk is required to enable any one to assign an exact date to materials which only remodelled their style three times.

Dr. Rock's rules for deciphering these three dates may, however, be easily learned, as they are broad and simple. In his comprehensive "Introduction to the Textiles in the Kensington Museum" (p. lxvii) he says that the three defined periods of silk-weaving in Sicily are: First, from the time of Justinian to the Hohenstaufen (from the sixth to the twelfth century); secondly, from the accession of Frederick I. (Barbarossa), 1152, to Charles IV., 1347 (twelfth to fourteenth centuries); the third period is of one century only, from 1347 to 1456.

The first period especially shows African animals, such as the giraffe and the different kinds of antelopes, mixed with Arabian mottoes; and the patterns are generally woven with gold. This is merely gilt parchment, the silk being mingled with cotton.

Pl. 35.

See larger image
Peacock Pattern. Silk Wrapping on the body of St. Cuthbert. Durham.

The second period, beginning in the twelfth century, shows the arrival of Count Roger's Persian and Greek [163]workmen, captives from Thebes, Corinth, and Athens. The fresh designs show fragments of Greek taste, such as masks and foliage, and give one a slight foretaste of the Renaissance.[260]

These semi-classical echoes are contemporary in the Sicilian looms with such Norman motives as a crowned sovereign riding with a hawk upon his wrist.

This description singularly applies to the relics removed from the tomb of St. Cuthbert, at Durham, in 1827; among which are fragments of three wrappings, or garments of silk, so suggestive of the artistic traditions of many nationalities, and the long descent of patterns, recognizable after the lapse of centuries, that a description of them, accompanied by illustrations, can hardly fail to be interesting. They are all now reduced by time to a rich golden brown, though there are indications that blue, green, and red have been woven into their fabric, and there are also on one of them traces of gilding. The first (plate 35) shows Oriental conventional peacocks, double-headed and collared, framed within circles which slightly intersect each other, thus giving the opportunity for varying the original motive by breaking up the rolling arabesqued pattern, and uniting the stems and flowers contained in the border. The spaces between the circles are filled in with gryphons in pairs, of the Babylonian stamp, thick limbed with strongly-marked muscles. There is a border or guimp, Persian in character, in which are small crosses surmounting repetitions of the crenelated pattern found in Assyrian ornament.

The second piece of silk contains a large rosace. Scattered about it are repetitions of the Persian leaf [164]or tree of life, and the border consists of kneeling hares or fawns between a Persian arabesque and a corded line. The mixture of Egyptian and Assyrian styles is remarkable throughout, till we come to the centre of the rosace, where we find a most incongruous man in armour on horseback with a hawk on his wrist, giving the Norman stamp of the reigning house and influence in Sicily. The central subject is exactly repeated on an embroidered twelfth century chasuble in the treasury of the Cathedral of Bamberg, only that a royal crown and robes are worn by the horseman (pl. 36).[261]

The third specimen is the most noteworthy (plate 37). There is nothing of Assyrian here, but it reminds one of Egyptian and Greek art, and at once suggests Count Roger's Greek slaves at the Sicilian looms, but the design is probably of a much earlier date, and the subject is puzzling. A piece of drapery resembling an Egyptian sail with its fringes[262] (pl. 38) is looped up on each side to the head of a thyrsus, and above it hangs a large cluster of fruits. The lower part of the drapery rests upon water, and is somewhat like a boat, with ducks swimming towards it, and fish disporting themselves in the rippling waves. Between the circles the ducks are repeated, facing a shield enriched with rows of the crenelated pattern surmounted by a vine.

These fragments have belonged each to a very large and freely woven silk shawl or mantle. The circles are about two feet across. There is a different arrangement of the threads in each web, giving different fine diapers, and the last described has a raised pattern which might have been intended to represent water.

Pl. 36.

See larger image
NORMAN AND PERSIAN TYPE.
A Silk Wrapping on the body of St. Cuthbert. Durham.

Pl. 37.

See larger image
GRÆCO-EGYPTIAN STYLE.
A Silk Wrapping on the body of St. Cuthbert. Durham.

Pl. 38.

Boat with coloured sail, from the tomb of Rameses III. at Thebes. (Wilkinson's "Ancient Egyptians," iii. p. 211.) Explanatory of the design on St. Cuthbert's silk shroud, pl. 37.

[165]It is most likely that in the twelfth century, or even a little later, the body of St. Cuthbert was wrapped in these shawls, and so left when at the Reformation, his shrine was destroyed, and the coffer containing his remains buried in the same place, and piously concealed till our own day. I shall describe the beautiful embroideries in which the body had been clothed in the tenth century when I come to the subject of English work.

The third period of silk-weaving art is unmistakably Sicilian. At the end of the thirteenth century and beginning of the fourteenth, Palermo struck out her own line. The Greek cross appears in various forms. The designs are of a wonderful richness and capricious ingenuity. They show alike Asiatic, African, and European animals, and every kind of mythological creature—griffins, dragons, dogs, and harts, with large wings; swans, pheasants, and eagles, single or double-headed, often pecking at the sun's rays; beautifully drawn foliage and flowers, and heraldic emblems and coats-of-arms. One peculiarity of the third period is the frequent use of green patterns on "murrey"-coloured grounds.

All this splendour of design was commonly lavished on poor material. The silks continued to be mixed with cotton, and the gold, or rather the gilding, was so base that it has almost always become black on the foundation strips of parchment or paper.[263]

[166]The heraldic silks are mostly of the time of the Crusades, when the distinguished pilgrims and warriors, especially the English, made Sicily their half-way house to the Holy Land, and brought from thence fabrics woven to suit their tastes. In Auberville's book we find, under the dates of many centuries, the most remarkable fragments now known. On portrait-tombs and in some very ancient pictures are figured beautiful silks woven in gold, which are recognizable at once by their Arab-Sicilian style. Of this type, the remarkable fragment of the dress of Richard II., in the Kensington Museum, dates itself, by carrying the cognizances of his grandfather and his mother, and the portrait of his dog Math.[264]

The last period of the Sicilian silks is especially marked by the inscriptions being mostly nonsense, and only woven in as ornament, with the forms of Arab lettering.[265]

Sir G. Birdwood says that whether the Saracens found the manufacture of silk already established in India or not, they certainly influenced the decorative designs. He adds that kincobs are now woven at Ahmedabad and Benares, identical in design with the [167]old Sicilian brocades; while the Saracenic Sicilian silks abound in patterns which prove their origin in Assyrian, Sassanian, or Indian art.

We know that the Saracens introduced colonies of Persian, and probably Indian workmen into Spain, after the beginning of the ninth century, to assist them in their architecture and textile manufactures, and in return the Mogul emperors of Delhi invited many Italian and French designers into India.

The Taj and other buildings in Rajpootana are decorated with exquisite mosaics coeval with those of Austin of Bordeaux. Their styles of art in textiles, and in other materials, have acted and reacted upon each other; and nothing throws more light on the affinities and the development of the modern decorative arts of Europe than the history of the introduction, under Justinian, of the silk manufactures from the East into the West.[266]

From Palermo, all the stages of the manufacture of silk spread themselves over Italy and into Spain. According to Nicolo Tegrini, the flourishing silk-weavers of Lucca having been ejected from the city in the early part of the fourteenth century, carried their art elsewhere, and even to Germany, France, and Britain.[267]

Italian weavers went to Lyons in 1450, and so started the silk industry that it has steadily increased till now. It gives employment to about 31,000 looms and 240,000 workpeople of both sexes.

The Moors, when they overflowed into Iberia, carried with them all their Orientalisms, traditions, manufactures, and designs; thus disobeying their prophet, who forbade the use of silk except to women.

[168]Senhor F. de Riano tells us that from the ninth to the eleventh centuries, Spain was producing fine silk tissues. The Moorish Cordovese writer, Ash-Shakandi, who lived in the beginning of the thirteenth century, says, "Malaga is famous for its manufactures of silks of all colours and patterns, some of which are so rich that a suit made of them will cost many thousands. Such are the brocades with beautiful designs and the names of the Caliphs, Ameers, and other wealthy people woven into them."[268]

The same author, speaking of the manufactures of silk at Almeria, says that thence came the brightest colours; and Al-Makhari adds a list of precious silk tissues, naming the "Tiraz," the "Iscalaton," and the robes called each by its own special name.[269] Ash-Shakandi also mentions the looms of Murcia, and its carpets.[270]

When the Moors were driven from Spain, the silk works of Malaga and Almeria were ruined. But those of Valencia became famous, and flourish to this day. Talavera della Reina also produces fine ecclesiastical fabrics, and at Toledo the ancient traditions are preserved, and they still weave sixteenth-century designs.

In Italy, Genoa, Florence, and Milan followed the Sicilian silk manufactures, and each has left specimens of the craft, of which Rock has pointed out the marked individualities.

The rich stuffs with inscriptions inwoven in gold, in the Middle Ages, were called "literatis."

[169]The designs of Lucca at first imitated the Moorish Sicilian type; and introduced as their speciality, white figures, such as angels in white garments, and exchanged the Oriental intricate patterns for a bolder and simpler style.

Venice, of course, also showed at first the Oriental impress; but she soon struck out a line of her own; and her especial invention was shown in weaving, from the thirteenth to the sixteenth centuries, square pieces of silken tissue, representing sacred subjects.

Florentine tissues, especially their velvet and gold brocades, were particularly splendid, and can be recognized by the loops of gold thread drawn to the surface and left there. Of these early Florentine gold brocades we have still beautiful examples in the palls of our City companies and in ancient ecclesiastical vestments. The loops of gold have been the custom since the thirteenth century, and still prevail in certain traditional fabrics, for instance, in the banners woven annually for the prizes at the horse races in Florence. The Corsini family, who have for many generations and for hundreds of years competed in these races, had, in their princely palace at Rome, a room entirely hung with the silk of these gorgeous banners.

In Hungary, Queen Gisela, in the eleventh century, established looms for weaving silk; and many convents throughout Europe and in England wove silken tissues for the service of the Church, till the great manufactures absorbed these partially private enterprises.[271]

Individual exertion produced copies, or motives that are taken from Eastern, Southern, or Northern inspirations; but it is only in large national schools of arts or crafts that an absolutely recognizable style becomes [170]apparent. For example, the early French silks from monastic establishments are not remarkable for either style or texture till the sixteenth century, when they came to the front as a national manufacture, and have held the highest place in silk-weaving ever since.

The Flemish towns of Ypres, Ghent, and Mechlin were known for their silken webs in the thirteenth century, and at that time innumerable small schools of the craft seem to have covered Europe. They are constantly named in the lists of fine furnishings in Germany. In England, France, and Germany, as well as in the Low Countries, each convent had, besides its silk-weaving looms, its workshops for embroideries on silk, woollens, and linens, borrowing from the Byzantine Empire, Sicily, and Spain, their designs and patterns.

About this time (the thirteenth century), Marco Polo resided and travelled in Asia. He visited the principal cities of Syria, Persia, Khotan, and Cathay, and from him we have information of the different Asiatic textiles, generally bearing the name of the city where they were woven. He names, for instance, the mediæval "baudas" and "baudakin" (with endless modifications in the spelling), from Baghdad. This afterwards gave the word baldachino to the awning or canopy over the altar, which it retained even when textiles had given place to marbles and mosaics.[272]

Satin is only found named in catalogues about the fourteenth century. But the dalmatic of Charlemagne, at Rome, is embroidered on a stout blue satin, and has never been transferred; and at Constantinople, Baldwin II., at his coronation in 1204, was shod and clothed in vermilion satin embroidered with jewels; while all the [171]Venetian and French barons present were clad in satin.[273] Semper and Bock believe that it had been a Chinese material long before it reached Europe.

Satin was often called "blattin," in connection with the colour of the cochineal insect (blatta), whose dye was invariably used for satin. We cannot tell, however, which was certainly named from the other.[274]

In the poem of "The Lady of the Fountain," translated by Lady Charlotte Guest from the Welsh ballads of the thirteenth century, silk and satin are often named. At the opening of the poem, King Arthur is described seated on a throne of rushes, covered with a flame-coloured satin cloth, and with a red satin cushion under his elbow.

Fiery red was the orthodox colour for satin. In old German poems we find it described as "pfellat," always as being fiery. One kind of pfellat was called salamander.[275] Bruges satins were the most esteemed in the Middle Ages. Chaucer speaks of "satin riche and newe."[276]

Satin and velvet are the contrasting silken materials. In satin the threads are laid along so that the shining surface ripples with every ray of sunshine, and the shadows are melted into half-lights by the reflections from [172]every fold. It makes a dazzling garment, splendid in its radiant sheen; whereas in velvet, where each thread is placed upright and shorn smoothly, all light is absorbed and there are no reflections, and the whole effects are solemn, rich, and deep.[277] Some of the oldest velvets resemble plush in the length of their pile, and have not the dignity of velvet.

Semper, from the different derivations that have been suggested, selects the connection of the word "velvet" (German, Felbert) with "welf," the skin or fur of an animal.[278]

Among the gifts to Charlemagne (ninth century) from Haroun el Raschid were velvets; and the earliest existing specimen we know of is named by Bock as being in the Pergament Codex at Le Puy, in Vendôme, where, amongst other curious interleaved specimens of weaving, is a fine piece of shorn silk velvet.[279]

Marco Polo, in the thirteenth century, frequently speaks of velvet as an Asiatic fabric. It is first known as a European textile in Lucca, about 1295, and we may therefore say that it was imported from the East.[280]

In the next chapter on colour I have noticed the curious fact that the word purple was sometimes used to mean colour, and sometimes to express the texture of velvet, thus confounding the two; but I have also pointed out that it had other meanings, and had become a very comprehensive word for everything that expressed richness and warmth.

[173]While examining and judging embroideries, we must be careful not to be deceived by the different dates often occurring in the grounding and the applied materials. Much embroidery was worked on fabrics that were already old and even worn out; and

others have been transferred centuries ago, and perhaps more than once, to fresh grounds.[281]

This sometimes causes a good deal of difficulty in dating specimens. One should begin by ascertaining whether the needlework was originally intended to be cut out (*opus consutum*), and so laid on a ground of another material, and worked down and finished there.

Of course it is always evident and easily ascertained, whether the work has been transferred at all. If so—and from each succeeding transference—small fragments may be found showing on the cut edges. You will often see remains of two or more of these layers, reminding you of the three Trojan cities dug up at different depths under each other at Hissarlik.

In judging each specimen the acumen of the expert is needed to obtain a correct opinion, and he should not only be an archæologist, but a botanist and a herald besides;[282] and, in fact, no kind of knowledge is useless in deciphering the secrets of human art. But even when so armed, he is often checked and puzzled by some [174]accidental caprice of design or mode of weaving, and after wasting trouble and time, has to cast it aside as defying classification.

It is, however, as well to note these exceptions, as, when compared, they sometimes explain each other.

What I have said regards, of course, the historical and archæological side of the study of textiles, and I have treated of them as being either the origin or the imitations of different styles of embroidery, and so inseparably connected with the art which is the subject and motive of this book; and not only in this does the connection between them exist, but in the fact that as embroideries always need a ground, silken and other textiles are an absolute necessity to their existence.

For these reasons alone I have given this chapter on materials, short and imperfect, but suggesting further research into the writings of the authors I have quoted, and, I hope, exciting the interest of the reader.

FOOTNOTES:

[130]Periplus of the Erythrean Sea.

[131]It is described by Yates as having the appearance of a flat ribbon, with the edges thickened like a hem.

[132]This rough bark is probably the reason that it absorbs colour into its substance (perhaps under the scales); and it may also account for its being capable of felting.

[133]It may be laid down as a fundamental rule in technical style, that the product shall preserve the peculiar characteristics of the raw material. Unfortunately, the artist is often ignorant of the qualities of the fabric for which he is designing, and the workman who has to carry it out is a mechanic, in these days, instead of a craftsman.

[134]Molochinus, or malva silvestris (wild hemp), Yates, pp. 292-317, is sometimes spoken of as a mallow, sometimes as a nettle. In the Vocabulary of Papias (A.D. 1050) it is said that the cloth called molocina is made from thread of mallow, and used for dress in Egypt. Garments of molochinus were brought from India, according to the Periplus (see Pliny, 146, 166, 170, 171). It was seldom used by the ancients, but both Greeks and Romans made it serve for mats and ropes. The Thracians wove of it garments and sheets. It is not named in the Scriptures.

[135]See Gibbs' "British Honduras."

[136]Spartum was a rush. Pliny says it was used for the rigging of ships.

[137]The bark of trees such as the Hybiscus Tiliaceus, and that of the Birch (see Yates, p. 305-6). Birch bark was embroidered, till latterly, by the Indian women in North America with porcupines' quills. Pigafetta says (writing in the sixteenth century) that in the kingdom of Congo many different kinds of stuff were manufactured from the palm-tree fibre. He instances cloths on which patterns were wrought, and likewise a material resembling "velvet on both sides."

[138]"Camoca" or caman in the Middle Ages is supposed to have been of camels' hair, mixed with silk. Edward the Black Prince left to his confessor his bed of red caman, with his arms embroidered on each corner. Rock (p. xliv) gives us information about the tents and garments of camels' hair found throughout the East, wherever the camel flourishes

and has a fine hairy winter coat, which it sheds in the heat. The coarser parts are used for common purposes, and the finest serve for beautiful fabrics, especially shawls. Marco Polo tells of beautiful camelots manufactured from the hair of camels; and of the Egyptian coarse and very fine fabrics woven of the same materials.

[139]"Le Chevalier à Deux Epées" (quoted by Dr. Rock), and Lady Wilton, "Art of Needlework," p. 128.

[140]See p. 359, *post*, for Boadicea's dress.

[141]See Mr. Villiers Stuart's "Funeral Tent of an Egyptian Queen."

[142]The Moors in Spain excelled in leather-work and embroidery upon it; and Marco Polo describes the beautiful productions of the province of Guzerat, of leather inlaid and embroidered with gold and silver wire. Yule's "Marco Polo," p. 383.

[143]See chapter on Stitches.

[144]See Chardin, vol. i. p. 31.

[145]Tin, called "laton," was used to debase the metal threads in the Middle Ages. It is also named as a legitimate material for metal embroideries.

[146]For all information about asbestos, see Yates, pp. 356, 565.

[147]There is one at the Barberini Palace at Rome. A sheet, woven of asbestos, found in a tomb outside the Porta Maggiore, is described by Sir J. E. Smith in his "Tour on the Continent" (vol. ii. p. 201) as being coarsely spun, but as soft and pliant as silk. "We set fire to it, and the same part being repeatedly burnt, was not at all injured."

[148]See Yule's "Marco Polo," vol. i. pp. 215, 218, and Yates, p. 361.

[149]There are specimens of bead-work pictures at St. Stephen's at Coire, in the Marien-Kirche at Dantzic, and elsewhere. See Rock, p. cv. This is, in fact, mosaic in textiles, without cement.

[150]Witness the stone whorls for the spindles in our prehistoric barrows, and the "heaps" of the lake cities.

[151]Yates, "Textrinum Antiquorum," p. 129.

[152]An Egyptian Dynasty called themselves the Shepherd Kings.

[153]Yates gives endless quotations to show how ancient and how honourable an occupation was that of tending sheep.

[154]Semper, i. p. 139. The cover of the bed on which was laid the golden coffin in the tomb of Cyrus was of Babylonian tapestry of wool; the carpet beneath it was woven of the finest wrought purple. Plautus mentions Babylonian hangings and embroidered tapestries. See Birdwood's "Indian Arts," i. p. 286.

[155]Joshua vii.

[156]Ezekiel xxvii. 22.

[157]Semper, "Der Stil," i. p. 138.

[158]Yates, pp. 79, 91, 93, 99, 102, 445. Lanæ Albæ.

"The first, Apulia's; next is Parma's boast;And the third fleece Altinum has engrossed."

Martial, xiv. Ep. 155.

Martial also speaks of the matchless Tarentine togæ, a present from Parthenius:—

"With thee the lily and the privet paleCompared, and Tibur's whitest ivory fail;The Spartan swan, the Paphian doves deploreTheir hue, and pearls on the Erythrean shore."

Martial, viii. Ep. 28.

[159]The sheep of Tarentum, from the days of the Greek colonists, were famed, as they are still, for the warm brown tints on their black wool. Pliny says that this is caused by the weed *fumio*, on which they browsed. Swinburne says, in his "Travels in the Two Sicilies," that there the wool is so tinged by the plant now called *fumolo*, which grows on the coast.

[160]See Blümner's "Technologie," p. 92; also "Comptes Rendus de la Commission Impériale Archéologique" of St. Petersburg, 1881; also the Catalogue Raisonnée of Herr Graf'schen's Egyptian Collection of Textiles at Vienna.

[161]See Pliny's "Natural History," viii. 74, § 191. Tanaquil is credited with the first invention of the seamless coat or cassock.

[162]The Gauls in Britain wove plaids or tartans. See Rock, p. xii; Blümner, pp. 152-54; Birdwood, p. 286.

[163]Pliny, "Natural History," book viii., 73, 74.
[164]"Georgics," iv. 334; Yates, p. 35.
[165]"Comptes Rendus de la Commission Impériale Archéologique," St. Petersburg, 1881. Much of this Gobelin weaving has lately been found in Egypt. See "Katalog der Teodor Graf'schen Fünde in Ægypten," von Dr. J. Karabacek.
[166]Semper considers that the famous Babylonian and Phrygian stuffs were all woollen, and that gold was woven or embroidered on them. See "Der Stil," i. p. 138.
[167]Worcester cloth was forbidden to the Benedictines by a Chapter of that Order at Westminster Abbey in 1422, as being fine enough for soldiers, and therefore too good for monks. See Rock's Introduction, p. lxxviii.
[168]Both these fabrics are represented in Egyptian and Greek fragments, and are equally well preserved.
[169]Boyd Dawkins, "Early Man in Britain," pp. 268, 275.
[170]See Wilkinson, "Ancient Egyptians," vol. iii. p. 116; Yates, p. 23.
[171]It appears that the art of printing textiles was known in Egypt in the time of Pliny. See Yates, p. 272, quoting Apuleius, Met. l. xi.; also see Wilkinson, "Ancient Egyptians," vol. ii. p. 196, pl. xii.
[172]See Yates, "Textrinum Antiquorum," pp. 268, 335; Herodotus, ii. 86. Herodotus and Strabo speak of Babylonian linen, cited by Yates, p. 281.
[173]"Textrinum Antiquorum," pp. 267-80. A peculiarity of Egyptian linen is that it was often woven with more threads in the warp than in the woof. A specimen in the Indian Museum, South Kensington, shows in its delicate texture 140 threads in the inch to the warp, and 64 to the woof. Another piece of fine linen has 270 to the warp, and 110 to the woof. Generally there are twice or three times as many threads, but sometimes even four times the number. Wilkinson gives a probable reason for this peculiarity. See Wilkinson's "Ancient Egyptians," vol. i. chap. ix. pp. 121-226. See Rock's Introduction, p. xiv.
[174]De Somniis, vol. i. p. 653. Yates, p. 271.
[175]Philo, cited by Yates, p. 271.
[176]Paulinus ad Cytherium, cited by Yates, p. 273.
[177]Herodotus, l. ii. c. 182, l. iii. c. 47. Rawlinson's Trans.
[178]Proverbs vii. 16.
[179]Yates, p. 291. Denon describes a tunic found in a sarcophagus, which he examined, and says: "The weaving was extremely loose, of thread as fine as a hair, of two strands of twisted flax fibre."—Auberville's "Ornement des Tissus," p. 4. Some marvellously fine specimens of such cambric may be seen at the South Kensington Museum and the British Museum.
[180]Not that we have any remains of flax linen from their tombs.
[181]It was carried thence, at a prehistoric date, to Assyria and Egypt.
[182]There is no proof that it was grown in Egypt till the fourteenth centuryA.D., when it is mentioned for the first time in a MS. of that date of the "Codex Antwerpianus." See Yates, Appendix E, p. 470.
[183]Birdwood, p. 241.
[184]Puggaree. Yates says that cotton has always been supposed to be the best preserver against sunstroke, p. 341.
[185]*Carpas*, the proper Oriental name for cotton, is found in the same sense in the Sanskrit, Arabic, and Persian languages. Yates, p. 341.
[186]In the Æneid, the garment of Chloreus the Phrygian is thus described:—
"His saffron chlamys, and each rustling foldOf muslin (*carpas*), was confined with glittering gold."
Æneid, xi. 775.
[187]Dakka muslins are the most esteemed. Their poetic names, "running water," "woven air," "evening dew," are more descriptive than pages of prose. See Birdwood, ii. p. 259.
[188]Chintzes, calicoes, fine cloths, and strong tent-cloths, cotton carpets, &c., &c. Forbes Watson classifies the calicoes as being white, bleached and unbleached, striped, &c., printed chintzes, or pintadoes. See Birdwood, p. 260.

[189]For Buckram and Fustian, see Rock, pp. lxxxv, lxxxvi. In Lady Burgeweny's (Abergavenny) will, 1434, she leaves as part of the furnishings of her bed "of gold of swan," two pairs of sheets of Raine (Rennes), and a pair of fustian. Anne Boleyn's list of clothes contains "Bokerams, for lining and taynting," gowns, sleeves, cloaks, and beds. Rock, lxxxvi. Renouard, in his "Romaunce Dictionary," quotes the following: "Vestæ de Polpia e de Bisso qui est bacaram." For the antiquity of this fabric, see Herr Graf'schen's Catalogue of Textiles from the Fayoum.

[190]See Yates, p. 300, citing "Herod's silver apparel."

[191]"Indian Arts," ii. p. 237.

[192]Rock, p. xxv. Yates (p. 3) says they cut their gold for wearing apparel into thin plates, and did not draw it into wire, as it is translated in the Vulgate (Exodus xxxix.). The ephod made by Bezaleel was of fine linen, gold, violet, purple, and scarlet, twice dyed, with embroidered work. This tradition must have guided the artist who designed the ephod in the National Museum at Munich, in the seventeenth century, for a prince boy-bishop.

[193]Quintus Curtius says that many thousands, clothed in these costly materials, crowded out of Damascus to meet Alexander.

[194]There is a very ancient local tradition at Shūsh, that A.D. 640, in the reign of the Kaliph Omar, the body of the prophet Daniel was found, wrapped in cloth of gold, in a stone coffin; and, by order of the victorious general, it was placed in one of glass, and moored to the bridge which spanned the branch of the Euphrates flowing between the two halves of the city, so that the waters flowed over it. See "Chaldea and Susiana," by Loftus, and Sir G. W. Gore Ouseley's translation of a Persian version of "The Book of Victories." Alexander is said to have been buried in a glass coffin. (See Wilkinson's "Ancient Egyptians," ii. p. 102, note †.)

[195]Yates, pp. 367-70; Rock, p. xxvi.

[196]"Aura intexere eadem Asiâ invenit Attalus Rex unde nomen Attalicis."—Pliny, viii. c. 48, and Yates, p. 371. The reign of Attalus II. was B.C. 159-188.

[197]"And they did beat the gold into plates, and cut it into wires, and work it into the blue, and the purple, and the fine linen."—Exod. xxxix.

[198]See Yates, p. 371; and Bock, xxxiii.

[199]Pliny, xxxiii. In the Museum at Leyden there is a shred of gold cloth found in a tomb at Tarquinia, in Etruria. This is a compactly woven covering over bright yellow silk.

[200]Gold wire is still worked through leather at Guzerat. See Birdwood, p. 284, Ed. 1880. Marco Polo mentions this embroidery 600 years ago. Bk. iii. chap. xxvi. (Yule). The hunting cuirass of Assurbanipal (pl. 1) appears to be so worked, and of such materials. Also see Wilkinson, "Ancient Egyptians," vol. iii. p. 130. This gold for weaving was beaten into shape with hammers.

[201]Pope Eutichinus, in the third century, buried many martyrs in golden robes.

[202]"Liber Pontificalis," t. ii. p. 332.

[203]See Rock, pp. xxvii, xxxv; and Parker's "Use of the Levitical Colours," p. 49.

[204]See Yates, p. 376.

[205]Rock, p. xxxv. The toga picta, or trabea, part of the official dress of her sons.

[206]Hoveden's "Annal." p. 481, Ed. Savile; Rock, p. xxx.

[207]See "Archæologia," 1880, pp. 317, 322; also Pl. 74, No. 20 (*post*).

[208]Bock, "L. Gewänder," taf. ix. vol. i.

[209]Rock, p. xxxvii.

[210]Ciclatoun, according to Rock, p. xxxix, is a common Persian name for such tissues in the East. This, in common with nasick, nak, and many other beautiful tissues, was wrought in gold with figures of birds and beasts.—Yule's "Marco Polo," ed. 1875, i. p. 65.

Dr. Rock quotes the old ballad,—

"In a robe right royall bowne,Of a red ciclatoune,Be her fader's syde;A coronall on her hede sett,Her clothes with byrdes of gold were betteAll about for pryde."

[211]In St. Paul's in London there was formerly an amice adorned with the figures of two bishops and a king, hammered out of silver, and gilt. Dugdale, ed. 1818, p. 318. See also Rock, pp. xxix-xxxii.

[212]Museum at Berne.

[213]A piece of Venetian work to be seen at the South Kensington Museum is an altar frontal, worked in coral, gold beads, seed pearls, and spangles. All jewellers' work, including enamel, was much admired and introduced into their embroideries. (See Rock's Introduction to Catalogue of the Kensington Museum, pp. civ-cviii, ed. 1870.)

[214]On this gorgeous piece of Italian art there are added a number of buttons (for we can give them no other name), with crosses and hearts under crystal, which seem to have belonged to another period and workmanship, or else are to be attributed to a superstitious feeling on the part of the maker, who placed these Christian signs, perhaps, surreptitiously, and for the good of his own soul.

[215]The Museum of National Art at Munich has a fine collection of gold and silver, spangled, and black bead head-dresses, now mostly antiquated, though in peasant dress it yet survives.

[216]It is embroidered in gold, with red silk and gems; and I have elsewhere said that it probably issued from the Hotel de Tiraz at Messina.

[217]Terry, in his "Voyage to the East Indies," speaks of the rich carpets (p. 128): "The ground of some of these is silver or gold, about which such arabesques in flowers and figures as I have before named are most excellently disposed."

[218]These of late years have been the most gorgeous objects at exhibitions of old needlework, and the ambition and despair of collectors.

[219]Gold thread was also made of gilt paper, equally by the Moors and the Japanese.

[220]In Aikin's "Life of James I.," p. 205, we have a curious account of the monopoly of gold thread, that had been granted, with others, to George Villiers, Duke of Buckingham. The thread was so scandalously debased with copper as to corrode the hands of the artificers, and even the flesh of those who wore it. This adulterated article they sold at an exorbitant price, and if they detected any one making a cheaper or better article, they were empowered to fine or imprison them, while a clause in their patent protected themselves. The manufacturers of this base metal thread were two Frenchmen, Mompesson and Michel, and Edward Villiers, the Marquis' brother, was one of the firm. Doubtless they drove for a time a roaring trade, as gold embroideries were then universally worn, both by men and women; but the House of Commons interfered, and the monopoly was abolished.

[221]Mitre of white satin, with two figure subjects in flat gold—the martyrdom of St. Stephen, and that of St. Thomas of Canterbury.

[222]The School of Gold Embroidery at Munich produces work of a richness and precision which has, perhaps, never been excelled. The raised parts of the design are first cast in soft hollow "carton," and the gold is worked on it and into the recesses with the help of a fine stiletto, which pioneers the needle for each stitch. This is embroidery "on the stamp," but without padding.

[223]Bock, "L. Gewänder," vol. i. p. 48. Prizes are offered at Lyons for the best mode of manufacturing gold and silver thread that will not tarnish.

[224]Yates says, pp. 160-162: "Whether silk was mentioned in the Old Testament cannot, perhaps, be determined. After fully considering the subject, Braunius decides against silk being known to the Hebrews in ancient times ('De Vestitu Heb. Sacerdotum,' i. c. viii.)." The contrary opinion is founded on the passage, "I clothed thee with broidered work, and shod thee with badger-skins. I girded thee about with fine linen, and covered thee with silk" (*meshi*).—Ezekiel xvi. But the translation is disputed.

[225]"Code of Manu," xi. 168; xii. 64. Yates, "Textrinum Antiquorum," p. 204.

[226]Auberville, "Ornement des Tissus," p. ii.

[227]Yates (pp. 173, 174) believes that "Cos" should always be read for Cios, about which there seems to be some confusion. Chios has also been substituted for the name of "Cos," the island.

There is no doubt that the Roman ladies obtained their most splendid garments from Cos—perhaps of wool as well as of silk.

[228]Birdwood, "Textile Arts of India," ii. p. 269.

[229]Yates, "Textrinum Antiquorum," p. 204.

[230]Yates, "Textrinum Antiquorum," note (*), p. 184. Aristotle (fourth century B.C.), however, had already given evidence respecting the use of silk, which was adopted and repeated by Pliny, Clemens Alexandrinus, and Basil. Aristotle tells the story of Pamphile. One thousand years later Procopius (sixth century A.D.) says the raw material was then brought from the East, and woven in the Phœnician cities of Tyre and Berytus. See Yates, pp. 163, 164.

[231]Ibid., note (*), p. 184.

[232]Yates, "Textrinum Antiquorum," p. 181.

[233]I have mentioned this already, to prove the antiquity of the art of embroidery. Here I repeat it in reference to the first mention of silk. (See p. 38 *ante*.)

[234]"Bibliothèque Orientale de M. Herbelot," ed. 1778, vol. iii. p. 19.

[235]Auberville, p. 2; Yates (pp. 172, 173) calls her Si-ling, wife of Hoang-ti, and quotes the "Resumé des Principaux Tractes Chinois," traduits par Stanislas Julien, 1837, pp. 67, 68.

[236]Auberville, "Histoire des Tissus," pp. 2-4; "Du Halde," vol. ii. pp. 355, 356 (8vo edition, London, 1736).

[237]Related by Klaproth, the Russian Orientalist.

[238]Yates, p. 238. "History of Khotan," translated by M. Abel Rémusat, pp. 55, 56.

[239]Khotan or Little Bucharia would, in common parlance, be included in Serica; and therefore silk exported thence to Europe would have been perfectly described as coming from the Seres. Yates, p. 231, 232.

[240]Yates, p. 231.

[241]While in Europe the arts of daily use and decoration were struggling for life after many interruptions and revolutions, the civilization of Japan, which is nearly contemporary with Christianity, spent itself in perfecting to the most exquisite finish the arts which had been imported from China and Corea. Japan also inherited the power and the tradition of concealment, and so Europe remained unconscious, until the last century, of the miraculous arts which a semi-barbarous people were cultivating—*not* for commercial purposes. Auberville, "Tissus," pp. 2-4.

[242]Yates, pp. 175-184.

[243]Yates, p. 176. The silken flags attached to the gilt standards of the Parthians inflamed the cupidity of the army of Crassus. The conflict between them took place 54 B.C. About thirty years after this date, Roman luxury had reached its zenith—

"The insatiate Roman spreads his conquering armO'er land and sea, where'er heaven's light extends."

"Petronius Arbiter," c. cxix.

After these words he says that among the richest productions of distant climes, the Seres sent their "new fleeces."

[244]Yates, p. 183.

[245]"Holosericum," whole silk; "subsericum," partly cotton, hemp, or flax. The longitudinal threads or warp, cotton; the cross threads, silk. Rock, "Textile Fabrics," p. xxxvii (ed. 1870).

[246]Yates, p. 195.

[247]Yates, p. 198. For the value of the denarius, see Waddington, "Edit. de Diocletien," p. 3.

[248]Gruter, tom. iii. p. 645; Yates, p. 205.

[249]Yates, p. 246. The words "silk" and "satin" are spoken of by Yates as having two derivations—the one imported to us through Greece and Italy, the other from Eastern Asia, through Slavonia, by the north of Europe.

[250]Yates, p. 231; who remarks, p. 203, that the laws of Justinian are not directed against the use of silk as a luxury, but rather as appropriating it as an imperial monopoly and source of revenue.

[251]Tom. ii. p. 106 (ed. 1630). See Yates, p. 213.

[252]Yates, p. 214.

[253]Auberville, Plate 4. Amongst these are what he calls "Consular silks." These are, or may be, included in the palmated class, as they are evidently woven for triumphal

occasions. One of the most remarkable has every mark of Oriental design. It represents a picture in a circle, repeated over and over again, of a warrior in his quadriga. Black or coloured slaves drive the horses, either running beside them or standing upon them; and other slaves carry beasts on their shoulders, and are stooping to give them drink at a trough. The space between the circles is filled in with the tree of life, growing out of its two horns. The colours are purple and gold. He places this between the first and seventh centuries (see pl. 34).

[254] There are, however, a few that have not had the security of the tomb, and yet have survived, such as the chasuble and maniple at Bayeux, of the seventh century, and Charlemagne's dalmatic.

[255] Roger de Wendover, "Chronica," t. iv. p. 127, ed. Coxe. Quoted by Rock from Ralph, Dean of St. Paul's. See Rock, Introduction, p. lv.

[256] Roger de Wendover, "Chronica," t. iv., ed. Coxe; also Yates, "Textrinum Antiquorum," pp. 243, 244.

[257] In the twelfth century. Semper, i. p. 38.

[258] See illustration from the portrait of Sultan Mahomet II., by Gentil Bellini. *Ante*, p. 146, Plate 33.

[259] See Semper, p. 157.

[260] The Sicilian type of design in silk-weaving was carried into Germany about the end of the second period. We are informed by Auberville that there existed at that time a manufacture of ecclesiastical stuffs at Leipzig, from which he gives us fine examples.

[261] See Bock's "Liturgische Gewänder," vol. ii. Taf. xxxiii. The pattern is twelfth century "metal work," embroidered in gold.

[262] See Wilkinson's "Ancient Egyptians," iii., pl. xvi.; v., pl. xxxiv. In general, a scarf floats from the prow or from the oars.

[263] The Crusaders carried away splendid booty from the towns they took and ransacked. As it was the great gathering-place of all Eastern and Western nations, Jerusalem was a mart for rich merchandise from Persia, Arabia, Syria, and Phœnicia, till the times of the Latin kings. Antioch, as well as Jerusalem, yielded the richest plunder. Matthew Paris (a contemporary historian), speaking of what was taken at Antioch, 1098, says, "At the division of costly vessels, crosses, weavings, and silken stuffs, every beggar in the crusading army was enriched." Alexandria, as early as the middle of the sixth century, A.D., had been the depôt for the silken stuffs of Libya and Morocco. Here is a wide area opened to us for suggestions as to the origin and traditions of patterns in silk textile art. See Bock's "Liturgische Gewänder," vol. i. pp. 29, 30.

[264] Rock, Introduction, p. ccxlviii, and p. 268, No. 8710.

[265] The weaving of inscriptions in textiles is not a Saracenic invention. Pliny says it was a custom among the Parthians. See Rock's "Textile Fabrics," p. lxi.

"In allusion to lettered garments, Ausonius thus celebrates Sabina, of whom we otherwise know nothing:—

"'They who both webs and verses weave,The first to thee, oh chaste Minerva, leave;The latter to the Muses they devote.To me, Sabina, it appears a sinTo separate two things so near akin;So I have writ these verses on my coat.'"

See Lady Wilton on "Needlework," p. 53.

[266] Birdwood, "Indian Arts," p. 274.

[267] Yates, "Textrinum Antiquorum," p. 244; Tegrini, "Vita Castruccii," in Muratore, "Ital. Script.," t. xi. p. 1320.

[268] Riano, "Cat. of Loan Exhibition of Spanish Art in South Kensington Museum," 1882, p. 46.

[269] In Hoveden's account of the fleet of Richard I. coasting the shores of Spain, he speaks of the delicate and valuable textures of the silks of Almeria. Rog. Hoveden, Ann., ed. Savile, p. 382. Rock, p. xx.

[270] Bock, pp. 39, 40, quotes from Anastasius and the Abbot of Fontenelle, proving that silken rugs were manufactured in Spain by the Moors.

[271] Auberville, "Histoire des Tissus," p. 14.

[272]Yule's "Marco Polo," p. 224. "Baudakin" from Baghdad, "damask" from Damascus. "Baudakin" was woven with beasts, birds, and flowers in gold.

[273]"Récit de Robert Clari." He was one of the companions of Ville d'Hardouin, and a witness to the coronation of Baldwin II. See Auberville's "Histoire des Tissus," p. 21.

[274]Satin is called by Marco Polo "zettani," and he says it came from Syria. The French called it "zatony;" the Spaniards named it "aceytuni," which is probably derived from "zaituniah," the product of Zaiton. Yates (p. 246) gives the derivations of the words satin and silk; the one imported to us through Greece and Italy, the other from Eastern Asia, through Slavonia and Northern Europe.

[275]Ibid. In the Wigalois, a story is told of a cavern in Asia full of everlasting flames, where costly fellat was made by the Salamanders, which was fireproof and indestructible.

[276]"Man of Lawe's Tale: Canterbury Pilgrims."

[277]"Ohitos terciopelos" (three-piled-velvet eyes) is a pretty Spanish phrase, describing the soft, dark, shadowy eyes of the Spanish girls.

[278]The Italian word *velluto* means "shaggy."

[279]Bock, i. pp. 99-101.

[280]Buckram was sometimes a silken plush, but generally was woven with cotton. This was also Asiatic, and named by travellers of the twelfth and thirteenth centuries. I have already mentioned it as a textile in the chapter on cotton. When woven of silk it belongs to the class of velvets.

[281]Elsewhere I have spoken of the embroideries of the early Christian times found in the Fayoum, in Egypt. These afford notable examples of the ancient method in putting in patches on a worn or frayed garment. They invariably embroidered them, and so added a grace to the old and honoured vestment, and justified the classical appellation, "Healer of clothes" for a darner. The comparatively modern additions of the restorer, are in ancient as in later specimens, often a puzzle to the archæologist.

[282]The specimens in the South Kensington Museum, where Dr. Rock gives their approximate dates, are most useful to the student of this subject.

[175]

CHAPTER V.
COLOUR.

"My soul, what gracious glorious powersTo hue and radiance God has given!"
Cautley, "Emblems," p. 21.

It is my intention to confine myself to the discussion of colour, in as far as it belongs to the dyes of textiles and the materials for embroidery. I will adhere as closely as I can to this part of what is a great and most interesting subject—one which the science of to-day has opened out, and by the test of experiment, cleared of erroneous theories; revealing to us all its beauty and fitness for the use and delight of man.

As through all ages the eye has been gradually educated to appreciate *harmony* in colour, so *dissonance*—that is, what errs against harmony—hurts us, without apparently a sufficient reason; and we have to seek the causes of our sensations in the scientific works and lectures of Professor Tyndall and others.

There is no doubt that the appreciation of colour has belonged in different degrees to the eye of every animal, but especially to that of man, ever since light first painted the flowers of the field. The eye is created to see colour, as well as form. But we know that men, being accustomed to acquiesce in the powers with which they find themselves gifted by nature, enjoy and use them, long before they begin to study, classify, and name them.

When we recollect that the circulation of the blood was not known within the last three hundred years, and [176]that Albert Dürer painted the skeleton Death on the bridge of Lucerne, with one bone in the upper and one in the lower arm, we shall be surprised to find that the ancients had named the colours they saw, with some degree of descriptive and scientific precision. The word "purple," for instance, covered a multitude of tints, which had not as yet been differentiated, either in common parlance or in poetry,[283] though as articles of commerce the purple tints had been early distinguished.

What names have we now, in this present advanced day, for defining tastes or smells? We say that something smells like a violet, or a rose, or a sea breeze, or a frosted cabbage. We say a smell is nice or nasty, that a taste is delicious or nauseous; but beyond calling it sweet or sour, we have no descriptive words for either smells or tastes, whereas the nations who traded in the materials for dyes exchanged their nomenclatures, which we can recognize from the descriptive remarks of different authors.

Colour, as an art, was born in those lands which cluster round the eastern shores of the Mediterranean—the northern coasts of Syria and Arabia, and the isles of Greece. All art grew in that area, and all its adjuncts and materials there came to perfection, though often imported from more southern and eastern sources.[284]

E. Curtius says that the science of colour came into Europe with the Phœnicians and accompanied the worship of Astarte. This, of course, applies to artistic textiles, as the Greeks had already acquired the art of dyeing for plain weaving. Numa, in his regulations for necessary weaving, refers also to colour. The Italians[177]therefore must at that time have made some advance in the art, especially the Etruscans.[285]

The infinity of variation in colour is difficult to imagine. The chemists of the Gobelins have fixed and catalogued 4480 tones. Besides, we must not forget that it is now all but ascertained that the same colour is probably appreciated differently by nearly every eye.[286]

How the eye accepts colours and conveys them to the mind is still a question in dispute, though the theories of Tyndall, Helmholz, Hering, Charpentier, and others, aided by experiments, are drawing ascertained facts into a circle, which will ere long be complete, and the mysteries of colour may be ascertained.

Probably the effects of colour on educated minds are as various as the tints and shades of tones of the many substances which receive them,—reflected from all surrounding objects, blazing in light, or softened by shadow,—fresh and glowing, or permanently faded—shining with modern varnish, or sobered by the dust of ages.

It is the art of the colourist, whether he paints pictures, or dyes textiles, or embroiders them, to reduce the tints of the prism to an endurable and delightful lowness of tone, while preserving as far as possible all their light and purity.

Prismatic colours are so radiantly glorious, that when we see the rainbow in the sky it is each time a joyful surprise. The most stolid natures are moved by it; we have even seen our dog staring at it.

When, in experiments on light, the shafts of colour are [178]thrown on the wall, they are greeted with shouts of admiration; but these glories are veiled to us by the fact that the eye cannot dissect the prismatic ray without the assistance of the instrument that has revealed it. This is a merciful arrangement; for we are not fitted to live in a prismatic display, any more than in a continuity of lightning flashes. We should go mad or blind if exposed to either.

Science has shown us the perfect beauty of colour without form, the soothing pleasures of its harmonies, and the delightful surprises of its contrasts. From the glimpses we have of its nature and laws, we may hope for fresh inspiration for the art of the colourist.

Though it is true that each eye, even when educated, retains its own special appreciation of the colours that gratify its seeing nerve, yet there are certain standards which give almost universal pleasure.[287]

The blind and the colour-blind must remain exceptions for all time; and there are many gradations in colour-blindness, till we come to the normal class of seeing eyes; and passing them by, reach to those few men, gifted beyond all others with that fund of sensitive eye-nerve and mental power, which enables them to create new thoughts in colour.[288] Titian and his school arose from the inherited science and tradition, and carefully prepared pigments of his immediate predecessors, acting on an [179]exceptional eye and mind, imbued with the splendours of the early mornings and the sunsets in the glowing atmosphere of Venice.

Colour has long been supposed to convey certain impressions to the mind. The absence of all colour, which we call "black," symbolizes in dress, grief, pride, or dignity; according as it drapes the mourner, the Spanish grandee, or the priest.[289] Yellow being the colour of the sun and of corn and gold, represents riches, generosity, and light. Red stands between the dark and the lively colours, and represents warmth and animation, dignity, splendour, life, love, and joy.

The expression of blue is that of purity. It recalls the distant sky, the calm ocean, and has an immortal and celestial character. It ascends to the highest and descends to the lowest tones of *chiaro-oscuro*. Nothing so nearly approaches pure white as the palest blue; nothing is so nearly black as the darkest.

Green has been assigned by nature the place of the universal background. It is the complementary colour of red, softening and assimilating it by reflected shadows, and setting off the glory of every flower and fruit. The expression of green is gaiety and modesty, light and tenderness, shadow and repose, to both the eye and the mind.[290]

It must be allowed that it is by the earliest associations of the individual, or by those derived from the family, the tribe or the nation, that colours are connected with such attributes welded by art and time into traditional meanings, which they absolutely possess,[291] and from which fashion [180]cannot disconnect them; such, for instance, is the royalty of purple.

The word purple is so indiscriminately used as a poetic epithet, rather than as a distinctive appellation, that much confusion has been caused by it. Historically, among the Persians, Greeks, and Romans it appears to have been simply the royal colour, varying from the purest blue, through every shade of violet, down to the deepest crimson. Sometimes, poetically, "purple" seems to have described only a surface. The breezy or stormy sea was purple; the sky was purple; the hyacinthine locks of Narcissus, the rosy lips of Venus were purple. As a textile, velvet was purple, even when it was white.[292]

The epithets "purple" and "wine-coloured" are often bestowed on the Mediterranean Sea, and are justified by its occasional hue:—

"As from the clouds, deep-bosom'd, swell'd with showers,A sudden storm the purple ocean sweeps,Drives the wild waves, and tosses all the deeps."

Pope's Homer, "Iliad," b. xi. v. 383.

Professor Tyndall suggests that the soft green of the sea, shadowed by clouds, assumes a subjective purple hue. Homer must have observed this before he became blind.

[181]Pliny gives us much information about this colour; he enumerates the different sea-shores and coasts, Egyptian, Asiatic, and European, whence came the shell-fish (the murex and pelagia) that produced the so-called Tyrian purple dyes.[293]

He says that Romulus wore the purple, and that the dyed garments, all purple, were sacred to the gods in those days. After saying that it was still a colour of distinction, he continues: "Let us be prepared to excuse the frantic passion for purple, though we are impelled to inquire why such a high value is placed on the produce of this fish, seeing that in the dye the smell of it is offensive, and the colour, of a greenish hue, resembles the sea when tempestuous." He describes purples[294] as being differently coloured according as to whether these "conchylia" inhabited the sea mud, the reefs, or the pebbly shores, the last being the most [182]valuable.[295] This purple, said to have been imported from the coasts of Tyre, was till lately sold in Rome for its weight in gold; it gave the burning rosy red dye of the Cardinal's robes, and was called "Porpora encarnadina," purple incarnadine. It is full of light and freshness, and never fades; in fact, it has all the qualities ascribed to it by Pliny. It intensifies in the light.[296]

After purple, scarlet was the colour most esteemed by the ancients. The Israelites must have carried with them the dyes which coloured the hangings, woven or embroidered, belonging to the sanctuary in the wilderness, of which the outer covering of rams' skins was [183]dyed scarlet, and was probably of the nature of red morocco.[297]

There was the mineral dye, (cinnabar or red sulphate of mercury), and the insect dye; the first was probably used in mural painting. It is translated in our Bible as vermilion, in the account given by Jeremiah of a "house, ceiled with cedar, and painted with vermilion."[298] Also Ezekiel gives us another instance of house-painting in vermilion.[299] Homer, who as a rule does not describe colouring, says the Greek ships were painted red.

It is probable that cinnabar was tempered, by admixture of white or other colours, for the monochrome painting of the Egyptians and Greeks. It was called by the Greeks miltos, by the Romans minium.

The dye of the red portions of the funeral tent of Queen Isi-em-Kheb, Shishak's mother-in-law, is found by analysis to be composed of hematite (peroxyde of iron) tempered with lime. This is a beautiful pink red.[300]

The mineral red now called vermilion must have borrowed its name from the insect dye which the Greeks and Romans called "kermes." In the Middle Ages the dye from the kermes was still called "vermiculata," of which the word vermilion is a literal translation.

We should be fortunate if we could find how the Greeks and Romans prepared the cinnabar for mural painting, of which we find remnants in ruins and tombs—a lovely and pure red, with a tender bloom on it like a fragment of the rainbow, and not the slightest shade of yellow.

[184]One of the most beautiful specimens of this scarlet that I am acquainted with, is a small drinking-cup (a "rhyton") at the British Museum, in the form of a sphinx, with a white face, gilded hair, and a little cap of pure cinnabar, which is so soft in tone that it suggests the texture of scarlet velvet.

Cochineal, which was first brought from America in the sixteenth century, has now replaced almost every other scarlet dye for textiles.

Crimson is once mentioned in Chronicles as karmel,[301] which may mean the dye of the kermes insect;[302] and from this the word crimson is legitimately derived. Whether the scarlet coupled with it is a vegetable, mineral, or insect colour, we have no means of ascertaining. "Though your sins be as scarlet, they shall be as white as snow; though they be red as crimson, they shall be as wool."[303]

From what Pliny says, it appears that some green dyes were produced from a green clay; others from metals. Copper furnished the most beautiful shades.

Blue has always been extracted from indigo. Pliny tells us that the Phœnicians brought it from Barbarike, in the Indies, to Egypt; and he quotes the "Periplus" on this subject. He gives an amusing report that indigo is a froth collected round the stems of certain reeds; but he was aware of its characteristic property, that of emitting a beautiful purple vapour when submitted to great heat; and he says it smells like the sea. The Egyptians likewise extracted blues from copper.

[185]Yellow was anciently, in Egypt, sometimes a vegetable and sometimes a mineral dye. Browns and blacks were prepared from several substances, especially pine wood and the contents of tombs burned into a kind of charcoal.

We find that lime, chalk, white lead, and other mineral substances were employed by the ancients for the different approaches to dazzling whiteness. That of the lily, the emblem of purity, can only be emulated in textile or pictorial art by opaque substances reduced as much as possible by bleaching to the last expression of the colour of the raw material. Nothing that is transparent can be really white, as colours are seen through it, as well as the reflected lights on the two surfaces.

In painting, we can produce the effect of whiteness in different ways, leading by the gradation of tender colours and shadows up to a high light. But in textile art, which is essentially flat, it is necessary to pursue a different method, and that of isolation is the most simple and effective, and was well understood in Egypt, Greece, and India. The white pattern, or flower, is surrounded with a fine dark line (black is the best), which effectually separates it from all the surrounding colours, and gives it the effect of light, even when the whiteness retains enough of the natural colour of the raw material to tone it down very perceptibly. The eye accepts it as white, and ignores the tint that pervades it, and is hardly to be expelled from silk or wool. Linen and cotton are the whitest of materials, after passing through the hands of the chemist or the bleacher.

It is amusing to observe that Pliny regarded colours, whether vegetable or mineral, rather as useful for the pharmacopeia of his day, than as dyes or artistic pigments. He speaks contemptuously of the art of his time, and yet he gives some curious hints that are well worth collecting [186]for experiment. His fragmentary information, though often inaccurate, is most valuable to those who are seeking once more to find lasting colours, and despair of discovering mordants that will fix the aniline tints. From him we learn more of the Egyptian colouring materials than of any others, as he named their sources, European, Asiatic, or African; and there is no doubt of the perfection of their mural pigments and textile dyes, which have remained unimpaired to the present time.

Renouf says that "painting, as it is now understood, was totally unknown to the Egyptians; but they understood harmony of colour,[304] and formulated in it certain principles for decorative uses. They made the primary colours predominate over the secondary by quantity and position. They introduced fillets of white or yellow in their embroideries, as well as in their paintings, between reds and greens, to isolate them; and they balanced masses of yellow with a due proportion of black." They never blended their colours, and had no sense of the harmony of prismatic gradations, or the melting of one tint into another; each was worked up to a hard and fast edge line. If in one part of a building, one set of colours predominated, they placed a greater proportion of other colours elsewhere, within the range of sight, so as to readjust the balance. Those they employed were mostly earthy mineral colours (used alike for frescoes and for painting cotton cloths, though vegetable dyes were needed for woollens and linens). These were: for *white*, pure chalk; for *black*, bone-black mixed with gum; for *yellow*, yellow ochre; for *green*, a mixture of yellow ochre and powdered blue glass; for *blue*, this same blue glass mixed with white chalk; for *red*, an earthy pigment containing iron and [187]aluminium.[305] They understood the chemistry of bleaching, and the use of mordants in dyeing.[306]

The statistical records of China of the time of Hias (2205 B.C.), according to Semper, mention colours as being of five tints, and all the produce of the Chinese Empire.[307]

In the unchanging art of India, the ancient colours are used now. Therefore, when we give the following list, we must suppose that it embraces all that have been known from the beginning.

Indian dyes are mostly vegetable. For *yellow*, akalbir, the root of the Datiscus Canabinus; also yellow is dyed with asbarg, the flower of the Cabul larkspur (*Delphinium sp.*).

Orange. Soneri dyed with narsingar, the honey-scented flower of nyclanthes (*Arbor Tristis*).

Scarlet is first dyed with cochineal (formerly with kermes), which gives a crimson colour; next with narsingar, which turns it vermilion.

Purple is dyed first with cochineal (formerly kermes), afterwards with indigo.

Lilac. Ditto, only paler.

Blue. All shades of indigo.

Green. With indigo first, and next the various yellow dyes.

Brown. Sandal-wood, called "sandali;" almond colour (Badami).

Grey. Sulphate of iron and gold.

Black. Deepest shade of indigo.[308]

Speaking of Indian coloured textiles, Sir G. Birdwood [188]says: "All violent contrasts are avoided. The richest colours are used, but are so arranged as to produce the effect of a neutral bloom, which tones down every detail almost to the softness and transparency of the atmosphere." He says that in their apparel both the colouring and the ornaments are adapted to the effect which the fabrics will produce when worn and in motion. "It is only through generations of patient practice that men attain to the mystery of such subtleties."

An outline, in black or some dark colour that harmonizes with the ground, or else worked in gold, is common in Indian work, not only for the purpose of isolating the colours of the design, but also to give a uniform tone to the whole surface of the texture. Their traditional arrangements of tints were thoroughly satisfying to the eye. But degenerated by European commerce, the artistic sense of beauty itself is disappearing throughout our Indian Empire.

Persian carpets (the fine old ones of the fourteenth to the seventeenth centuries) give us lessons in the art of isolating colours. In these, a flower will lie upon a surface which contains two or more other tints, and as the design passes over them, the outline colour is changed, so as to isolate the flower equally on the different grounds. This is done with such art that the eye ignores the transition till it is called to remark it. For instance, as a white, or no-coloured pattern, wanders over a green and red ground, the outline changes suddenly from green to red, and again to green as it leaves the opposite colour on the ground pattern.

Mr. Floyer speaks of the brilliancy and lasting qualities of the dyes which the Persians, by slow and tedious processes, extract from plants; from the "runaschk" (madder), a fine red; from the "zarili" (the golden), which is a yellow flower from Khorasan, and also from the [189]leaves of the vine, a bright yellow.[309] They import indigo from Shastra (or from India), by the Khurum river. He says these dyes are perfectly fast, leaving no trace on a wetted rubber, whereas the European dyes they sometimes use come off freely.

Pliny says the Gauls had invented dyes counterfeiting the purple of Tyre; also scarlet, violet, and green, all of these were dipped in the juices of herbs.[310]

Vitruvius says the Romans extracted dyes from flowers and fruits, but he neither specifies nor describes them.

The ancient Highland tartans were dyed with bark of alder for black, bark of willow for flesh colour. A lichen growing on stones supplied their violets and crimsons.[311] The lichen on the birch-tree gives a good brown; heather gives red, purple, and green.[312]

Thus we see that pure colours for dyeing textiles have been extracted from vegetable substances—herbs, wood, seeds, flowers and fruits, mosses and sea-weeds;[313] mineral substances—earths, sands, ores, metals, rusts, and stones; animal substances—both of land, water, and air; beasts, fishes, shells, birds, and insects.

It is evident, from the derivation of the word, that [190]there were chromatic scales in colour before the phrase was ever applied to music.

The Greeks and Romans are supposed to have understood chromatic scales of tints—animal, vegetable, and mineral—and except with the intention of producing startling effects, they did not mix them. They felt that each was harmonious as a whole, and, unlike the Egyptians, they studied harmony. They arranged their scales according to the materials from which they were extracted, and kept those from different chemical sources apart, as being discordant.[314]One scale was that of the iodine colours, of and from the sea. Marine products are mostly iridescent. To comprehend this, think of the harmonious interchange of delicate tints, called by the ancients "purple," on a string of pearls. Shells and shell-fish, sea-weeds and fish, furnished these dyes. They were called "conchiliata."

The chemistry of the arts of bleaching was not unknown to the ancients; but they reserved and regulated it for certain purposes, preferring to retain at least a part of the original colouring, as shades of grounding which served, as a surface glaze does in painting, to connect and harmonize the superinduced tints.

Experiments with the object of reviving this mode of producing harmonious combinations, have been made lately at the Wilton Carpet Works, by dyeing shades of colour on unbleached goat's and camel's hair, and sheep's wool; and the tones produced are beautifully soft and rich.

[191]M. Edouard Charton ascribes the great change in the modern scales of colours to the discovery by the French, in the Gobelins, of a pure scarlet dye, the use of which made it necessary to raise the tone of all other colours. He says that scarlet was formerly represented by the dye called kermes, which indeed was not scarlet, but altered from crimson to something approaching it by the addition of narsingar, of which the bright yellow gave the scarlet effect.

M. Chevreul, director of the dyeing department of the Gobelins, has succeeded in composing the chromatic prism, to which I have already alluded, containing 4420 different tones. We may take it for granted, that from these may be selected any possible scale of tints required for decorative work. This vast area for choice of our material will impose on the artist of the future fresh responsibilities.

In the typical Oriental colouring, the whole arrangement was traditional, and it was irreligious to depart from what had been fixed by statute many centuries before, and only perfected by the experience of many generations of men; and this veneration for traditional custom has hitherto been prevalent in European art to a certain point. But the old conservative perfection of unadulterated colour has already been done away with. The freedom of experimental art is chartered, and mercantile interests now, as ever, govern the supply of materials.

Our normal bad taste and carelessness has been cast back on the lands which were the cradle of art, and we receive, to our surprise, gaudy, vulgar, and discordant combinations from the East, whence we drew our first inspirations. For the future we shall have to study ancient specimens, and correct our errors by the help of their teaching to the eye and mind.

Gas colours are at present our worst snares. They are [192]in general very beautiful; but they are so evanescent, and fade into such unexpected and contradictory tones, that we cannot reckon upon them. When embroidering with the coloured materials of the day, we are in constant dread of what disastrous effect may be produced by the first shaft of sunshine that may fall from our moderately illuminated sky, through the uncurtained window.

The trade in colours can hardly be an honest one, till the means of fixing each tint permanently is ascertained.[315] At any rate, something should be done towards grouping them, with respect to their enduring qualities, so that when they fade, if fade they must, they may do so harmoniously, and in sympathy with each other; and while they are in their first glow they should be selected, as much as possible, from what Pliny calls natural colours,[316] which recall the exquisite effects of nature, searched out and displayed by every sunny gleam, reflected on each other in lovely tones, and subdued and veiled by passing shadows. It is said that Mr. Wardle, of Leek, is now seeking for dyes of pure unadulterated colours, and mordants to fix them. He deserves all success.

The reason I have entered, in even so cursory a manner, into the history of colours is my desire to point out the great value placed, long ago, on the careful preparation of those used in ancient textile art; and to [193]show how our forefathers sought them out in many lands and waters; how they noted their varieties; how they classed and prized them for their endurance as well as for their pristine beauty; how they paid their weight in gold or silver for certain culminating tints; and how they, therefore, produced works which became matters of history and landmarks in civilization.

FOOTNOTES:

[283]"Seeing, they saw not, neither did they understand."

[284]See Pliny's "Natural History," which gives much information on the subject.

[285]E. Curtius, "Greek History;" Engl. Trans., i. p. 438; Blümner's "Technologie," p. 216.

[286]Charpentier "differentiates in every normal eye a sensibility for light, a sensibility for colour, and a sensibility for form (a visual sensibility)."—See "Modern Theories of Colour," *The Lancet*, August 19th, 1882, p. 276. We can perceive, by studying works of art, how variously these gifts are distributed, or, at any rate, how differently they are received and acted upon by individual minds.

[287]The effect of colour on the brain is a subject only just now beginning to attract attention. Experiments on the insane have been made in Italy, especially, I believe, at Venice; and it is said to be ascertained that red and green are irritants, whereas windows glazed with blue glass alternating with white have sensibly calmed the nerves of the patients.

[288]Let us compare the beautiful creations of the Venetian school with the demoralizing brightness of aniline colours, or the opaque, earthy tints which some call beautiful, mistaking their dulness for softness and sobriety of colouring. But they, too, have their uses.

[289]Black and red are, in ecclesiastical work, the emblems of mourning.

[290]The Bardic rules in early Britain enjoined three simple colours: sky blue, the emblem of peace, for the bard and poet; green, for the master of natural history and woodcraft; spotless white (the symbol of holiness), for the priest and Druid.

[291]The blind man said that red was like the sound of a trumpet, which shows what a soul-stirring colour it was in his mind's eye.

[292]"Purpura" is supposed to mean crimson velvet. It came, like "cramoisi," to be a name for a tissue. Fr. Michell quotes velvet of Vermeil-cramoisi, "violet and blue cramoisi, and pourpre of divers colours," but he says he never met with "pourpre blanche." Yule, ed. 1875, i. p. 67. Plano Carpini (p. 755) says the courtiers of Karakorum were clad in "white purpura;" and that on the first day of the great festival in honour of the inauguration of Kuyuk Khan, all the Mogul nobles were clad in pourpre blanche, the second day in ruby

purple, and the third in blue purple: on the fourth day they appeared in Baudichin (cloth of gold). (Yule, "Marco Polo," vol. i. p. 376.) White purple is also named in the inventories of Sta. Maria Maggiore at Rome, and those of Notre Dame in Paris. "Histoire du Tissu Ancien, à l'Exposition de l'Union Générale des Arts Décoratifs."

[293]François Le Normant, in his "Grande Grèce," tells of the dye of the purple of Tarentum from the murex, found in the Mare Piccolo. He says that Tarentine muslins, woven from the filaments of the pinna dipped in the dye of the murex, rivalled those of Cos. Le Normant laments the total neglect of the murex in these days (could its trade be revived?) Plutarch says that Alexander the Great, having made himself master of Susa (Shushan), found, amongst other riches of marvellous value, "purple of Hermione" worth forty thousand talents (Quintus Curtius says fifty thousand), which, though it had been stored 190 years, retained all its freshness and beauty. See Plutarch's "Lives," edited by J. and W. Langhorne, vol. ii. p. 739; Blümner, i. p. 224-240. The reason assigned for their dye being so perfect was that the Susanians knew how to comb the wool to be dipped, and prepare it with honey. According to Aristotle the dress of Alcisthenes, the Sybarite, was dyed with this purple from Shushan (Ciampini, Vet. Mon.).

[294]Semper gives us an account of iodine colours. Some, he says, were extracted from sea-weeds, green and yellow; the purples, when finest, from the shell-fish. The Phœnician coasts gave the best purples; those of the Atlantic the best blacks and browns. And thus he completes the scale of iodine colours. See Semper, "Der Stil," i. p. 206.

[295]Heaps of the shells of this "murex trunculus" have been found at Pompeii, near the dyers' works. Hardouin says that in his time they were found at Otranto, and similar remains have been noticed at Sidon. Sir James Lacaita informs me that the living shells are still found along the shores of the Adriatic, as well as on the wash near Argos. No doubt the Phœnicians traded first in the produce of the Sidonian and Tyrian coasts, though they afterwards went farther afield in collecting their dyes. Auberville says that the purple of the Romans was a deep violet (double dyed, purpuræ dibaphæ), and that this colour was Asiatic. The Phœnicians traded in it, and sold it for its weight in silver. Instead of fading in the sunshine, its colour intensified. The enduring nature of this colour is proved by the purple fragments from a Greek tomb in the Crimea of about 300 B.C., described in chapter on stitches, p. 217. See "Histoire du Tissu Ancien, à l'Exposition de l'Union Générale des Arts Décoratifs."

[296]Though really red of the purest colour, it doubtless received its name of Tyrian purple as being one of the materials of the amethystine double dye. The web or fleece was first dipped in the dye of Purpura, and then in that of the Buccinum, or they reversed the process to give a different tint. This is Pliny's account of the process of dyeing, which is very simple, and gives no details. Semper says that the ancients called black and white the two extremes of purple—white the thinnest, and black the thickest or most solid layer of colour. Both were thus considered as colour. (Semper, i. pp. 205-7.) As long as there is light, black always appears to be either blue, or brown, or green, till with darkness all colour disappears.

[297]Exod. xxv. Semper (i. p. 103) suggests that these rams' skins were dyed with the periploca secamone—a plant still used for this purpose in Egypt.

[298]Jeremiah xxii. 14.

[299]Ezekiel xxiii. 14: "The images of the Chaldeans." "The men portrayed in vermilion on the wall."

[300]Villiers Stuart, "Funeral Tent of an Egyptian Queen." See Appendix.

[301]2 Chron. ii. 7.

[302]The Arabs received the kermis from Armenia, and the name was originally "Quer-més," "oak-apple." Sardis was famed for its kermes dye. See Birdwood, "Indian Arts," p. 238, ed. 1880, and Yule's "Marco Polo," i. p. 67.

[303]Isa. ii. 18.

[304]Renouf's Hibbert Lectures, p. 67-69. It may be called balance, rather than harmony.

[305]Wilkinson, "Manners of the Ancient Egyptians," vol. iii. pp. 301-3.

[306]Blümner, p. 220. See Pliny, "Natural History," xxxv. 42.

[307]Semper, i. p. 248.

[308] See Birdwood's "Indian Arts," p. 272. In the Code of Manu, black garments are sacred to the Indian Saturn, yellow to Venus, and red to Mars. See Birdwood, p. 235.

[309] See Floyer's "Unexplored Baluchistan," pp. 278, 373, 406. The Persians produce their deep yellow from the skin of the pomegranate, by boiling it in alum. Major Murdoch Smith describes the Persian processes for dyeing patterns red and black in textiles. The Italian women dye their own dresses in the pomegranate yellow; also in turmeric yellow, and other vegetable dyes.

[310] Pliny, "Natural History," xxii. 3. Unfortunately, Pliny seldom condescends to give us the recipes for dyeing processes.

[311] Logan's "Scottish Garb."

[312] See Elton's "Origins of English History."

[313] The Cretan tincture was extracted from a plant which Theophrastus, Dioscorides, and Pliny respectively name. The last calls it the *Phycos thalassion*. This was not a sea-weed, but a lichen—probably the same from which the orchid purple of modern art is prepared. See Birdwood, "Indian Arts," i. p. 238.

[314] The same scale of colour varies as much on the different textiles employed, as it does from the colours extracted from other chemicals. Silk, wool, cotton, flax, give very different results. The colouring matter may be identical, yet you cannot place them side by side without being aware that they may be repellant, instead of harmonious in tone. The scale is sometimes removed to another pitch, and they will no more harmonize than instruments that have not been attuned to the same diapason. See Redgrave's Report on Textile Fabrics.

[315] With the changes in colouring materials has arisen the necessity for discovering new mordants. The gas colour of madder is exactly the same chemically as that extracted from the vegetable, but the old mordant does not fix it, and it changes very soon to a dull blackish-purple hue.

[316] Pliny, "Natural History," ix. 12. The most unnatural, and the most disagreeable dyes, are the magentas. Sir G. Birdwood tells us that the Maharajah of Cashmere has adopted a most efficient plan for the suppression of magenta dyes within his dominions—first, a duty of 45 per cent. on entering the country, and at a certain distance within the frontier, they are confiscated and destroyed.

[194]

CHAPTER VI.
Part 1.
STITCHES.

Stitches in needlework correspond to the touches of the pencil or brush in drawing or painting, or to the strokes of the chisel in sculpture. The needle is the one implement of the craft by which endless forms of surface-work are executed. With a thread through its one eye, it blindly follows each effort of its pointed foot, urged by the intelligent or mechanical hand grouping the stitches, which, being long or short, single or mixed, slanting, upright, or crossed, are selected as the best fitted for the design and purpose in hand. The word "stitches" does not, however, in this chapter represent merely the plural of one particular process of needle insertion, but the produce and effect of each different kind of stitch by grouping and repetition, according to its most ancient nomenclature. That which is astonishing is the endless variety of surface, of design, of hints and suggestions, of startling effects, and of lovely combinations, resulting from the direction of the needle and manipulation of the materials, and differing from each other according to the power or the caprice of the worker. But the machine is always the same—the threaded needle strikes the same interval, forming the "stitch."

This venerable implement, *the needle*, has, through the ages, varied but little in form. The attenuated body, the sharp foot, the rounded head, and the eye to hold the thread, are the same in principle, whether it is found [195]in the cave-man's grave, formed of a fish's bone or shaped from that of a larger animal; hammered of the finest bronze, as from Egypt, or of gold, like those found in Scandinavia. A bronze needle was lately discovered in the tomb of a woman of the Vikings in Scotland, and its value is shown by its being placed in a silver case. Steel needles were first made in England in 1545, by a native of India. His successor, Christopher Greening, established a workshop in 1560 at Long Crendon, in Bucks, which existed there as a needle factory till quite lately. The rustic poetic drama, entitled "Gammer Gurton's Needle," performed at Ch. Coll., Cambridge, in 1566, was a regular comedy, of which a lost needle was the hero. In those days the village needle was evidently still a rare and precious possession.

Fig. 20.
1, 2, 3, 4, 5, Bronze needles from Egyptian tombs now in British Museum.
6. Cave-man's needle from the Pinhole, Churchfield, Ereswell Crag.
7. Bone needle from La Madeleine, Dordogne.

The art of embroidery consists of a design, which includes the pattern, and the handicraft or stitches—the "motive" and the "needlework."

In painting, as in sculpture, the first idea, as well as [196]the last touch, must come from the same head and hand. But in needlework it is not so. The pattern is the result of tradition. It is almost always simply a variation of old forms, altered and renewed by surrounding circumstances and sudden or gradual periods of change.

However much the design may alter, rising often to the highest point of decorative art, and as often falling back to the lowest and most meaningless repetitions and imitations, the *stitches* themselves vary but little. The same are to be found in Egyptian and Greek specimens, and the classical names are those used by mediæval writers, and have come down to us, "floating like bubbles on the waves of time."

Sir George Birdwood[317] thinks that every kind of stitch is found in traditional Indian work. I confess that I have not been able hitherto to trace any of the "mosaic" stitches to India, nor do we ever see them in Chinese or Japanese embroidery, which shows every other variety. They are, however, occasionally found in Egyptian work.

The following is a list of stitches, under the nomenclature of classical, Roman and mediæval authors:—

Opus Phrygionium or Phrygium.	Passing or metal thread work.
Opus Pulvinarium.	Shrine or cushion work.
Opus Plumarium.	Plumage or feather work.
Opus Consutum.	Cut work.
Opus Araneum or Filatorium.	Net or lace work.
Opus Pectineum.	Tapestry or combed work.

Here are two English lists of stitches; their quaintness must be my excuse for copying them. The first is from Taylor, the water-poet's "Praise of the Needle" (sixteenth century):—

"Tent work, raised work, laid work, prest work,Net work, most curious pearl or rare Italian cut work,[197]Fine fern stitch, finny stitch, new stitch, and chain stitch,Brave bred stitch, fisher stitch, Irish stitch, and queen's stitch,The Spanish stitch, rosemary stitch, and maw stitch,The smarting whip stitch, back stitch, and the cross stitch.—All these are good, and these we must allow,And these are everywhere in practice now."

The second list is from Rees' "Cyclopædia" (Stitches), 1819:—

"Spanish stitch,
Tent stitch on the finger,
Tent stitch in the tent or frame,
Irish stitch,
Fore stitch,
Gold stitch,

Twist		stitch,
Fern		stitch,
Broad		stitch,
Rosemary		stitch,
Chip		stitch,
Raised		work,
Geneva		work,
Cut		work,
Laid		work,
Back		stitch,
Queen's		stitch,
Satin		stitch,
Finny		stitch,
Chain		stitch,
Fisher's		stitch,
Bow		stitch,
Cross		stitch,
Needlework		purl,
Virgin's		device,
Open	cut	work,
Stitch		work,
Through		stitch,
Rock		work,
Net	work,	and
Lent work.		

"All which are swete manners of work wroughte by the needle with silke of all natures, purls, wyres, and weft or foreign bread ('braid'), etc., etc."

Part 2.
PLAIN WORK AND WHITE WORK.

We are told that the primal man and woman sewed in Paradise.

To "sew," in contradistinction to the word to "embroider," is derived from the Sanskrit *su, suchi*, and thence imported into Latin, *suo*.[318] To prove how highly [198]esteemed needlework was among the Romans, I may mention that the equivalent of the phrase "to hit the right nail on the head" was *rem acu tangere*, "to touch the question with the point of the needle."

"Plain work" is that which is necessary. As soon as textiles are needed for covering and clothing, the means are invented for drawing the cut edges together, and for preventing the fraying where the material is lacerated by the shaping process. Hence the "seam," the "hem," and all the forms of stitches that bind and plait. These necessary stitches constitute plain needlework, and are closely followed by decorative stitches, which in gradation cover the space between plain needlework and embroidery.

Semper has given us his archæological theories for the origin of needlework and its stitches.

These are his arguments, if not always his words. He says: "The seam is one of the first human successful efforts to conquer difficulties."[319]

A string, a ribbon, a band, may serve to keep together several loose things; but by means of the seam, small things actually become large ones. For example: a full-grown man can, by its help, cover himself with a garment made of the skins of many small animals. When Eve sewed fig-leaves together, she made of these small pieces a garment of patchwork.

Acting on the principle of making a virtue of necessity, accepting and adorning the severe facts of life, seams [199]came to be an important vehicle of ornament. The Gauls and Britons embroidered the seams of their fur garments. "We may judge of the antiquity of the seam by its universal and mythological meaning. The seam, the tie, the knot, the plait, and the mesh are the earliest symbols of fate uniting events."[320]

We find but little mention of plain work in mediæval writings. When linen was worked for some honourable purpose, such as a gift to a friend or a royal personage, it was generally embroidered or stitched in some fancy fashion. Queen Elizabeth presented Edward VI., on his second birthday, with a smock made by herself. Fine linen was about this time constantly edged with bone laces.

Mrs. Floyer has written so well, and given us so much practical information on plain needlework, that I feel it unnecessary to enter at any length into the principles of plain sewing, as my theme is needlework as decorative art.

Mrs. Floyer has, as it were, unpicked and unravelled every stitch in plain work, till she has discovered and laid bare its intention, its construction, and effect. She, has also given us rules made clear to the dullest understanding, instructing us how to teach the young and ignorant. She shows us the quickest and most perfect way of working different materials for different purposes, and tells us how to select them. I will, therefore, refer my readers to her most useful and instructive books,[321] and pass on at once from the craft of plain needlework, to stitches as the art of embroidery.

The link between plain and decorative work deserves [200]attention. This link is "white embroidery." I imagine it was not a very ancient form of the art, and was practised first in mediæval days; when we begin to have constant notices of it. The first white laces appear to have followed close upon the first white embroideries.

There is a tomb of the fourteenth century in the Church of the Ara Cœli at Rome, where the effigy of a knight lies on his bed, draped with a sheet and a coverlet, both embroidered. These are evidently of linen worked in white.[322] I give a drawing of them in illustration (pl. 39).

From that date we find continually mention of such work by nuns and ladies.[323]In England it was especially called "nuns' work" (plate 42). There is a great survival of this stitchery in Italy amongst the peasantry. They have always adorned their smocks and aprons, and their linen head-coverings, and the borders of sheets for great occasions, with patterns in "flat stitches," "cut stitches," and "drawn work." The Greek peasants do the same. In Germany will be found much curious white embroidery, of designs which show their antiquity; and from Spain we get "Spanish work" in black, on white linen, which is nearly allied to the stitches of white work.

Pl. 39.

See larger image
Embroidery imitated in marble on the tomb of a knight, in the Church of the Ara Cœli, Rome.

Lord Arundel of Wardour possesses a linen cover for a tabernacle (or else it is a processional cloak) which is of the purest Hispano-Moorish design, and unrivalled in [201]beauty. It is embroidered in Spanish stitches in white thread, on the finest linen, and is intersected with fine lace insertion (pl. 40). It is said to have been found in the time of Elizabeth with some other articles in a dry well; among them a little satin shoe, of which the shape proves its date to be of the end of Henry VIII.'s reign. Russian embroidery, consisting of geometrical patterns in red, blue, and black thread, is of this class.

Pl. 40.

See larger image
Processional Cloak, time of Henry VIII., belonging to Lord Arundel of Wardour.

In England alone, the peasantry do no white work for home use, and we must suppose it has never been a domestic occupation. Indeed, the love of the needle is by no means an English national tendency, in the lower classes. Nothing but the plainest work is taught in our schools. Anything approaching to decorative art, with us, has been the accomplishment of educated women, and not the employment of leisure moments in the houses of the poor.

Semper, in "Der Stil,"[324] gives rules for white embroidery, and the reasons from which he deduces them are good. He says, that allowing it as a maxim that each textile has its own uses and its own beauties, we should place nothing on linen which would militate against its inherent qualities and merits; and that, as the great beauty of flax is its smoothness and purity, all projections and roughnesses should be avoided which would catch dust or throw a shadow. Carrying out this idea, it would appear that satin, and not lace stitches are therefore, the most suitable for this kind of decoration. The accepted rule for selecting the stitch for each piece of work is this: on stout grounds the thread should be round and rich, whereas delicate materials carry best the most refined and shining thread work; and in embroidering the smooth surface of linen fabrics, the flattest stitches are the most appropriate.

[202]

Part 3.
OPUS PHRYGIUM (*or gold work*).

Gold embroideries were by the Romans attributed to the Phrygians. All gold work was vaguely supposed to be theirs, as all other embroidery was included in the craft of the Plumarii in Rome.

It has been disputed whether needlework in gold preceded the weaving of flat gold or thread into stuffs, or whether it was an after-thought, and an enrichment of such textiles. I imagine that the embroidery was the first, and that the after-thought was the art of weaving gold. Babylonian embroideries appear to be of gold wire, as we see them in the Ninevite marbles.

An instance of the way golden embroideries were displayed among the Greeks is that of the Athenian peplos, which, as I have already said (p. 32), was worked by embroideresses under the superintendence of two Arrhephoræ of noble birth. It was either scarlet or saffron colour, and blazed with golden representations of the battles of the giants, or local myths and events in the history of Athens.[325]

The art of the Phrygians, who gave their name in Rome to all golden thread-work, has come down to us through the classic "auriphrygium" and the "orphreys" of the Middle Ages. Semper thinks that the flat gold embroidery was the first invented.[326]

The Phrygians had attained to the utmost perfection in tissue ornament when the Romans conquered them, and finding their art congenial to the growing luxury of Rome, they imported and domesticated it; both the people and their work retaining their national designation. Pliny, ignorant of the claims of the Chinese, gave to [203]the Phrygians the credit of being the inventors of all embroidery.[327] The garments they thus decorated were called "phrygionæ," and the work itself "opus Phrygium." The term "auriphrygium," at first given to work in gold only, was in time applied to all embroidery that admitted gold into its composition; and hence the English mediæval term, "orphreys."

All the gold stitches now called "passing" came from Phrygia; Semper attributes all the "mosaic stitches" to the Phrygians, calling them "opus Phrygionium."[328] Gold stitches are splendidly exemplified in the embroidered mantle of St. Stephen, of the ninth century. The only somewhat earlier piece of mediæval gold embroidery with which I am acquainted is the dalmatic of Charlemagne in the Vatican, richly embroidered in fine gold thread; and the mantle of the Emperor Henry II. in the Museum at Munich, worked by his Empress Kunigunda, who appears to have been somewhat parsimonious in her use of the precious material.

Almost all ecclesiastical and royal ancient embroideries were illuminated with golden grounds—golden outlines or golden flat embroideries. Later still, raised gold thread work has imitated gilt carvings or goldsmiths' jewellery; and we feel that it was at once removed from its place as embroidery, and became an elaborate imitation of what [204]should belong to another craft.[329] Such deviations from the proper office and motive of needlework are so dangerously near to bad style and bad taste, that they always and inevitably have fallen into disrepute.

Part 4.
OPUS PULVINARIUM (*or cushion work*).

This "opus pulvinarium" is not only to be found in Oriental work, but it has also survived in a very few fragments from Egypt.[330] One of these, in the British Museum, is worked on canvas, in wool and flax; another in a white shining thread, resembling asbestos, on linen or fine canvas. They are regular "canvas" or "cross" stitches, and therefore, under mediæval nomenclature, would be classed as "opus pulvinarium." This name must include all stitches in gold, silk, and wool, whether Phrygian, Egyptian, or Babylonian in their origin, excepting the flat and lace stitches (plate 41).

Pl. 41.

See larger image
MOSAIC STITCHES.
1. Italian Pattern, sixteenth century. From Frida Lipperheide's Musterbuch. 2. Scandinavian. Bock, i. taf. xi. 3. Egyptian. From Auberville's "Tissus," p. 1.

Semper's term, "mosaic" stitches, is a good one, as it covers all that are relegated into patterns in small square spaces, counted by the threads of the textile on which they are laid.[331] He believes that the mosaic patterns and [205]cross stitches in needlework preceded the tesselated pavements, and formed their first motive, though the stitch now refers itself back to the mosaic, at least in name.

It is remarkable that in Chaldea and Assyria there still exist some ruined walls, which are adorned with pilasters, panels, and other architectural forms, covered with some sort of encaustic, imitating textile patterns.[332] The effect is produced by means of a kind of mosaic work of small nails or wedges of baked clay, with china or glazed coloured heads. These are inlaid into the unbaked clay or earth, of which the walls are constructed, and while binding it together, give the effect of the surface being hung with a material which has a pattern worked all over in cross stitch.

The Chinese, the Chaldeans, and the Assyrians long continued to show in their buildings the tradition of this style of decoration. In Egypt there has been found some unfinished mural painting where the plaster has been previously prepared by dividing it into small rectangular spaces, apparently on the principle of the canvas ground for cross stitches.

The name "mosaic" stitch does not interfere with, or militate against the classical appellation of *opus pulvinarium*, which means "shrine work" or "cushion stitches." These appear to have been from the first considered as the best suited for adorning cushions, chairs, footstools, and the beds on which men reclined at their feasts, as they are firmly-set stitches which will stand friction.

[206]Most of the work now done in Syria, Turkey, Greece, and the Principalities, shows different forms of the mosaic stitches; so also does the national Russian work, which is Byzantine. All these designs are conventional and mostly geometrical.

This work, in the East, is generally the same on both sides. We may infer that the spoil anticipated by Sisera's mother, "the garments embroidered on both sides, fit for the necks of those who divide the spoil," was of this kind.

Thus we see that the "opus pulvinarium" has a very respectable ancestry; and though it had somewhat degenerated in the early part of our century, and had languished and almost died out under the name of Berlin wool work, yet it has done good service through the days of mediæval art down to the present time, both in England and throughout Europe (pl. 42); and it will probably revive and continue to be generally used.

Though the least available for historical or pictorial work, and not by any means the best for flower-pieces (as the squareness of the stitches refuses to lend itself to flowing lines or gradations of colour, unless the stitches are extremely fine, and the work, in consequence, very laborious), yet it finds its especial fitness in all geometrical designs. It is also particularly well suited to heraldic subjects.

A remarkable example of the use of cross stitches exists in the borders of the Syon cope, in which the coats-of-arms are so executed. This is of the thirteenth century; and besides these cushion stitches, it exhibits all those which are grouped in the style called opus Anglicum or Anglicanum.

Pl. 42.

See larger image
Italian "Nun's Work," from a pyx cloth, sixteenth century.

Many charming designs for this kind of stitch may be found in the old German pattern-books of the Renaissance [207](Spitzen Musterbücher), and also in those Venetian "Corone di Vertuose Donne" lately reprinted by the Venetian publisher Organia. These are worthy of a place in every library of art.

It would seem best to place the chain stitch named "tambour" in this class, as it naturally assimilates with the plaited and cross stitches. It is so called from the drum-shaped frame of the last century in which it was usually worked.

Part 5.
OPUS PLUMARIUM (*or plumage work*).

The "Opus Plumarium" is one of the most ancient groups, and includes all flat stitches, of which the distinguishing mark is, that they *pass* each other, overlap, and blend together. "Stem," "twist," "Japanese stitch," and "long and short" or "embroidery stitch," belong to this class, to which I propose to restore its original title of plumage work.

The origin of the name is much disputed, but it is supposed to have pointed to a decoration of plumage work, and we find that feathers have been an element in artistic design from the earliest times. There were patterns in Egyptian painting which certainly had feathers for their motive (fig. 21, p. 208).

Semper, finding that birds'-skins were a recognized article for trade in China, 2205 B.C.,[333] believes that they were used as onlaid application for architectural decoration; and this is possible, for we still obtain from thence specimens of work in different materials partly onlaid in [208]whole feathers, whereas sometimes the longer threads of the feathers are woven by the needle into the ground web. In Her Majesty's collection there are some specimens from Burmah—creatures resembling sphinxes or deformed cherubim, executed in feathers, applied on silk and outlined in gold. We have likewise from Burmah, in the Indian Museum, two peacocks[334] similarly worked; the legs and beaks are solidly raised in gold thread; and the outlines also are raised in gold, giving the appearance of enamelling. The *cloisonné* effect of brilliant colours, contrasted and enhanced by the separation of the gold outlines, can be seen to perfection in specimens of the beautiful Pekin jewellers' work, where the feathers are inlaid in gold ornaments for the head and in the handles of fans. Nothing but gems can be more resplendent.

Fig. 21.
Feather patterns, Egyptian.

These survivals help us to understand the casual mention we find in classical authors, of the works of the Plumarii, which appellation was given at last to all embroiderers who were not Phrygians.[335]

[209]We have other glimpses of Oriental feather-work in different parts of India.[336]

The use of feathers is common in the islands of the Pacific. It is native to the Sandwich islanders; and M. Jules Remy describes the Hawaiian royal mantle, which was being constructed of yellow birds' feathers through seven consecutive reigns, and was valued in Hawaii at 5,000,000 francs. A mantle of this description is the property of Lady Brassey.

In Africa, ancient Egyptian art furnishes us with traditional feather patterns and head-dresses; and Pigafetta tells us of costumes of birds' skins, worn in the kingdom of Congo in the sixteenth century for their warmth; sea-birds' feathers being highly esteemed.[337]

In America, where birds are most splendid, the art of the feather worker was carried to the greatest perfection. It was found there by the Spaniards, and recorded in all their writings for its beauty of design and execution, and for its great value, equal to that of gold and precious stones.

Though now looked down upon, as being a semi-barbarous style of decoration, because it exists no longer except in semi-barbarous countries, we must consider [210]feather work as a relic of a past higher civilization which has died out, rather than simply as the effort of the savage to deck himself in the brightest colours attainable.

Feather-work is a lost art, but the name of "opus plumarium" remains, and proves that it was still recognized as such in the days of Roman luxury. The name survived when the practice was all but forgotten in Europe,[338] and the art itself disused, probably, because the birds of our continent rarely have any lovely plumage to tempt the eye.

But the glory of feather-work was found again in Mexico and Peru, and the surrounding nations, in the sixteenth century—praised, exalted, demoralized, and crushed out by the cruelties of conquest. The Spaniards at first brought home beautiful garments and hangings, representing gods and heroes, all worked in feathers.[339] Under their rule the natives produced pictures agreeable to the taste of their masters. Pope Sixtus V. accepted a head of St. Francis, which had been executed by one of the ablest of the "amantecas" (the name for an artist in feathers). Sixtus was struck with surprise and admiration at the beauty and artistic cleverness of the work, and, until he had touched and examined it closely, would not believe that plumage was the only material used.

There are beautiful hangings and bed furniture at Moritzburg, near Dresden, said to have belonged to Montezuma. They were given to Augustus the Strong, King of Poland, by a king of Spain.

In the seventeenth century, and later, feather work was still an art in Mexico, the convents continuing to preserve its traditions. Bustamente says that this industry was still in operation in the beginning of our [211]century. The Mexican Museum preserves specimens of the last three hundred years, from the time of the conquest of Mexico.

There is in the Cluny Museum, in Paris, a beautiful triptych, evidently of the sixteenth century. It is worked in feathers, with delicate outlines in fine gold thread. Nothing can exceed the tenderness and harmony of the colouring in shades of blue, and warm and cool brown tints. This is probably a survival of that lost art of Mexico which was carried on in their convents, and may have been a copy of a treasured relic of European art.

Among the few noteworthy specimens that have survived, is the mitre of St. Carlo Borromeo at Milan, described by M. F. Denis as being both artistic and beautiful. He tells us in his Appendix that even now, a tissue of feathers is woven in France, as soft and flexible as a silk damask; and rivalling the Mexican scarlet feather fabric, which the Spaniards admired so greatly. He also speaks of the inlaid feather work, invented by M. Le Normant of Rouen, in the last century, and afterwards continued in Paris by his English pupil, Mr. Levet, who sold two of his works to the then Duke of Leeds, in 1735. The first is a vase of flowers, the second a peacock, designed by M. Oudry (peintre du Roi). Both of these, framed as screens, are now at Hornby Castle.

Unfortunately feathers are, by their nature, most attractive to that greatest destroyer, next to Attila—the moth. Ghirlandajo called mosaic in marble and glass, "painting for eternity;" we may call feather work, "painting for a day."

From the essays of M. Ferdinand Denis,[340] much may be learned of the *arte plumaria* of the Mexicans and their neighbours of Brazil, Guatemala, Peru, and Yucatan, [212]and the land of the Zapotecas, &c., where it was also cultivated. He says that their civilization is so mysterious that we have as yet no means of judging whence came their art.

Fergusson suggests the similarity between Central Asian and Central American art, both in architectural forms and plastic and sculptured remains. He thinks that its tradition was transmitted from Asia to America in the third and fourth centuries of our era. If so, it was an unlucky moment for the recipients, as the art of Asia, as well as that of Europe, was then at its lowest and most debased phase; perhaps, however, the more fit for the fertilization of that of a perfectly barbarous people. There is something fascinating in the suggestions on this subject in Mr. Donelly's "Atlantis;" but when conjecture is only founded on tradition, and without proof, we must not take it into serious consideration.

Having proved the universal use of feathers, it is not difficult to appreciate the causes which suggested everywhere the transfer of this decorative art to another craft, employing less perishable materials. Embroidery probably followed it closely and absorbed it throughout Asia and in Egypt; and the survivals now are only an accidental specimen, a tradition, and a name.[341]

The name "Plumarii," for the embroideries, is thus fully accounted for, and we need seek no further elucidation. [213]It was commonly used in classical Roman times. "Opus plumarium" seems to have become the legitimate term for all needlework. The Plumarii were the embroiderers, whether their work was in wool, or thread, or in silk (at a later period),[342] with or without admixture of gold or silver (as the Argentarii were the jewellers).

The article on the word "plumarius" in Hoffman's Lexicon,[343] after describing two kinds of Plumarii, Phrygians and Babylonians, proceeds to say, "These latter, who wove garments and hangings of various colours, were called 'Plumarii;' but though this name was at first confined to craftsmen who wove patterns in the shape of feathers, in course of time the name was extended to those artists who, with the needle or by painting, embellished robes."[344]

The "opus plumarium" included, as I before said, all flat stitches; and I repeat that "feather application" was certainly its first motive; and next came the stitches that conveyed the same desired effect, though a new material was employed, fitted for the needle, which, having served its apprenticeship in "plain work," now came to the front as a decorative agent.

Painting with the needle began with an attempt to model with it; the lay of stitches being so arranged as to [214]give the whole effect of light and shadow, so as to delineate the forms without changing the shades of the material used. I give on the opposite page some Japanese birds, which will explain what I mean. The stitches are so intelligently placed as absolutely to give the forms of the birds imitated. They represent plumage, and a more artistic representation cannot be imagined. (Pl. 43.)

The same stitch which we find prevailing in China and Japan as plumage work, is employed in embroidering flowers. Here satin, stem, and plumage stitches are blended together, and excellent decorative effects are produced; but the texture of flowers is not to be imitated, as is that of the plumage of birds. "Satin" stitch is a more restricted form of plumage stitch; and "stem" is another variety of these flat stitches, very useful in its place. I therefore have assigned the name of "plumage stitch" to that hitherto called "embroidery" or "long and short" stitches; and I give the term "plumage work" to include all the "flat" stitches.

Practically, it is allowed that these flat stitches, especially the plumage stitch, give most scope for freedom in needlework, as they are laid on at once, and according to the inspiration of the worker, and may cover the outline and efface it. The stitches are not counted, and have more of the nature of touch than any others, as their length, thickness, and closeness may be varied at will. The artist's design thus admits of interpretation according to the taste and feeling of the needlewoman.

Pl. 43.

See larger image
Japanese Opus Plumarium.
Part 6.
OPUS CONSUTUM (*or cut work*).

This is "Patchwork," or "Appliqué" ("inlaid" and [215]"onlaid"). Vasari calls it "Di commesso," and says that Botticelli invented it for the use of Church banners, as being much more effective than any other style of work, or even than painting, as the outlines remained firm (non si stinguano), and were not affected by the weather (as in painted cloths) and were visible on both sides of the banner. Botticelli drew with his own hand the baldachino of Or San Michele, and the embroideries on a frieze carried in procession by the monks of Santa Maria Novella; he died 1515. Perhaps he may have revived the art of application in his own day.

There are, however, much earlier examples of patchwork, of which the first and most remarkable is the Egyptian funeral tent of Queen Isi-em-Kheb, mother-in-law of Shishak, who besieged and took Jerusalem three or four years after the death of Solomon, B.C. 980. It may be described as a mosaic, or patchwork of prodigious size, made of thousands of pieces of gazelles' skins, dyed, and neatly sewn together with threads of colour to match, resembling the stitching of a glove, the outer edges bound with a cord of twisted pink leather, sewn on with stout pink thread (pl. 44). The colours are described as being wonderfully preserved, when it is remembered that they are nearly as old as the Trojan War; though perhaps their preservation is less surprising than that the flowers wreathed about several royal mummies of the same period should have shown their colours and forms when the cases were first opened, so as to be recognized as blue larkspur, yellow mimosa, and a red Abyssinian flower, massed closely together on the foundation of a strong leaf cut in zigzags. Among the flowers lay a dead wasp, whose worthless little form and identity were as perfectly preserved as those of the mighty monarch on whose bosom it had completed its short existence. The tent itself consists of a centre or flat top, divided down the [216]middle, and covered over one half with pink and yellow rosettes on a blue ground; on the other half are six large vultures, each surrounded with a hieroglyphic text which is really an epitaph. The side flaps are adorned first with some narrow bands of colour; then with a fringe pattern; then with a row of broad panels, red, green, and yellow, with a device or picture and inscription in the two other colours; on this border there are kneeling gazelles, each with a pink Abyssinian lotus blossom hanging to its collar. The rest of the side flaps and the whole of the front and back flaps are composed of large squares, alternately pink and green. This, for its antiquity, its style, its stitchery, materials, and colours, is a most interesting work of early art, and an example of the perfection to which it had attained. It is remarkable how much variety of effect has been produced with only four colours, by the artistic manner of placing and contrasting them. To our more advanced taste, however, the whole effect of the contrasting colours is inharmonious and gaudy, though certainly striking and typical.[345]

Another piece of Egyptian application, from the Museum at Turin, is a pretty leaf pattern cut out in red stuff, laid on a white ground, and worked down with a darker outline of the same colour.[346]

Fig. 22.
Piece of appliqué in red stuff and red outlines from Egypt.

Pl. 44.

See larger image
Funeral Tent of Isi-em-Kheb. From Villiers Stuart's "Funeral Tent of an Egyptian Queen."

We have an instance of ancient "application" of about [217]600 years later, Greek in its beauty of design and execution. Alas! we can only ascertain, from tattered fragments taken out of a tomb in the Crimea, that it was parsemé with figures on horseback or in chariots. The border is very beautiful. Compare the fragments of which we have obtained a copy with the mantle of Demeter, from a Greek vase, and you will perceive how the styles correspond (Pl. 16, Fig. 23). The ground material is of the finest woven wool, of a deep violet or purple colour, enriched with application of another fine woollen fabric of a most brilliant green, worked down, outlined and embroidered in white, black, and gold-coloured wool, apparently in stem stitches.[347] The accompanying illustration gives the effect and general design of the outer border only, in which the applied leaf is worked down in red, gold, and white.

It is much to be regretted that the centre of the mantle is so tattered and discoloured that it is impossible to do more than ascertain that the design that is embroidered on it consists of figures on horseback or in chariots, in spirited attitudes. The second and broader border is to be found (pl. 17).

Fig. 23.
Narrow border of a Greek mantle.

"Opus consutum" cannot in any sense perhaps be the name of a stitch or stitches. But it applies to a peculiar [218]style of embroidery employing certain stitches. It is the term given to all work cut out of plain or embroidered materials, and applied by "working down" to another material as grounding. It includes all raised and stuffed application in silk, woollen, and metal thread work. It has been given to all work in which the scissors are active agents, whether in cutting out the outlines or in incising the pattern, as in much of the linen and muslin embroideries of our day, now called "Madeira work," of which a great deal was made in the first part of the century by English ladies who designed and collected patterns from each other, and gave the produce of their industry as gifts to their friends for collars, cuffs, and trimmings.[348]

"Cut work" is named by Chaucer, and is constantly to be found in inventories from his time to the beginning of the last century. At Coire, in the Grisons, is a very beautiful chasuble, of which the orphrey is of the school of the elder Holbein or Lucas Cranach, applied and raised so as to form a high relief. The figures are covered with satin and embroidered. The chasuble itself is of fine Saracenic silk, woven with golden inscriptions in broad stripes. The colours are brown, crimson, and gold.

See larger image

Wall Pilasters
Appliqué Cut-work, Italian XVI. Cent^{ry}
Property of Countess Somers

In the later Middle Ages, a good deal of this work was executed in Germany for wall hangings; figures were cut out in different materials, and embroidered down and finished by putting in the details in various stitches. As art they are generally a failure, being more gaudy than beautiful. This, however, is not necessarily the case, for there is at the Hotel Cluny a complete suite of hangings of the time of Francis the First, partly applied [219]and partly embroidered, which are beautiful in design and colouring, especially the fruit and trophies in the borders.

In the sixteenth and seventeenth centuries cut work was much employed in Italy for large flowered arabesque designs, commonly in velvet or silk, making columnar wall hangings, which are often very effective; giving the rooms an architectural decoration, without interfering with the arrangement of works of art, pictures, statues and cabinets, placed in front of them. Besides, it was supposed that the utmost effect of richness was thus accomplished with the least labour, and very large spaces and very high walls covered, without losing anything of beauty by distance, as must be the case when the work's highest merit is in the delicacy of the stitches and the details of form. (Pl. 45.)

The Earl of Beauchamp has inherited a most beautiful suite of hangings of "appliqué work;" silks of many kinds are laid on a white brocade ground with every possible variety of stitch, forming richly and gracefully designed patterns; and showing to what cut work can aspire.

A great deal of "opus consutum" has been done in the School of Art Needlework, in the way of restoration of old embroideries. Here may be seen copies of different models of many periods; amongst other British specimens, part of a bed at Drumlanrig, in which James I. slept. In this work the application is cut out, raised and stuffed, and "couched" with cords, and the whole thing is as stiff, strong, conventional, and enduring as if it were a piece of upholstery that was carpentered yesterday, instead of being needlework of at least 250 years ago.

One of the most remarkable large works of this style that exists was shown in 1881, at the South Kensington Museum, during the Spanish Exhibition.[349] It was of the [220]kind called "on the stamp." This was a landscape seen between columns wreathed with flowers and creepers. In the foreground couched a stag, the size of life—a wonderful reproduction of the hide of the creature in stitches. The relief is so high that the columns appear to be circular by the shadows they throw; and the stag is stuffed so as to be raised about six inches. The work is superb, and causes pleasure as well as wonder; and yet, in spite of the beauty of the design, and the richness of the materials—gold, silver, silk, and wool profusely used—it is a divergence from the legitimate art of embroidery, and is simply the attempt of the needlewoman to combine again the arts of sculpture and painting with the help of so inadequate an implement as the needle. Therefore, except as being a marvellous and beautiful curiosity, it is a failure; it is not art.[350]

Practically, cut work is the best mode of arriving at splendid effects by uniting rich and varied tissues.[351] The Italian curiosity vendors know this well, and often cut up the remnants and rags of rich stuffs, old faded silks, and scraps of gold and silver tissues, and with them copy fine old designs, and sell them as authentic specimens of such and such a date.

I was once requested to give an opinion as to the date of a curtain border bought in Italy, and on consideration I gave the following verdict: "The design is of the sixteenth century; the applied velvet and [221]gold cord, of the seventeenth century; the brocaded silk ground, eighteenth century; the thread with which the whole was worked—machine-made silk thread (English)—middle of nineteenth century." The whole effect was excellent, and very antique.

This art of "application" is the distinctive part of the "opus consutum," and it is the best and most economical method for restoration of old embroideries, of which the grounding material is generally worn out long before the stitches laid upon it. Much beautiful work has thus been rescued from annihilation, and restored to use from its long imprisonment in the boxes and drawers of the garret and store-room. But it is cruel to transfer historical or typical works, and so puzzle the artist and the historian.

It is so troublesome to embroider on velvet or plush, or gold tissues, that application is the easiest and most effective mode of dealing with these fabrics.[352] The outlines laid down in cord have the best effect, while binding the edges and securing them from fraying, and it is almost certain that the eye receives most pleasure, in flat art, from a defined outline, which satisfies it; where there are no cast shadows, it lifts the work from the background, and separating the colours, it enhances their beauty. It would appear, however, as a rule, that either black or gold metal should invariably be employed, because they do not interfere with any colour they approach. White is distracting and aggressive. The Greeks sometimes used gold colour instead of gold, as we see in the mantle from the Crimea already referred to; but this is not nearly so agreeable to the eye as pure gold.

[222]A great deal of modern "opus consutum," or application cut work, has been done in Constantinople of late years. The designs in general, are not artistic; nor are the colouring and materials very commendable. The onlaid material is, in general, sewn down with chain stitches, and cut out afterwards.

Part 7.
LACE.—OPUS FILATORIUM OR ARANEUM.

Mrs. Palliser says that from the earliest times the art of lace-making has been so mixed up with that of needlework, that it is impossible to enter upon the one without naming the other. This is, in fact, what she has done, showing the intimate connection between the two in her charming work on lace, where much information about embroideries in general, may be found in the introduction.[353]

M. Blanc also considers that there is but a slight transition between embroidery and guipure, which he says was the first lace.[354] As all the earliest specimens and designs for guipure were Venetian, the art was, therefore, probably an Italian invention, though an Oriental origin has sometimes been attributed to it. The objection to this last theory is that we find no ancient specimens, and no modern continuation of such work in the East.

The word "guipure" is a stumbling-block. It has been applied to many forms in the varying art of [223]lace-making; which same variableness has caused its nomenclature to assume the terms belonging to other textile arts where they approach or touch each other, (as in netting, fringes, or embroideries). The nearest approach to laces before the thirteenth century was more in the nature of what we now call guimp.[355]

Embroidery differs from lace, in that it is worked on already woven tissues; whereas lace is manufactured at once, both ground and design.[356] But the link between the two is not missing.

In the twelfth century they worked "opus filatorium," which consisted of embroidery with the needle on linen, of which half the threads had been drawn out, and the remainder were worked into a net by knotting them into groups, then dividing, and knotting them again. [224][357] There is a piece of work described in an old catalogue quoted by Rock. "St. Paul's, London, had a cushion covered with knotted thread: Pulvinar copertum de albo filo nodato." Here lace and embroidery touch each other.[358] Sir Gardiner Wilkinson notices some early Egyptian work in the Louvre as "a piece of white network pattern, each mesh containing an irregular cubic figure." This sounds much like lace-work.

It may be fairly asserted that the term "embroidery" embraces the craft of lace-making, as almost all ancient and much modern lace is simple embroidery, and formed entirely by the needle.

Some kinds of lace, however, are made by plaiting and twisting the threads attached to bobbins round pins which are previously arranged in the holes of a pattern, pricked on parchment or glazed paper.[359] The original motive and idea of lace is a net. The patterns called by the ancients "de fundata," are netted designs meshed. You will see them constantly in Egyptian and Greek art, both in wall painting and textile decoration. Homer [225]speaks of golden cauls, and so does Isaiah,[360] as adorning women's heads. They also mention nets of flax.

The capitals of the brazen columns adorned with "nets of chequer work" in Solomon's Temple are very curious.[361] And the author of "Letters from Italy, 1776," tells of the garment of a statue at Portici, edged with a border resembling fine netting. Egyptian robes of state appear to have been sometimes trimmed with an edging of a texture between lace and fringe.[362]

Lace has been made of many materials in many ways. We may instance "passementerie," made with bobbins (bone lace), with or without pins, or with the needle only, by hand. The materials have been gold, silver, silk, thread (these two last white or coloured), the fibres of plants, and human hair.[363] A lace called "yak" is made of wool or hair.

Bone laces in gold and silver, or the two mixed and interchanged, are continually mentioned in the inventories of the fifteenth, sixteenth, and seventeenth centuries. Bed hangings, chair and cushion covers, and table cloths were constantly trimmed with gold and silver bone lace, and fringes of the same.[364] Laces in coloured silks were [226]made in Spain and the Balearic Isles late in the last century.[365]

In 1542, a sumptuary law was passed in Venice, forbidding the metal laces embroidered in silk to be wider than "due dita," i.e. about two inches. This paternal interference in the details of life is truly Venetian. It was intended to "protect the nobles and citizens from injuring themselves and setting a bad example."

Perhaps this strict rule was relaxed in favour of crowned heads and royal personages; for there is at Ashridge, among the relics of Queen Elizabeth's enforced visit, a toilet-cover of red and gold striped silk, with a trimming of lace, four inches broad, of Venice gold and silver lace embroidered in coloured silk. Specimens of these laces are rare, owing to the intrinsic value of the metal. We must suppose the origin of these golden trimmings to belong to a very early period. A piece of gold wire lace guimp was lately found in a tomb near Wareham, and is supposed, with reason, to be Scandinavian.[366]

M. Blanc describes lace as a "treillage" or network, and says it is made in three ways. You may complete the ground first, and then work the pattern with the needle. This he calls lace "pure et simple;" and he considers that it differs from guipure in that the latter consists of flowers and arabesques worked separately, and then connected with bars, lines, or meshes. This guipure is the second mode of lace-making.[367] The third is by machinery; but this has the inherent defect of all machine-made fabrics, to a practised eye; i.e. a certain rigidity and coldness in the exactly repeated forms, in which [227]the human touch is wanting. It is curious how in art, even a "pentimento" is valuable, recalling the hand that erred as well as created; the attention that strayed, or reconsidered the design.[368]

M. Blanc, speaking of the beauty of point d'Alençon, praises it especially as being entirely needlework. He names the different modes of lace-making, and judges their merits. Of needle-made lace he says: "And the value of this lace not only arises from its representing a considerable amount of labour, but also because nothing can replace in human estimation the fabrics produced by a man's, and still less by a woman's handicraft. However the hand may have been restrained by the necessity of faithfully following, on green parchment, the designs imagined and traced by another person, there is always, even in copying an outline, an individuality, an imperceptible deviation to the right or to the left, above or below the tracing, which impresses on the design the accent of strength or weakness, of indecision or determination."[369] I would add, of intelligence or stupidity; of knowledge or ignorance.

This is not the first time, and will certainly not be the last, that I shall have sought to impress on the needlewoman the fact that her individuality cannot fail to be strongly marked in her work; and I would urge her to carry out the suggestions that her experience and her taste afford [228]her, while seeking to render faithfully the original motive of the designer. In lace-making, as in all art, the interest and the life, as it were, is imparted to each specimen by the attention and thought bestowed upon it.

Mrs. Palliser shows us, by her beautiful illustrations, how much variety may be given to designs for lace-making, which have changed with each period of contemporary art, and are markedly distinctive of their nationalities.

Mr. A. Cole's lectures on lace, his volume of photographs, and M. Seguin's valuable work, are full of information.

M. Urbani de Gheltof's "Technical History of Venetian Laces," translated into English by Lady Layard, is a beautiful little book and a worthy imitation of the ancient lace-books of the sixteenth and seventeenth centuries.[370]

The subject has been so thoroughly discussed by adepts in connection with its revival as a local industry in its original cradle, that I will confine myself to a few observations on its history and its place in decorative art.

Fringes, Knotting, Netting, Knitting, Crochet, Tatting, and Lace-making, are all parts of the same branch of ornamental needlework. They are all "trimmings," in the sense of being decorative edges to more solid materials. They are not available as coverings for warmth or decency; but they serve to give the grace of mystery to the object they drape or veil. They soften the outlines and the colours beneath them, while they permit them to peep through their meshes. They are hardly to be included in what is called high art, having more affinity with grace, refinement and coquetry, than with æsthetic culture or noble thought.

[229]This tendency in lace work may be the reason that the masculine mind does not, in general, appreciate these lovely textures, but rather despises them (even when the designs are beautiful and ingenious), as being flimsy and deficient in honest intention; whereas women have always greatly prized them for their delicacy and refinement, and their great value, on account of the time, trouble, and eyesight expended upon them. Their knowledge of stitches also enables them to appreciate their variety, and the taste shown in their selection and arrangement for carrying out each design.

Lace stitches are almost innumerable.[371] Upwards of a hundred are named, and their variations are endless. But a volume would not suffice us for entering into the details of the craft; many of its stitches have been imported into embroideries in gold, silk, and crewels; and such adaptations are always allowable, provided the effect is good.

We have every reason to believe that the claims of Venice as the first and original school of lace-making have been satisfactorily proved.[372] Genoa, Florence, Milan, especially the last,[373] followed suit. Germany, France,[374] [230]and Spain soon started their schools; but Lady Layard believes that Spain received all her inspiration and the greater part of her laces from Venice, which likewise sent teachers to France and to Brussels—or rather, we may say, had many first-class workwomen decoyed from her manufactories to assist in starting rival industries in other countries.[375]

The first pattern-books were printed in Venice in the sixteenth century; and these "Corone di belle e virtuose donne," as they are sometimes entitled,[376] were imitated in France and Germany.

Venice was proud of her industry, and of the noble ladies who fostered it. It is recorded in the "Virtù in Giocco of Giovanna Palazzi" that Giovanna Dandolo, or "la Dandola," (wife of the Doge Malapiero,) was the first patroness of Venice laces. She also fostered the art of printing in Venice, and is spoken of as a "principessa di gran' spirito, ne di private fortune," and her memory is cherished in connection with these proofs of her patriotism. We hear also that Morosin or Marosin, wife of the Doge Marin Grimani, patronized Venetian lace-making. Her forewoman, or *maestra*, was a certain Cattina Gardin, and through her the art was settled at Burano, where it has been so lately revived.

At the Cathedral of Burano, is kept in the sacristy, perhaps the finest existing piece of artistic lace of the sixteenth century. It contains many groups of figures from the history of our Lord, beautiful both in [231]design and execution, worked in "Punti Fogliami," and filled in with exquisite tracery. This was the border of an antipendium.

Mrs. Palliser laments the extinction of the art in Venice, and says that but one woman of the old craft had survived; but her elegy was premature, as that old woman, by name Cencia Scarpariola, has lived to see hundreds of girls at Burano reviving all the old traditions, having learnt from her the secrets of the "mestiere," or "mystery." Under the patronage of the Princess Margherita, now Queen of Italy, and with the active help and superintendence of Countess Adriana Marcello and Princess Giovanelli, most beautiful laces are now made in every old point, French and Flemish, as well as Venetian. Pezzi, merli, and merletti are executed in the different styles which include all lace-making, and of which we here give a list from M. de Gheltof's book:—

Net		lace.
Cut		lace.
Open		lace.
Flowered		lace.
Knotted		lace.
Darning	or square	netting.
Venice		point.
Burano		point.
Drawn		lace.[377]

Embroidered linen.[378]

The price of these laces is very high, but not beyond their value when we consider the vast amount of skilled labour bestowed on them. We are often told that old lace is cheaper than new, as an absurd fact, because the antiquity of lace is supposed to add to its value. Yes, but principally as an object of archæological interest; whereas that which is being made now is supporting by its daily wage the needlewoman and her family, and perhaps [232]providing for her old age; and as the strain on the eye is very heavy, many lace-workers early in life lose their sight, at least for all the purposes of their craft.[379] For these reasons we cannot say that the prices required for such luxurious trimmings are unreasonable. Zanon da Udine gives us an idea of how costly they were in old times. He says that Giuseppe Berardi, a lace merchant in Venice, made a profit of 75,000 francs on a commission for a set of lace bed-hangings for the wedding of Joseph II., Emperor of Germany, which proves the high prices paid for the new laces of their day.

Blond laces, which take their turn occasionally as fashionable trimmings, veils, and Spanish mantillas, are so called from their original Venetian name, "merletti biondi," pale laces. De Gheltof derives this appellation from the celebrated collar of Louis Quatorze, and fancies it was made of the fair hair of the workers; but this is only vague conjecture. The term was applied in the seventeenth century to laces in silk, gold, and silver—never to thread laces. I confess I do not find the reason for the name, but accept De Gheltof's information that it was given by the authority of the magistrates of Mercanzia in 1759.

This is but a very slight sketch of the history of lace. Venice being its birthplace, and likewise the busy scene [233]of its rehabilitation, I have lingered over its school, and left but little space for the discussion of those of Spain, Flanders, Belgium, and France. But these have been thoroughly investigated, and their individual merits are well appreciated, both as antique and modern dress decoration.

I have already said that the lace schools in France were instituted by Colbert, who placed one at Auxerre, under the especial care of his brother, the bishop of that city. Louis Quatorze made it one of his splendid caprices, and not only set the example, but forced the fashion into this luxurious and extravagant channel.

In Spain, lace was made to look its best by being worn stretched over the great hoops of the "Guard-Infante;" and the fashion spread all over Europe. The white laces, resembling carved ivory or those in gold and silver, which remind one of solid jewellers' work, when spread over the surface of these fortified outworks, guarding from all approach the persons of the Infantas of Spain, assume in the portraits by Velasquez, a dignity which is in keeping with their value. The splendid designs show brilliantly on a background of scarlet, rose colour, or black silk; and that which, hanging loosely, looks only tawdry and ragged, had a magnificent effect when thus displayed.

For ecclesiastical purposes, these grand solid laces seem most appropriate, being effective in large spaces, and easily seen at a distance, hanging over the edge of the altar, as a border to the linen cloths, or finishing the white alb of the officiating priest.

One cannot but agree with M. Blanc, who points out that each piece of lace had its intention, and that a fashionable ball-dress trimmed with the edging of an antique altar-cloth in loops, is in false taste, to say no worse of the misappropriation.

[234]Though we have had no schools of lace in England (unless we can call our imitative industries schools), we have samplers of the time of Queen Elizabeth, and down to the middle of the last century, showing that drawn lace and cut lace were regularly taught, probably as an accomplishment, by Italians. The laces of Devonshire and the Isle of Wight

(called Honiton) form a group totally distinct from those of Northamptonshire, Bedfordshire, and Oxfordshire, which last are very simple cushion bobbin-laces.

From the sixteenth century English ladies have, for their amusement, made cut laces. Still, we must confess we have no national style of lace, and the only enduring ones have been those of France and Belgium, which have always kept the lead since their establishment, though fluctuating in design with the varying fashions of each epoch. Perhaps the reason of their longevity is that they have followed always the taste of their day. That of our time being decidedly archæological, ancient patterns are now the most successful.

There is a kind of embroidery darned-work, called "Limerick lace," which is said to be only made in Ireland, and being partly machine-made, is not pure lace, and therefore little esteemed. Very fine thread laces have been produced at Irish work schools; but no commercial result has followed. Clever imitations of Venice point have come from Ireland lately, called "raised crochet." This is a novelty, and it is extremely fine and beautiful work.

Pl. 46.

See larger image
Egyptian "Gobelins," Woven and Embroidered.

The Exhibition of Irish Lace in London (June, 1883), shows how widespread have been the efforts of Irish ladies to employ the peculiar genius of the sister island for delicate work with the needle, which has always been shown in their beautiful embroideries on muslin and cambric. It appears that every kind of lace, except, [235]perhaps, Brussels point, has been made in Ireland within the last 180 years; but as in each case the effort was always that of one individual woman, the school fell away when she died.

The names of these ladies are now worthily recorded in the official catalogue of the exhibition, with photographs of the specimens produced under their superintendence and care. Perhaps a permanent industry may crown, however late, their exertions to help the women of Ireland.

Part 8.
TAPESTRY—OPUS PECTINEUM.

It is necessary to define precisely what is meant by the word "tapestry."[380] The term has been applied to all hangings, and so caused confusion between those that are embroidered with a design, on a plain or brocaded woven material, and those which are inwoven with the design from the first.[381] This latter was called in classical language, "opus pectineum," because it was woven with the help of a comb (the "slay"),[382] to push the threads tight between each row of stitches; and the individual stitches were put in with a sort of a needle, or by the fingers only, and laid on the warp. It was thus practised by the Egyptians, by the Persians, Indians, and Peruvians; and in Egypt was often finished by embroidery. (Pl. 46.) In Egyptian tombs we have evidence of their tapestry, from the mural paintings representing men and women weaving pictures [236]in upright looms. The comb which served to push the threads together after the stitches were laid in is sometimes found in the weaver's tomb.

We have, in the British Museum, pieces of "opus pectineum" from Saccarah, in Egypt; and also fragments from a Peruvian tomb, of barbarous design, but the weaving is equal to the Egyptian; and both resemble the Gobelins weaving of to-day. Whence came the craft of the Peruvians?

Tapestry is woven in two ways, by a high or by a low-warp loom (*haute-lisse* or *basse-lisse*), vertical or horizontal. The "slay" is the implement which is peculiar to the craft. I shall not enter into any description of the mode of working the looms, as this has been thoroughly well done by masters of the art.[383] But I would call attention to the Frontispiece, copied from a Greek vase, where Penelope is portrayed sitting by her *haute-lisse* frame. I also refer the reader to the illustration from the Rheims tapestries, in which a mediæval artist shows the Blessed Virgin weaving at one that is horizontal or "basse-lisse." (Pl. 47.)

Pl. 47.

See larger image
Portion of a Tapestry Hanging. Cathedral. Rheims. The Virgin weaves and embroiders at a *basse-lisse* frame.

For the best information I have been able to obtain regarding tapestry weaving, I must acknowledge my indebtedness to M. Albert Castel's "Bibliothèque des Merveilles."[384] He has given great care to the consideration of this subject, and has collected good evidences to prove his conclusions, which I willingly accept*en bloc*. Of course he has chiefly dealt with the French branch of the art, and with the Flemish, from which it immediately descends. He begins, however, by quoting Pliny, to prove the antiquity of weaving, and gives a verse of Martial's to this effect: "Thou owest this work to the [237]land of Memphis, where the slay of the Nile has vanquished the needle of Babylon."[385]

Homer makes Helen weave the story of the siege of Troy; this may have been partly embroidered; and there are some pieces of woven tapestry introduced most ingeniously into the web of a linen shirt or garment, of which the sleeve is in the Egyptian department of the British Museum, proving that figures were pictured by weaving quite as early as the date of Troy, and unmistakably finished with the needle (Plate 18); at any rate, as early as the days of Homer. Arachne's web was interwoven with figures. She and Minerva rivalled each other in ingenious design and perfect execution. The description of the beautiful hangings they wove, the glorious colours with their tenderly graduated tints, and the graceful borders, appear to be almost prophetic of the highest efforts of the looms of the Gobelins.[386][387] Arachne's [238]name is derived from the Hebrew word for weaving, "Arag."

It appears that the town now called Arras, but anciently Nomenticum, was always a centre of the trade of the weavers;[388] for Flavius Vopiscus, writing in A.D.282, says that thence came the Byrri—woven cloaks with hoods, which were much in vogue amongst all classes in the later Roman Empire. The craft of weaving, which flourished in the Flemish and other adjacent countries, seems to [239]have become native to that soil, and to have clung to it, surviving many historical cataclysms.[389]

Though in the fifth century the inhabitants of that country were transported wholesale to Germany by the Vandals, and among them those of the town of Arras, yet, thanks to the monasteries, there was a survival and a revival; the craftsmen grouping themselves round the religious houses. Specimens as models were brought from the East. Aster, Bishop of Amasis (a town in Asiatic Turkey), describes these Oriental hangings in one of his homilies. He says that animals and scenes from the Bible were woven on white grounds.[390]

Sidonius Apollinaris, Bishop of Clermont Ferrand,[391] says that some foreign tapestries are "pictured" with the summits of Ctesiphon and Nephates, "wild beasts running rapidly across void canvas, and also by a miracle of art, the Parthian of wild aspect with his head turned backwards." This might be a description of a Chinese composition, and probably it is so.[392]

Woven tapestry is also called "Arras,"[393] because that town in the Netherlands was the home and school of the art of picture weaving in the Middle Ages. It has been hitherto excluded from the domain of needlework, because of the different use of the needle employed in it. [240]It has always been woven on a loom, and is, in fact, embroidery combined with the weaving; for the shuttle, or slay, or comb completes each row of stitches. It belongs as much to our art as does tambour work, which is done with a hook instead of a needle. Tapestry weaving is the intelligent craft of a practised hand guided by artistic skill. The forms of the painted design must be copied by a person who can draw; and the colours require as much care in selection, as in painting with oils or water-colours. Such a thing as a purely mechanical exact copy is impossible in any art; and the difficulties are increased a hundredfold when it is a translation into another material, and another form of art. Besides, in this case, the copies are worked from the back, and the picture is reversed. The question is this: Can it be claimed as belonging to the same craft as embroidery? I answer in the affirmative, and I claim it.

"When the Saracens began to weave tapestry we cannot tell; but the workers in woven pictures were called Sarassins, and their craft, the 'opus Saracenicum.'"[394] The French and Flemish artisans who continued to weave in the old upright frames (*haute-lisse*) were, whether Christians or not, called "Sarassins." Probably they came through Spain, possibly from Sicily to Flanders and to France, or else from Byzantium. Viollet-le-Duc says that the "Saracinois" was a term applied to the makers of velvety carpets (*tapis veloutés*).[395] This is [241]possible.[396] Woven carpets of Oriental type were spreading themselves as articles of luxury through Europe early in the Middle Ages; and the Persian style of design was much the same then, when the first models were brought to Spain, and thence to Arras, as it is now in the carpets we buy just woven in Persia.[397] The oldest specimens known here have been exhibited in the Indian Museum, and may be of the thirteenth and fourteenth centuries. The perishable nature of the material makes us dependent on the sculptured records of all artistic design for our knowledge of carpets and hangings of more than a thousand years ago; and we must confess that we find nothing really resembling a Persian pattern in any classical tomb or sculpture of the Dark Ages.[398]

[242]I have allowed myself to touch upon carpet weaving, as it is germane to tapestry; though it is a branch that soon loses itself and leaves artistic work in the distance. Except the first design, it has become purely mechanical.

After what has been quoted from Ovid's "Metamorphoses," and bearing in mind the pictured webs described by Homer, and likewise the evidence of the frescoes in Egypt, and the woman weaving on the Greek fictile vase found at Chiusi, we may be justified in concluding that, like all other arts, that of tapestry existed in very early days, died out, and had to begin afresh, and gradually return to life, during the Middle Ages.

Bishop Gaudry, about 925, possessing a piece of tapestry with an inscription in Greek letters surrounded by lions "parsemé," was much put about till he obtained something to match it, to hang on the opposite side of his choir at Auxerre.[399] And it is known that the monks of St. Florent, at Saumur, wove tapestries about 985, and continued to do so for two centuries. St. Angelme of Norway,[400] Bishop of Auxerre, who died in 840, caused many tapestries to be executed for his church. At Poitiers this manufactory was so famous in the eleventh century, that foreign kings, princes, and prelates sought to obtain them, "even for Italy." The rules of their order of the monks of the Abbey of Cluny, dated 1009, were followed by those of St. Wast and of the Abbey of Fleury, and others in France, who all wove wool and silk for tapestries. Le Père Labbé, from whom much of this information is drawn and acknowledged by M. Charton (my authority), says that in 876, at Ponthièvre, in presence of the Emperor Charles [243]the Bold, the hall of the council-chamber was hung with pictured tapestries, and the seats were covered with them.[401]

Pl. 48.

See larger image

Order of the Golden Fleece. Tapestry at Berne, taken from Charles the Bold at the Battle of Grandson, 1476.

Sufficient has been said to show that during the dark ages hangings were woven in France, Germany, and Belgium,[402] and that England was not behind the rest of the civilized world in this craft. I think, also, that we have indicated its Oriental origin.[403]

Arras continued to lead as the great tapestry factory till the end of the fifteenth century, when the commercial failure of the city began, at the death of Charles le Téméraire, Duke of Burgundy.[404] Plate 48 shows a [244]portion of his tent hangings woven with the order of the golden fleece taken at the battle of Grandson—now in the museum at Berne. Till then Arras had supplied most of the splendid decorations of which we find such marvellous lists. Every possible subject—religious, romantic, historical, and allegorical—was pressed into the service, and pictured hangings were supposed to instruct, amuse, and edify the beholders. The dark ages were illuminated, and their barbarity softened, by these constant appeals to men's highest instincts, and to the memories of their noblest antecedents and aspirations, which clothed their walls, and so became a part of their daily lives. The great Flemish and French workshops became the illustrators of the history of the world, as it was then read or being enacted. It is a record of faiths, religious and political; and of national and family lives and their changes. The Exhibition at Brussels in 1880 showed, by its "Catalogue Raisonné," how much could be extracted from its storied tapestries of both archæological and artistic information.[405]

Though the art continued to be the servant of refined luxury in the fifteenth century, Arras itself had done its work,[406] and was superseded as the greatest weaver of [245]artistic tapestry by a neighbour and rival, Brussels, which had been gradually asserting itself as a weaving community, from that date absorbed most of the trade of Arras, and thence forwards, till Henri IV. established the works of the Savonnerie, Brussels led European taste, and employed the best artists. Brussels employed Leonardo da Vinci and Mantegna, Giovanni da Udine, Raphael, and later, Rubens and the great Dutch painters, to design cartoons for tapestry works. Raphael's pupil, Michael Coxsius, of Mechlin, superintended the copying of his master's cartoons. Shortly afterwards, Antwerp, Oudenarde, Lille, Tournai, Valenciennes, Beauvais, Aubusson, and Bruges all had their schools;[407] and the adept can trace their differences and peculiarities, and name their birthplace, without referring to their trade-mark, or to that of the manufacturer, which is usually to be found in the outer border. Poitiers, Troyes, Beauvais, Rheims, and St. Quentin likewise had their schools, and became famous.

Want of space prevents my entering more fully into this subject of the northern tapestries, and I must refer my readers to the authorities I have quoted from so largely.

ITALIAN TAPESTRY.

The word Arrazzi shows us whence the Italians drew [246]their art. Doubtless there were looms in the Italian cities, and especially under ecclesiastical patronage, through the dark ages. Rome was in communication with the Atrebates in the third century, by whom she was supplied with the Byrri, or hooded cloaks then worn; and as it had been a centre for weaving commerce, it is probable that Rome received from Arras the craftsmen as well as the produce of their looms. At the Renaissance we find factories for pictured webs in Florence, Rome, Milan, Mantua, and elsewhere. The best artists of the Italian schools—Mantegna, Leonardo, Raphael and his scholars, &c., &c.—gave their finest designs to be executed in Italy, before they were sold to Arras, Brussels, France, or England, and they are accumulated in the treasure-room of every palace in Italy. But the finest collections are those of the Vatican, and of the Pitti in Florence. A splendid volume might be edited of these grand artistic works; such a record would be invaluable. Vasari[408] and Passevant give us occasional glimpses of local factories for tapestry, but, as we have before said, this subject has still to be investigated.

FRENCH TAPESTRY.

In France, as elsewhere, tapestry was probably woven in private looms and in the religious houses from early days. M. Jubinal believes that it was made at Poitiers, Troyes, Beauvais, Rheims, and St. Quentin as early as 1025.[409] Froissart describes the entry of Isabel of Bavaria [247]as a bride into Paris, when the houses were covered with hangings and tapestries representing historical scenes.[410]The Cluny Museum possesses a most curious mediæval suite of hangings from the Chateau de Boussac, of the early part of the fifteenth century. They tell the story of the "Dame au Lion," and are brilliantly coloured and charmingly quaint and gay in design. Hangings designed by Primaticcio were woven at Fontainebleau, where Francis I. started the manufacture in 1539. However, the first national school of tapestry weaving was that at Chaillot, under the experienced teaching of workmen from Arras; afterwards transferred to the town of Gobelins, 1603, by Henri Quatre.[411] Louis Quatorze and his minister Colbert splendidly protected this manufacture by law, privilege, and employment; so did Louis Quinze. Before the Revolution, other considerable tapestry works were flourishing at Aubusson in Auvergne, at Felletin in the upper Marches, and at Beauvais. These two last were especially famed for velvety tapestries (*veloutés*).

As usual, the French have surpassed all other nations in this textile art. The pictorial tapestries of the Gobelins have carried the beauty of wall hangings to the utmost perfection. Nothing can be more festive than a brilliantly lighted hall, glowing with these woven pictures or arabesques, framed in gilded carvings or stuccoes. Still we must acknowledge that, in choice of worthy subjects, the Flemish ideal, which had been left far behind, was the highest. The weavers of the time of Louis Quatorze [248]aspired only to teach the glories of France, not the moralities of society and civilization, in their historical compositions, which were then superseded by classical mythology, or else by scenes from rustic life, of the Watteau School. La Fontaine's fables gave some of the prettiest and gayest designs, and were generally the centres of splendid arabesques. The drawing and execution were perfect.

It is to be feared that in the future, great works of textile decoration will be few and far between. It is only when the State, or the monarch that represents the dignity of the State, protects and fosters these artistic factories, that they can continue to thrive. Without such powerful encouragement, fashion, commercial depression, or a war will stop for a time the orders without which funds fail, discouragement sets in, and ruin quickly follows; and the best workman when unemployed, or forced for some years to wield the sword, loses his practised skill never to be restored. In France, whatever has been the form of government, the old traditions of protection for the Gobelins have been acted up to and maintained. The consequence is that science and art still contribute their efforts in the machinery, the colouring, and the designing of hangings of which the materials[412] and the execution are unrivalled. Probably there will never again be a Tuileries or a Versailles to adorn, but an Hôtel de Ville, especially if it is occasionally destroyed, may give from time to time opportunity for such decorations.

ENGLISH TAPESTRY.

When we consider the antiquity and the excellence of the art of tapestry on the Continent, we cannot pretend [249]that there can be the same general interest in that of our English looms. But to ourselves it naturally assumes the greatest importance; and I have tried to trace the efforts of our ancestors in this direction, by noting every certain sign of English production, in what must have been an imitation of Flemish or Oriental weaving. The few facts here collected may be of service to the future writer of the history of English tapestries.

Comnenus, Prince of Arras, fled before the Romans from Nomenticum to England; and he and his Atrebates settled themselves between Silchester and Sarum, and the Belgæ and Parisi did the same. The Romans found them here when they invaded England. Wherever the Belgic tribes spread themselves, the art of weaving was established. Comnenus probably brought over, and left to his descendants, the inheritance of this craft.

Dr. Rock thinks that pictured tapestry was woven at an early period in the Middle Ages by the monks in England. The earliest proof of this that we possess, is the notice by Matthew Paris (thirteenth century) describing the three reredos for St. Alban's Abbey; the first, a large one, depicting the finding of the body of the Protomartyr; the others, "The Prodigal Son" and "The Man who fell among Thieves." All these were executed by the orders of Abbot Geoffrey.[413]

While in London in 1316, Simon, Abbot of Ramsay, bought for the use of his monks, looms, shuttles, and a slay. "Pro weblomes emptes xx^d. Et pro staves ad [250]eadem vj^d. Item pro iiij Shittles, pro eadem opere vj^d. Item j sloy pro textoribus viii^d."[414]

In Edward II.'s time there were hangings woven in England which appear to have been absolutely tapestries. They were much valued abroad, and were called "Salles d'Angleterre." Charles V. of France (1364) possessed among his articles of costly furniture, "Une salle d'Angleterre vermeille brodée d'azur, et est la bordure a vignettes, et le dedans de Lyons, d'Aigles, et de Lyopars."[415]

Our trade with Arras must have improved our tapestries. We are told of Edward III. selling his wools to that town, and being therefore called by Philip de Valois, his "Marchant de Laine." Horace Walpole refers to an act, "De Mysterâ Tapiciarorum," of the time of Edward III., 1327, "regarding certain malpractices of the craft," which proves its existence in England at that period.[416]

Mr. French, in his catalogue of the Exhibition in London, 1851, quotes the tapestries of St. Mary's Hall at Coventry, to prove that there was a manufactory in England, *temp.* Henry VI. There were certainly individual looms, though we doubt whether it had yet become a national industry, as we have so few specimens remaining. The St. Mary's tapestries contain portraits of Henry VI., Cardinal Beaufort, &c., and are probably contemporary works. The subject is the marriage of Henry VI.

There is also a piece of tapestry at Bude, in Cornwall, the property of Mr. Maskell, which came from a royal sale. Here the marriage of Henry VII. is depicted, and [251]the style resembles that of the Coventry hangings. The costumes are certainly English, and the original pictures must have been English, though they might have been wrought at Arras, reminding one of the groups of figures and the dresses on the Dunstable Pall (see Plate 78).

Dr. Rock also quotes the reredos belonging to the Vintners' Company, representing St. Martin sharing his cloak with a beggar. He thinks this is executed by the monks of St. Alban's, and attributes to those of Canterbury the fine tapestries of the legends of the Virgin at Aix, in Provence, of which we have the history. They were originally given to Canterbury Cathedral by Prior Godstone, and were called Arras work. There is no doubt that there were looms and artists in the convents and monasteries before there was any recognized school of such work in England. Probably till the Reformation such hangings were being woven all over Europe, and only then ceased in Germany and England. One cannot but regret that the weight of the evil which preponderated over the good in the Houses of the Church, should have caused so much that was beautiful in art to be crushed by their ruin.

Chaucer speaks of "tapestry of verd."[417] This green tapestry seems to have been intended to give a bowery effect to the room it hung; and one can imagine that it pleased the taste of the poet of the "Flower and the Leaf." It seems to have been much the fashion in England and elsewhere about that period, and generally represented landscapes and woody foregrounds only; but sometimes figures and animals were portrayed, and always in the same tints of bluish-green.

Dr. Rock gives us an extract from the wardrobe accounts of Edward II., containing the following items: [252]"To a mercer of London for a green hanging of wool, woven with figures of kings and earls upon it; for the king's service upon solemn feast days in London;" therefore the "tapestry of verd" was not a novelty even in the time of Chaucer.[418]

Oudenarde was famous for these "hallings" or "salles." All the specimens mentioned in the catalogue of tapestries exhibited at Brussels in 1880, are said to be from thence. But we see no reason why it should not have been an English style of weaving also. The first establishment of a permanent manufactory in England, did not, however, take place until the latter end of the reign of Henry VIII., when Robert Sheldon "allowed" his manor-house at Barcheston, in Warwickshire, to "one Hicks," whom he signalizes in his will as "the author and beginner of all tapestry of Arras in England." This will is dated 1576.[419]

See larger image
SUMMER
English Tapestry, Temp. Henry VIII. at Hatfield

There are four pieces of tapestry representing the Seasons, removed from an old family house and placed by Lord Salisbury at Hatfield House, where they hang in the great corridor. These were probably woven in Barcheston. (Plate 49.) The style is English Renaissance, and the design full of intention; in fact, they have the seal of the time of Henry VIII. Only one [253]characteristic reminds one of Flemish art, and that is the mode of drawing the plants and flowers, which might have been taken out of an old German herbal. The landscapes and peasantry are unmistakably English. The pictures are worked with strong black outlines which emphasize every detail and give the effect of a highly coloured outlined engraving; reminding one of the children's books by Marcus Ward or by Walter Crane.[420]

The tapestries called the "Spanish Armada hangings" were probably woven here late in Elizabeth's reign. In her time we find in catalogues of household goods, descriptions of splendid hangings, furnishings of palaces and private houses. The MS. inventory of the Earl of Leicester's belongings, in the library at Longleat, astonishes us with the abundance of suites of hangings of tapestry that it enumerates, as well as those embroidered by hand, and others of stamped and painted leather.

It was in the reign of James I. that the manufacture [254]was set up at Mortlake, in Surrey. Aubrey, in his "History of Surrey, i. p. 82," however, dates the institution in the subsequent reign; but Lloyd[421] is not only positive for the former date, but affirms it was "of the motion of King James himself," who gave £2000 towards the undertaking; and we have further proofs extant that he spent largely, and encouraged it in every way. He gave to Sir Francis Crane, who erected the house at Mortlake, "the making of three Baronets" towards his project for manufacture of tapestry.[422]

Another curious item which we quote, shows that the funds for the enterprise were not easily forthcoming. It is a warrant "to Sir Francis Crane: £2000 to be employed in buying £1000 per ann. of pensions or other gifts made of the king, and not yet payable, for ease of

His Majesty's charge of £1000 a year towards the maintenance of Sir Francis Crane's tapestry manufacture."[423]

Apparently this little arrangement did not succeed, for there is an acknowledgment by Charles I., in the first year of his reign,[424] that he is in debt to Sir F. Crane: "For three suits of gold tapestry we stand indebted to Sir Francis Crane £6000. Also Sir F. Crane is allowed £1000 annually for the better maintenance of said works for ten years to come." The king also granted the estate of Stoke Bruere, near Stamford, in Northamptonshire, as part payment of £16,400 due to him on the tapestry works at Mortlake.[425] The great value of these tapestries is shown by the prices named in the Domestic Papers of the State Paper Office, [255]and in private inventories; they were woven in silk, wool, and gold, which last item accounts both for their price and for their disappearance.

William, Archbishop of York and Lord Keeper, gave £2500 for four pieces of Arras representing the four Seasons.[426] Their value, however, fell during the civil wars, for the tapestries of the five Senses from the Palace of Oatlands, which were from the Mortlake looms, were sold in 1649 for £270. The beautiful tapestries at Houghton were woven at Mortlake: these are all silk, and contain whole length portraits of James I. and Charles I., and their Queens, with heads of the royal children in the borders. A similar hanging is at Knowle, wrought in silk, containing portraits of Vandyke and Sir Francis Crane.[427]

Francis Cleyne was a decorator and painter employed in the works at Mortlake by Charles I., who, while he was still Prince of Wales, brought him over to England from Rostock, in Mecklenburg (his native place), while the Prince was in Spain wooing the Infanta. Cleyne was great in grotesques, and also undertook in historical designs.[428]

Three of the Raphael cartoons were sent to be copied at Mortlake.[429] The purchase of these cartoons by the king, showed how high was the standard to which he tried [256]to raise the art in England. The "Triumph of Cæsar," by Mantegna, was obtained for the same purpose in 1653; and certain Dutch prisoners were forwarded to the manufactory to be employed on the work.[430] It was entrusted to the care of Sir Gilbert Pickering, who was either an artist or the superintendent of the works.

After the death of Sir Francis, his brother, Sir Richard Crane, sold the premises to Charles I. During the civil wars, the property was seized upon and confiscated as having belonged to the Crown. It occupied the site of what is now Queen's Head Court. The old house opposite was built by the king for the residence of Cleyne the artist. Gibson, the dwarf, and portrait painter, who had been page to a lady at Mortlake, was one of his pupils.[431]

The value of the king's collection of tapestries was well understood during the Protectorate. The tapestry house remained in the occupation of John Holliburie, the "master-workman." After the Restoration, Charles II. appointed Verrio as designer, intending to revive the manufactory. This was not, however, carried out; but the work still lingered on, and must have been in some repute, for Evelyn names some of these hangings as a fit present among those offered by a gallant to his mistress.[432]

Arras is said to have been woven at Stamford, but we have no data of its establishment or its suppression. Burleigh House contains much of it; and there is a suite of hangings at Belton House, near Grantham, of which there are duplicates at Wroxton House, in Oxfordshire, all having the same traditional origin at Stamford. Possibly Sir Francis and Sir Richard Crane may have [257]received orders at their house at Stoke Bruere, which lay near enough to Stamford to account for the magnates of the town and neighbourhood obtaining furnishings of their tapestries, and, perhaps, vying with each other in decorating their apartments with them.[433]

In Northumberland House there was a fine suite of tapestry, woven in Lambeth, 1758.[434] This is the only sample of that loom of which we ever find any mention. There were also works at Fulham, where furniture tapestry in the style of Beauvais was made. This manufactory was closed in 1755.[435] It may be hoped that the revival of tapestry weaving at Windsor in our own day may be a success, but without the royal and noble encouragement it receives, it would probably very soon fall into disuse.

Unless it is supported by the State, such an exceptionally expensive machinery cannot possibly be kept at work. It requires the superintendence of the best artists, and the weavers themselves must needs have the highest technical education to enable them to copy really fine designs. These artistic requirements, besides the extreme tediousness of the work, make it the most expensive of all luxurious decorations—even more costly than embroideries by the hand, covering the same spaces. However, the two styles of hangings never can [258]enter into competition, except in a financial point of view. Tapestries are the best fitted for wall coverings, and embroideries for curtains of all kinds—for beds, for windows, and for portières.

The old hangings are now again having their day, and we are striving to save and restore all that remain to us. We must continue to guard these treasures from the moths, their worst enemies; and science should be invoked to assist us in the preservation of these precious works of art, of which the value is now again understood and appreciated, and which increases with every decade that is added to their antiquity.

Tapestry, as art, has its own peculiar beauties, and one of them is the softening, yet brilliant effect of the alternate lights and shadows of the ridge-like surface; the separation of each stitch and thread also casting minute shadows in the opposite direction, and giving an iridescent effect. It is a mistake to struggle against this inherent quality, instead of seeking to utilize it. The coarser and simpler tapestries of our ancestors are really more beautiful and effective in large spaces—flat in the arrangement of colours, and sharply outlined—than the imitations of paintings of the last two centuries, in which every detail of form and colour is sought to be expressed.[436]

M. Blanc says that tapestries were intended to cover the bare walls, but not to make us forget their existence. The wall being intended for comfort and defence, the mind is solaced with the idea it conveys. It is a mistake, therefore, to substitute a surface picture, so real that it at [259]once does away with this impression of security, while a certain conventional art should amuse the mind with shadowy representations and suggestions.

It is, perhaps, fortunate that the possibilities of tapestry weaving are restricted, and thus its very imperfections become the sources of its best qualities as decoration and comfort. One element of textile weaving, the use of gold, both in the backgrounds and in the draperies, takes it at once out of the region of naturalism, while giving it light and splendour.

The designer for tapestry need not be a great genius. Harmony, repose, grace, and tender colouring are the qualities most valuable to such an artist. Battle-pieces, and other exciting and awful subjects, are only bearable in apartments that are used for state occasions, or for hanging corridors and anterooms. They are painful to live with.

All tapestries are liable to suffer by the double nature of their materials—their woollen surface and linen threads which are affected by both damp and heat crinkling the forms and puckering the faces, and bringing out unexpected expressions and deformities. For this reason the design should be as flat and as simple in its outline and shading as is consistent with beauty.

FOOTNOTES:

[317]Birdwood, "Indian Arts," p. 283.

[318]"The word in Sanskrit for a needle is *suchi*, from *such*, to sew or pierce. This is the same word as the Latin *suo*, to sew; so probably the common word used by the Aryans in their primeval habitations was *su*, and they clearly knew how to sew at that remote period. Eve sewed fig-leaves together. Adam sewed also. The Hebrew word is *tafar*, and clearly meant *sewing*, not *pinning* together with thorns. Sewing is the first recorded art of our forefathers."—Letter from Mr. Robert Cust.

[319]Semper, "Der Stil," Textile Kunst, i. pp. 77-90.

[320]Semper, Textile Kunst, "Der Stil," i. p. 77. The German word "naht," here literally translated, would be, uniting, weaving, bringing together.

[321]"Handbook of Plain Needlework," by Mrs. Floyer. See also her "Plain Hints for Examiners," &c.

[322]Dr. Rock, "Introduction," pp. cix, cx, calls it "thread embroidery," and names some specimens in the South Kensington Museum. He says it was sometimes done in darning stitches for ecclesiastical purposes, for instance, for coverings for the pyx. It is

mentioned in the Exeter inventory of the fourteenth century. There is notice of white knotted thread-work belonging to St. Paul's, London, in 1295, by Dugdale (p. 316).

[323]St. Catherine of Sienna's winding-sheet is described as being cut work (punto tagliato) on linen. This sounds like embroidery of the type now sold as "Madeira work," the pattern being cut out and the edges overcast.

[324]Semper, "Der Stil," i. pp. 132, 203.

[325]See Semper, "Der Stil," i. p. 289.

[326]Ibid. He cites Athenæus, iv. 64.

[327]Phrygia in general, and especially Babylon, were famed for their embroideries. "Colores diversos picturæ intexere Babylon maxime celebravit et nomen imposuit."—Pliny, lib. viii. 74. See D'Auberville, "Ornement des Tissus," p. 7.

[328]"Der Stil," i. p. 196. "Opus Phrygium," in the Middle Ages, included all gold work in flat stitches. The cloak worked by Queen Gisela in the ninth century, for her husband, St. Stephen, King of Hungary, the imperial mantle at Bamberg, of the date of 1024, and the robes of Bishop William de Blois (thirteenth century), in the library at Worcester Cathedral, are all "opus Phrygium," and resemble each other in style.

[329]In the Museum at Munich are two remarkable examples of these imitations. There is an embroidered badge of the Order of the Dragon, worked in gold and woven over with coloured silks, so as to present the appearance of enamel (sixteenth century). The second is a dress for a herald of the Order of St. Hubertus, which is richly embroidered in gold and silver, and the badge and collar are imitated in the most extraordinary manner, and laid on entirely in gold needlework. This is of the seventeenth century.

[330]In Salt's collection from Saccarah (British Museum); also at Turin, in the Egyptian Museum; and in the collections in the Louvre, figured by Auberville in the "Ornamentation des Tissus."

[331]Hence the French name, *pointes comptées*.

[332]See Semper, ii. p. 213, for wood-work at Panticapæum, Kertch, in the Crimea, which evidently has descended in style from panelled needlework hangings. Chaldean wall decoration at Khorsabad and Warka, near Nimroud, recalls the effect of "opus pulvinarium" according to Loftus. See Semper, i. p. 327.

[333]"Der Stil," i. pp. 196, 248. This is known from the archaic books of imperial commerce.

[334]Peacocks' feathers, either woven or onlaid, are those most commonly used in China and Japan. "Ka Moolelo Hawaii," by M. Jules Remy, Paris, 1861. See Ferdinand Denis, "Arte Plumaria," p. 66.

[335]Yates, "Textrinum Antiquorum," p. 373, translates from Publius Syrus the word *plumata*, "feathered." The word "embroidered" would have here improved the sense, even though it is a peacock that is described.

"Thy food the peacock, which displays his spotted train, As shines a Babylonian shawl with feather'd gold."

He also quotes Lucan, who is praising the furnishings of Cleopatra's palace: "Part shines with feathered gold; part sheds a blaze of scarlet."—Yates, p. 373.

[336]Sir G. Birdwood, with all his enthusiasm for Indian art and its forms, yet cannot resist a touch of humour when he describes a state umbrella, of which the handle and ribs are pure gold, tipped with rubies and diamonds, the silken covering bordered with thirty-two fringed loops of pearls, and "also appropriately decorated with the feathers of the peacock, heron, parrot, and goose."—Birdwood, "Indian Arts," ii. p. 182.

[337]"History of the Kingdom of Congo," c. viii. p. 55, by Filippo Pigafetta (translated by Mrs. M. Hutchinson).

[338]In the Tyrol certain embroideries are called "Federstickerei."

[339]For the feather hangings at Moritzburg, see Appendix 2.

[340]"Arte Plumaria," by M. Ferdinand Denis. Paris, 1875.

[341]The Plumarii mentioned by Pliny were craftsmen in the art of *acu pingere*, or painting with the needle. Though Seneca speaks of the "opus plumarium" as if it were absolutely feather-work, yet it may have been at that time undergoing its transition into embroidery, suggested by feathers, and imitating them in gold, silver, wool, or thread. When

Lucan describes the extraordinary change introduced into Roman habits and luxury by Cleopatra's splendours, his use of the words, "pars auro plumata nitet," probably means their imitation or mixture with gold embroidery, and would, therefore, come under the head of "opus Phrygium."

[342] It is said that the work, named "Plumarium," was made by the needle; and the Greeks, from the variety of the threads, called it "Polymitum." "Plumarium dicitur opus acu factum quod Græci a licionum varietate multiplici polymitarium appellant."—Robert Stephan. "Thesaurus Linguæ Latinæ," s.v. Plumarius.

[343] Blümner, i. p. 209. "The Plumarii were a class of persons mentioned by Vitruvius, and found likewise in inscriptions. It cannot be decided with certainty what was their occupation; their name would lead us to suppose that it has something to do with feathers."—Becker's "Gallus," ii. p. 288. But see Marquardt, "Handbuch d. Röm. Altert." vii. pt. 2, p. 523.

[344] "Plumarium qui acu aliquod depingit super culcitris plumeis."—R. Steph., "Thesaur. Lat."

[345] See "The Funeral Tent of an Egyptian Queen," by Villiers Stuart.

[346] See Auberville's "Tissus," Plate i.

[347] "Compte Rendu de la Commission Archéologique, St. Petersburg, 1881." Pl. iii. pp. 112,119.

[348] In the British Museum is the lining of a shield which shows the arms of Redvers, third Earl of Albemarle (who died 1260), applied in different coloured silks.

[349] Lent by the Archæological Museum at Madrid.

[350] Rees' Cyclopædia speaks of embroideries "on the stamp or stump," as being so named "when the figures are high and prominent, supported by cotton, wool, or hair;" also in "low and plain embroideries, without enrichment between." He speaks of work "cut and laid on the cloth, laid down with gold, enriched with tinsel and spangles." Rees' Cyclopædia, "Embroidery," 1819.

[351] "Opus consutum." The way in which this applied work is used in India, for the special adornment of horse-cloths, saddles, and girths, is very interesting.

[352] The chapter on "application," in the Handbook of Embroidery of the Royal School of Art Needlework, will be useful to those who need instruction in the most practical, and therefore the quickest way of doing cut work.

[353] Mrs. Palliser's "History of Lace." The origin of needle-made lace-work is attributed by M. de Gheltof to the necessity for disposing of the frayed edges of worn-out garments. This I think somewhat fanciful. *Fringes* may have been so suggested.

[354] See M. Blanc's "Art in Ornament and Dress" (p. 200).

[355] Mrs. Bayman (late Superintendent in the School of Art Needlework) writes thus: "I see no reason to doubt that the word guipure is derived from 'guipa' or 'guiper,' a ribbon-weaver's term for spinning one thread round another; and that guipure was originally more like what we now call 'guimp,' or like 'point de Raguse,' first being made of thread, of more or less thickness and commoner material, wound round with a finer flax, silk, or metal; then they cut shapes, bold scrolls, and leaves out of cartisane, vellum, or parchment, winding and covering them over with the more precious thread. These figures were then connected by brides, only as close as was required to hold them together, and leaving large open spaces, thus forming the large scroll patterns seen in so many old pictures." No doubt the heavy "Fogliami" and "Rose point" laces developed themselves from these still older kinds of point. As the cord and card lace disappeared, the name slid on to all laces with large, bold patterns and open brides, though the special method which first created it had been effaced. Latterly, embroidered netting or laces have been called "guipure d'art." Littré gives the derivation of the word; he says it is from the Gothic *Vaipa*, or German *Weban* or *Weben* (*g* and *p* replacing the *w* and *b*).

[356] The word lace came from France, where it was called *lacis* or *lassis*, derived from the Latin *laqueus* (a noose). These words originally applied to narrow ribbons—their use being to lace or tie.

[357] The Venetians early made much lace for furniture or ecclesiastical linen adornment, of what they called "maglia quadrata," which was usually squared netting,

afterwards filled in with patterns in darned needlework. This somewhat primitive style of lace trimming was popular on account of its simplicity, and descended to the peasantry for their domestic decorations in Spain, Germany, France, and Italy. There are specimens of this work believed to be of the thirteenth century. At the time of the Renaissance the simple geometrical designs developed into animals, fruits, flowers, and human figures.

[358]See Rock, p. cix, cx. He says that a sort of embroidery was called network, and certain drawn work he calls "opus filatorium." See Catalogue of Textiles in the South Kensington Museum, by D. Rock, p. cxxvii.

[359]Reminding us of the description of a net—"holes tied together by a string." As a contrast in descriptive style, we would quote Dr. Johnson on network: "Anything reticulated or decussated at equal distances, with interstices between the intersections."—Johnson's Dictionary.

[360]Isaiah iii. 18, xix. 9.

[361]The nets of chequer work which hung round the capitals, with the wreaths of chain work, were designed by Hiram of Tyre, at Solomon's desire (1 Kings vii. 17).

[362]A fringe lace is made on the Riviera, of the fibres of the aloe, and is called "macramè," which is an Arabic word. Mrs. Palliser's "History of Lace," p. 64.

[363]A collar of fine white human hair was made in point lace stitches at Venice, and worn at his coronation by Louis Quatorze. It cost 250 pieces of gold. "Scritti di V. Zanon da Udine" (1829). Cited by Urbani de Gheltof, "Merletti di Venezia," pp. 22, 23.

[364]See, for example, the inventory of the household goods of the great Earl of Leicester at Longleat; also the lists of the possessions of Ippolito and Angela Sforza (sixteenth century).

[365]Coloured thread and silk laces are still made in Venice.

[366]In the British Museum.

[367]M. Blanc's use of the word "guipure" is different from that found in the notices of the art by other authorities.

[368]The first lace-making machine was contemporary, or nearly so, with the stocking-making frame. About the year 1768 it was altered, and adapted for making open-work patterns. In 1808, the Heathcot machine was started for bobbin net. In 1813, John Leaver improved on this idea, with machine-woven patterns. The Jacquard apparatus achieved the flat patterns, and the new "Dentellière" has perfected the art. Lace-making by machinery employed by the latest official returns in 1871, 29,370 women in England, and 24,000 in France. See Encyclopædia Britannica, 9th edition, p. 183-5.

[369]M. Charles Blanc, "Art in Ornament and Dress," p. 211.

[370]The information contained in these volumes is most valuable, for the lace-worker as well as the collector.

[371]Lady Layard suggests that the cut lace work, which was the earliest made in Venice ("punto tagliato," "point coupé"), simply consists of button-hole stitch with purl ornaments. These are varied with geometrical stitches and needle-weaving in those solid laces called "punti tagliati Fogliami," and "Rose point de Venise," of the finest kinds.

[372]Urbani de Gheltof, in his book, "Merletti di Venezia," p. 9, says that Venetian laces and fringes were furnished thence for the coronation of Richard III. (1483). I fancy that gold guimps or braid, rather than netted laces, must be here intended, as we have no other notice of lace so early. See *Ibid.* pp. 10-20.

[373]Henry VIII. had a pair of hose of purple silk, edged and trimmed with a lace of purple silk and gold, of Milanese manufacture. Harl. MSS., 1519.

[374]The manufacture of point d'Alençon was created under the special orders of Louis Quatorze, by Colbert, in 1673. Now more than 200,000 women, besides the machinists, are employed in lace-making in France. Colbert imported the teachers from Venice.

[375]Yriarte says that Alençon, Argenton, Sedan, Mercourt, Honiton, Bedford, Buckinghamshire, Oxfordshire, Mechlin, Bruges, Brussels, all followed in imitation of Venice. Yriarte's "Venise," p. 250.

[376]Titian drew the designs for one of these books for "punti tagliati." The laces made in the Greek islands probably owe their origin to Venice, showing the same "punti in aria."

[377]I have already spoken of "lacis" as either darned netting or drawn work. Of this there is an English specimen at Prague, said by tradition to be the gift of Queen Anne of Bohemia, wife of Richard II. It originally trimmed or bordered an ecclesiastical garment.

[378]For further information, we refer the reader to M. Urbani de Gheltof's book on Venice laces already cited (Organia, Venice, 1876), and Lady Layard's translation (1882).

[379]I am assured on the best authority that this is unknown as yet at Burano; but the workers, as well as the revived industry, are very young. The modern school of Burano has only been established eleven years. It is certainly delightful to see the 320 happy faces, singing, chattering, and smiling over their graceful occupation; and the beauty of the Buranese women, which is celebrated, has not suffered from their occupation. There is a charming little article of the *Revista di Torino*, 1883, which describes the improvement in the social condition of Burano, morally and physically, and the way it is recognized by the inhabitants. Instead of signs of miserable poverty, the promoters of the lace school are greeted by the women leaning from the windows with, "Siestu benedetta!" ("Be thou blessed!").

[380]The word "tapestry" comes from the Greek *tapes*, which is used equally for hangings or carpets. The Italians call carpets "tapeti" to this day. It is believed to have been originally an Egyptian word for such fabrics.

[381]For instance, the embroidered hangings of the eighth century at Gerona, in Spain, have been more than once quoted as proofs of tapestries having been manufactured there at that period.

[382]The "slay" means the "strike." The word had the same meaning originally: to slay a man was to strike him.

[383]See De Champeaux, South Kensington Museum Art Handbook, 1878.

[384]"Bibliothèque des Merveilles" (sur les Tapisseries), publié sous la direction de M. Edouard Charton, à Paris, 1876.

[385]Martial, xiv. 150.

[386]Minerva accepts the challenge of the Mæonian Arachne, who will not yield to her in the praises of being first in weaving wool. The girls desert the vineyards round the little town of Hypæpa, to look at her admirable workmanship. She boasts that hers is finer than that of Pallas, and, desiring a vain victory, rushes upon her own destruction. "... They stretch out two webs on the loom, with a fine warp. The web is tied to the beam; the slay separates the warp; the woof is inserted in the middle with sharp shuttles, while the fingers hurry along, and being drawn with the warp, the teeth (notched in the moving slay) strike it. Both hasten on their labour, and girding up their garments to their bosoms, they move their skilful arms, their eagerness beguiling their fatigue. There are being woven both the purples, which are subjected to the Tyrian brazen (dyeing) vessel with fine shades of minute difference; as in the rainbow with its mighty rays reflected by the shower, where, though a thousand colours are shining, yet the very transition eludes the eyes that look upon it; to such a degree is that which is adjacent the same, and yet the extremes are different. The pliant gold is mingled with the threads, and ancient subjects are represented on the webs." Then follows the list of the subjects. The web of Pallas had a large central design, and a smaller one on each corner, surrounded with a border of olive leaves. Arachne's contained nineteen pictures, of two or more figures each, and was surrounded by a border of flowers, interwoven with the twining ivy. Ovid's "Metamorphoses," book vi.

Through the kindness of my friend, Lord Houghton, I am enabled to give the sequel of the story—Arachne's transformation into the Spider, as—

A PARAPHRASE AND A PARABLE.

Lo! how Minerva, recklessly defied,Struck down the maiden of artistic pride,Who, all distraught with terror and despair,Suspended her lithe body in mid-air;Deeming, if thus she innocently died,The sacred vengeance would be pacified.Not so: implacable the goddess cried—"Live on! hang on! and from this hour beginOut of thy loathsome self new threads to spin;No splendid tapestries for royal rooms,But sordid webs to clothe the caves and tombs.Nor blame the Poet's Metamorphoses:Man's Life has Transformations hard as these;Thou shall become, as Ages hand thee down,The drear day-worker of the crowded town,Who, envying the rough tiller of the soil,Plies her monotonous unhealthy toil,Passing through joyless day to sleepless nightWith mind enfeebled and decaying sight,Till some good genius,[437] kindred though apart,Resolves to raise thee from the vulgar mart,And once more links thee to the World of Art."

[387]Appendix 3.

[388]Guicciardini ascribes the invention of woven tapestry to Arras, giving no dates; so we do not know whether he attributes it to the Belgic Atrebates or to their successors, the Franks. In either case the craft was probably imported from the East.

[389]The Atrebates were the inhabitants of that Belgic region till the fifth century; now it is the province of Artois, probably a corruption of the name "Atrebates." Taylor, "Words and Places" (1865), pp. 229-385.

[390]Castel, "Des Tapisseries," p. 30.

[391]Sidonius Apollinaris, Epist. ix., 13. Cited in Yule's "Marco Polo," p. 68.

[392]Castel, "Des Tapisseries," p. 31.

[393]The commentators of Vasari, MM. Lechanché and Jenron, believe that this art was coeval in the Low Countries with Roman civilization and Christianity; but it would appear that the weavers had fled to Britain to escape from the Romans. Ibid. p. 52. Traces of the name Arras have been found by Bochart and Frahn in Ar-ras, the Arabian name for the river Araxes and the people who inhabit its shores; but this may be accidental, and is at best an uncertain derivation.

[394]Rock, Introduction, p. cxii. This "Saracenic work" is really so like what is called by the Germans "Gobelins" when found in Egyptian tombs that one can hardly doubt whence the Moors brought their art. There are several Egyptian specimens in the British Museum. See also the catalogue of Herr Graf'schen's collection of Egyptian textiles, from the first to the eighth century. "Katalog der Teodor Graf'schen Fünde in Ægypten, von Dr. Karabacek. Wien, 1883."

[395]Viollet-le-Duc, "Dictionnaire du Mobilier Français, Tapis," p. cxii; also M. Jubinal, "Tapisserie Historique." It is difficult absolutely to assign to any known specimens a date anterior to the fifteenth century; although M. de Champeaux thinks that the "Sarazinois" were mostly or entirely carpet-weavers about the eleventh century. He says there is documentary authority to prove that these were woven with flowers and animals. There is a very deep-piled velvety carpet at Gorhambury (the Earl of Verulam's place). Here Queen Elizabeth's arms and cypher appear on a Persian or Moresque ground pattern surrounded with a wreath of oak leaves. It may have been a gift from Spain,—left after one of her visits to her Chancellor.

[396]"Tapisseries des Gobelins," A. L. Lacordaire, p. 10 (1853). He considers that the Sarazinois were embroiderers as well as weavers—and this theory is supported by extracts from an inventory of Charles VI.'s hangings of 1421.

Every detail of the art and its materials was carefully regulated by the French statutes of 1625-27, containing many laws for the perfecting of the manufacture of new as well as the restoration of old tapestries—and fines were imposed for not using materials as nearly as possible matching the original ones; and likewise for any other dereliction from the rules of the craft. Ibid. pp. 9, 10, 14.

[397]At the Poldi Bezzoli Museum in Milan there are some very fine carpets; one especially, a Persian, is supposed to be of the fifteenth century. This is very finely woven of pure, tender colours, and the whole composition, flowers and animals (most beautifully drawn lions, &c.), is delicately outlined in black on a white ground. The colouring is rich and harmonious, and has the iridescent effect of mother of pearl.

[398]In the San Clemente frescoes at Rome there are hangings which show a semi-Asiatic style.

[399]"Mémoires Historiques et Ecclesiastiques d'Auxerre," par M. l'Abbé Lebœuf, i. pp. 178, 231.

[400]There are very interesting Norwegian tapestries of the sixteenth century, which show distinctly an Eastern origin.

[401]Jubinal, "Tapisseries," pp. 25, 26; Viollet-le-Duc, "Dic. de Mobilier Français," p. 269.

[402]There is much splendid tapestry—German, and especially Bavarian,—to be seen at Munich; and, indeed, the more one seeks, the more one finds that private looms were constantly at work in the Middle Ages for votive offerings. There is a tapestry altar-piece at Coire, in the Grisons, of the Crucifixion, which is evidently of the fourteenth century. The colours are still brilliant, and the whole background is beautifully composed of growing flowers. No sky is seen. There is at Munich an altar frontal of tapestry, Gothic of the fifteenth century, exquisitely beautiful. The weaver has introduced a little portrait of herself at her loom, under the folds of the virgin's cloak at her feet.

[403]M. Albert Castel ("Tapisserie," p. 53) believes that the taking of Constantinople, when Earl Baldwin was elected to the throne of Byzantium, had a great effect on Flemish art, which then received a strong impulse from Oriental designs and traditions. See M. Jubinal's very interesting account of the tapisserie de Nancy which lined the tents of Charles the Bold at the siege of Nancy (p. 439). These tapestries are an allegory against gluttony. "Tapisseries Hist.," pp. 1-5.

[404]Charles the Bold has left us records of his taste in tent hangings of Arras at Berne, as well as at Nancy. These are the plunder from his camp equipage after the battle of Grandson. The whole suite, of many pieces, represents battles and sieges, and sacred subjects also, such as the adoration of the Magi. They are finely drawn and splendidly executed with gold lights, and are of the most perfect style of the fifteenth century. The National Museum at Munich contains most valuable specimens of very early and very fine tapestries; amongst others, a Virgin, which was certainly designed in the school of Dürer, and is of the greatest perfection of its art, both as to colour and drawing and the general effect, which has a soft, dreamy beauty, only to be seen in fine woollen tapestries, and differing from pictorial design and intention.

[405]See Rock, cxii: Among the remarkable suites of tapestry of which we find historical mention are the following: In 1334, John de Croisette, a "Tapissier Sarazinois, demeurant à Arras vendit au Duc de Touraine un tapis Sarazinois à or: de l'histoire de Charlemagne" (Voisin, p. 6). Of the many recorded as belonging to Philip, Duke of Burgundy and Brabant, one piece, "Haulte lice sanz or: de l'histoire du Duc de Normandie, comment il conquit Engleterre."—"Les Ducs de Bourgogne," par le Comte de Laborde, ii. p. 270, No. 4277.

[406]M. de Champeaux, the author of the "Handbook of Art Tapestry" belonging to the series of the Kensington Museum, 1878, says that the history of Arras has yet to be written. He, however, gives a great deal of interesting information, especially about the French tapestries, on which subject we fancy there is little more to tell. Their art does not come from such a distant time as that of the Belgian manufactures. After Louis IX. had decimated the inhabitants, and dispersed the remainder, Arras yet made a gallant struggle to revive her industry and compete with the rising prosperity of Brussels; but France had decreed against her.

[407]"Encyclopædia Britannica" ("Art Tapestry"), pp. 17, 97.

[408]Vasari vividly describes the design for a tapestry for the King of Portugal—the history of Adam—on which Leonardo da Vinci, then aged twenty, was engaged. He lingers tenderly over the picture of the flowery field and the careful study of the bay-trees. Vasari, tom. vii. p. 15; ed. Firenze, 1851.

[409]See M. Jubinal's "Tapisseries Historiées," p. 26; Viollet-le-Duc, "Mobilier Français," i. p. 269.

[410]Froissart's "Chronicles," iv., chap. 23; Johnes ed. 1815.

[411]M. de Champeaux, "Handbook of Art Tapestry," p. 24; also Rock, "Textiles," p. 122. M. Lacordaire, "Tapisserie des Gobelins," p. 15, tells us that under Louis XIII. the statutes of 1625-27 contain many regulations for the perfection of the materials employed in weaving new as well as in restoring old tapestries. Fines were imposed for not matching the colours carefully.

[412]English wool is still used for the finest tapestries at the Gobelins. The wool from Kent is considered the best.

[413]"Vitæ St. Alban. Abbatum," p. 40; Rock, p. cxi. That the walls were covered with tapestry in the thirteenth century is supposed to be proved by the description of Hrothgar's house in the Romance of Beowulf. We are told that the hangings were rich with gold, and a wondrous sight to behold. "History of Domestic Manners, &c., in England during the Middle Ages," by Thomas Wright, p. 2.

[414]Matthew Paris, in Dugdale Monast., ed. 1819, ii. p. 185.

[415]Quoted by Michel from MSS. in the Imperial Library, Paris.

[416]This was a writ to the Aldermen and Sheriffs of the City of London, principally levelled against the dealings of "certain Frenchmen which were against the well-being of the trade of the Tapissiarii ... by petition of Parliament at Westminster." Calend. Rot. Pat. Edward III., p. 148, "De Mysterâ Tapiciarorum," Lond. M. 41.

[417]Called "verdures" in French inventories.

[418]Rock's Introduction, p. lxxix.

[419]"The art of weaving tapestry was brought to England by William Sheldon, Esq., about the end of the reign of Henry VIII."—See Dugdale's "Warwickshire" ("Stemmata:" Sheldon), 2nd edition, folio, vol. i. p. 584; also Lloyd's "State Worthies," p. 953, quoted by Manning and Bray, "Hist. of Surrey," vol. iii. p. 82. But we have an earlier notice of a spirited attempt to make fine tapestries at Kilkenny. Piers, Earl of Ormonde, married the daughter of Fitzgerald, Earl of Kildare, "a person of great wisdom and courage." They brought from Flanders and the neighbouring provinces artificers and manufacturers, whom they employed at Kilkenny in working tapestries, diaper, Turkey carpets, cushions, &c. Piers died 1539. Carte's Introduction to the "Life of James, Duke of Ormonde," vol. i. p. 93 (Oxford, 1851).

[420]William Sheldon at his own expense brought workmen from Flanders, and employed them in weaving maps of the different counties of England. Of these, three large maps, the earliest specimens, were purchased by the Earl of Orford (Horace Walpole), by whom they were given to Earl Harcourt. He had them repaired and cleaned, and made as fresh as when out of the loom, and eventually gave them to Gough, the antiquary, who bequeathed them to the University of Oxford. The Armada tapestry, which is stated to have been designed by Henry Cornelius Vroom, the Dutch marine painter, and woven by Francis Spiering, appears to have been, in 1602, in the possession of Lord Howard, Lord High Admiral and the hero of the Armada. Fuller particulars are given in Walpole's "Anecdotes," i. p. 246, under the name of Vroom, Sandart being the principal authority. Part of them were in the House of Lords till 1834, when they perished in the fire. These had been engraved in 1739 by John Pine, but it appears that at that time there were in the royal wardrobe other pieces, now lost.

[421]Lloyd's "Worthies."

[422]Calendar of State Papers, cx. No. 26, James I., 1619-23.

[423]Calendar of State Papers, vol. clxxxi. No. 48.

[424]Rymer, "Fœdera," vol. viii. p. 66, ed. 1743.

[425]Brydges, "Northamptonshire," i. p. 323, under the head of "Stoke Bruere," pt. 1, p. 48.

[426]Manning and Bray's "History of Surrey," vol. iii. p. 302.

[427]Horace Walpole, "Anecdotes of Painting in England," vol. ii. p. 22.

[428]Macpherson, "Annals of Commerce."

[429]There is in Brydges' "Northamptonshire," under the head of "Stoke Bruere" (the estate which King James gave to Sir F. Crane as part payment of the deficit of £16,400 in his tapestry business), mention of the cartoons of "Raphael of Urbin, ... had from Genoa," and their cost, £300, besides the transport. M. Blanc says, with great justness, that Raphael, when he prepared these cartoons for tapestry, made designs for weaving, and *did not paint pictures*. If they had been intended for oil pictures, they would have been very differently treated.

[430]Calendar State Papers, Domestic, Sept. 28th, 1653.

[431]Horace Walpole's "Anecdotes of Painting," vol. iii. p. 64.

[432]See Evelyn's very scarce tract, entitled "Mundus Muliebris," printed 1690, p. 8.

[433]Lord Tyrconnell, Lord Exeter, and Lord Guildford had married three of the Brownlow heiresses of Belton, who had a winter residence at Stamford.

[434]Designed by Francesco Zuccarelli. Rock, Introduction, p. cxiv.

[435]It has been at different periods the crowning glory of the craft of the weaver to place different patterns or pictures on the two sides of the web. This would almost appear to be impossible, but that it has been done in late years, according to Rock, who tells us that he saw a banner so woven, with the Austrian eagle on one side and the Virgin of the Immaculate Conception on the other. He says that the same manufacturer was then being employed in producing ecclesiastical garments with the colours and patterns so varied.

[436]In old tapestries three tints only were employed for the complexions of men, women, and children—the man's reddish, the woman's yellow, and the child's whiter than either. It is an agreeable economy of colours, simple and effective, and avoids the pictorial imitation that one deprecates. See M. Charles Blanc's "Grammaire des Arts Décoratifs: Tapisserie," p. 112.

[437]The poet here refers to H.R.H. the Princess Christian.

CHAPTER VII.
HANGINGS.

"... Her bedchamber was hang'dWith tapestry of silk and silver...."
"Cymbeline," Act II., Scene IV.

The most important works that have been executed in embroidery, have been hangings or carpets. We may look upon these as belonging to the history of the past. Never again will such works be undertaken. Their *raison d'être*, as well as the means for their production, have ceased to exist. We have very ancient historical evidence of the use of hangings (or tapestries), either as curtains to exclude prying eyes, or as coverings to what was sacred or else unseemly, or as ornamental backgrounds in public and private buildings.

There is no doubt that in pillared spaces the enclosures and subdivisions were completed by hangings from pillar to pillar, from the earliest times of Asiatic civilization. In Assyria, and afterwards in Greece and Rome, the open courts and rooms were shaded from the sun and rain by umbrella-like erections with hangings stretched over them. From the Coliseum's vast area to that of the smallest atrium in the Pompeian house, the covering principle was the same.

Palace-halls and temples alike were furnished in this way, and the cold splendour of the polished marbles was enhanced by contrast with the shadowing folds of soft textures richly embroidered in bright colours and gold. The statues, the gold and silver vessels, the shrines heaped with votive offerings, were all brought into higher relief and effect by the screens, the curtains, and the veils which classical perfect taste would plan so as to carry out the decorator's intention. Babylonians, Persians, Assyrians, Egyptians, Greeks, and Jews, each adorned their sacred places in similar fashions.[438] Clemens Alexandrinus says that behind the hangings of the Egyptian temples were hidden their "foolish images."[439]

The word "hangings" was applied to all large curtains and tapestries, tent coverings, screens dividing empty spaces, or pendant between pillars; also sails,[440] banners, and decorations for processional purposes covering walls or hanging from windows; all these have been embroidered or woven with pictures and patterns. Carpets, from having originally the same name, "tapete," are to be added to this list, and, in fact, their uses are often interchanged. Kosroes' famous hangings were used as a carpet, and Persian and Babylonian carpets have been hung on the walls. A Babylonian hanging must have resembled, in its style (of which we have descriptions), the Persian carpet of to-day.

Semper gives excellent reasons for his theory that, next to dress, hangings (the clothing of architecture) were the earliest phase of art.[441] He looks upon the most ancient paintings on architecture as absolutely representing textile coverings. Some of the earliest Babylonian decorations show men supporting draperies, which he believes to be the tradition of the time when the tallest slaves held up the hangings to their own height; and above them, in tiers, were men, dwarfs, and even children fastened on brackets, carrying the hangings up to the roofs. This was an Assyrian custom, and was adopted by the Romans as a mode of disposing of their prisoners of war. Woltmann and Woermann appear to lean to the suggestion that permanent imitations of hangings were carried out in painted or encaustic tiles covering the masonry of Chaldean buildings at Nimroud and Khorsabad. The pale ones associated with low reliefs, and really resembling them, as they were partly raised, and the reliefs in alabaster and stone, which were partly coloured, were in harmony, and yet in contrast, with the brilliant tiles of Babylon.[442]

We know exactly what were the purple, scarlet, and white hangings of the Sanctuary in the wilderness, designed by Bezaleel, and that the veil of the Temple was blue, purple, crimson or scarlet, and white, i.e. worked on white linen; and we know from Josephus, that "the veil of the Temple, which was rent in twain" sixteen centuries later, was that dedicated by Herod, [263]and was Babylonian work, representing heaven and earth[443] (see p. 23 *ante*). Its colouring was scarlet, white, and blue. Scarlet and white hangings seem indeed to have been an Oriental fashion; and fashion then was not ephemeral, but lasted hundreds of years. The embroidered curtains of the Tabernacle are repeated in the hangings of Alexander's wedding tent, after 1500 years; and a thousand years later still they reappear in the seventh century, when Pope Sergius gave curtains to the high altar (baldachino) in the basilica of St. Peter's at Rome of this same scarlet and white embroidery.

In early Oriental art, the enormous expenditure of work is appalling to think of. Abulfeda describes the palace of the Caliph Moctader, on the banks of the Tigris, as being adorned with 38,000 pieces of tapestry, and of these 12,000 were of silk worked in gold. What a wealth of women had to be wasted in creating such a wealth of embroideries![444]

There is a Bedouin romance which describes the tent of Antar, and shows the taste for large works. Five thousand horsemen could skirmish under its embroidered shade; and Akbar's largest tent held 10,000 persons.

Nadir Shah's gorgeous tent, which was of the end of the seventeenth and the beginning of the eighteenth century, was of scarlet cloth on the outside, lined with [264]violet satin embroidered with gold and precious stones. The peacock throne was placed within it, and was kept there during the remainder of Nadir Shah's reign.

Sir John Chardin says that "The Khan of Persia caused a tent to be made which cost two millions: they called it the house of gold;" and it was resplendent with embroideries.[445] These are comparatively modern works, and sound commonplace and vulgar compared to those of Greece and Egypt.

The Greeks imitated the tents and temporary buildings of the Eastern monarchs. This phase of Oriental luxury was imported by Alexander the Great, and we have the description of two of his gorgeous creations at Alexandria, where he outrivalled the ancient traditional glories of Assyria and Persia. His own tent was supported by fifty golden pillars, carrying a roof of woven gold, embroidered in shimmering colours, and divided from the surrounding court, filled with guards and retainers, by scarlet and white curtains of splendid material and design.

But more gorgeous is the account of the tent in which he entertained ninety-one of his companions-in-arms on the occasion of his marriage. This tent was supported by columns twenty cubits high, plated with silver and gold, and inlaid with precious stones. The walls of the court were formed by curtains adorned with figures worked in gold, and were hung from beams plated with the precious metals, to match the columns. The outer court was half a mile in circumference.[446]

Yet Alexander's wedding-tent was exceeded in splendour by that erected by Ptolemy Philadelphus for his great pomp at Alexandria, described by Kallixenos, as cited by [265]Athenæus.[447] This tent, crowned with golden eagles, was supported by pillars fifty cubits high. They upheld an architrave with cross-beams covered with linen, on which were painted coffers, to imitate the structure of a solid roof. From the centre was suspended a veil of scarlet bordered with white. The pillars in the four angles represented palm-trees of gold, and the intermediate columns were fashioned as thursi, and were probably wreathed with golden vines and bunches of grapes made of amethysts, as we know of a Persian tent so adorned, and the whole idea of the erection was evidently fresh from the East.[448] A frieze eight cubits high was composed of niches containing groups of tragic, comic, and Satyric figures "in their natural garb;" and nymphs and golden tripods from Delphi. The tent was separated from the outer peristyle by scarlet hangings, covered with choice skins of wild beasts. Upon these were hung the celebrated Sikyonian pictures, the heritage of the Ptolemaic dynasty, alternating with portraits and rich hangings, on which were embroidered the likenesses of kings, and likewise mythological subjects. Between these and the frieze hung gold and silver shields. Opposite the entrance, vessels of the most costly materials and workmanship, valued at 10,000 talents of silver, were ranged, so as to strike the eye of all who entered there. Golden couches supported by Sphinxes were placed along the sides of the tent, furnished with soft purple woollen mattresses, and coverings gaily and exquisitely embroidered. The floor was strewn with fresh blossoms, [266]except where a most costly Persian carpet covered the centre. In the doorways and against the pillars stood a hundred precious statues by the greatest artists.

This description dazzles the imagination! To be an upholsterer (a vestiarius) in those days was to be an engineer, architect, and artist! Semper, from whose translation we are quoting, remarks that the luxurious "motive" of such an erection naturally arose from the desire to make use of the mass of artistic materials acquired by conquest, and the effort to reduce them to certain architectural principles already accepted.[449]

That Alexander did not purposely destroy the Persian embroideries is evident from the fact that Lucullus speaks of them 200 years later.

Rome accepted and adopted all the Oriental uses of hangings, in the Temple and the house for temporary festive occasions.

By both Greeks and Romans hangings were used in triumphal processions, covering immense moving cars or draping the temporary buildings which lined the avenues of their progress. Also the funeral pyres which Greece and Rome copied from Assyria were hung with [267]splendid materials and embroideries. Without describing one of these awful erections, it is impossible to give any idea of how much artistic treasure was thrown into the flames which consumed the remains of a great man. The funeral pyre dedicated by Alexander to his friend Hephæstion recalls that erected by Sardanapalus in one of the courts of his own palace, on which he perished, surrounded by his wives and his treasures. Hephæstion's catafalque was built of inflammable materials, 250 feet high, raised in many stories, and hung with pictorial tapestries, painted and embroidered. Each story was adorned with images of ivory and gold. In the upper story were enormous hollow figures of Sirens, filled with singers, who chanted the funeral odes.[450] It is to be hoped that they were released before the conflagration.

The records of such extravagant funeral ceremonies teach us how much of human thought, how much of art and beauty which had helped to civilize the world, were torn from the places they were intelligently designed to decorate, heaped up by the conquerors, and as ruthlessly spent and destroyed for the boast of a day.[451]

Christian Rome adopted the traditions of Pagan decoration, and introduced them in her worship, processions, and shows. A great religious procession like that of the "Corpus Domini" in our own times, has [268]reminded us of a Roman triumph. The baldachini and the banners; the torches; the streets, festooned with draperies; even the Pagan emblems, which have been converted into Christian symbolism—all these were the echoes of classical days; but they are fast disappearing. Two thousand years will have worn out and effaced these customs, and our children will not see them.

I have not space to linger over the many descriptions of Oriental, Grecian, and Roman work to be gathered from classical authors, but from them this lesson is to be learned that the first principle which guided those great decorators was the individuality and appropriateness of each design to the purpose for which it was intended and the place it was to fill. But even their peculiar excellences did not save them from the universal law of destruction. When the hangings were worn, or became for any reason distasteful, they were replaced by others, often by gifts or spoils from friendly allies or conquered kings. The quantity of gold laid upon these great religious or national works was the cause of their destruction as soon as they were withdrawn and superseded by something of a newer fashion. The intrinsic value in precious metals of such works is proved by Pliny's statement that Nero gave four millions of sesterces for covers of couches in a banqueting-hall.[452] The hangings or carpets taken by the Caliph Omar from Kosroes' white palace (A.D. 651) must have been some of the finest and most valuable embroideries ever known.

They formed a tapestry carpet or hanging, representing all the flowers of spring, worked in coloured silks, gold, and precious stones. Kosroes entreated Omar to keep it intact for himself, but he was so virtuous that he cut it up into little bits and divided it amongst his generals. Gibbon [269]describes this wonderful piece of work.[453] We have heard much of a marvellous carpet, given lately by the Guicowar of Baroda to the tomb of Mahomet at Medina, which, from its description, recalls the style of Kosroes' hangings; and their history gives us a notable instance of how works of art in the time of war and conquest come to be considered only for the value of their materials. War, the enemy of culture, all but effaces whole phases of art when a country is overrun and plundered. But there is almost always a residuum, which has influence whenever there is a revival, beginning with the smaller arts of luxury in more peaceful and prosperous days.[454]

To return to the classical veils and hangings. You may see them on Babylonian bas-reliefs, on Greek fictile vases, or painted in frescoes on the walls of Egyptian tombs and temples; in the houses in Pompeii and Herculaneum, and in the remains of Roman villas and tombs everywhere. From all of these we may learn something.

The obvious intention of hangings in household decoration is to cover bare walls, so as to adorn at once that which was rough or common, without delay or trouble.[270]They were also used as curtains to shut out the cold or the heat, and to give privacy to rooms without doors or windows. Hangings on bare walls have always been meant to hang straight down, undisturbed by folds, whereas curtains and portières would probably have to be looped up or continually drawn aside. The designs to be worked upon them should necessarily be regulated by their shape and use.

Semper considers that a square is an expressionless form, and that it should be avoided.[455] If you wish to give dignity to a room, its hanging decorations should be divided into panels of greater height than breadth, so as to elevate the spaces they cover. Horizontal stripes bring down the ceiling, and even in furniture, look ill except as borders. Nothing can be more ugly or inartistic than the curtains one finds in old illuminations, covered with bands of the same pattern throughout the surface, but even this is less unpleasant on the walls than lines crossing each other at right angles. The Romans looked on chequers as barbarous national characteristics, and left them to the Gauls and Britons. Chequers should be avoided unless they express a meaning, as in Scotch tartans. Semper observes that the striped stuffs, especially those of Oriental fabrics, were never intended to be spread out flat, but to be draped in folds and loops, and the lines only seen broken up. He continues:—"One rule, which cannot be neglected with impunity, is this: that whether the hanging or screen is supposed to stand or to hang, there must be an above and a below to every pattern, and it must, moreover, be upright." All foliage designs, and those containing animals, must start from below, and grow upwards. Another of his laws is that the heaviest colours should be placed below, and the palest and brightest above. This may be disputed. It [271]must be first determined where contrast is needed. If the darkest part of the pattern is below, it may be necessary to give it the lightest background, on the principle of balancing quantities in colour. The dado, or lowest border, will often give the necessary weight to the design. Semper goes on to say, "A surface may be made to appear to stand, or to hang down, according to its decoration. For instance, a triangle will hang or stand, according as its apex points downwards or upwards. But in draped curtains all symmetry of design is lost, and the rich forms and fulness of folds rather tend to destroy the effect of elaborate patterns, and to take their place."

Another important difference between standing and hanging tapestries is their finish or edge, the upper one being an upright continuous border, and the lower one a fringe. In both cases it is a continuation of the main threads of the material, and these belong exclusively to the hanging tapestries and curtains. The fringe is so essential a part of hanging decoration, that we must pause and give it our best consideration. In Babylonian art it is most important. The extreme solidity of the knotted fringes in their dress and hangings show either the thickness of the woven substance, or that the fringes were made by enriching the warp and adding to it. They are almost always, on the Assyrian sculptures, simply knotted fringes; but the little portable Chaldean temple on the bronze gates from Balawat (near Nimroud), in the British Museum, shows fringes of bells or fruit like those of the Jewish tabernacle in the wilderness (fig. 2). On Egyptian linen we sometimes see, woven or worked, a reticulated pattern which imitates a fringe.

The carpets of the Egyptians, Babylonians, and Persians were evidently used sometimes as hangings, though many of their designs would not have served both[272]purposes equally well. That the Babylonian weavers, however, understood that a carpet lying on the ground should be covered with an even pattern, and be finished with a border all round, is evident from the exquisitely chiselled designs, imitating carpets, on two portions of pavements in the British Museum (pl. 27); and we may compare these with the different treatment of designs for the veils of the temples, both in Babylon and Egypt, on which were represented the signs of the zodiac and all the heavenly bodies, and other symbolical and unconventional forms. The Atrium of the Greek and Pompeian houses, which was modelled on the same idea, was separated from the Court by curtains, hung on rods or nails. On festive occasions these may have been garlanded with natural flowers. If so, we may be sure that the little wreaths worked on them, as we learn from frescoes, would combine with the gala day's decorations, and would be designed with that view. The Greek artist would never have approved of natural flowers or trees, embroidered as if growing out of a dado, simulating a garden worked in wool. This would have been considered a bad attempt at pictorial art.

M. Louis de Ronchaud, in his "Tapisseries des Anciens," speaks of the hangings which he supposes to have decked the recess that contained the chryselephantine statue of Athenè Parthenos in her temple at Athens. He says these votive hangings dressed the pillars that surrounded the Hecatompedon, and formed a tent over the head of the goddess. M. de Ronchaud believes that among the subjects of the Delphic embroideries, described by Euripides in the tragedy of Ion, may be recognized some derived from the designs on saffron-coloured hangings, spoken of by the poet as "the wings of the peplos."[456]

[273]The downfall of decorative art, domestic as well as national, kept pace with the downfall of the Roman Empire. During the Dark Ages, of such art there seems to have been very little; and of that the best was Celtic or Anglo-Saxon. But the darkness shrouds from our view the artistic life of the world, and the dawn was very long in breaking. We must therefore return to the subject of hangings, after a gap of nearly a thousand years, when the first stirrings of the European revival came, in the twelfth century.[457] Symonds says: "The arts and the inventions, the knowledge and the books, which suddenly became vital at the time of the Renaissance, had long lain neglected on the shores of that Dead Sea which we call 'The Middle Ages.'"[458]

There can be no doubt that, during the Dark Ages, hangings woven and embroidered continued to be the custom throughout Europe. Our own Anglo-Saxon records prove that such furnishings were employed to mitigate the cold bareness of our northern homes from the earliest times. Sir G. Dasent informs me that in Icelandic Sagas, as early as the eleventh century, there are frequent notices of hangings both in churches and in the halls of houses; such, for instance, as the Saga of Charlemagne, i.e. scenes out of Charlemagne's life, worked on hangings 20 ells long. In Scaldic poetry, a periphrasis for a "lady" is "the ground of hangings," or "the bridge of hangings," all pointing to embroidery.

From illuminated MSS. engraved in Strutt's "Antiquities of the English," and contemporary European work of the tenth to the thirteenth centuries, we find that the favourite style of embroidery, when not representing [274]historical or sacred subjects, was a *parsemé* pattern. Armorial bearings were generally reserved for cushions, chair-backs, and the baldachinos of altars, beds, and thrones.[459]Richer and more flowing designs were later introduced.

In the fifteenth, sixteenth, and seventeenth centuries, splendid tapestries of Arras, and hangings even of cloth of gold, were common as palatial decorations. Sometimes we have a glimpse of less ambitious hangings; for instance, in the London house of Sir Andrew Larkynge, Knight, in the fifteenth century, the hall was hung with sage-green panels, bordered with gold "darned work," and the "parler" with sage-green, bordered with crimson.

French embroidered hangings were very fine in the sixteenth century. Jeanne d'Albret, the mother of Henri IV., was a great patroness of such works. Miss Freer tells us that—

"When Jeanne and Antoine took possession of the Castle of Pau, they found their new abode rich in works of art and splendid decorations. The refined taste of Marguerite d'Angoulême was visible everywhere. Jeanne's presence-chamber was adorned with hangings of crimson satin, embroidered by the hand of Marguerite herself. The embroidery represented a passage from the history of the Queen's own life."

"During the hours which the Queen allowed herself for relaxation, she worked tapestry, and discoursed with some one of the learned men whom she protected."

"The Queen daily attended the afternoon sermon, preached by her chaplains in rotation. Often, however, [275]weary with the excess of her mental labours, and lulled by the drowsy intonation of some of these ministers, the Queen slept during part of the discourse. Jeanne always felt severe reproach of conscience when she had thus involuntarily yielded to fatigue; and finding the inclination grow upon her, she demanded permission from the Synod to work tapestry during the sermon. This request was granted; and from thenceforth, Queen Jeanne, bending decorously over her tapestry-frame, and busy with her needle, gave due attention to the rambling addresses of her preachers."

"Comme elle (Jeanne d'Albret) estoit grandement adonnée aux devises, elle fit de sa main de belles et grandes tapisseries, entre lesquelles il y a une tente de douze ou quinze pièces excellente qui s'appelle *les Prisons brisées*, par lesquelles elle donnoit à connôistre qu'elle avoit brisé les liens et secoué le joug de la captivité du Pape. Au milieu de chaque pièce, il y a une histoire du Vieu Testament qui resent la liberté, comme la délivrance de Suzanne, la sortie du peuple de la captivité d'Egypte, l'élargissement de Joseph. Et à tous les coins il y a des chaisnes rompues, des menottes brisées, des strapades et des gibbets en pièces, et par-dessus en grosses lettres ce sont ces paroles de la deuxième aux Corinthiens, ch. iii.: *Ubi spiritus, ibi libertas.*"[460]

Cluny boasts a most curious suite of hangings from the Chateau de Boussac, of the early part of the fifteenth century, which are charming, quaint, and gay, and historically and archæologically interesting. They tell the story of the "Dame au Lion."

Modern French tapestries, from the manufactories of the Savonnerie, the Gobelins, and elsewhere, are decorative to the highest degree. Nothing can be more festive than these works of the time of Louis XIII., XIV., and XV., [276]framed in white and gold, carved wood, or stucco, reflected in mirrors, and lighted by crystal or glass chandeliers and girandoles. Such hangings have nothing in common with those of early times; they are not temporary coverings of bare spaces, but panels in decorated walls, where they form an integral part of the architectural composition and design. They do not merely serve to give warmth, comfort, and colour to desolate halls, as did those ancient tapestries belonging to the furniture of the great man who sent them on before him from palace to palace, carrying them away with his baggage lest some one else should do so in his absence. These were probably merely attached by loops and nails, as one sees in country villas or castles in Italy to this day.

We find that the Italians in the sixteenth and seventeenth centuries often hung their walls with upright strips of work, in the guise of pilasters. The walls were thus divided into panelled spaces, which separated pictures, statues, and cabinets, of which the style did not agree in juxtaposition. These pilasters were generally of "opus consutum," or "appliqué" in its different forms. Above, next to the cornice, and below, next to the dado, or even touching the floor, they were connected by borders of similar work. The spaces between were mostly filled with rich brocades or velvets of one colour, so as to make the best backgrounds for the artistic treasures grouped against them. Sometimes fine tapestries filled the intervening spaces, and sometimes splendid embroideries. There is a beautiful example of this sort of decoration at Holland House, where the dining-room is adorned with pilasters worked on velvet in gold and coloured silks, with tapestries between them. This is Florentine work, of the sixteenth or beginning of the seventeenth century.

[277]Hangings entirely in needlework, to cover large spaces, are rare, but a few are to be found all over Europe in museums, palaces, and private houses, which are interesting as objects of art. The genealogical tree of the Counts of Kyburg, designed in the sixteenth century, and carried to France as plunder, and now restored to its home near Zurich, is a remarkable instance of a piece of needlework that deserved the value placed on it. Many

splendid pieces of embroidered tapestries are at the Cluny Museum. The beatitudes of St. Catherine, from the castle at Tarrascon, and the hangings worked in appliqué and flat stitches with portraits of Henri IV., Jeanne d'Albret, &c., are monuments of industry, and design; and are very beautiful.

There, is a large room at Castle Ashby hung with tapestry in cross stitches, worked by the ladies of the family, and finished 150 years ago. The industry shown here is indubitable, but the designs are barbarously bad and funny. In the Palazzo Giustini at Florence there is a suite of hangings worked also in cross stitches of the same period, of which the design is very clever and graceful, and the effect beautiful and artistic. An irregular bank of brown earth is crowded with grasses and small flowers about a foot above the dado, and from this grow rose-bushes, covered with blossoms of different shades, held back to a treillage of delicate "cane colours." The leafage is brown, against a sky that is not blue, but which rather reminds one of blue than of grey. It is conventionally treated, and the effect is singularly rich and harmonious. Had it been a little more naturalistic, it would have looked too much like a painted picture; but as it is, the decoration is charming, and so universally admired that we cannot but wonder it has never been imitated. In the Borghese Palace at Rome there is a ball-room hung with white satin embroidered with wreaths [278]of flowers, and a similar one in the Caetani Palace, on crimson satin. These are about 150 years old, and are so far above being mere objects of fashion, that they must be placed by their beauty of design and execution amongst objects of art, and so will probably survive more centuries of change, holding their own, and increasing in value and esteem.

For hangings in church decoration, the reader is referred to the chapters on ecclesiastical art and on tapestry.

Having discussed the origin and reason for hangings, and having tried to draw from what has been accepted as beautiful and perfect in taste, some guidance in hanging our modern rooms, supposing always that the spaces are fitted for really fine decorations, I yet would add a few more words on this subject. There are in general some previous conditions which will help us to choose the style and design of such furnishings. In the first place, we should study what is appropriate to the persons who will first inhabit the rooms. The bride's apartment may be white and gold, garlanded with roses, and gay with groups of Cupids; but such prettinesses would not be suitable to the home of a mourning Queen. Tender or subdued colouring equally sets off groups of young and lovely faces, and the bent form robed in black. Embroideries are always agreeable on such backgrounds, and it is as a vehicle for needlework that I now allude to the design of the artist in hangings. We are somewhat restricted, or we ought to be, when there are treasures of art already in the house, by the desire to exhibit them to the best advantage. The hangings should be of a colour which suits all pictures, and if the walls are either embroidered or tapestried with woven designs, they should be very much subdued, both in form and colour, so as not to prevent the eye from perceiving at [279]once the precious objects hung against them. A fine brocade or velvet of one colour suits pictures best; but if our object is to show off our cabinets, which are generally black, and our statues, which are mostly white, then richly embroidered backgrounds in brilliant colours are the best, compensating the eye in variety and splendour.

FOOTNOTES:

[438]The "women who wove the hangings for the grove" were probably priestesses of the worship of Astarte (2 Kings xxiii. 7).

[439]He says that within the sacred shrine was revealed their god—a beast rolling on a purple couch—veiled with gold embroidered hangings; and he describes the magnificent temples, gleaming with gold, silver, and electrum. Quoted from Clemens Alexandrinus, in Renouf's "Hibbert Lectures," p. 2.

[440]"Fine linen with broidered work from Egypt was that which thou spreadest forth to be thy sail."—Ezekiel xxvii. 7. Egyptian sails were woven and painted; sometimes they were blazoned with embroidered patterns. The Phœnix was set there to indicate the traveller's return. See Wilkinson's "Ancient Egyptians," vol. iii., ed. 1837, p. 211.

[441]See Semper, "Der Stil," vol. i. p. 273.

[442]The figure-painting of the nations we have spoken of, successful so far as it concerns its special purpose of exhibiting a clear and comprehensive chronicle of events, is

at the same time no more, so far as it concerns its artistic effect, than a piece of tapestry or embroidery done into stone, and can only be estimated ... as a piece of coloured wall decoration. Woltmann and Woermann, "History of Painting," Eng. Trans., pp. 23-30. See also Perrot and Chipiez, "Histoire de l'Art dans l'Antiquité," for tile decorations at Nimroud; vol. ii. p. 704.

[443]Compare this record with Solomon's veil for the Temple, of blue, and purple, and crimson, and fine linen (2 Chron. iii. 14), and the hangings designed by Bezaleel, of scarlet, blue, purple, and embroidered with gold (Exod. xxxix. 2, 3, 5; see also Josephus, "Wars of the Jews," Whiston's trans., p. 895).

[444]As cited from Abulfeda by Gibbon, chap. lii. ix. p. 37, ed. 1797. When one is moved to pity, thinking of the enforced labour of thousands of captive women, fallen, perhaps, from high estate, and only valued for the toil of their hands, it comforts one to believe that they would hardly have produced beautiful works without enjoying some happiness in the creation of that beauty.

[445]Yule's "Marco Polo," vol. i. p. 394, note 7.

[446]See Semper, "Der Stil," i. pp. 310, 311; Chares, ap. Athen. xii. 54, p. 538.

[447]Semper's "Der Stil," i. p. 311; Athen. v. 25, p. 196.

[448]Phylarchus, ap. Athen. xii. 55, describes a Persian tent in which were golden palm-trees, and vines fruited with precious stones, under which the Persian kings held their state. On an Assyrian sculpture at the British Museum is seen Assurbanipal on a couch, the queen opposite to him, under an arbour of jewelled vines; unless it represents a rural entertainment, which is unlikely.

[449]The art of the "tapezziere," "tapissier," "tapestry-hanger," is not a recognized one with us, though it is in Italy and France, where the hangings for special occasions in churches and houses are stored away, treasured for hundreds of years, cleaned and mended, and hung and placed to the best advantage by men educated for the purpose. In poor churches which possess no fine materials for decoration, one has often wondered at and admired the picturesque effects extracted from yards of muslin, gold tinsel, and box wreaths, artistically combined. Our house carpenter is the only representative we have of the vestiarius, and he is but a feeble descendant from the ancestors of his craft, who were expected to study and evolve the adornments of the building for its completion, the materials of decoration for special occasions, and lastly, the mechanical means for hanging and stretching the draperies. These were sometimes movable frames or posts—"scabella" (whence "escabeau," échafaudage, scaffolding).

[450]Semper, "Der Stil," i. pp. 314, 315.

[451]Never again will such great works be executed with the needle. In civilized countries, sovereign splendours are at a discount. The East occasionally produces something fine, because there they still have harems and slaves; but even these ancient institutions are losing their stability and in the interest of humanity, if not in that of needlework, we may soon hope there will be neither the one nor the other. We must allow, however, that the purple and gold embroideries now being executed for the King of Bavaria in his school at Munich are royally splendid, and, by their execution, worthy of past days.

[452]Pliny, viii. 44, 196.

[453]Gibbon's "Roman History," ix. c. 51, p. 370, ed. 1797; also see Crichton's "History of Arabia," i. p. 383.

[454]The utter dispersal of accumulated family and household treasures has had a sad illustration in the loads of Turkish and Slav embroideries which have flooded the markets of Europe since the Russo-Turkish war. Work, treasured for generations, sold for a piece of bread, robbed from the deserted home or the bazaar, stolen from the dying or the dead. These are so suggestive of the horrors of war, and touch us so nearly in connection with the rights and wrongs of the Eastern question, that they cause us more pain than pleasure when we study these beautiful specimens of well-blended colours and designs, that show their Aryan (Persian or Indian) origin. Lady Layard's residence in Constantinople was, perhaps, the "happy accident" which will have preserved the secrets and practice of this work for future generations, by her active and generous institution of a working organization for the poor exiled and starving women, and for the sale of their work in England.

[455]Semper, "Der Stil," i. p. 30, § 10.

[456]This subject has been ably treated in the Introduction to "La Tapisserie," by Eug. Müntz; Paris, 1885.

[457]I refer to the chapter on "English Embroideries" for the *parsemé* patterns of our mediæval hangings, and to the section on tapestry in the chapter on "Stitches."

[458]"Renaissance in Italy," J. A. Symonds, p. 4.

[459]But to this rule there are notable exceptions, of which Charles the Bold's hangings for his tent (now at Berne) furnish a brilliant example. Here the Order of the Golden Fleece is repeated on a field of flowers, exquisitely designed.

[460]"Life of Jeanne d'Albret," by Miss Freer, pp. 68, 123, 330.

[280]

CHAPTER VIII.
FURNITURE.

"Jane, I hate æsthetic carpets;High-art curtains make me swear.Pray cease hunting for the latestQueen Anne chair.I care nothing for improvements,On the simple style of Snell,Which will suit both you and me ex-tremely well."

ROBERT CUST, "Parody of the Last Ode of the First Book of Horace."

"First, as you know, my house within the cityIs richly furnish'd with plate and gold;Basons and ewers, to lave her dainty hands;My hangings all of Tyrian tapestry;In ivory coffers I have stuff'd my crowns;In cyprus chests my arras, counterpoints,Fine linen, Turkey cushions boss'd with pearl,Costly apparel, tents and canopies,Valance of Venice gold, in needlework;Pewter and brass, and all things that belongTo house, or housekeeping."

SHAKESPEARE, "Taming of the Shrew," Act II., Scene I.

The last chapter on hangings, their history and uses, and the preceding account oftapestries, naturally lead to the consideration of the furniture which may accompany them.

Homer's description of Penelope's bridal couch is very curious. The central idea is the bedpost, fashioned out [281]of the stem of an olive-tree growing in the court, and inlaid by Ulysses himself with gold, silver, and ivory, and bands of dyed purple ox-hide. The stone walls and roof were built over to cover it in, as it stood yet rooted in the ground.[461]

The illustration is a very quaint delineation of a Chaldean four-roomed house, where the rooted tree with its stem and branches is suggestive of the state of the domestic art of the architect and the upholsterer in those Archaic days.[462]

Fig. 24.
Assyrian delineation of Chaldean House.

Furniture has been the excuse and the vehicle for embroideries, from the footstool and the cushion to the window curtain and the bed-hangings.[463]

Such curtains are the most permanently important features in the economy, or rather the luxury of the [282]house. Let us begin with the decorations of the state bedroom.

Now the shape of the bed must regulate the design. If there is only a canopy—like that over a throne—one may have fine work for the head of the bed inside the canopy, and a rich border round its valance; this should contrast with the walls; and the curtains should marry the two together, by the embroidered borders belonging to the fashion of the bed, and accompanying the window curtains; while the plain surface should match with the wall hangings. Another method is to have the bed and curtains hung with plain materials, to contrast with embroidered or tapestried hangings on the walls.

This style of bed canopy absolutely belongs to the decoration of the wall to which it is attached. But when we have to deal with a large four-post bed—"a room within a room," as poor Prince Lee Boo said—the bed may, in its own decoration, be totally independent of the wall hangings; and care must be taken that we do not injure the effect of both by too much contrast or too much similarity. Every room has its own individuality, and the first beginning of its decoration must be the key-note to guide the rest of the furnishing and adornment. I am anxious to point out that the bed and its belongings are a most important element in the beauty and dignity of style of the room and the house that contains it. It is a splendid opportunity for displaying the embroideries of the women of the family, and for exercising their taste. "The chamber of Dais," as it was called in old times, was always carefully adorned for the welcome of the honoured guest. The bed-hangings, and even the linen, were embroidered,[464]and the greatest care and the [283]most artistic work were lavished on the coverlet in firm stitches and twisted threads, while on the curtains the frailest materials and most delicate stitches were freely bestowed, as they were safe from friction. We may employ floss-silk and satin-stitch for such works with safety.

As a rule we should avoid too great a variety of design in the decoration of a bedroom, and at the same time beware of its becoming monotonous.

I should say that a change in the design, though not in the style, of the different parts of the bed is admissible, and gives opportunities for rich and graceful work. For instance, a parsemé pattern may be varied judiciously on the curtains, the valance, and the heading; provided there is a connecting link (say a cypher) found throughout. If the back of the Baldachino is embroidered, it admits of totally different treatment, and the valance must include a border according to its outline.

The ingenuity and magnificence of the Elizabethan bedroom furnishings are proved by the inventories to be found in old houses. Those describing the property of the Earl of Leicester, in the Library at Longleat, are so characteristic of a time when each room contained artistic furniture, that I cannot help making here some extracts, and pointing out that embroidery was usually employed to individualize each decoration.

"At Killingworth (Kenilworth) Lord Leicester's Bedsteads." "A fayre, rich, standing Square Bedstead of carved walnut-tree wood: painted with silver hearts, ragged staves and roses. The furniture and teste crimson velvet embroidered with silver roses, and lined throughout with Buckram." There was apparently a [284]second set of curtains inside of striped white satin, trimmed and fringed with silver, and the velvet curtains were also fringed with silver with long "buttons and loops."

Another bedstead is described, with the pillars painted red, and varnished. The teste and curtains of red silk edged with gold and silver bone lace, and embroidered "in a border of hops, roses, and pomegranates."

Another "Bedstead painted red and gold, and varnished; with crimson velvet, gold and silver in breadths, embroidered over with red, gold, and silver,—lined with Milion (Milan) fustian," &c., &c. The catalogue of the tapestries and embroidered hangings include fifteen suites at Kenilworth only; and three other houses are equally well provided. The ground of one of these suites of five pieces of embroidery, of animals and flowers, is described as being "Stannel cloth lined with cannevois" (canvas). Each room has chairs, cushions, carpets (which appear to have covered the floor and the tables), and "Cabinutts" (cabinets) covered with embroideries.

In a Florentine Palace (the Alessandri), there is a state apartment,[465] where the bed, the walls, the curtains, and the furniture are entirely decorated with the same splendid materials, i.e. gold brocaded with crimson velvet. The eye longs for some repose amidst the gorgeous reiterated forms and colours. If the bed and curtains had been either plain crimson velvet or embroidery, it would have been much more beautiful. This sort of example is a lesson and a warning, which is valuable even under less splendid conditions.

Amongst our fine Indian embroideries, those of Lucknow, Gulbargah, Aurungabad, and Hyderabad are well [285]fitted for beds and furniture. These we can study in the Indian Museum, and it seems a pity not to profit by, and encourage the resources of our own Empire.

Carpets and rugs were sometimes embroidered as well as woven in patterns. They were anciently spread on thrones, couches and sofas, at entertainments;[466]and used for covering the catafalques at funeral ceremonies, or for laying over tombs, as is still the custom in the East. We who restrict their use to domestic purposes, are beginning to understand that these decorations look best when the patterns are geometrical, and that natural objects, such as rabbits and roses, even when conventionalized, are unpleasant to tread upon.

The sofa and chairs are so often the vehicles for embroidery that we must give them a separate share of our attention. The square shapes of the chair-backs repeated several times give us an opportunity for balancing colours and introducing forms of decoration which may be made to contrast with everything else in the room, and so enhance the general effect. Say that the carpet is red, and the furniture and hangings are of tender broken tints, it will be a pleasure to the eye if the cushions on the sofa and the chairs and seats are panelled with a deeper or lighter colour than the carpet, but always reposing the eye by contrasting plain surfaces with richness of design. Then the footstool or cushion should break away entirely from the carpet on which it lies, that the poor thing may be spared the kick it invariably receives, when the master of the house has tripped over its invisible presence.

For furniture, the cushion stitches, i.e. canvas and cross [286]stitches, are certainly the best. They are the most enduring, as they bear friction without fraying; and are therefore, in this case, preferable to satin stitches, which are liable to be spoilt by contact, and give the lady of the house, who is probably the artist, a pang each time an honoured guest occupies the comfortable chair embroidered in floss silk, unaware that it is an æsthetic investment, and that a percentage of its beauty is disappearing every time it is brought into collision with broadcloth.[467] This brings us to the subject of the covers called "housses" by French upholsterers, and which may come under the head of small decorations, or rather, of petty disfigurements. The things which went by the horrid name of "antimacassars" have, however, given way to "chair-backs," and crochet has been displaced by linen veils worked in crewels. This is a step in the right direction. No well-regulated eye could do otherwise than suffer from the glaring white patterns of crochet-work, mounted aggressively on the back of every chair in the room, as a buffer between it and the human head and shoulders. The suggestion was disagreeable, and the present chair-back still recalls it. To reconcile us to its use, it must be sparingly used, and artistically disposed. The "antimacassar" is a remaining sign of the overlap of dress and manners. Our great-grandmothers embroidered the chairs, and valued them exceedingly, and never would have contemplated that they should be soiled by a male or female head lying back upon them. True, they wore powder and pomatum then—but they never leant back; such a [287]solace, and solecism in manners, was reserved for the privacy of the bedroom and the arm-chair covered with cotton piqué or washing chintz. Under the new manners, and since the introduction of the graceful lounge, the antimacassar doubtless has saved many ancestral works, but nowadays we wear neither powder nor pomatum. On the contrary, we dye, dry, and frizzle our hair till it might serve as a brush to remove any dust it encountered, and it spoils nothing.

The table-cover is a source of endless variety;[468] on the whole I should recommend here plain surfaces and deep borders. The articles thrown on the table are best set off by plain grounds. The colour of the table-cover may be a test of artistic taste, and may make or mar the whole effect of the furnishings of the room, especially if it is newly acquired, in order to enliven the fading glories of ancestral taste.

The Screen.—This evidently began its existence as a curtain hung on a movable frame for the purpose of dividing large chambers for separate uses.[469] The Chinese seem to have been the first to stretch the curtain tight over the frame, making it a fixture, and often an actual partition, painted with pictures by brush or needle.

To our modern home, the screen in a large room, gives a sense of snugness, and is an actual necessity for keeping off the draughts drifting in through ill-fitting window-frames and doors; and at the same time serving æsthetically as a background to high chairs and tables heaped with objects of art, and tall vases of flowers. [288]The high screen groups and unites the pictures of active and still life around it; and meanwhile the little fire-screens are performing the merciful service of saving the complexions of our daughters from being sacrificed to Moloch in front of our scorching coal fires. I need not recommend these as fit surfaces for embroidery—they offer themselves to it; and the School of Art Needlework is a living witness to how much they are appreciated and how largely employed. On the screen, decorative ambition is permitted to rise to pictorial art. Nothing in furniture is prettier than the screen covered with refined needle painting, either arabesqued or naturalistic. You may vary the designs to any extent, either as large pictures covering many folds, or in small pictures repeated or varied on each. Here design to individualize the living-room comes into play, and is most conspicuous for good or for evil effect.

Amongst the occasional furnishings of the home, we would instance embroidered curtains to veil pictures, which are perhaps too sacred to expose to the general eye. We know how often in churches and sacristies on the Continent, one, or even two veils have to be withdrawn before the holy and precious picture is displayed. We have seen these little curtains beautifully worked so as to form by their design a picture in the space they cover. Crimson silk is perhaps worked in gold and colours for a gilt frame, and white and silver within ebony or walnut settings. I would recommend this style of work to the consideration of our decorators. It is interesting to find in an old catalogue at Hampton Court, how pictures of sacred subjects were thus decently veiled, in the profaner moments of court gaieties.[470]

[289]Embroidered book coverings were often very beautiful, either as simply clothing the boards, or when finished with metal-work corners, backs, and clasps.

I quote the following lines, said to have been written by Tasso on a case for a book, embroidered for him by Leonora d'Este:—

"Questo prezioso dono,Ch' ornar coll' ago ad Eleanora piacque,Lo vidde Aracne, e tacque.Or se la mano, che la piaga fè al core,Si bello fè d' amore il dolce laberinto,Come uscirne potro, se non estinto?"

In the catalogue of Charles V.'s library, the materials used for bindings are thus named: Soie veluyau, satin damas, taffetas, camelot, cendal, and drap d'or; and many were embroidered.

Tact, discretion, and knowledge are required when we undertake to adorn the home to be lived in; and while employing the art of embroidery to embellish it, we must never forget that harmony, and the absence of anything startling, tends to the grandiose as well as the comfortable. Bright bits of colouring should be reserved for pictorial art, or for small objects, such as cushions and stools. If for the general tint blue be chosen, let it be either pure pale colour, like the æther, or a soft one, pale or dark, such as indigo; but the startling aniline blues should be avoided as being offensive to the nerves of the eye. If red be the foundation colour, let it be Venetian red, part scarlet, part crimson; or pure crimson (Tyrian purple), or pure scarlet (cochineal). Never employ scarlet with a yellow tinge; it may not affect yourself, but it is blinding to many eyes. Avoid brickdust, which is simply a dirty mixture of earthy colours. Of green there are few shades that are not beautiful, soothing, and more or less fitted for a background to needlework. Olive-green, sea-green, pea-green, emerald-green, [290]and sage-green,—Nature teaches us how these harmonize together and with all other colours. Only arsenical green is impracticable and repulsive. Yellow, pale as a primrose, glowing as gold, or tender as butter, is always beautiful; but one tint we would exclude from our list, called "buff," which never can assimilate with any other colour, and is often the refuge of the weak-minded man that cannot face the responsibility of choosing an atmosphere in which he will have to spend many hours of his existence, when the walls, the ceiling, and the hangings will inevitably obtain a subtle, but real influence on his nerves; which, in the case of buff, will be that of a yellow fog, while pale primrose will have the effect of early sunrise, and pure gold that of sunset.

A rule to be respected is that decoration should be reposing instead of exciting. The unexpected, which is an element in the enjoyment of what is new, should be such as to become the more agreeable the longer we are accustomed to it. Mr. Morris's golden rule is this: "Have nothing in your houses that you do not know to be useful or believe to be beautiful."[471] In decorative art, and therefore in embroidery, the first object to consider is beauty—beauty in conception, proportion, drawing, and colour. I would not have it thought that I am placing our secondary art too high, and giving it too much importance, when I apply to it the first essential rules of art; but one of these furnishes my excuse. It is that "the simplest and smallest creation should be as faultless as the greatest and grandest." Now beauty cannot be obtained, even in little works, without proportion in size, harmony and balance in colour, and correctness in form, and these require the careful study of first principles.

[291]Proportion in size is most important, both as regards ourselves and our surroundings—objectively and subjectively. When our masters, the Greeks, wished to express force and majesty, they sculptured their gods of unearthly size, larger than their heroes, who yet exceeded in stature their human models. The statue of the god placed in the temple was the largest object seen, and the delicacy and refinement of the details in dress, throne, and base only enhanced the effect of majestic proportion.

In the temple men were to be reminded of their own nothingness. In the gymnasium, and on the racecourse, and at the public games, the surrounding pictures and statues were all intended to excite ambition by showing men the heroic size to be attained by the awards of fame. But at home, in the house, man is already supreme, and needs no incentive to assert himself, and no tall standard by which he may be measured. The Lares and Penates themselves were very small objects to look at, whatever may have been the thoughts they suggested. Nothing is so alarming or unpleasant as gigantic figures worked in tapestry or embroidery.

And if even the guardian gods of the house were kept in due subjection as to size, why not all decorations, and especially those representing the flowers of the field? Certainly in worked decorations flowers should be no larger than in nature—perhaps on the whole they are best rather smaller. Botanical monstrosities on the wall dwarf the flowers in a bow-pot near them, and nature has her own lovely proportions, which should be studied and respected. These remarks, of course, apply exclusively to domestic decoration, which is the special object of our art, and for the guidance of which the suggestions contained in this chapter are intended.

[292]I would strongly advocate the return to the old system for the production of large embroideries. If ladies would design, or have designed for them, curtains or tapestries, and let the work-frame be the permanent occupier of the morning sitting-room, they might at least commence works that members of the family or friends might continue and complete at their leisure; and should they at any time hang fire, a needlewoman or clever professional worker might be called in to help to finish it. Thus ladies might assist the art of needlework by their own original ideas, and give individual beauty to their homes, and an impetus to the occupation which helps to support so many of our struggling sisters. The frame or métier is always a pretty object in the drawing-room or boudoir. The French understand this well; and make it one of their most useful "properties" in their scenic representations of refined home life.

I will conclude this chapter with two quotations. The first is part of Sir Digby Wyatt's advice in a Cambridge Lecture. "You can never hope (he says) to have the means of supplying yourself with what is beautiful unless you take pains to add to the production of that beauty. The colour which the decorative painter" (and the embroiderer also) "may cast around you is neither more nor less than an atmosphere in which your eye will be either strengthened or debilitated. If you accustom your eye only or mainly to contemplate what is satisfactory in colour and form to the highest tastes, it will gradually become allured to such delicacy of organization as to reject unintentionally all that is repugnant to perfect taste."

Mr. Morris, in a lecture to the "Birmingham Society of Arts and School of Design," says of ugly furnishings: "Herein the rich people have defrauded themselves as well as the poor. You will see a refined and highly [293]educated man nowadays, who has been to Italy and Egypt and where not, who can talk learnedly enough (and fantastically enough sometimes) about art and literature of past days, sitting down without signs of discomfort in a house that, with all its surroundings, is just brutally vulgar and hideous. All his education has done for him no more than that."

"You cannot civilize man unless you give him a share in art." But the man must be civilized by education to accept that share of art that his life offers to him. It must be admitted that though a man may be educated enough to enable him to theorize, he may yet be too poor to furnish with taste. If he is able to act up to his theories, and to surround himself with what is refined, and fail to do so, and is contented not to stir in this matter, he is not truly educated.

"Now that which breeds art is art. Any piece of work that is well done is so much help to the cause." "The cause is the Democracy of Art, the ennobling of daily and common work."

FOOTNOTES:

[461]Odyssey, xxiii., l. 190.

[462]Layard's "Monuments," 1st series, pl. 77; see "Histoire de l'Art," ii., Perrot and Chipiez.

[463]A bed may be absolutely without any hangings or tester, and yet carry embroidery, as in the curious funeral couch of a sepulchral monument in painted terra-cotta in the Campana Museum of the Louvre. Here the mattress is worked to resemble ticking, striped, and the cushions have embroidered ends; and are made in the form of bolsters. There is a similar sepulchral monument in the British Museum. Both of them were found at Cervetri, and are quaint examples of early Etruscan art. See Dennis' "Etruria," 2nd ed., p. 227.

[464]The thread embroideries in counted stitches were worked in an endless variety of beautiful designs, of which the collection in Franz and Frida Lipperheide's "Musterbücher für Weibliche Handarbeit" is most interesting and exhaustive; including Italian and German "Lienenstickerei," Berlin, 1883.

[465]Of the seventeenth century.

[466]The carpets used by the Romans were called Triclinaria Babylonica, for the use of the triclinium, and Polymata cubicularia, for the cubiculum. These were dyed crimson, scarlet, and purple. See Horace's Satires, ii. 6; also Smith's "Dictionary of Greek and Roman Antiquities," s.v. Tapes., p. 102-106, Triclinium.

[467]"Marco Polo," p. 92, ed. Yule, speaking of the ladies of Caramania in the thirteenth century, says they produced exquisite needlework on silk stuffs of divers colours, with figures of birds, beasts, trees, and flowers. They worked hangings for the noblemen's use, as well as cushions, pillows, quilts, and all sorts of things.

[468]Lampridius ("Antonin. Heliogab." cap. xxvi. see Bock, p. 129) says, in the life of Heliogabalus, that table-covers were embroidered for the emperor, representing the dishes which were to be placed upon them at the festal table of this epicure.

[469]See the screen on the Assyrian bas-relief in the British Museum, placed round the back of the throne on which the king is seated. This is apparently a frame on which hangings are fixed.

[470]See inventory Of Henry VIII.'s goods, &c., I. Ed. VI. (Bib.) Harl. 1419, quoted by Felix Summerley in his "Handbook of Hampton Court."

[471]I would add, "except that which is consecrated by time or sentiment."

[294]

CHAPTER IX.
DRESS.

"Whatever clothing she displays,From Tyre or Cos, that clothing praise;If gold show forth the artist's skill,Call her than gold more precious still;Or if she choose a coarse attire,E'en coarseness, worn by her, admire."

OVID, "Ars Amat." ii. 297, 300 (Yates, p. 180).

Having glanced at the decoration of the house, I must now proceed to say a few words on Dress. Semper, Labarte, and Sir Digby Wyatt all take it for granted that the Art of Dress preceded all other arts.

Every ancient record shows how early decoration of dress by needlework began, and how far it had gone; and when we read of festal hospitalities and marriage gifts, embroidered garments are invariably named. Solomon in all his glory, though he praised the lily, yet shone in splendid apparel. The Greeks refined the gold, and painted the lily.

Pl. 50.

See larger image
Italian Knight dressed for conquest, by Gentile da Fabriano. Academia at Florence.

As soon as dress became an art, and not merely an acknowledged necessity for warmth and decency, I see no reason to deny that the same decorative genius that embroidered the garment might at the same time have imagined the carving of the chair and the inlaying of the sword and bow; but as regards the precedence of the arts, we can only guess at what is probable. Beauty in dress is certainly a universal instinctive passion. Perhaps the birds (which Mr. Darwin and others credit with [295]preening their plumage, conscious that their spots are the brightest, and their feathers the glossiest, and that they are therefore adored by the hens, and the envy of the shabbier cocks) suggested to men the same method for securing the preference of the other sex, who in return willingly helped to adorn the idols of their hearts and homes. (Plate 50.) This natural state of things still prevails in Central Africa, where Schweinfürth describes a king dancing before his 100 wives costumed in the tails of lions and peacocks, and crowned with the proboscis of an elephant. It appears, however, that, unlike Cleopatra, "custom had staled his infinite variety," and the 100 ladies looked on the splendid display with blank indifference.

This is only a barbarous illustration of the fact that in the earliest civilizations magnificent garments were worn by men to dazzle and awe the beholders by the splendour which represented wealth and conquest. How glorious a man could appear apparelled to represent majesty and dominion, may be learned by studying Canon Rock's book on the coronation dresses of the Emperors of Germany—a book great in every sense of the word. The portrait of Charles V. robed and crowned is a dazzling example of the arts of dress, embroidery, and jeweller's work. These garments have for ages been treasured at Vienna, Aix-la-Chapelle, and in the Vatican at Rome.

The coronation garments of the Emperors of Russia are said to be gorgeously beautiful.

It seems hardly necessary to assert that embroidery has always been especially applicable to dress. Each garment, being individualized by the design depicted on it, was fitted for individual uses and occasions. The conqueror's palmated mantle, the coronation robe, the bridal garment, the costume of the peasant for festival days, and the officiating vestments of the priests for [296]special services of prayer and praise—these were loyally or piously worked; they descended from generation to generation as family treasures or as historical memorials, and sometimes as holy relics,[472] till they and the call for them, were swept away at once by social changes; yet some still remain and hold their place. Priestly garments, together with Church decorations, never laid aside in the Roman and Greek Churches, are being partially revived in our own; and for secular adornment the embroiderer is often called upon to work a garland, to enwreathe the form of a pretty woman, to lie on her shoulders and encircle her waist.

The greatest loss to the art is that men as a rule have ceased to individualize themselves, or their position or office by dress,[473] and have left entirely to the women the pleasure and duty of making themselves as lovely and conspicuous as their circumstances will permit. The same linen and broadcloth are cut in the same shapes, of which the only merit is that they are said to be comfortable, and whose highest aim is to be spotless and unwrinkled; these show the altered conditions of the highly [297]civilized man, and woman too, for he has long left behind him the idea of dazzling the female eye or heart by the attraction of colour. This applies only to European costume at home or in the colonies. The East still retains its pleasure in gorgeous combinations, in which man enfolds his person, and shows how beautiful he can make himself when thus clothed, in accordance with the classical axioms, as to how much of the human form should be revealed, and how much concealed.

The principle on which the ancients embroidered their garments was like that of the Indians, the large surfaces plain, or covered with quiet diapers or spots, the rich ornaments being reserved for the borders, the girdles and the scarves. Their garments hung loose from the shoulders or girdle; whether long or short they clung to the figure or fluttered in the wind. The long flowing robes to the feet veiled the form completely, and were only thrown off for the battle or the chase, or in the struggles for victory in the races and games. Dress, in the supreme reign of beauty, was intended to flow around, or to conceal, but never to *disguise*, the human frame it enclosed.

Homer thus describes Juno's toilet before calling on Jupiter:—

"Around her next a heavenly mantle flow'd,That rich with Pallas' labour'd colours glow'd;Large clasps of gold the foldings gather'd round;A golden zone her swelling bosom bound."

Iliad, xiv. v. 207.

The Greeks certainly wore delicate and tasteful embroidery on their garments, frequently finished with splendid borders, while the large space between was dotted with stars or some simple pattern. We learn this from the paintings on Greek fictile vases. In the

British Museum there is a little bronze statuette of [298]Minerva (with twinkling diamond eyes). She has a broad band of embroidered silver foliage from her throat to her feet.

As the beauty of Greek forms acted and reacted on the beauty of their "Art of Dress," so we may be certain that all deformity of dress has been produced by deformity of race in mind or body, and that climate is an important factor in both. The cold of the farthest north has produced people short, fat, and hairy; which natural gifts have been supplemented by their warm clothes or coverings, in the same way that a "cosy" covers a teapot. Flowing garments there would be utterly out of place, petticoats are unknown, and the Lapp hangs out nothing that can be the vehicle for carrying an icicle. Their dresses, or cases, are planned to keep out the cold, and to place another atmosphere between the heart of the breathing mass, and the cruel, cutting, outer wind. Hence, the materials used are not only woven hair, but the furry skins themselves. In the south, under the sunshine, dress is for the greater part of the year only needed for decency and beauty. The flowing and delicate cottons and silks and fine woollens, are shaped to cover and adorn the beautiful forms, which for entire isolation take refuge in the never-failing mantle. The mantle was the great opportunity for the embroiderer's craft. Alkisthenes, the Sybarite, had a garment of such magnificence that when it was exhibited in the Temple of Juno at Lacinium, where all Italy was congregated, it attracted such universal admiration that it was sold to the Carthaginians by Dionysius the Elder for 120 talents. The ground was purple, wrought all over with animals, except the centre, where were seen Jupiter, Juno, Apollo, Minerva, Venus, and Themis. On one border was the figure of Alkisthenes himself, on the other was depicted the emblematic figure of his native city, Sybaris. The size of [299]the garment was Homeric—it was fifteen cubits, or twenty-two feet in breadth.[474]

That the ladies of Greece in the fourth century carried down the historical and Homeric traditions of the embroidery frame, and made it part of their daily lives, while the Persian women of rank left such work to their slaves, is evident from the pretty legend told of Alexander the Great, who desiring to beguile the weariness of his prisoners, the wife and family of Darius, sent them some of his garments to embroider. When it was reported to him that these princesses were much mortified, believing it was a suggestion of their fallen fortunes, Alexander hastened to reassure them—saying that his own mother and sisters occupied themselves in embroidering dresses.

The Persians and Babylonians seem to have preferred subjects for their embroidered dresses somewhat in the style of the mantle of Alkisthenes, which was probably Oriental, and suggests the Babylonian mantle in Jericho; "which tempted Achan to sin." The Egyptian frescoes on the other hand, sometimes give us women and goddesses dressed in small flowery patterns that remind one of Indian chintzes. These were probably woven, painted, and embroidered, and filled in with threads of gold. The Romans varied their fashions, but they preferred for a time striped borders on their garments,[475] and called them "molores," "dilores," "trilores," up to seven. The Greeks but seldom departed from the rule of plain or quietly patterned surfaces with [300]rich borders in their delineations of dress, though there are examples of large designs covering the whole garment.

The embroidered dresses of early Christian times are to be judged of by mosaics and frescoes—mostly Italian. Those of the dark ages were till lately only names and guesses. But a hiatus in our knowledge has been filled up lately by the store of entombed textiles discovered in the Fayoum in Egypt, and now at Vienna, in Herr Graf'schen's Collection. Here we have a variety of shapes, designs, and stitches, and every kind of subject, sacred and profane, Christian and Pagan, and the missing links between Indian and Byzantine fabrics are revealed. They cover nearly 400 years, from the third to the seventh century, and many of them may be looked upon as apart from any ecclesiastical or even Christian suggestions. I have spoken of them in the chapter on Woollen Materials.[476]

After the seventh century, we again come into the dawning light of history—and find here and there an illustrative fragment, nearly always ecclesiastical, taken from the graves of priests and monarchs. Charlemagne's mantle and robe embroidered with elephants and with bees, preserved at Aix-la-Chapelle—his dalmatic in the Vatican—the Durham embroideries, are rare and precious examples of that early period.

Semper describes the difference between "the covering" and the "binding." This seems to be little considered in modern costume, but it is so essential that I would impress it on my readers. He says that "the covering seeks to isolate, to enclose, to shelter, to spread around, over a certain space, and is a collective unit," whereas binding implies ligature, and represents a "united plurality,"—for example, a bundle of sticks, the *fasces* of the lictors, &c. "Binding is linear, in dress it [301]is either horizontal or spiral." What can the united plurality be that justifies the binding often bestowed on the figure in fashionable costumes? more fitted for binding together the bones of the dead, than for permitting the agility of the muscles of the living. Semper continues,—"Anything that goes against this important axiom is wrong."[477]

I think we must all agree that the objects of dress are decency, isolation, warmth, grace, and beauty. As long as fashion takes the place of taste, and extravagant*chic* supersedes grace and beauty, we must not hope that fine designs to individualize dress will be called for. The French machine-made embroideries are so beautiful, and comparatively cheap, that we cannot compete with them. The best artists design them, and the only fault to be found is this, that as they are made by thousands of yards, and can only be varied by interchange of colours, they become common the day they are produced. It has been said that "fashion is made for a class, but taste for mankind."[478] Fashion is the enemy of taste, though she makes use of her services. The gown, of which the fashion is in every sense imported from France, will probably never again be the vehicle for home embroideries. But there are other articles of personal adornment which will always be available for the fancies of decorative taste—the fan, the purse or satchel, the apron, the fichu, the point of the shoe, and the muff—all these are objects on which thought and ingenuity may well be expended, and which will remain as records of personal feeling when the workers and givers of such graceful mementoes are far away. Carriage-rugs and foot-muffs, and embroidered[302]letter-cases, and book-covers, must be placed somewhere between furniture and personal ornament. In all these the "*imprévu*," or "unexpected," is what is valuable, including all that is original and quaint.

Embroidery will, however, probably continue occasionally to be employed in the adornment of dress—and will leave of each phase and period of art some fine examples on which the archæologist of the future may pause and reason.

There are in most old houses some specimens of old secular work—few earlier than the date of Henry VIII. Gothic dress is very rare, except the ecclesiastical. But from the fifteenth century till now, there remains enough to exercise our curiosity, our artistic tastes, and our power of selection and comparison; and hints for beauty and grace may often be found and adapted to the style of our own day.

Planché's "Dictionary of Dress," and Ferrario's "Costumi antichi e moderni di tutti i Popoli," are great works on dress and costume, and both are splendidly illustrated and worthy of study.

FOOTNOTES:

[472]Elsewhere I have spoken of dress being continually offered to the images of the pagan gods in the temples. Herodotus (ii. p. 159) tells us that Pharaoh Necho offered to the Apollo of Branchidæ the dress he happened to have worn at both his great successes (the victory of Magdalus and the taking of Cadytis). In the procession of Ptolemy Philadelphus the colossal statue of Bacchus and his nurse Nysa were draped, the former in a shawl, the latter in a tunic variegated with gold. See Yates, "Textrinum Antiquorum," p. 369. Old clothes were sent as votive offerings to temples, and inscriptions recording lists of such decorations are still extant. See Appendix 1. The Greeks honoured the menders and darners, and called them "healers of clothes." Blümner, p. 202.

[473]Men in former days preferred to show by their dress their station and the company they belonged to. Guilds had their ceremonial dresses, and their "liveries," and their cognizances, and considered it an honour to wear them. See Rock, "Church of our Fathers," ii. p. 115.

[474]Aristotle, De Mirab. Auscult., xcvi.

[475]Asterius, Bishop of Amasis, in the fourth century, describes both hangings and dress embroidered with lions, panthers, huntsmen, woods, and rocks; while the Church

adopted pictorial representations of Christian subjects. Sidonius alludes to furniture of like character. See Yule, "Marco Polo," p. 68.

[476]"Katalog der Theodor Graf'schen Fünde in Ægypten," von Dr. J. Karabacek, Wien, 1883.

[477]Semper, "Der Stil," p. 28.

[478]Unfortunately this axiom may be reversed. Taste only belongs to a small class, and mankind follows it, whether good or bad, if it only be the fashion.

[303]
CHAPTER X.
ECCLESIASTICAL EMBROIDERY.

"And now as I turn these volumes over,And see what lies between cover and cover,What treasures of art these pages hold,All ablaze with crimson and gold....Yes, I might almost say to the Lord,Here is a copy of Thy WordWritten out with much toil and pain;Take it, O Lord, and let it beAs something I have done for Thee!How sweet the air is! how fair the scene!I wish I had as lovely a greenTo paint my landscapes and my leaves!How the swallows twitter under the eaves!There, now, there is one in her nest;I can just catch a glimpse of her head and breast,And will sketch her thus, in her quiet nook,For the margin of my Gospel-book."

LONGFELLOW, "The Golden Legend" ("The Scriptorium"), p. 176.

"Upon Thy right hand did stand the queen in a vesture of gold, wrought about with divers colours.... The king's daughter is all glorious within: her clothing is of wrought gold. She shall be brought unto the king in raiment of needlework."—Psalm xlv. 10, 14, 15.

If the Bride is the type of the Church, how truly has she been, for eighteen centuries, throughout Christendom, adorned with gold, and arrayed in raiment of needlework.

By ecclesiastical embroideries, we mean, of course, Christian work for Christian churches. The first [304]pictured decorations of our era, in early frescoes, mosaics, and illuminated MSS., and the first specimens that have come down to us of needlework and textiles, testify by their *naïveté* to their date.[479]

The prosperity of the Church's hierarchy was founded on the ruins of the Empire, over which Attila had boasted that where his horse trod no grass grew; and truly the cultivated art of those splendid days had lapsed at once to a poverty of design and barrenness of ideas which would soon have dwindled into mere primitive forms, had not a fresh Oriental impulse arrived from Syria, Egypt, and Byzantium,—and then the arts were born anew.[480] The continuity was broken; yet, being devoted to the service of the Church, the new arts were by it moulded and fostered. Little lamps twinkled here and there in monastic houses. Hangings for the churches, coverings for the altars, robes for the priests, occupied the artist and the embroiderer.

[305]The forms, the colours, the uses, were adapting themselves to become the symbols of orthodoxies and heresies, and thus became a part of the history of the Church. The links are many between them and the history of the State; and here ecclesiastical embroideries come in as landmarks.

Royal and princely garments, which had served for state occasions, were constantly dedicated as votive offerings, and converted into vestments for the officiating priest, and so were recorded and preserved.[481]

Royal and noble ladies employed their leisure hours in work for the adornment of the Minster or the home church or chapel. Gifts of the best were exchanged between convents, or forwarded to the holy father at Rome, and were often enriched with jewels. The images of the Virgin and saints received from wealthy penitents many costly garments,[482] besides money and lands.

This dedicatory needlework has preserved to us the records of classical, Byzantine, and Arab-Gothic design, which otherwise must have been lost.

The Church records and illuminated MSS. give us [306]most trustworthy information of the way in which the altars, the priests, and even the kings were arrayed; and the catalogues of royal wardrobes are also very instructive, as we find how often princely gauds became, as gifts to the Church, commemorative of historical events, such as a victory or an accession, a marriage or a coronation.

Woltmann and Woermann say that the efforts of the Christians in the time of Constantine tended to delay the extinction of classical design in Rome. Of the fourth century they give as examples the mosaics of "Sta. Pudenziana," where we can still find antique beauty of design. We may also mention the church of "St. Agnese fuori le mura," which once contained the sarcophagi of Constantine and his mother Helena, and of which the decorations in the ceilings are entirely classical, though the motives had been transferred to Christian symbolism.[483]

The total disappearance of Greek art did not occur till the eighth century, when the new blood infused from foreign sources began to assert itself.[484]

Rome had succeeded to Greece as being the centre of Christian art, which assumed the phase commonly called the Romanesque. This was a conglomerate of Oriental, Byzantine, and Græco-Roman, varied in different countries. Then there were the Scandinavian, and Runic, and Celtic styles drifting from the North; the Lombardic, of Central Italy; the Ostro-Gothic, of Ravenna; the Byzantine, of Venice, all acting and reacting upon each other.

All these rough and inchoate attempts at the beautiful, [307]prepared the world for the acceptance of the Arabic influence, which is said to have been imported at the end of the eleventh century by the Crusaders, to whose pious enterprise some attribute the whole of the splendid Gothic art of the three succeeding centuries. But the marking characteristic of the Arabic arch is wanting; the ogee shape is seldom to be found in Christian architecture;[485] and the pointed arch so naturally results from the intersection of the round arches, that we cannot but look upon these causes as co-incident.

I have elsewhere remarked how often in art different causes co-operate to form a style. The father and mother are of different nationalities, and the result shows the characteristics of its double parentage. The learned antiquaries, who draw their arguments mainly from the form of the arch, must settle whence and how Gothic art in stone came into Europe. It was doubtless the effect or result of more than one cause.

But in as far as it influenced textile art, we have come to the period when it must be studied in Sicily, the half-way house and resting-place of the Crusaders on their highroad to the Holy Land.

Sicily, which had succeeded to Constantinople as being the great manufacturing mart during the Middle Ages, was, in the hands of the Moors, the origin and source of all European Gothic textile art. Yet even at Palermo and Messina they were controlled by the traditions of the schools of Greece, ancient and modern, and by Babylonian, Indian, and African forms and symbolisms.

Byzantium furnished many of their designs, which were [308]sometimes of very remote date, though pressed into the service of the new style and the Church.

These and all the streams of ecclesiastical decoration throughout Europe flowed towards Rome, and were re-issued with the fiat and seal of the Central Church, which also afterwards presided over the art of the Renaissance.[486]

By studying what remains to us of fragments and records we know all the materials which clothed the primitive and mediæval Church, and we find that there was but little originality in textile decoration or in the forms of dress, which either resembled those of the priests in the Jewish synagogue or those of the heathen temples; and were adapted from traditional patterns.

The constant repetition of the cross and the signs of the Passion, with the emblems of saints and martyrs, were interwoven with the ancient classical forms, mixed up with the old symbolisms partially altered to suit their new service of Christian art. Of course such changes were inevitable, while the old motives were being translated to the new uses.

The corselet of Amasis (the Egyptian corselet, p. 20, *ante*) closely resembles the Jewish ephod, which probably was borrowed from Egypt.[487]

In Rock's "Church of Our Fathers," vol. i. p. 409, we find mention of the consular trabea, profusely worked in gold, as being the origin of the cope.

Pl. 51.

See larger image
St. Mark. Anglo-Saxon Book of the Four Gospels in the Cathedral Library at York.

It has been suggested and disputed that the stole was an adaptation of the latus clavus; indeed, if we compare [309]the examples given by Bock[488] we can hardly doubt that the consular trabea and the latus clavus either served as the models for the Christian Bishop's dress, or were derived from the same traditional sources. Such is the intimate chain of design from century to century, from age to age; from Egypt to the Holy Land, and thence to Rome.

Bock gives his authorities for saying that the clavus was sometimes an applied border, sometimes a loose stripe hanging down in front, as may be seen in two consular diptychs given in plate 70. Much has been written on this latus clavus, its origin and meaning, and I shall return to it in reference to the chrysoclavus pattern, p. 337, *post*, and I refer the reader, who may wish to enter more fully into the questions raised by conflicting opinions regarding the clavus, to Marquardt's "Handbuch Röm. Alterthümer," vii. p. 2, pp. 528-533, where great learning and ingenuity have been expended, without arriving at any satisfactory conclusions.[489]

This keeping to the old lines and outward appearance as much as possible was mainly due to a regard for safety during the persecutions, and also to the Christian spirit of adoption and conversion, rather than that of antagonism, which influenced all their early manifestations.

This unchanging character of art was also partly owing to the absolute sterility of the ashes of Roman Imperialism.

It is true that through the Dark Ages individual genius occasionally flashed and left a mark here and there; [310]but such phenomena are so rare, that when they occur we hesitate before we assign them to that age.

The Anglo-Saxon art of illumination shows these inspired moments; I would point to their drawings in the books in the Bodleian at Oxford, and the "Book of the Four Gospels" (of the tenth century) in the Minster Library at York, which are original and graceful, and have a reflection from the classical traditions. To an artistic eye they are beautiful. (Plate 51.)

The conscientious colouring of the Anglo-Saxon MSS. is liturgical. Mr. Clapton Rolfe[490] says that the Levitical traditions in the earlier system of decoration in the Christian Church had a far stronger hold on the popular mind than we are willing now to admit; and that the five Levitical colours, gold, blue, purple, red, and white, were retained in the Christian ritual. Whenever we come across figures of Anglo-Saxon bishops, the liturgical vesture entirely agrees with the Biblical description.

Embroideries before the twelfth century generally preserve a semi-Roman, semi-Oriental character, which is nearly related to the art which is called Lombardic. This differs from what we know of Scandinavian and Celtic design through illuminated books,[491] carving on stone crosses throughout the north of Europe, Great Britain, and Ireland, and the remains we possess of their metal work. I am not aware of any ecclesiastical embroideries which show a Celtic origin,[492]unless the intertwined [311]patterns on Italian dresses in paintings of the thirteenth and fourteenth centuries may be supposed to be derived from that source. (See p. 91,*ante*.)

Fig. 25.

In accounting for the instances of evident Oriental influence on Christian art, which came through Byzantium, we must not restrict ourselves to searching out the Arabian traditions, but we must remember also how much Babylon and Persia, as well as India, had given to the Empire of the East, and these influences were in full force at the time that Christian art was being organized.

We know, for example, that the great veil of the temple at Jerusalem, given by Herod, was Babylonian.

The materials—linen, silk, and woollen—on which ecclesiastical embroideries were worked at Rome and Constantinople were accepted all over the Christian world. The fabrics were plain, striped, and figured; and came from Persia and India, Greece, Alexandria, and Egypt. Even Chinese and Thibetian stuffs are often named. Cloths of gold and silver also came from the East, as in the days of Attalus. All these furnished the grounds on which needlework was lavishly spent.

[312]The great veils which divided the pagan and Jewish temples were at first adopted in the Christian churches, but they gradually disappeared from common use, in spite of occasional survivals and revivals during the Dark Ages.

Records exist of the hangings of the ancient basilica of St. Peter at Rome, spread between the pillars supporting the baldachino over the high altar and those of the choir; and at the Ostro-Gothic imperial court of Ravenna, in the fifth century, Maximianus ordered a set of similar splendid curtains (tetravela) to be worked for the altar. Anastasius Bibliothecarius (ninth century), in his biographies of the popes, mentions curtains and embroidered altar-pieces worked in the sixth and seventh centuries.[493]

Sergius (A.D. 687) ordered four white and four scarlet curtains, and Pope John (701) hung white ones between the pillars on either side of the altar at St. Paul's. St. Zacharias[494] gave similar hangings to the churches of St. Peter and St. Paul. Stephen IV. placed immense silver curtains at the entrance of the basilica of St. Peter's, and in 768 gave to it sixty-five curtains of figured Syrian stuffs.[495] The same hangings prevailed at intervals in England, France, and Germany, till the twelfth and thirteenth centuries, when the new Gothic style of high, pointed arches altered the decorative customs.

Pl. 52.

See larger image

Fragments of Silk to be seen at Coire in Switzerland, also in the South Kensington Museum.

[313]From Anastasius's mode of speaking of ecclesiastical garments, it appears that they were named in the treasury catalogues after the animals represented on them—"the peacock garment," "the elephant casula," "the lion cope." Evidently these were Oriental gold brocades, Indian or Persian, or else reproductions of their designs, and from Auberville's and Bock's books of engravings we can judge how they repeated and varied their motives. One woven subject, which evidently started its textile career as one of the labours of Hercules, was gradually transferred to Samson, or to Daniel in the lions' den. (Plate 4, Auberville's "L'Ornement des Tissus.") (Plate 52.)[496]

However, in Russia and throughout the Greek Church the ancient Byzantine use of hangings still remains in force.

The art of embroidery has always given its best efforts to these church draperies.

Rome was so laden with splendid embroideries by her eastern conquests, that probably the Christian decorators would have availed themselves of some of the accumulated stores; but we have no record of such adaptations, unless the splendid curtains and the silver hangings of Pope Stephen IV. were taken out of some imperial treasure-house.

The contrast between early ecclesiastical art and that which immediately preceded it in the palaces of the Cæsars (at Rome, Tivoli, and wherever we find their ruined glories) is most remarkable.

[314]The lovely and the lively had been suddenly abandoned for the heavy earnest solemnity and inartistic drawing of the frescoes of the underground church of St. Clemente in Rome, and that of the early Christian mosaics.

It is as if the arts which had lent, nay, given themselves to the glorification of idols, had suddenly died out, leaving behind them neither an artist, nor a skilled artisan, scarcely a tradition.

The new Christian ideas had to be painfully recorded on sacred buildings and their furnishings for more than a thousand years; with all the patient acquiescence of untaught ignorance, and the struggling uncertainty of genius pursuing a distant glimmering light, apparently unconscious of all that had preceded it in Egyptian and classic art. The great political and religious revolutions in Europe had crushed and buried the arts under the ruins of the Empire over which Time himself seemed to have broken his hour-glass, so little was there to show any memory of their past, or hope for their future. The alternate progress and destruction of the arts in European civilization strike the student, in vivid contrast with the immutability of those of the East, especially in India and China, where the old forms were still being maintained by the swaddling bands of codified custom[497] that had restricted their development, but prolonged their existence, and so they had survived, while Greece conquered and robbed the East and Egypt, and Rome crushed Greece and was in her turn despoiled by the Goths and Huns.[498]

[315]Christian art had to begin at the very beginning, and collect its own traditions, and organize its own forms. These gradually accumulated, availing themselves of accepted symbols, and adding to them hidden meanings. The Reformation checked this development in the north of Europe, but after 300 years we are now witnessing its revival, which is not merely owing to a religious impulse, but also to the archæological tendency of our day and to the historical interest we attach to the ceremonials of the East.

As the Reformation in Germany was less sweeping and iconoclastic than our own, we find there many more remains of ecclesiastical art collected in the churches to which they have always belonged, or in museums into which they have drifted;[499] and the Germans have thus been enabled to do more than even the French, in training the different schools of work throughout the Continent.

They have proved the Oriental character of the fabrics employed through the Dark and Middle Ages, i.e. for about 1400 years, whether they were Syrian, Indo-Chinese, Indian, Alexandrian, Greek, Sicilian, or Spanish, or whether they had come from Asia by the north or the south of Europe. The same traditional forms governed them all. But an adept is able generally to class and [316]name each specimen by the texture of the webs, by the way gold or gilt thread is inwoven in them, whether the metal is pure or alloyed, round or flat; also by the mode of twisting and dyeing the wool, flax, or silk, and its quality and colouring matter.

Among the earliest historical church embroiderers the foremost figure is that of the Empress Helena, the mother of Constantine, claimed in Wales and in the Welsh ballad of "The Dream of Maxen Wledig" as being a Welsh princess married to the Emperor Constans. She is said to have embroidered an image of the Virgin, which Muratori speaks of as existing in the Church of Vercelli in the seventeenth century. Bock says it is still there, and he quotes an ancient inventory of the treasures of Phillip the Good, of Burgundy, which names a "Riche et ancienne table d'autel de brodeure que on dit que la première Emperriez Christienne Fist."[500] The Empress Helena died in the fourth century.[501]

Then after a long interval comes "Berthe aux grands pieds" the mother of Charlemagne, who in the eighth century was famed for her needlework, which is celebrated in a poem by Adhelm in the eighth century, quoted by Mrs. Palliser,[502] "a ouvrir si com je vous dirai meillior ouvriere de Tours jusqu'a Cambrai," and her grand-daughter Gisela followed in her footsteps. Nearly contemporary, is Aelfled's Durham embroidery,[503] described in the chapter onEnglish work.

[317]Christian art before the twelfth century is very often rich, usually picturesque, from its fulness of intention; sometimes beautiful, when it recalls some echo from the East, or some tradition of Greek art;[504] but the embroideries of those centuries are almost always quaint; this is invariably the archaic phase of all early art. Born in the catacombs of Rome—roused by impulses from the north, by education in the south, and everywhere encouraged by the fostering hand of the Church, and the patronage of papal and of royal and imperial houses,—it evolved its forms, and emancipated itself at last from its poor and sordid condition; and the Gothic phase of each nation attained to its own peculiar growth and characteristics; and among them the foremost in the world's estimation was theEnglish school of embroidery, to which the next chapter is devoted.

There has been much controversy as to the date of the dalmatic of Charlemagne in the Vatican treasury. Like every good early piece of Gothic work in Italy, it is allotted to the days of Pope Boniface VIII. (thirteenth century). But when we examine this splendid relic we cannot doubt that it is of a much earlier time, as there is nothing Gothic to be found in it. It is full of the lingering traces of Greek art (not Byzantine). It reminds us most of the mosaics of Santa Pudenziana, which are always quoted to prove that Greek art still survived in Rome in the eighth century.[505] The dalmatic has been much restored, but, I believe, most carefully [318]kept to the old lines. It is worked on a thick, dark-blue, or purple, satiny silk, which had entirely fallen into little stripes, but has been skilfully mended, and the embroidery has never been transferred. On the front is our Lord in glory, saints below, and angels above, with a border of children playing, which is truly Greek. The motive of this is the "Ibi et Ubi." On the back is the Transfiguration, and on the humerals are the sacraments of bread and wine. The whole, as art, is beautiful; and it is historically most interesting. Lord Lindsay tells us that in the dalmatic of Charlemagne, (called that of Leo III.) Cola di Rienzi robed himself over his armour, and ascended to the Palace of the Popes after the manner of the Cæsars, with sounding trumpets before him, and followed by his horsemen—his crown on his head and his truncheon in his hand—"Terribile e fantastico."[506]

This dalmatic must be ranked first and highest among ecclesiastical embroideries. (Plates 53, 54, 55.)

Some of the details are curious. The whole of the blue satin ground is worked with crosses "parsemé." Parts of the design are so adorned with larger and smaller Greek crosses—and others with the starry cross. On the shoulder is once embroidered the mystic swastika.[507]

See larger image
Charlemagne's Dalmatic
The Vatican, Rome
See larger image
Charlemagne's Dalmatic
The Vatican, Rome

Pl. 55.

See larger image
Details of Charlemagne's Dalmatic. Vatican Treasury.

Pl. 56.

See larger image
Cope called "of St. Silvester." Treasury of St. John Lateran, Rome. English Embroidery, thirteenth century.

Rock says, "Those who have seen, in the sacristy of St. Peter's at Rome, that beautiful light-blue dalmatic said to have been worn by Charlemagne when he sang the gospel at High Mass, at the altar vested as a deacon, [319]the day he was crowned Emperor in that church by Pope Leo III., will remember how plentifully it is sprinkled with crosses between its exquisite embroideries, so as to make the vestment a real 'staurac̣in.'"[508]

Pl. 57.

See larger image
Portion of the Cope at St. John Lateran, showing its condition.
See larger image
Pluvial, English, XIII. Century
Museum at Bologna

Pl. 59.

See larger image
The Daroca Cope. Museum at Madrid. Opus Anglicanum, fourteenth century.

Pl. 60.

See larger image
Portion of the Cope of Boniface VIII., twelfth century. From Anagni. Now in the Vatican Collection.

Pl. 61.

See larger image
Altar Frontal from Anagni, Italy.

Signor Galletti, Professor of Embroidery to the Pope, says it is undoubtedly of the eighth century. It has been suggested that the design is of the date of the Exarchate. It is, however, something of infinitely finer style; it is noble, simple Greek.

Charlemagne's dalmatic is embroidered mostly in gold—the draperies in basket-work and laid stitches; the faces in white silk split-stitch, flat, with finely-drawn outlines in black silk. The hair, the shadowy part of the draperies, and the clouds are worked in fine gold and silver thread with dark outlines. The hands, feet, and draperies have a fine bas-relief effect. (Plate 53, 54, 55).

The "pluvial of St. Silvester," in the church of St. John Lateran at Rome, is probably, from its Gothic style, of the time of Boniface VIII. (thirteenth century).[509] It never served

St. Silvester, except as being perhaps dedicated to him. On seeing it, one is convinced that it is English. It has one peculiarity of English Gothic design in the canopies being supported by twisted pillars of vine-stems, in this case intersected by green shoots, and carrying leaves. The angels, the two cherubim clothed in peacocks' feathers, the fine split-stitch, the gold grounding, and the drawing are also distinctly English.

I give an outline of the pluvial from photographs,[510] and a finished woodcut of the centre to show the style and condition of the work. The design is most beautiful, and we can only regret the loss of the border, which has [320]been entirely cut off. This shows how elaborate is the design, yet how artistically arranged as a whole composition. (Plate 56, 57.)

It is difficult to settle the precedence between this splendid piece of church decoration and the rival pluvial of Bologna in the Museo Civico, said to have come from the church of San Giacomo. It resembles in style and execution that of St. Silvester, but its architectural arrangement contains six circles of subjects, worked like the other in silk and gold, with gold groundings; and both are embroidered on linen. On careful examination of this splendid work of art, I have come to the conclusion that it is English. (Plate 58.)

The Daroca cope (lately belonging to the Archæological Museum at Madrid) is undoubtedly English. We can claim it by its peculiar shrine-work, and the twined columns on the orphreys; by the cherubim, by the peacock-feathered angels, and by the form of the panels enclosing the different subjects, from the "Life of Our Lord." (Plate 59.)

The cope of Boniface VIII. in the Vatican came from the church of his native place, Anagni (plate 60), where are still very curious old embroideries (see Hon. and Rev. I. Clifford's list of embroideries in Appendix 5). Some appear extremely ancient, but there is no sign by which they may be dated. Some are probably of the thirteenth century, and are very coarse Italian work, though finely designed (plate 61). There are doubtless many interesting specimens still to be found in the sacristies of Italian churches. But they have generally been transferred to museums.

Pl. 62.

See larger image

1. From Tomb in Worcester Cathedral, of Bishop Walter de Cantilupe, consecrated 1236.
2. Embroidered Cope at Aix in Switzerland.

Pl. 63.

See larger image

Mitre of Thomas à Becket at Sens, showing the Scandinavian Fylfot Cross (thirteenth century).

Jewelled Cross on Rose-coloured Cope at Rheims (twelfth century).

In the tomb of Walter de Cantilupe (eighteenth century) at Worcester, were found the remains of a dress which is decidedly of an earlier date—evidently of Oriental material, but Anglo-Saxon work—so exactly resembling in style that [321]at Aix given by Bock,[511] that we can hardly doubt that they proceeded from the same workshop, or at least are of coeval design. Both are worked with a dark red outline on a red silk ground. The faces and hands are in white silk—all the rest between the outlines is gold thread, flat stitch. Bock places its date as antecedent to the tenth century, and indeed there is no reason to doubt that this is correct, though the Worcester fragment was taken out of a tomb of two centuries later. As these garments were stored in the church treasuries; and as antiquity (without an historical interest) was then of no value, these old clothes, holy by their use and office, yet by their shabbiness unfit for public show, may have been reverently disposed of in clothing the bodies of departed priests, who probably had worn those very vestments, when officiating at the altar near which they were laid to rest. When the date of the wearer of the garment is ascertained, the dress cannot be of a later period, but it may have belonged to a much earlier one. The architectural part of these two embroideries, i.e. the canopy work, resembles that of the Bayeux tapestry. Both appear to be English. (Plate 62.)

Pl. 64.

From Tomb of Bishop William of Blois, died 1236. Worcester Cathedral Library.

Pl. 65.

See larger image
A portion of the Mantle embroidered by Gisela for her husband, St. Stephen of Hungary. From Bock's "Kleinodien."

In the eleventh century, and for some part of the twelfth, needlework design in England, France, and Germany first assumed a phase, which may be called the metal-work style. It is to be found on the robes and mitres of St. Thomas of Canterbury (Thomas à Becket) at Sens[512]—on the famous rose-red cope of satin embroidered with gold and pearls at Rheims (which we should incline to believe is English)[513] (plate 63). The fragment of the cope [322]of William of Blois, found in his tomb, is in this style. (He died in 1236.) The fragments of this curious garment, worked in gold on a purple silk material, evidently Oriental, are also preserved under glass in the Cathedral Library at Worcester (plate 64).

Amongst the finest instances of ecclesiastical needlework, and, indeed, we may say, of ecclesiastical art of the twelfth century, is the coronation robe of St. Stephen of Hungary, decorated by his queen, Gisela,[514] which is preserved in the Imperial Treasury at Ofen (plate 65).

Of this authentic historical work we have the whole story. The original design,[515] drawn on linen, carefully coloured, is to be seen at the Benedictine convent abbey of Martinsburg, near Raab in Hungary. The care with which the work was carried out shows the value then placed on such undertakings considered as art, and it has been justified by its survival of 800 years; time having spared it owing to its perfect materials and manipulation, till it received cruel injuries by being carried off and thrown into the bog of Orsava during the revolution under Kossuth. It was, however, recovered and restored, and was worn by the present emperor at the splendid and picturesque ceremonial of his coronation at Pesth. The design reminds us of the mosaics in the apse of Santa Maria Maggiore and other churches at Rome, and it is extremely beautiful. It consists of an arrangement of medallions and inscriptions, with "metal-work" ornaments in bands alternated with smaller medallions. Yet the figures are not so finely drawn as those of the Durham relics of the beginning of the tenth century. The drawing of the figures of the Gisela mantle resembles those on the garments of Walter de Cantilupe (plate 62), which, from their design and stitches, seem to be of this [323]period. The architectural parts are very like in design to those of the Bayeux tapestry, though they are infinitely better, and they have Lombardic characteristics.

Pl. 66.

See larger image
Portion of the Coronation Mantle of Henry II. of Germany, embroidered by the Empress Kunigunda. From Bock's "Kleinodien."

It appears that Queen Gisela had personally embroidered this many-figured, richly-embroidered representation of the "Ibi et Ubi"—The Saviour in His glory as Victor over death and hell, seated on the bow of heaven, surrounded by choirs of angels and saints, and prophets of the Old Testament; below on thrones, are the twelve Apostles. The figures are worked in Oriental gold thread on Byzantine crimson silk.

In contrast to the Ubi, the heavenly hereafter, the queen, in the lowest broad hem (border) has represented the Present, the then "Ibi," by the leaders of the Hungarian magnates and the half-figures of the royal givers in large gold-embroidered medallions.

The next finest specimen of eleventh century needlework was the gift of Henry II., Emperor of Germany, and his wife Kunigunda, to the cathedral of Bamberg, where it still exists[516] (plate 66).

This, again, consists of medallions great and small, of which the borders, gracefully intertwined, form a large composition[517] covering the whole surface of the imperial pallium it once adorned. But in the fifteenth century it was transferred from its original purple silk ground to one of dark-blue damask, and altered to the form of a chasuble, as we see it now. The general design resembles that of the mantle of Gisela.

Bock calls the style of these works Romanesque; and he thinks that they show a Saracenic influence. [324]They appear, however, as I said before, to be rather Lombardic than anything else. The reader is referred to Dr. Bock's preface for further lists of Continental works and workers.

Abbé Martin considers that in the thirteenth century the opening out of Gothic art was extended to the laity, and was really the sign of a great social revolution. Gothic art had till then only served the Church, and had been by circumstances closed to the people, who were yet unfitted, by their want of education, for artistic life.[518]

Art was till then almost exclusively produced by the monastic orders, into which all talent had drifted. But about this time it fell into the hands of architects and other originators of design, who presently banded themselves together into brotherhoods and guilds.[519]

Embroidery till the thirteenth century had been entirely in the hands of cloistered women, and the ladies who practised it learned their craft with the rest of their education in convents, and their work was simply ecclesiastical and dedicatory. At that period social burgher life in the towns had first begun to develope its love of luxury,[520] and to follow the fashions of other countries, and the changes of forms in dress and furnishing which came from foreign parts, though frequently checked by sumptuary laws. This social movement preceded everywhere political and religious revolutions. Embroidery then became customary in lay dress, [325]and lost its religious character, or rather its religious monopoly.

Pl. 67.

See larger image
The Syon Cope, South Kensington Museum (thirteenth century).

We find that about this time throughout the Church the forms of ecclesiastical garments were considerably modified, and made more comfortable for the officiating priest; and the old traditional trabea was cut down to the mediæval chasuble.

English needlework of the twelfth and thirteenth centuries had its own peculiar style of metal-work pattern, resembling the hinges and spreading central ornament branching across the wood-work on our church doors.[521]

When we meet with this kind of design on foreign church vestments, we feel inclined always to claim the merit of them for the English school. The foreign metal-work patterns are much lighter and more geometrical, and have not the firmness and at the same time the fancy that we find in our own of the twelfth century; and they remind us rather of the goldsmiths' than of the blacksmiths' craft. The English embroidery of this style has the character of "appliqué," i.e. one material laid upon another and fastened down.

There are differences of opinion as to the accepted characteristics of the "opus Anglicanum," which in the twelfth century began to be celebrated.[522] Some say that it was principally remarkable for its admixture of jewellers' work in the borders, or the imitation of it in gold thread. Some give the attempt to reproduce the effect of bas-reliefs in the embroidered groups of figures; others, again, point out the peculiarities of the "laid stitches" in gold, which so permeated the linen grounding, as to give the look of a material woven with gold thread. We may [326]fairly say that *all* these, which were then ingenious novelties, combined to give this opus Anglicanum its value, as well for its beauty as for its ingenuity.[523]

The Syon cope, (now one of the treasures of art in the Kensington Museum), is a perfect example of this work; and is also, according to Bock, "one of the most beautiful among the liturgical vestments of the olden period anywhere to be found in Christendom." Dr. Rock's study of this piece of thirteenth century work in his "Catalogue of the Embroideries in the South Kensington Museum" is most interesting, as exemplifying all the characteristics of the Gothic art of the period, in its historical, æsthetic, heraldic, liturgical, emblematical, and textile aspects. I have ventured to transcribe the whole of this notice in the Appendix.[524] I will only add here that the one error into which I think he has fallen, is in naming the stitches. The "diapers" are not opus plumarium, but opus pulvinarium, of the class of "laid stitches." This was ascertained by examining the back of the material under the ancient lining by a most competent judge[525] in my presence, and so a long-disputed point is set at rest (plate 67).

Ciampini says that in the twelfth century, the arts went hand in hand, each lending something to the design of [327]the others. This, however, has always been the case.[526] (Whether they greatly profited by such exchanges is another question.) I cannot but agree with Semper's often-reiterated theory, that textile art was a leading influence and constant suggestion to *all* art from the beginning. And the way that ecclesiastical decoration was so led in the twelfth century is very apparent. In the new art of stained mosaic glass in church windows we see the reflex of the flat illuminations and embroideries of that period; and while these were being influenced by metal-work, painting was being transferred again to textile art, pictures being woven as well as embroidered,[527] while textiles were seeking to emulate reliefs in a forced and unnatural manner, more ingenious than artistic.

While England in the twelfth and thirteenth centuries was exciting the admiration of all European artists by the imitation of bas-reliefs in needlework, by the arrangement of the light and shadows and by the "lay" of the stitches, and by a little help from the pressure of hot irons, to accentuate its apparent indentations, a similar inroad into the sister art of sculpture, or, perhaps, we should say a similar adaptation from the sister art, was going on in Switzerland and Germany, especially in Bavaria.

There was a clever and artistic mode of stuffing and raising of the important parts of the embroidered design, such as the figures, the coats-of-arms, or the emblems of the Passion, &c., in sacred subjects in imitation of high-relief. There are some beautiful specimens that [328]have been evidently designed in the School of Cranach. I will only mention the orphrey, of which the subject is the "Tree of Jesse," exhibited at Zurich, 1883, the chasuble at Coire in the Grisons, and the little triptych in the museum of the Wasser-Kirche in Zurich. This last is exquisitely pretty. The finest, however, is the altar-piece belonging to Prince Borghese at Rome, which is certainly German in its design.[528]

Beautiful as these few examples are, they yet show the mistake of mixing different forms of art. The designs are reduced to a compromise between painting, sculpture, and needlework, which excites interest and perhaps amusement rather than admiration.

Glass painting, of which we have no notice till the tenth century, shares many of the rules which hitherto had applied only to embroideries. It was intended to give colour and interest to those parts of a building which otherwise were cold and lifeless. *Flatness* in the composition, and the avoidance of pictorial effects (especially any perspectives) show that it was intended for conventional decoration, rather than as a rival to mural painting. There is no doubt that it generally superseded textile hangings, because it supplied the want of colour for the large traceried windows just coming into architectural design, toning down the crudeness of the masses of light, and tinting the walls and pavements on which it was cast.

When coloured glass came into general use, embroidered hangings mostly disappeared. Whatever may have been the cause, there is no doubt of the coincidence.

Pl. 68.
See larger image
An embroidered Panel, designed by Pollaiolo, and worked by Paulo da Verona.
In the Church of St. Giovanni at Florence (fifteenth century).

The applied embroideries of the north of Germany were evidently inspired by the newly-discovered art of [329]glass-painting, and resemble its designs, both in the compositions of figures and heraldic subjects. Of this we may remember examples in the Scandinavian Exhibition at South Kensington in 1881.[529]

All the most beautiful and picturesque needlework that we possess of the true ecclesiastical Gothic type, and which belongs to the perfect flowering of the art, is of the fourteenth and fifteenth centuries, just before the spirit of the Renaissance crept northward over Europe, preceding the Reformation and its iconoclastic effacements. This remark especially applies to England.[530] The art of representing Scriptural subjects in flat stitches, as medallions accompanied by beautiful foliage, and heraldic designs, is illustrated to us by the palls belonging to several London companies—and by those belonging to churches, especially that of the church at Dunstable, in which court ladies, knights, and saints form a most artistic border—the costumes being of the date of Henry VII. (see p. 378,*post*).

The perfection of the embroideries of Flanders of that period has never been exceeded, and it continues still to produce the most splendidly executed compositions in gold and silken needlework, of every variety of stitches. The Flemish work and its peculiar mode of laying golden grounds with flat-laid thread stitched down in patterns was carried into Italy, where great artists did not disdain to design for textiles. I give, as an instance, Vasari's account of the embroidered set of vestments designed by [330]Antonio Pollaiolo for the church of San Giovanni at Florence. These were carried out by Paolo da Verona, and took twenty-six years for their completion; and they were only one set of vestments, "embroidered by the most subtle master of the art, Paolo da Verona, a man most eminent in his calling, and of incomparable ingenuity (*ingenio*). The figures are no less admirably executed with the needle than drawn by Pollaiolo with the pencil,—and thus we are largely indebted to one master for his design, and to the other for his patience" (plate 68).

Towards the end of the fifteenth century the Gothic styles were replaced by the Renaissance, but the technical part of the art of embroidery for the churches lost none of its value. All the talent of the artist and the ingenuity of the craft continued to be lavished on altar decoration and priestly garments, in Flanders, Spain, France, and Italy. But the solemnity of these works was certainly impaired by their being emancipated from the traditional ecclesiastical forms and their accompanying symbolism, to which the old designers had so faithfully adhered. Ecclesiastical decorative art became, so to speak, unorthodox.

As a proof of this secular, I might almost say irreverent spirit, I quote Bock's accusation against Queen Mary of Hungary, who in her embroideries, preserved at Aix-la-Chapelle, is said to have represented herself as the Queen of Heaven, surrounded by her adorers on their knees.

There is no doubt, however, that needlework aspired in the fourteenth and fifteenth centuries to the highest place in art, and was enthusiastically cultivated by women of rank and position, of artistic taste, who still gave themselves to the productions of beautiful decorations, though they no longer confined themselves to ecclesiastical motives.

See larger image
Spanish Altar Frontal, Gold Embroidery XVII. Cen^y

[331]Gabrielle of Bourbon and Isabella, sister of Louis XI., spent their lives in preparing and overlooking fine works in their own apartments, and assembled around them noble damsels for this purpose. Anne of Brittany, who lived in an artistic atmosphere, had her own workshop of embroidery. Pictorial design now asserted its dominion over needlework, which accepted it, just as it had been influenced in the eleventh and twelfth centuries by metal-work motives, and, before then, by the art of mosaic.

In the sixteenth and seventeenth centuries the Spanish plâteresque embroideries (adopted and modified in Flanders and in France), consisting of heavy gold and silver arabesques of mutilated vegetable forms, superseded the graceful Renaissance of the classical taste.[531] These Spanish embroideries forced their way by their gorgeousness, in spite of their want of real beauty. They varied their effects with pearls, corals, and precious stones[532] (plate 69).

Spain, though she was much despoiled during the Peninsular War by her French invaders, yet still possesses some of the finest ecclesiastical work in the sacristies of Seville, Granada, Burgos, Toledo, Segovia, and Barcelona. Don Juan F. Riano[533] says that Toledo is a perfect museum of the work of the sixteenth century.

Sicilian and Neapolitan ecclesiastical needlework showed the Spanish taste of their masters, but not its [332]perfection. The use of pearls, coral, and beads[534]prevailed, and we may in general affix its date and its origin to each specimen by the silver largely used in the two kingdoms of Sicily and rarely elsewhere; also by the extreme brilliancy or rather the gaudiness of its colouring.

English ecclesiastical work came suddenly to an end at the Reformation. What was not destroyed is to be found in the possession of the old Roman Catholic families who have religiously collected the residue, preserved by concealment or by being overlooked; and in the wardrobes of Continental sacristies.[535]

But the church decorations of France, Germany, Flanders, Spain, and Italy have meantime, for the last 300 years, gone through all the variations of lay styles, emanating from anything but ecclesiastical motives. First, the Renaissance's semi-pagan (so-called) arabesques; then the Spanish plâteresque, which was a revolt against their own bastard Moorish-Gothic; next, the "Louis Quatorze," followed by the "Louis Quinze" and the

"Louis Seize," light, frivolous, and elegant, essentially social, and not serious.[536] Then a return to the classical of the Empire; and finally, since the beginning of this [333]century, to a conglomerate, lawless imitation of forms and styles, utterly meaningless and uninteresting, as well as wanting in ecclesiastical dignity and decorum. We are glad to believe that we are ourselves striving to reconstruct some sort of style that shall be able to express poetical and religious ideas, especially in our church decorations. At any rate, it must be of some use to understand the hidden springs which once raised ecclesiastical embroideries, and especially those of England, so high as objects of beauty, worthy to adorn the house of God, and to be for centuries valued as monuments of pious industry and thoughtful art.

One of these hidden springs and ancient underlying motives was the symbolism which gave a religious intention to the smallest design for the humblest use, provided that its purpose was the service of the Church.

Sacred symbolism is a subject to which I have alluded more than once; and it has played such an important part in the construction and growth of ecclesiastical art, that I cannot but give a short notice to the subject under this aspect.

Symbolism in art is what metaphor is in speech. It is the representation to the eye of an object which suggests something else besides itself.

Dr. Rock tells us that the symbolism of Scripture texts was given to the world in a book by St. Melito, Bishop of Sardis, A.D. 170. Its title is "The Key."[537] In the fourth century were produced two great works on Scriptural symbols, that of St. Basil in his homilies on the six days of the creation, and that by St. Ambrose; both entitled Hexameron.

[334]We meet this subject at every turn in the succeeding centuries, till in the twelfth we find it formulated and divided into branches—Bestiaria, Volucraria, and Lapidaria—and each type had frequently more than one meaning. Thus a lion represented power, sovereignty, dominion; also the "House of Judah;" a hare the emblem of man's soul; a peacock that of wisdom (many-eyed). The ruby represents love. The pearl, innocence. The twelve stones in a breastplate, the twelve tribes of Israel.[538] Trees and flowers had also their symbolical meanings, though we are not aware of their being recorded in any mediæval book. We know that the vine is the tree of life; the stem of Jesse, the sacramental emblem; that the lily stands for purity, the woodbine for chastity, and the rose for religious ecstasy. The crowned lily was always the special emblem of the Virgin.

These symbols had many of them a distant source, and had been, as I have already indicated, emblematic of other inner meanings in the expression of pagan faiths. The tree of life was Babylonian; the horn, Persian; the fire-sticks of the prehistoric cross, Egyptian or Indian; and the composite animals representing many qualities, Ninevite (probably Accadian).[539]

All these were utilized, so that their already accepted uses should be helps and adjuncts, instead of impediments to the appreciation of divine truths; in the same way that "all that was lovely and of good repute" in the belief and morals of the ancient peoples, reasserted [335]and purified, was claimed by the new teachers as types and antitypes. The symbolism of colours has been always considered very important in liturgical decoration,[540] and their meanings are discussed in the chapter on colour.

The mystical colours, as has been already stated, are five—red, blue, purple, white, and gold. These the Christian Church inherited from the Levitical law, and continued faithful to them till the modern Roman use introduced green and black. The Church of England before the Reformation never allowed any but the original five mystic colours.

The symbolism of ecclesiastical embroideries, as well as that of all Christian art, being intended to illustrate the truths of Christianity by the teaching of the eye, the great symbol of our faith, the *Cross*, naturally drew to itself all its prehistoric forms as being the prophetic types of the "true cross."

The earliest form of the prehistoric cross, , is supposed to refer to the worship of the sun, and is said to be formed of two fire-sticks (for producing fire by friction) laid across each other. This is almost universal in prehistoric, archaic, classical, and Christian art to the thirteenth century. The next most ancient form is a broken cross, thus, , said to be the double of the Tau, or Egyptian sign of life, and claimed by the Rabbins as having been the sign in blood, which stopped the hand of the angel of death, over the doors of the Israelites at the first Passover. This afterwards was called the [336]"Gammadion," from its likeness to a doubled Greek gamma, and it was also said to symbolize the "corner-stone."[541]The third commonest form, apparently a modification of that of the fire-sticks, , is to be found throughout Celtic and Scandinavian art, and was called in England "the fylfote" (from its likeness to the arms of the Isle of Man), and likewise "the Gammadion," though it shows another source than the Greek letter.

From these three forms already in use, added to that of the Crucifixion, endless varieties were composed to suit the ecclesiastical taste and requirements of different national styles of symbolical decoration. I refer my readers to plate 26 in the chapter on patterns for a few of these from different sources. They are extremely suggestive. I have there entered more fully into the subject, regarding it as a fertile pattern motive in textile art.[542]

The cross "bearing twelve fruits for the saving of the nations"[543] is so like some of the representations of the Persian or Indian Tree of Life, that the transmission and adoption of the symbolic form is evident. The cross (plate 63) is a good mediæval example, and is taken from the celebrated rose-coloured cope at Rheims, embroidered with gold and pearls on a rose-coloured satin ground.

Pl. 70.

See larger image
IVORY CONSULAR DIPTYCH.
1. In the Wasser-Kirche Museum, Zurich. Sixth century.
2. Of an earlier period, and finer workmanship, at Halberstadt. No date given.

The Roës is an ecclesiastical pattern of wide use and of very long descent, often named in ancient Church [337]inventories. It is sometimes called the "Wheel and Plate." Its origin is probably Oriental, but it certainly was adopted by the Romans as the motive of their triumphal garments, the *togæ pictæ*, worn in the processional return of a conqueror, whether he were a general or a sovereign. The first motive was a surface covered with circles, closely touching each other, and containing figures which had a reference to their purpose. In Christian times the heads of saints were sometimes inserted, especially in that form of the Roës called the chrysoclavus, from the intersticial ornament between the circles.

I have written (p. 308-9) about the Trabea, which on the Roman consular ivory diptychs of several centuries is so invariably embroidered with this same clavus pattern (plate 70) that we must conclude that it had a meaning and a tradition.

The very ancient superstition that driving in a nail is a fortunate rite, may have been connected with the pattern called the clavus; and the chrysoclavus, from being merely a nail pattern, became consecrated in Christian art as representing the heads of the nails of the Crucifixion, and hence its early Christian name.[544]It was originally filled in with a radiated ornament like the sun; (probably the first motive of this pattern, which seems to be the same as the Egyptian sun-cross,) and its peculiar decoration remained in possession of the descriptive name "palmated," though it is difficult to discover in it any likeness to the palm branch or [338]tree, unless it is supposed to resemble it as seen from above.

The toga triumphalis was also called the toga picta, because its precious purple fabric was covered with gorgeous embroideries. After it had been worn at the triumph or festival, by the victorious general, the distinguished noble, or the Emperor, it was laid by and dedicated in the temple of Jupiter Capitolinus. Thus these palmated triumphal patterns, and their traditional decorations, having by their dedication to the gods assumed a religious character, were woven for Christian ecclesiastical use during the dark ages, and were repeated in Sicily and Spain down to the beginning of the fifteenth century.[545]

I have elsewhere spoken of the "cloud pattern," which is very ancient, Chinese, Indian, and mediæval. Its use has always been for celestial subjects in embroidery, either isolating or supporting spiritual figures. This was appropriated by ecclesiastical art, and we find it nowhere else in Europe.

This sketch of the history of ecclesiastical needlework, (necessarily incomplete from want of space), is founded on the works of Semper, Bock, Rock, and the comparison of many specimens in collections and exhibitions in London and elsewhere. Auberville absolutely places before us the materials as well as the patterns of the weaving of the Christian era, as well as fragments of Egyptian textiles, in his beautiful book on Tissues.

For forms and patterns we cannot do better than study Bock's liturgical chapters and their illustrations, as well as Dr. Rock's "Church of our Fathers."

The stitchery of Christian art has been discussed [339]in the chapter on stitches, and I repeat that there is nothing new in the treatment of solid embroideries, (lace stitches having been the only innovation of the last 400 years), though many of the ancient stitches have lost their distinctiveness, and fallen into a pitiful style by gradual descent which reached its lowest point in the early part of this century, as is shown by the robes embroidered for the coronation of Charles X. in the museum of the Louvre.

In the commencement of this our nineteenth century, there was a total cessation of embroidery, which had, for nearly 2000 years held its own as an art, apart from all others; perhaps a secondary one—yet mixed up with every refinement and luxury of civilization.

Its revival in England, especially, is owing to many causes. As ecclesiastical decoration I have already attributed it to the archæological tendencies of our day, as well as to the æsthetic sentiment which protests, after so long a period of abstention, against the puritanical bareness and coldness of our national forms of worship. The obliteration of embroidery from the list of the arts was more complete in England than elsewhere; as the church of Rome still continued to be adorned with beautiful work on altar-cloths and frontals, and priest's dresses, which, though too much regulated in design by the lay tastes and fashions of the time, have combined to keep up a traditional school of needlework throughout the Continent.

Exhibitions abroad and at home have shown us what a latent power in art embroidery still preserves, and architects have employed the women's needles to give colour and beauty to the decaying churches, which have been restored to their original architectural effects by careful copies of what remained in wood, stone, and glass.

[340]The number of new churches has also given rise to the production, in more than one semi-conventual establishment, of beautiful and effective works, such as the altar-cloth at Durham, and those at Canterbury and Worcester. Such works have revived the impulse of artistic and ecclesiastical taste, and in many small churches we have seen beautifully embroidered altar decorations.[546]

There are, however, many amateurs who are perhaps mistresses of the craft of needlework, and who are yet not educated sufficiently to design a really thoughtful and beautiful work of art, and to these a few remarks may be addressed, which may help the struggling aspirants, and show them how they fail, and where to seek for assistance.

I shall begin by pleading for more careful design, and less parsimony in expenditure upon the usual church adornments. It is once more a received dogma in ecclesiastical art, one in which all religious opinions agree, that the building in the parish which is set apart for the first public duty, that of worship, should show as much beauty as the means and taste of the community can command.

Perhaps the little church has just been restored, or completely rebuilt from the foundations; the consecration is imminent. The white stone, carved or plain, shines fresh and cold, and the whole space looks poor and bare.

The rich woman of the neighbourhood sees and feels that colour is wanting (for the windows must wait till their use as pious memorials fills them with glowing tints). The central point of the whole edifice, the altar, calls for the first key-note in colour to be struck, and a splendid altar-cloth is the fitting instrument.

She consults the architect, who probably is also an artist, and the design is agreed upon, and hurriedly [341]drawn and carried out; for there is not a moment to lose if it is to be ready for the opening day. It may be beautiful, and it sometimes is so, but the mere want of time for due consideration often results in the commonplace ornamentation, which neither satisfies the eye nor the mind. It is often only a mere bit of colour and a mediæval pattern, and has no apparent motive or meaning to give it value.

One sometimes finds that a conventional form has been selected, of which the emblematic intention it originally expressed has been forgotten or overlooked. Therefore, while to the unlearned it conveys no meaning, it is read as absolute nonsense by the ecclesiastical archæologist, simply because it is worked in a language of undeciphered hieroglyphics—unknown to the worker—meaningless, reminding us of the Græco-Egyptian inscriptions, of which the pictured words seem to have been copied at random for their prettiness, or the Arabian lettering on some of the ancient Sicilian textiles, which is nonsense. The sense and the emblematic meaning are forgotten, and the conventional form—an empty shell—is alone retained, conveying no idea, and reduced to the low purpose of being a pretty pattern, vague and unintelligent.

I have so often said that a pattern always originally possessed, and should always retain a meaning, that I fear to become tiresome; but I repeat it here, as in ecclesiastical design it is more important than elsewhere; the meanings are deeper, and convey more essentially solemn traditions and allusions. If the motive of the designer is evident, and is conscientiously worked out, its value receives an enduring quality, and its present interest is enhanced.

Embroidery is not less eloquent than her sister-arts in the teaching of divine lessons, and appealing through the [342]beauty of form and colour to the poetical instincts of the congregation, of which the least educated members almost unconsciously feel the influence; and besides, the people are always alive to the charms of symbolism, when it is placed within their reach. As a proof of this, among our own peasantry and mechanics, I would point to their universal enjoyment of the "Pilgrim's Progress."

In the symbolism of art, the thoughts which are individual to the artist can only be expressed by known forms and colours, even as the poet must employ the words and the metres already accepted by the literature of his language.

Hurry is fatal to art. But another and very serious cause of its deterioration is its costliness.

In the dark and mediæval ages, time was of no account. Skilled labour, such as was needed for carving, illuminations, and embroideries, was freely given as the duty of a life, for one particular object, the good of a man's soul. The cloistered men and women worked for no wages; neither to benefit themselves nor their descendants; hardly for fame,—that was given to the convent which had the credit of patronizing and producing art,[547] while the very name of the artist was forgotten.

It was from pure love of the art as a craft, and the belief that it was a good work in which they were engaged, and from their abundant leisure, that they were enabled to evolve the lovely creations which delight and astonish us when shown in the sacristies and treasuries of foreign religious houses and churches, where they have been cherished for centuries. Like the silkworm they spent themselves; and by their industrious lives were surrounded in their living graves by the elaborated essence of their own natures, a joy and consolation to themselves, [343]and a legacy to all time. To them, also, art appeared as the consoler.

But to return to the grievances of to-day—cheapness and hurry, economy of pence and hours—these often are the bane of the work which we give to the Church, sometimes as a memorial, sometimes as a thank-offering. The colours are bad, because cheap dyes fade, and none others can be had without much trouble, and we have only time to select among those that are for sale. The work is poor because it must be done quickly, and we cannot afford to delay and pay for the extra hours necessary to make the stitches worthy and capable of lasting. Possibly we cannot give the time ourselves, nor can find any one effectually to organize and overlook the work.

Though the design, the motive, the colours and materials, as well as the stitches, need to be each carefully studied, yet we perhaps accept an ancient drawing intended for a different place and use; and thus we fail to produce any effect, with uncongenial surroundings. Sometimes we feel obliged to take the design forced upon us by a shopwoman as ignorant as ourselves, with the submissive hope "that it will do."

Now to a truly artistic mind it would appear that each little church, however simple and devoid of ornament, requires its own special colours and design, besides the individual motive of the giver; and people forget that the whole effect in any such compositions must be comprehensive, and that one careless mistake spoils all.

The High Church, in its love of ritualistic vestments, has sometimes been prejudicial to the general adoption of properly studied altar decorations; as there is a common suspicion that a clergyman's personal wish for ornament, akin to a woman's addiction to fine clothes, governs all his attempts to adorn the altar; whereas [344]there should be, and there often is, a real artistic feeling for the fitness of things, in the furnishings of the most beautiful building set aside by the community for the glory of God. But it is not necessary for beautiful effects that there should be any coloured vestments. When the clergy are duly robed in the orthodox surplice and scarves, there is, perhaps, something funereal in the white linens and black Geneva silk, but yet the traditional white and black have their own value against a background of altar-cloth and reredos splendidly coloured.

Now that, in spite of prejudice, church decoration is so much the custom of our day, it is worth our while to consider seriously how best to carry it out, and search into the principles which may apply to all ecclesiastical embroideries, whether they are to be dedicated in the Minster, the village Church, or the home Chapel.

We must begin by remembering that in these days, if we cannot do the work ourselves, it must be highly paid for. The skilled artisan who is no artist, receives enough to feed his family, according to the higher wages of the time. The woman's slow stitchery has to support probably as many claims, and yet it is always grudged as being too costly. The sculptor or the painter who succeeds in obtaining employment, is highly paid, but the designer for metal-work or embroideries occupies an unrecognized place in art, and barely earns enough to live by. The illuminator has ceased to exist; he would starve—probably has been starved out long ago.

The decorative designer, having, therefore, no status, has no education; and it is almost impossible to find in England an artist to accept orders for thoughtful ecclesiastical designs. Hundreds of boys and girls are taught "freehand drawing," and having copied some casts and lithographs and drawn some flower-pieces, without any particular aim, find a precarious living by [345]designing frightful wall-papers for the million. These poor creatures, from whose lives all ambition and originality have been effaced, are our decorative artists.

Still a beautiful original design can sometimes be obtained, and if that is beyond our reach, we may courageously copy from ancient models, selecting judiciously what is most suitable for our purpose.

The ecclesiastical artist should be well informed in the modes of working a design. The stitch if selected without experience may mar the effect of the whole composition, as some stitches of themselves convey the meaning of shadow, and others that of light.

In ecclesiastical work which is intended to be effective in the distance, as well as perfect in detail, it is worth while to weigh the claims of the architectural low-relief motive, i.e. a flat raised surface, with an edge sufficiently accentuated to catch a light on one side, and cast a sharp shadow on the other. All flat *raised* stitches conduce also to this effect, especially if edged with a cord, and it is much more striking than in stuffed work (on the stamp), which has not the incisive effect that is given by the tool to the sharp edge of stone or wood carvings.

If we can afford to give to our church without stint, let us seek for the most beautiful textiles, such as are again woven in imitation of the old fabrics; gratefully acknowledging all that Pugin, Ruskin, and the foreign manufacturers, especially those at Lyons, have done in the revival of woven designs. Let us avoid those materials which are easily spoiled by sunshine, dust, and smoke, and all those that fray easily. Woollens are not long lived. Crewels, beautiful as they are, are not salient in their effect. Silks, satins and velvet, and gold brocades,[548]or groundings worked in with gold thread, are [346]the only materials worthy of bearing fine embroidery, fit to receive them, and capable of keeping them for centuries. Plushes and worsted velvets are unworthy, indeed they are worthless.

The gold we employ must be either pure "passing," or else the Chinese or Japanese gold threads which differ in colour, but have each their own value, and never tarnish, even in the coal smoke of London. Pure silver, too, is beautiful, and if it is really pure, can be kept bright with bread crumbs.

In composing the altar decoration for the cathedral or the village church, we ought to take into consideration what is suitable for the surrounding architecture. In great spaces, the majestic altar-cloth or frontal, shining with gold and silver, and glowing with silken embroideries, recalls the splendid altar "palli" encrusted with gems in St. Mark's, St. Peter's, and other ancient churches; and is in perfect keeping with the high and gorgeous reredos, the rich screen, the fretted roof and clustered ornaments of a great cathedral choir. Such glories are unattainable in the modest village church.

But though we may subdue the brilliancy of our decoration, we should try to make it yet a work of art. The design may have as much intention, the work be as refined and individual, and the gold as pure, as in larger works. The precious metals may be confined to small spaces in the parts we desire to accentuate, such as the cross in the centre, or the edges of the orphreys, or they may be entirely replaced with fine silk work.

The altar-cloth we desire to present, may be simply a gift, so that we may choose any design that will agree [347]with the date of the building. We may prefer any subsequent style, but not one anterior to that of the architecture. It would be a mistake to imitate Anglo-Saxon ornaments in a church of the flamboyant style.

Perhaps the altar-cloth we are discussing may be intended as a sort of votive offering, a memorial of a baptism, a wedding, or a funeral.

For the first, white silk worked in gold and silver, or gold-coloured silk, or parsemé with conventional spring flowers would be appropriate. For a marriage, crimson, rose-colour, blue and gold, or a mixture of all these, to produce a festive and gorgeous effect. For a funeral, purple or violet silk or velvet, with palms and the crown of thorns in gold or silver.[549] These would serve at the festivals of the Church: the purple for Good Friday,[550] the crimson for Saints' days, the white for Christmas and Easter Sunday.

The reredos, or the screen curtain behind the altar, should be made available for enhancing its effect, as well as for enlarging the area of textile coloured decoration.

As this is intended for a background, it should be either subdued or else contrasting, in juxtaposition with that which it is intended to supplement. Woollen embroideries or tapestries are the most usually selected for this purpose. The softness of fine crewels is well shown near the more glowing tints of silk, velvet, and gold of the altar frontal. If this is white, or light coloured, the reredos hanging should be of dark or richly [348]worked material; if the frontal is dark, the contrast should be preserved by hangings of tender shades.

The pulpit and reading-desk, with their small cushions and veils, and beautiful worked covers for the books, give opportunities for repetition of colour which is often required for picturesque effect.

I should recommend the young ecclesiastical designer to study the principles which guided the authors of some of the fine Gothic examples remaining to us, such as the great Stoneyhurst cope, and the palls of the different London companies, as well as the very few fine altar-cloths still existing. All these have their brilliant and effective treatment; they are intended to be glorious, and either represent massive jewellers' work or tissues of wrought gold.

Anciently, the ornaments for the different church services, which we timidly reduce to floral decorations (often, however, very beautifully planned and executed), gave the opportunity for displaying costly embroidered hangings.

The paschal of the choir of Durham, for example, was a marvellous construction of wood and gilding, metal-work, and (probably) hangings. It was as wide as the "lateral" of the choir, and as high as the building, so that the central and seventh candlestick (that from which the new fire for the year was kindled) was so near the roof that there was a "fine convenience through the said roof of the church for the help of lighting it." I quote from a rare book printed by G. S. Ross for Mrs. Waghorn, 1733.

This little book is full of interesting matter regarding Durham Cathedral, though the author is most concerned in relating the vandalisms committed by the dean's wife, Mrs. Whittinghame, who evidently had "no culture," and a strong turn for appropriating odds and ends, such as [349]tombstones, embroidered silk, and other curiosities which she deemed valueless except for her own purposes,—such a woman is a real archæological misfortune!

The corporax used in celebrating the mass by St. Cuthbert in the seventh century (he died and was buried at Holy Isle in 657) was supposed to be endowed with miraculous powers and was carried into battle on many occasions as a banner.

This banner was of crimson velvet on both sides, wrought with flowers in green silk and gold, and fringed with red silk and gold. The corporax cloth was inserted in the centre, and covered with a square of white velvet, having on it a cross of red velvet, "most artificially worked and fringed, with little silver bells in the fringe." This was carried into battle, till Dame Whittinghame "did most injuriously destroy the same in her fire."

One feels as if this woman were spiteful, as well as stupid. But for her punishment, her memory is kept quite the contrary to green by Mrs. Waghorn's careful record of her iniquities; which has at the same time fortunately preserved to us the description of the banner of St. Cuthbert, and gives also an idea of "the good and sumptuous furniture of changeable suits," and of "the divers vestments wrought and set round about with pearls, both stoles and flannels, &c."

Looking at it from a distance, it appears that the "fair white linen" for the communion service always requires the softening of the edges by fringes, by cut work embroidery, or by thick lace edgings. If a white ground for embroidery is required, nothing is more beautiful than linen, especially if it is not over-bleached. White, in art, should be represented by the nearest approach to no colour; but it is more agreeable to the eye by its being tempered with a suggestion of the natural tint, of which all textile substances possess something (excepting cotton) [350]before they have passed through the hands of the fuller or the chemist.

Corporals and veils for the pyx used to be of white linen, embroidered with white silk or linen thread; the silk gives a beautiful, varied, shining brightness.

I think a few words should be said about the fringe.[551] Its motive and *raison d'être* is the disposal of the threads of the warp when it is cut out of the frame; these being tied and knotted symmetrically, become an artistic decoration instead of an untidy tangle of threads and thrums. Edging the material and finishing it with its own loose ends is a very ancient custom; and we can see from the sculptures of Nineveh that they were great in that city in the art of fringe-making, and the Israelites, when they made their hangings for the sanctuary, trimmed them with fringes. It stands to reason that an added fringe should be arranged with reference to the origin of the decoration, and the moment we think of it, the eye is annoyed by seeing a deep fringe of one or two colours traversing the whole widths of the frontal and super-frontal, quite irrelevantly, and without any reference to the masses of colours, woven or embroidered, above them; and the consequence of this carelessness is, that it makes it look as if this part of the decoration, came from another source, independent of the composition which [351]it ought to supplement. The fringe should belong to the whole design, and be carefully fitted to the spaces occupied by the colours above it, each of its compartments or divisions being filled in with those tints which are most conspicuous in the general design and would show effectively in the warp. It is not necessary to account for all the colours, as the threads employed to form the woof would naturally disappear at the sides of the web. The sections of the fringe should be skilfully arranged so as to reappear at equal distances, or at least they should be so balanced as to produce that effect. If this is impossible, the fringe should be all of one shade, matching exactly the ground of the textile. It may be relieved by clustered knobs, or hanging beads or cups of different colours and gold. The celebrated pluvial at Aix-la-Chapelle has a fringe of gold bells hanging to a gold cord, which amalgamates with the pattern.[552] The veils of the Sanctuary in the wilderness were fringed with attached ornaments, bells, blossoms, knops, flowers, and fruit, which sounds extremely pretty.

To resume, let me once more urge that in church work neither time nor trouble be spared; nor yet money grudged, if possible. The design should be full of intention, the stitching perfect, and the materials most carefully chosen for tints, for endurance and smoothness. Remember that no inferior substitute will serve to give present effect, nor will it last into the future.

Design, as I have elsewhere said, is all the better for being to a certain degree circumscribed, relegated, and regulated by the laws of traditional usage, as well as those of good taste, and this applies especially to ecclesiastical design.

These laws serve as the frame which encloses the [352]motive thought, and makes it a complete whole, that can admit of no amplifications.

New symbols should not be adopted except for the expression of new facts or altered circumstances, and these can but seldom enter into liturgical art.

There is so much already formulated and admitted, and the area in which we may gather our materials is so large, that we need not seek for more than we find under our hand, ready for use.

Besides the symbolism of dogma, we have all the heraldry of the Saints; and can repeat and vary the emblems of those to whom the church we are working for is dedicated. The keys of St. Peter, the sword of St. Paul, the lilies of the Virgin, the cross of St. Andrew, the eagle of St. John,—I need hardly enumerate all these legitimate sources of decoration. Then there is the lay heraldry which belongs to the history of each church, and which memorializes the reign of the monarch when it was begun, finished, or restored, and the pious work and care of the founder and benefactor, the architect, and sometimes that of the sculptor.

Now as our forefathers accepted all this material for ecclesiastical design, remodelling it to their own uses in different centuries, so we cannot ourselves do better than imitate them, and profit by their experience; never missing an opportunity of studying ancient embroideries; and while we admire in them all that is admirable, and appreciate their historical and archæological value, we may yet extract greater benefit for ourselves, by criticizing what is imperfect, as well as what is possibly a descent and failure from a higher type.

We must make a judicious selection of what to imitate and what to avoid.

As a general rule, I should warn the young artist against the imitation of "naïveté" and so-called "quaintness;" [353]especially in our designs for Church embroidery as it is hardly a noble quality in art, though we look on it with a tender pity, half-way between admiration and contempt, when we find it inevitably in mediæval work; struggling to overcome the expression of something difficult, and expressing a difficulty only partly overcome. We find ourselves putting our minds into the attitude of the artist who conceived those figures with arms conventionally growing out of the encasing garment; conventionally holding a book, and giving a blessing with a conventional twist, not entirely ungraceful, nor devoid of a certain dignity, rather felt than perceived. Yet we contemplate them with a smile of conscious superiority, appreciating our own refined sense of their merits and infantine progress towards something good, that time—a long time—would, and did evolve. But those efforts at last culminated in a Christian art, such as is seen in the splendid forms and adornments in stone, gold, silver, glass, and embroideries of the thirteenth and fourteenth centuries. Such splendours as the windows of Bourges, the Sainte-Chapelle at Paris, or those of the Cathedral of Toledo, or King's College Chapel at Cambridge. Such sculptures and traceries as those of the Puits de Moise at Dijon, and the Chapter House at Southwell in Nottinghamshire. Such embroideries as the Syon cope, and the Borghese triptych. These are types worthy of all praise, and they are full of instruction to the student of ecclesiastical art.

The Kensington Museum offers us endless help and suggestions in its very interesting collection of liturgical vestments of every date and school; and its textiles, illustrated by the inventory of their learned collector, Dr. Rock, are most instructive.[553]

[354]In the library of that museum are to be found many of the learned works on these subjects by French and German *savants*. The exhibitions in the English counties are never without a case or a room full of embroideries, collected from the treasure-chests of the neighbouring churches and country houses, and especially from those of the ancient Roman Catholic families. The colleges of Oscott and Stoneyhurst have collected, by purchase or by gift, many fine relics of the craft, which are most liberally granted for exhibition.

For those who can go further afield there is instruction in almost every Continental town. Rome, Florence, Milan, Toledo, Sens, Rheims, Aix-la-Chapelle, Berne, Vienna, Halberstadt, Berlin, and Munich—each and all have stores of beautiful liturgical objects carefully preserved; of many dates, and many styles, and showing endless varieties of design, which can be employed on new works by careful selection and adaptation. Most of these belong to the eleventh and succeeding centuries; any earlier examples are fragmentary, and have generally been taken from the tombs of kings and bishops.

It seems to savour of desecration, this opening of shrines and disturbing the ashes of the illustrious dead, if only for the satisfaction of archæological curiosity. But except where it has hitherto been protected by the sanctity of the tomb, there is so little that remains to us,—so few textiles have survived the friction of use, or even that of the air, through as many as a thousand years or more, that we may plead the hunger for truth, and the [355]eager desire for proofs of identity and verification of historical legends, which are to be extracted from the shape of a garment, from the pattern on the border, or the lettering on the web of which it is composed; whence we reverently cut a fragment, and preserve it under glass.

"If studious, copie fair what time hath blurr'd,Redeem truth from his jawes."[554]

Before closing this chapter, I would wish to observe that I have entered into the subject of church decoration in no ritualistic spirit; I do not treat it theologically, but as art; and if these decorations are to be carried out at all, I feel that I am rendering a service to those whose duty or pleasure it is to provide them, by pointing out where they may find the principles which have been the spring and life of mediæval art, and the survivals which are now the best exponents of those principles to guide us in the works of our day.

FOOTNOTES:

[479]Figure-drawing in early Christian art was for nearly a thousand years primitively barbarous, with occasional exceptions. The rapid decline in Europe, through the art of the Catacombs and St. Clemente at Rome, and the frescoes and mosaics of Ravenna, down to the Bayeux tapestries, is very remarkable. In those inartistic compositions during the early Middle Ages, the figures were drawn facing the spectator, the head and feet in profile, differing in nothing from the Egyptian and Assyrian modes of representation. We can hardly account for this return to childish ways, from which Greece and Rome had so long been emancipated, except by supposing that they came from the imitations of Oriental textiles, which still retained very ancient forms; for instance, the motive of the sculptured lions over the gate of Mycenæ. We cannot say that Greek art in Rome was quite extinct till the eighth century. About that time there was a remarkable revival in England.

[480]Till very lately we have been entirely dependent on the frescoes in the Catacombs and in the underground Church of St. Clemente at Rome, and on monumental art and illuminations, for our knowledge of the textiles of the earliest days of Christianity. But Herr Graf'schen's discoveries in Egypt will, when published, add greatly to our information on this subject.

[481]The book by Parker on the "Liturgical Use" says that only the five liturgical colours were permitted in the use of the Church of England. Before the Reformation the Norman and English liturgical colours were different. (Rock, "Church of our Fathers," ii. p. 268.) Perhaps nothing was originally worked departing from this rule, but votive offerings are inventoried as being of all colours, having been accepted and used as decoration and for vestments.

[482]I have already spoken of the custom of clothing the images of the gods as a classical tradition. The Greeks draped their statues in precious garments, often the spoils of subjugated nations, offerings from the conquerors, or obsequious tribute from the conquered. Newton (Appendix 1) tells us of inscriptions containing inventories of old clothes offered in the Greek Temples. Ezekiel (xvi.) speaks of silk and linen embroideries given for covering the idols. The images of the saints in Roman Catholic churches are, we know, constantly draped in splendid embroideries, and hung with jewels.

[483]There is here an overlap of several centuries.

[484]Charlemagne's dalmatic, described hereafter, of which the pedigree is well ascertained, justifies Woltmann and Woermann's theory; as this eighth-century embroidery shows, by its design, that Greek art was still a living power.

[485]Of which we have yet examples on the Continent, here and there; for instance, in the Cathedral at Coire in the Grisons, and in the Romanesque church at Clermont in Auvergne (not the cathedral). I do not include in this statement of the rare occurrence of the ogee, the European countries which were subject to Moorish rule, i.e. Spain and Portugal.

[486]This, slightly modified, continued to prevail till the time of Louis XIV., when France took the lead, and gave a style to the world which entirely broke away from all mediæval tradition.

[487]Rock's "Church of our Fathers," i. p. 409. Compare Wilkinson's "Ancient Egyptians," i. p. 332 (see fig. 1); and Bock's "Liturgische Gewänder," taf. i., i. p. 130, fig. 6. Bock does not give his authority for the pattern on the ephod.

[488]Bock's "Liturgische Gewänder," i. taf. i., iii., vi.

[489]Yates' "Textrinum Antiquorum," pp. 203, 376, § 103. He quotes from Claudian the description of a trabea, said to have been woven by the goddess Roma herself, for the consul Stilicho. I give this as showing how forms and patterns become sacred by their being attributed to the inspiration of the gods. The name of Stilicho marks his tomb in Sant' Ambrogio's Church at Milan, on which is a curious moulding, carved with alternate roses and mystic crosses.

[490]Clapton Rolfe, "Ancient Use of Liturgical Colours."

[491]See the Book of Kells, Library, Dublin; also St. Cuthbert's Durham Book, British Museum, and the Celtic MSS. in the Lambeth Palace Library.

[492]Celtic and Scandinavian designs are characterized by meandering, interlaced, and knotted lines, which are described and discussed in the chapter on patterns. The forms of the Celtic stone crosses are very beautiful. See "L'Atlas de l'Archéologie du Nord, par la Société Royale des Antiquaires du Nord" (Copenhagen, 1857), where the metal remains are shown by careful engravings; also George Stephen's "Old Northern Runic Monuments."

[493]See Bock's "Liturgische Gewänder," i. p. 126, quoting Anastasius Bibliothecarius, pp. 153, 156, 189.

[494]Ibid. p. 189.

[495]The information here collected proves that these sovereign gifts to the great basilicas were by no means of costly materials, especially as compared with the preceding splendours of Rome, or the still more astounding luxury of Alexandria through the Greek conquests of the Eastern nations. To these rules of economical decoration, however, we find occasionally exceptions. We gather also from later lists that the embroideries of the Papal See were culled, in the thirteenth century, from France, Spain, Germany, and England.

[496]See also Bock's "Liturgische Gewänder," vol. i. pp. 9, 18, 56, 86, plate 2. At a later period the lion motive is supposed to have represented a Christian in the arena, and it certainly in time was symbolical of man struggling with the dominion of sin. However, Bock considers the design to have been originally classical Greek, and it survived to the seventh and eighth centuries, and was reproduced as late as the sixteenth.

[497]The Code of Manu in India, which 2500 years ago regulated all the crafts and ruled their decorations, is still in full force, and Chinese art was crystallized in the reigns of the first emperors of the Hia dynasty, 2197 B.C.

[498]We cannot but respect the memory of Attila, who checked the spoliation of Rome by his troops.

[499]The collections of needlework in Germany are very rich. The treasury of the cathedral at Halberstadt, the Markt-Kirche of Brunswick, the sacristy of the Marien-Kirche of Dantzic, and that of the Kaland Brethren at Strahlsund are especially quoted by Bock. At Quedlinburg are the tapestries of its famous abbess; at the Pilgrim Church of Marie at Zell are fine remains of stuffs and embroideries by the ladies of the imperial house of Hapsburg, of the thirteenth century; at the Abbey of Göss (near Lieben, Steiermark) is to be seen the remarkable needlework of the Abbess Kunigunda, and in the cathedral treasury of Heidelberg the antipendium of the fourteenth century, made for the church at Tirna. The museums of Berlin, Munich, and Vienna are very rich in textiles.

[500]See Bock's "Liturgische Gewänder," p. 133.

[501]Helen Lwyddawc. See "Mabinogion," by Lady C. Guest, pp. 279-284. This beautiful story is told in the language of the romance period, and yet has a certain Celtic colouring in it, which shows its origin. The ballad opens with a description of Helen watching a game of chess, clothed in white and gold, seated on a chair of gold, when Maxentius finds her in her father's palace.

[502]See Mrs. Palliser's "Lace," p. 4.

[503]See chapter on English embroidery, post.

[504]Early decorations of ecclesiastical dress are so thoroughly illustrated by the ancient frescoes and mosaics in Italy, that we can form an idea of the embroidered

vestments of each period by studying them, and the early illuminated books that are scattered over Europe. Dr. Bock gives authentic illustrations as well as information about the finest Continental specimens.

[505]For the mosaics of Santa Pudenziana, see Woltmann and Woermann, i. p. 167, "History of Painting." Translated by Sidney Colvin.

[506]Appendix 4. Lord Lindsay's "History of Ecclesiastical Art," i. p. 136. These gorgeous vestments are engraved by Sulpiz Boisserée in his "Kaiser Dalmatika in der St. Peterskirche," and far better by Dr. Rock, in his splendid work on the "Coronation Robes of the German Emperors."

[507]It is singular that we find the starry cross and the swastika filling alternate square spaces on the mantle of Achilles—playing at dice with Ajax—on a celebrated Greek vase in the Etruscan Museum at the Vatican. I have referred to this design elsewhere. (Plate 26.)

[508]Rock's "Introduction," p. liii.

[509]This date is assigned to it by Monsignor Clifford.

[510]Kindly supplied to me by the Father Superior of San Clemente in Rome.

[511]In the cathedral of Aix, Switzerland. Bock's "Liturgische Gewänder," i. taf. ii.

[512]One of these mitres has, it is said, been brought to England.

[513]Bock, "Liturgische Gewänder," ii. taf. xii. This is dyed in Tyrian purple (rosy red), and is simply the cross, representing the tree with twelve leaves, "for the healing of the nations."

[514]Bock, "Liturgische Gewänder," i. taf. iii. pp. 157-160.

[515]Bock, *ibid.*, p. 158, quotes the Jesuit Erasmus Fröhlich, (1754).

[516]See Bock's "Liturgische Gewänder," i. taf. iv. pp. 165, 166. "One of three costly garments."

[517]Modifications of the "wheel pattern" ("wheel and plate"). Of these works of the tenth and eleventh centuries the fine Roman lettering in the borders is a marking characteristic.

[518]See Bock's "Liturgische Gewänder," i. p. 214.

[519]There was no guild of embroiderers in England that we know of till that incorporated in the reign of Elizabeth. See chapter on English embroidery.

[520]Bock, i. 214, says that the splendid stuffs and embroideries were entirely consecrated to the use of the Church, till the luxurious arts invaded European domestic life from the seventh to the twelfth century.

[521]See the cross on the Rheims cope (plate 63).

[522]There is no doubt it was only used for church work.

[523]At Aachen, in Switzerland, there is a very remarkable pluvial of one kind of opus Anglicanum, which has been already alluded to. The border, of splendid gold embroidery, has the pattern completed in fine flowers of jewellers' work. (See Bock, "Liturgische Gewänder," ii. p. 297, taf. xli.-xliv.) Rock, "Textile Fabrics," Introduction, p. xxxi, cites from Mon. Angl. (ii. 222), the vestments given to St. Alban's Abbey by Margaret, Duchess of Clarence, A.D. 1429, as being remarkable for pure gold in its texture and the splendour of the jewels and precious stones set into it, as well as for the exquisite beauty of its embroideries. These are some of the characteristics of the opus Anglicanum.

[524]Appendix 6.

[525]Mrs. Bayman, of the Royal School of Art Needlework.

[526]If it is true that in the days of the Greeks and Romans the art of acupictura or needle-painting copied pictorial art, so likewise in the Egyptian early times, painted linens imitated embroideries. This we learn by specimens from the tombs. Painted hangings and embroideries appear to have been equally used for processional decorations. In the Middle Ages painted hangings imitated embroideries and woven hangings, and were considered as legitimate art.

[527]See Bock, vol. i. p. 10.

[528]Exhibited in the "Esposizione Romana" in 1869, in the cloisters of Santa Maria degli Angeli.

[529]See Woltmann and Woermann, who quote evidence as to works in painted glass as early as the ninth and tenth centuries in France and Germany ("History of Painting," vol.

[530]"Vasari," ed. Monce, taf. v. p. 101.

[531]See plate 69, which is a fine altar-frontal of the plâteresque Spanish.

[532]The dress of the "Virgin del Sagrario" at Toledo, embroidered with pearls, and the chasuble of Valencia, worked with corals, show how profusely these costly materials were employed.

[533]See "The Industrial Arts of Spain," pp. 250-264, by Don Juan F. Riano, and catalogues of Loan Exhibition by him for the South Kensington Museum series, 1881. The works of Spanish Queens and Infantas are to be seen at the Atocha, the church of the Virgin del Pilar at Madrid.

[534]There are most interesting examples of Scriptural subjects in Bock's "Liturgische Gewänder," i. taf. x. pp. 207, 208; taf. xi. pp. 239-278. These are of the thirteenth and fourteenth centuries; and we have some good fifteenth century bead-work in the South Kensington Museum.

[535]The splendid embroideries from Westminster Abbey, sold to Spanish merchants at the Reformation, now at Valencia, and the cope in the Museum at Madrid, are instances of these exportations. The Syon cope also was returned to England, after its long wanderings, about sixty years ago. I give its history by Dr. Rock in the Appendix 6.

[536]For examples of this ornate and graceful, but frivolous style, we may remember the mosaic altar frontals throughout the basilica of St. Peter's at Rome.

[537]See Dr. Rock's "Catalogue of Textile Fabrics," South Kensington Museum, Introduction, p. cxxxvi.

[538]Bock's "Liturgische Gewänder," i. taf. vi., vii., pp. 385-392. The emblematic meanings of stones is constantly alluded to in the Old Testament. Their symbolism has, therefore, a high authority and most ancient descent. In the Ashmolean Museum at Oxford is an illuminated copy of Philip de Than's Bestiarium, composed for Adelais, second wife of Henry I.

[539]"Cyclopædia of Bible Literature," vol. vii. p. 477.

[540]See Clapton Rolfe, "The Ancient Use of Liturgical Colours." (Parker, 1879.)

[541]See "Indian Arts," by Sir G. Birdwood, i. p. 97. He says this form is the sign of the Buddhist or Jainis, and that the fire-stick form was that of the Sakti race in India.

[542]See chapter on patterns, p. 103-4, ante.

[543]Revelations chap. xxii. v. 2.

[544]In mediæval times the cross in a circle was sometimes called the "clavus" . It was the same as an Egyptian sign, meaning "land" (plate 25). Donelly fancifully claims the sign as being that of the garden of Eden, and of the four rivers flowing from it (see "Atlantis").

[545]See plate 70, No. 1. In the upper part of the Halberstadt diptych, No. 1, the "gens togata" are sitting on Olympus, clothed in such purple garments embroidered with the chrysoclavus.

[546]I would instance the little church of St. Mary, built and adorned by the late W. E. Street, at Feldy, in Surrey.

[547]The art of illumination had in general kept a little in front of that of the painter, and illumination and embroidery went hand in hand.

[548]The fine brocades of velvet and gold, of which we find examples in the centres of palls, and a notable one in the celebrated Stoneyhurst cope, are still reproduced to order at Lyons, Genoa, Florence, and in Spain. The Florentine is distinguished by the little loops of gold thread which pervade it.

[549]In the English ritual gold was permitted wherever white was enjoined. This shows a true appreciation of the effect of the metal, separating and isolating all colours, and being of none.

[550]The purple is not one of the five mystic colours named; it is included in blue, and therefore the most ritualistic critic need not object to it.

[551] Under the Carlovingians, priestly garments were often enriched with splendid fringes, trimmed with bells. A Bishop of Elne, who died in 915, left to his church a stole embroidered with gold and garnished with bells. So rich were the fringes at that epoch, that King Robert, praying one day in the church, became aware that while he was lost in meditation a thief had ripped off part of the fringes of his mantle. He interrupted his proceedings by saying, "My friend, suppose you content yourself with what you have taken, and leave the rest for some other member of your guild." See "Histoire du Tissu Ancien," Union Central des Arts Décoratifs. For a fringe with bells, see the beautiful example in Bock's "Liturgische Gewänder" (plates xli. xlii. xliii. vol. ii. p. 297), already quoted.

[552] Resembling the fringe of St. Cuthbert's corporax, with its silver bells.

[553] This valuable collection of textiles is so ancient and therefore so frail, that it seems a pity to send portions of it continually travelling about the country for loan exhibitions. Change of climate—cold, heat, and damp—carelessness in packing and unpacking—above all, the reckless exposure to floods of sunshine even when they are protected from dust by glass,—all these endanger the preservation of what can never be replaced, and has only survived till now because of the quiet and darkness in which it has lain for centuries.

[554] George Herbert, "The Churchyard Porch," v. 15.

[356]
CHAPTER XI.
ENGLISH EMBROIDERY.

Through the preceding chapters I have tried to moderate my predominant interest in our national school of needlework, seeking to place it in its just position alongside of the coeval Continental schools. However, the more I have seen of specimens at home and abroad, the more I have become convinced of the great superiority of our needlework in the Middle Ages. As information about our own art must be valuable to us, I give a short account of English embroidery.

In England our art, like our language, is mixed. Our early history is one of repeated conquest, and we can only observe where style has flowed in from outside, or has formed itself by grafting upon the stem full of vitality already planted and growing. It is interesting to seek its root.

There is every reason to believe, from the evidence of the animal remains of the Neolithic Age (including those of sheep), that they came with their masters from the central plateau of Asia.

The overlap of the Asiatic civilizations over the barbarism of Northern Europe shows that Assyria[555] as well [357]as Egypt was a highly organized empire, and the Mediterranean peoples far advanced in the arts of life, while the Neolithic man survived and lingered in Britain, France, and Scandinavia. Yet, even at that early period, the craft of spinning and the use of the needle were practised by the women of Britain.[556]

Our first glimpses of art may have come to us by Phœnician traders, touching at the Scilly Islands and thence sailing to the coasts of Cornwall and Ireland. From Ireland we have curious relics as witnesses of their presence—amongst others, jewellery connected by, or pendant from, "Trichinopoly" chains, similar to those dug out of Etruscan tombs, and which were probably imported into Ireland as early as the sixth century B.C.[557]

[358]In the Bronze Age the chiefs and the rich men wore linen or woollen homespun. Fragments of these have been found in the Scale House barrow at Rylston, in Yorkshire. Dr. Rock says that an ancient Celtic barrow was opened not long ago in Yorkshire, in which the body was wrapped in plaited (not woven) woollen material.[558] Before this time the Cymri in Britain probably wore plaited grass garments; they also sewed together the skins of animals with bone needles.

Dyeing and weaving were well understood in Britain before the advent of the Romans. Hemp and flax, however, though native to the soil, were not employed by the early Britons. Linen perhaps came to us first through the Phœnicians, and afterwards through the Celts, and was naturalized here by the Romans.

Anderson ("Scotland in Early Christian Times") gives a high place to the forms of pagan art which prevailed in the British Isles, before the Roman civilization; and differing from and influencing that which came from Scandinavia. We must certainly allow that it was art, and that it contained no Greek or other classical element. His illustrations explain and give great weight to his theories.

Cæsar invaded England forty-five years B.C.[559] The [359]Romans gave us Christianity and the rudiments of civilization, but their attempts to Romanize us met with little success. Probably they imported their luxuries, and removed all they valued at the time of their exodus. From them we know what they found and what they left in Britain. Boadicea, Queen of the Iceni, the day of her defeat wore a tartan dress (polymita) and an "embroidered" or "fur" mantle; probably the fur was inside, and the skins embroidered outside. Dion Cassius,[560] who describes Boadicea's motley tunic, says that the bulk of the people wore what was apparently a chequered tartan. Semper says that the early tribes of Northern Europe, like the North American Indians of the present time, embroidered their fur wraps. The Emperor Honorius, in the fourth century, made it illegal for Roman nobles to wear extravagantly-worked fur robes; perhaps the report of Boadicea's dress had set the fashion in Rome.

During the first four centuries of our era, all art in Britain must have come from our Roman masters; and owing to their neglect of the people they conquered, we benefited little by their civilization.

All that we know of their decorative art in Britain, is that it was, with few exceptions, chiefly of small bronze statues, somewhat crude and colonial, as appears from the remains of their architecture, sculpture, mosaics, and [360]tombs.[561] Of their textiles we have no relics, and hardly know of any recorded, if we except the works of the Empress Helena. See p. 316, *ante*. We must remember that, as she was a British princess, it is likely that she had learnt her art at home, and therefore that the women of England were already embroiderers as early as the beginning of the fourth century.[562]

On the departure of the Romans, chaos ensued, till the Britons, who had called in the Saxons to help them, were by them driven into Wales, Brittany, and Ireland, which last they Christianized; and mingled the art of the Germans and Celts with that of the Danes and Norsemen[563]; all [361]which may be traced in the Irish remains to be seen in the College Museum at Dublin and elsewhere. From the time that England became Anglo-Saxon, literature, law, and art began to crystallize; and when, under Egbert, one kingdom was formed out of the heptarchy, order and a sense of beauty were in the course of development. Then came the invasion of the Danes (ninth century), who robbed, destroyed, and arrested all artistic improvement, till Alfred got rid of them for a time. Early in the seventh century the women of England had attained great perfection in needlework. This appears from a passage in a poem by Adhelme, Bishop of Sherborne. He speaks of their shuttles, "filled not with purple only, but with various colours, moved here and there among the thick spreading threads."[564] He had himself a robe "of a most delicate thread of purple, adorned with black circles and peacocks." This may or may not have been woven in England, but at that time weaving, as well as needlework, was the delight and occupation of the ladies of the court and of the cloistered nuns.[565] The thralls (slaves or serfs) [362]were employed in weaving in the houses of the nobles, probably they embroidered also.

Mrs. Lawrence sees reason to believe that in the seventh century, silk and fine linen were the materials for altar decorations, vestments, and dress; whereas the hangings of the house were of coarse canvas adorned with embroidery in thick worsted.[566] She says the term "broiderie" was reserved for the delicate works on fine grounds, in silk and gold and silver thread, and enrichments in metal work. Precious stones and pearls had already been introduced into the Byzantine and Romanesque designs imported from Greece and Rome.

The English Dominican Friar, Th. Stubbs, writing in the thirteenth century, describes in his notice of St. Oswald a chasuble of Anglo-Saxon work, which exactly resembles that of Aix.[567] This is splendidly engraved in Von Bock's "Kleinodien" amongst the coronation robes of the Emperors of Germany, and is adorned with the richest golden orphreys, imitating jewellers' work, enriched with pearls and silver bells.

There is an Icelandic Saga of the thirteenth century which relates the history of Thorgunna, a woman from the Hebrides, who was taken to Iceland on the first settlement of the country by Norway, A.D. 1000. She employed witchery in her needlework, and her embroidered hangings were coveted by, and proved fatal to, many persons after her death, till one of her inheritors burned them.[568]

Pl. 71.

One of the ends of the Stole of St. Cuthbert at Durham, which together bear the inscription,
"Aelfled fieri precepit pio Episcopo Fridestano."

English ecclesiastical art did not necessarily keep to Christian subjects; for it is recorded that King Wiglaf, [363]of Mercia, gave to Croyland Abbey his splendid coronation mantle and "velum;" and that the latter was embroidered with scenes from the siege of Troy.[569]

Pl. 72.

See larger image
Durham Embroideries, tenth century.

It was probably on account of such derelictions from orthodox subjects of design that in the eighth century the Council of Cloveshoe admonished the convents for their frivolous embroideries.[570]

In the eighth century our English work in illuminations and embroideries was finer than that of any Continental school; and therefore, in view of the great advance of these secondary arts, we may claim that we were then no longer outer barbarians, though our only acknowledged superiority over Continental artists was in the workrooms of our women and the cells of our religious houses.

During the terrible incursions of the Danes, and the many troubles that accrued from these barbarous and idolatrous invaders, the convents and monasteries, especially those of the order of St. Benedict, kept the sacred flame of art burning.[571] Both monks and nuns wrote, illuminated, painted, and embroidered. They evidently continued their relations with foreign art, for it is difficult to say at what period the Norman style began [364]to be introduced into England. It was the outcome of the Romanesque, and of this, different phases must have come to us through the Danes and the Saxons.

I cannot but dwell on the early life and springtide of our Anglican Christian art, which in many points preceded and surpassed that of other northern nations, as we arose from that period commonly called the Dark Ages. Ours was a gradual development, adding to itself from outer sources new strength and grace. The better perfection of details and patterns was succeeded by Anglo-Saxon ingenuity and refinement in drawing the human figure. The art, which was native to England, may be judged by the rare examples that we possess, and of which we may well be proud; though we must remember with shame how much was destroyed at the Reformation. Enough however, remains to prove that our English art of illumination of the ninth, tenth and eleventh centuries was very beautiful, and we are not surprised therefore to find in the embroideries of that period grace and artistic feeling.

The stole and maniple of the Durham cathedral library, which bear the inscription "Aelfled fieri precepit pio Episcopo Fridestano," are of the most perfect style of Anglo-Saxon design; and the stitching of the silk embroidery and of the gold grounding are of the utmost perfection of needlework art (plates 71, 72).

The history of this embroidery is carefully elucidated by Dr. Raine in his "Saint Cuthbert." He says that Frithestan was consecrated bishop in 905, by command of Edward the Elder, son of Alfred the Great. Aelfled was Edward the Second's queen. She ordered and gave an embroidered stole and maniple to Frithestan. After her death, and that of Edward, and of the Bishop of Winchester, Athelstan, then king, made a progress to the north, and visiting the shrine of St. Cuthbert, at Chester-le-Street, he bestowed on it many rich gifts, which are solemnly enumerated [365]in the MSS. Cott. Brit. Mus. Claud. D. iv. fol. 21-6. Among these are "one stole, with a maniple; one girdle, and two bracelets of gold." That the stole and maniple are those worked for Frithestan by the command of his mother-in-law,

Aelfled, may fairly be said to be proved. These embroideries, worked with her name and the record of her act, were taken from the body of St. Cuthbert in 1827.[572]

Pl. 73.
See larger image
St. Dunstan's Portrait of himself in adoration. From his Missal in the Bodleian Library, Oxford.

Another and earlier Aelfled was the widow of Brithnod, a famous Northumbrian chieftain. She gave to the cathedral of Ely, where his headless body lay buried, a large cloth, or hanging, on which she had embroidered the heroic deeds of her husband. She was the ancestress of a race of embroiderers, and their pedigree will be found in the Appendix.[573] At this time a lady of the Queen of Scotland was famed for her perfect skill in needlework, and the four daughters of Edward the Elder were likewise celebrated embroiderers.

St. Dunstan, Archbishop of Canterbury, is said to have designed needlework for a noble and pious lady, Aedelwyrme, to execute in gold thread, A.D. 924.[574] He prepared and painted a drawing, and directed her work.[575] I here give the portrait of our celebrated early designer [366]from the MS. in the Bodleian Library at Oxford, said to be by his own hand, and which represents him kneeling at the feet of the Saviour (plate 73).

Shortly before the Norman conquest, in the beginning of the eleventh century, we have notices of sundry other very remarkable pieces of work.

The Danish Queen Emma, daughter of Richard, Duke of Normandy, when she was wife to Ethelred the Unready, and again during her second marriage to Canute, gave the finest embroideries to various abbeys and monasteries. Canute, being then a Christian, joined her in these splendid votive offerings. To Romsey and Croyland they gave altar-cloths which had been embroidered by his first queen, Aelgitha,[576] and vestments covered with golden eagles. She worked one altar-cloth on shot blood-red and green silk,[577] with golden orphreys at the side and across the top. When one considers what the life of poor Queen Emma was, one hopes that "Art the Consoler" came to her in the form of her favourite craft, and that she did find consolation in it.

Croyland Abbey seems to have been most splendidly endowed by the Anglo-Saxon monarchs. There is continual mention in the records of those times of offerings of embroideries and other Church apparels. Queen Editha, the wife of the Confessor, dispensed beautiful works from her own workrooms, and herself embroidered King Edward's coronation mantle.

When in the eleventh century the Normans became our masters, they found cathedrals, churches, and palaces which almost vied with their own; likewise [367]sculptures, illuminated books, embroidered hangings, and vestments of surpassing beauty.

William of Poitou, Chaplain to William the Conqueror,[578] relates that the Normans were as much struck on the Conqueror's return into Normandy with the splendid embroidered garments of the Saxon nobles, as with the beauty of the Saxon youth. Queen Matilda, who evidently appreciated Anglo-Saxon work, left in her will, to the Abbey of the Holy Trinity, "My tunic worked by Alderet's wife, and the mantle which is in my chamber, to make a cope. Of my two golden girdles, I give the one which is adorned with emblems to suspend the lamp before the great altar."

I come now to the earliest large work remaining to us of the period—the Bayeux tapestry. We must claim it as English, both on account of the reputed worker, and the history it commemorates, though the childish style of which it is a type is indeed inferior in every way to the beautiful specimens which have been rescued from tombs in Durham, Worcester, and elsewhere. They seem hardly to belong to the same period, so weak are the designs and the composition of the groups. Though Mr. Rede Fowke gives the Abbé de la Rue's doubts as to the accepted period of the Bayeux tapestry, which he assigns to the Empress Matilda, he yet leans to other equally good authorities who consider the work as being coeval with the events it records.[579]

[368]Mr. Collingwood Bruce is of the same opinion, and for this reason—the furniture, buildings, &c., are all of the eleventh century, and our ancestors were no archæologists, and always drew what they saw around them. Mr. Bruce fancies the design to

be Italian, "because of the energetic action of the figures;" this seems hardly justified when we look at the simple poverty of the style. Miss A. Strickland suggests that the artist was perhaps Turold the Dwarf, who has cunningly introduced his effigy and name. That the tapestry is not found in any catalogue before 1369, is only a piece of presumptive evidence against the earlier date, and cannot compete with the internal evidence in its favour. On 227 feet of canvas-linen, twenty inches wide, are delineated the events of English history from the time of Edward the Confessor to the landing of the Conqueror at Hastings. The Bayeux tapestry is worked in worsted on linen; the design is perfectly flat and shadowless. The outlines are firmly drawn with cords on thickly set stem-stitches. The surfaces are laid in flat stitch. Though coarsely worked, there is a certain "maestria" in the execution.

The word "orphrey" (English for auriphrigium or Phrygian gold embroidery) is first found in Domesday Book, where "Alvide the maiden" receives from Godric the Sheriff, for her life, half a hide of land, "If she might teach his daughters to make orphreys."[580]

In the end of the eleventh century, Christina, Abbess of Markgate, worked a pair of sandals and three mitres of surpassing beauty, sent through the Abbot of St. Alban's to Pope Adrian IV., who doubtless valued them the more because they came from his native England.[581]

Pl. 74.

See larger image
English Patterns, chiefly from Strutt's "Royal and Ecclesiastical Antiquities of England."
1. 1066. 2. 1092. 3. 1100. 4. 1171. 5. 1171. 6. 1189. 7. 1189. 8. 1361. 9, 10. 1377. 11. 1399. 12. 1422. 13. 1426. 14. 1440. 15. 1445. 16. 1416. 17. 1445. 18. 1477. 19. 1530. 20. 1272.

Pl. 75.

See larger image
1. Panel of a Screen in Hornby Church. Painted fifteenth century.
2. Dress pattern from painted glass. St. Michael's Church, York. Fourteenth century.
3. A portion of the material of the Towneley Copes. Fifteenth century.

[369]Of the twelfth century (1170) we have the robes and mitres of Thomas à Becket at Sens; and another mitre of the period, white and gold, is in the museum at Munich, with his martyrdom embroidered on one side, and that of St. Stephen on the other. The gold needlework is so perfect that it resembles weaving. It is recorded that a splendid dress was embroidered in London for Elinor of Aquitaine, which cost £80, equal to £1400 of the value of to-day.[582]

Rock ("Church of our Fathers," t. ii. p. 279) truly says that it is shown by plentiful records and written documents, from the days of St. Osmond to the time of Henry VIII., that the materials employed in English ecclesiastical embroideries were the best that could be found in our own country or in far-off lands, and the art bestowed on them was the best we could learn and give. Various fabrics came from Byzantine or Saracenic looms, which are described as damasked, rayed, marbled, &c. The few surviving specimens fully justify the admiration bestowed on them throughout Christendom.

Matthew Paris, in the reign of Henry III., says that Innocent III. (1246), seeing certain copes and infulæ with desirable orphreys, was informed they were English [370]work. He exclaimed, "Surely England is a garden of delight! In sooth this is a well inexhaustible! And where there is so much abundance, from thence much may be extracted!"[583]

From the Conquest to the Reformation the catalogues of Church vestments which are to be found in the libraries of York, Lincoln, and Peterborough, show the luxury of ecclesiastical decoration. In Lincoln alone there were upwards of 600 vestments wrought with divers kinds of needlework, jewellery, and gold, upon "Indian baudichyn," samite, tartarin, velvet, and silk. Even in reading the dry descriptions of a common inventory, we are amazed by the lists of "orphreys of goodly needlework," copes embroidered with armorial bearings, and knights jousting, lions fighting, and amices "barred with amethysts and pearls, &c. &c." The few I have named will give an idea of the accumulation of riches in the churches, and the gorgeousness of English embroideries.[584]

I have collected from Strutt's "Illustrations"[585] and other sources a number of patterns for domestic hangings, copied from MSS. of contemporary dates, covering about

400 years, from the time of Harold to Edward IV. The hangings may have been more effective than appears at first sight, if the materials were rich and enlivened with gold. I give two textile designs which in their style are peculiarly English (plates 74, 75).

Now we enter on the age of romance and chivalry, when all domestic decorations began to assume greater [371]refinement. Carpets from the East covered the rushes strewn on the floors, and splendid tents were brought home by crusading knights; and the decorative arts of northern Europe were once more permeated with Oriental taste and design.

We know that in the so-called "days of chivalry," i.e. from the Conquest till the beginning of Henry VIII.'s reign, needlework was the occupation of the women left in their castles, while the men were away fighting for the cross, for the king, for their liberties, or for booty.

This period included the Crusades, the Wars of the Roses, wars with France, and rebellions at home; and yet there was a taste for art, luxury, and show spreading everywhere.[586]

The women were expected to provide, with their looms and their needles, the heraldic surcoats, the scarves and banners, and the mantles for state occasions.[587] They also worked the hangings for the hall and chapel, and adorned the altars and the priests' vestments. Alas! time, taste, and the moth have shared in the destruction of these gauds. The taste for the "baroc" is a new acquisition; no one cared for what was old, merely because it was old. The rich replaced their hangings and their clothes when they became shabby; the poor let them go to pieces, and probably burned the old stuff and the embroideries for the sake of the gold thread, which was of intrinsic value. But both in prose and poetry we read descriptions of beautiful works in the loom, or on the frame, executed by fair ladies for the gallant knights whose lives and prowess these poems have preserved to [372]us. I will give one quotation from that of Emare, in Ritson's collection: "Her mantle was wroughte by a faire Paynim, the Amarayle's daughter." This occupied her seven long years. In each corner is depicted a pair of lovers, "Sir Tristram and Iseult—Sir Amadis and Ydoine, &c., &c. These pictures were adorned with precious stones." The figures were portrayed—

"With stonès bright and pure,With carbuncle and sapphire,Kalsèdonys and onyx clere,Sette in golde newe;Diamondes and rubies,And other stones of mychel pryse."

The lady who owns this mantle is herself great in "workes of broderie."

From the Conquest to the Wars of the Roses, England may claim to have gradually acquired a higher place in art. Our architecture, sculpture, manuscripts, and paintings were not surpassed on the Continent: witness Queen Eleanor's crosses, and her tomb in Westminster Abbey; and the portrait of Richard II., surrounded by saints and angels, at Wilton House,[588] a picture which, preceding Fra Beato Angelico's works by at least a quarter of a century, yet suggests his style, refined drawing, and tender colouring. All who saw the frescoes found in the Chapel [373]at Eton College when it was restored, will remember their extreme beauty, and regret that they were effaced, instead of being preserved and restored. They were a lesson in what English art was in the end of the thirteenth, during the fourteenth, and into the beginning of the fifteenth centuries.

During the Wars of the Roses, when a duke of the blood-royal is said to have begged his bread in the streets of the rich Flemish towns, ladies of rank, more fortunate, were able to earn theirs by the work of their needle.[589]

The monuments of the eleventh and twelfth, thirteenth and fourteenth centuries, are our best authorities for the embroideries then worn. The surcoat of the Black Prince in Canterbury Cathedral is a noteworthy example. The sculptured effigy on the tomb over which it is suspended is absolutely clothed in the same surcoat, with the same accidents of embroidery, as if it had been modelled from it.

In Worcester, when the archæologists opened King John's tomb in 1797, they found him in the same dress and attitude as that portrayed on the recumbent statue.[590] Dress was then extravagantly expensive, and embroidered dresses were worn with borders richly set with precious stones and pearls.

The Librate Roll of Henry III. gives us a list of embroiderers' names: Alain de Basinge, Adam de Bakeryne, John de Colonia, &c.; and in the wardrobe accompts of Richard

II., William Sanstoune and Robert de Ashmede [374]are called the "Broudatores Domini Regis." These may have been the artists to whom the orders were delivered, for in the Librate Roll of Henry III. we find Adam de Baskeryne receiving 6s. 8d. for a "cloth of silk, and fringe, purchased by our commands to embroider a certain chasuble which Mabilia of St. Edmunds made for us." There were certainly then purveyors and masters of the craft. Stephen Vigner, in the fourteenth century, is so warmly commended by the Duke of Berri and Auvergne to Edward III., that Richard II. appointed him his chief embroiderer, and Henry IV. pensioned him for his skilful services.

John Garland, in the beginning of the thirteenth century, is a good authority for the use by our women of small hand-looms. In these they wove, in flax or silk (often mixed with gold), the "cingulæ" or "blode-bendes" so often mentioned, supposed to be gifts between friends for binding the arm, when blood-letting was so much in fashion that the operation was allowed to assume a certain air of coquetry. But the idea suggests itself that this was oftener the gift of the fair weaver to her favoured lover, to fold round his arm as a scarf in battle or tourney, to be ready in case it was needed for binding up a wound, and had possibly served as a snood to bind her own fair hair. There is an account of a specimen of this kind of weaving by M. Léopold Delisle.[591] He describes the attachment of a seal to a grant from Richard Cœur de Lion to Richard Hommet and Gille his wife, preserved in the archives of the Abbey of Aunai, in the department of Calvados. He considers it to be either French or English, and says it was a "lac d'amour," or "tie of love," cut up to serve its present [375]purpose. It is woven with an inscription in white on a ground of green, backed with pale blue, and the material is silk. The woven legend is thus translated from the old French—"Let him perish who would part us."

See larger image
Opus Anglicanum, XIII. Century
British Museum

The term "opus Anglicanum" is first recorded in the thirteenth century, and is supposed simply to mean "English work." But there is also good authority for its having been applied, on the Continent especially, to a particular style of stitchery, of which the Syon cope in the Kensington Museum is the best preserved great example known. Its peculiarity consists in its fine split-stitch being moulded so as to give the effect of a bas-relief; and this appears to have been generally reserved for the medallions representing sacred subjects, and especially employed in modelling the faces and the nude parts of the figures delineated. The effect of this work has often been destroyed, as time has frayed and discoloured the parts that are raised, exhibiting the canvas ground, reversing the high lights, and causing dark spots in their stead. This reversal of the intended effect is an additional practical argument for the flatness of embroidery.[592]

From the Librate Roll of Henry III. one can form an estimate of the value of the "opus Anglicanum" in its day.[593] In 1241 the king gave Peter de Agua Blanca a mitre so worked, costing £82. This would be, according to the present value, £230.

The finest specimens of this English work are to be found on the Continent, or have been returned from it. [376][594] They had either been gifts to popes or bishops before the Reformation, or they had been sold at that time of general persecution and pillage. Among the most remarkable are the pluvial (called) of St. Silvester at Rome, the Daroca pluvial at Madrid, the great pluvial at Bologna, and the Syon cope, of which I have already spoken. The general idea and prevailing design of these three great works are so singular, and yet so alike, that they must have issued from the same workshop, and that was certainly English.

In the Daroca cope the cherubim, with their feet on wheels, which are peculiar to English design, and the angels (in the vacant spaces between the framed subjects from the life of our Lord) have their wings carefully done in chain split-stitch representing peacocks' feathers, of which the silken eyes are stitched in circles, and then raised with an iron by pressure, so as to catch a light and throw a shadow. The ground is entirely English gold-laid work. This cope, so markedly national in design and stitches, probably drifted to the Continent at the time of the Reformation.[595]

Pl. 77.

See larger image

Characteristic English Parsemé Patterns for Ecclesiastical Embroideries.

Pl. 78.
See larger image
Dunstable Pall. Property of the Vicar of Dunstable *ex officio*.

A wonderfully preserved specimen of the "opus Anglicanum," of which a photogravure is here given, was lately presented by Mr. Franks to the Mediæval Department of the British Museum (plate 76). In this may be seen most of the characteristics of this work in the thirteenth century; such as the angels with peacock feather wings, moulded by hot irons; the features of all the figures similarly manipulated; the beautiful gold groundwork, which in this instance is covered with double-headed eagles; and lastly, the fashion of the beard on the face of our Lord and of all the men delineated—the upper lip and round the mouth being invariably shaven; whereas, [377]in Continental work, the beard is allowed to grow into the moustache, closely surrounding the mouth. There are other peculiarities belonging to English design—such as the angels rising between the shrine-work on the pillars out of a flame or cloud pattern, and the pillars very often formed of twined stems bearing vine-leaves or else oak-leaves and acorns. The compartments which frame the groups, when they are not placed in niches, are usually variations of the intersected circle and square. Plate 77 shows the cherubim which from the thirteenth to the sixteenth centuries are found on English ecclesiastical embroideries—also the vase of lilies (emblematic of the Virgin), and the Gothic flowers which are so commonly *parsemé* over our mediæval altar frontals and vestments.

Fig. 26.

It appears that in the reign of Edward III. the people ingeniously evaded the penalties against the excess of luxury in dress, by wearing something that looked as gay, but was less expensive than the forbidden materials; and which did not come under the letter of the law. They invented a spurious kind of embroidery which was, perhaps, partly painted (such examples are recorded). In the 2nd Henry VI. (1422) it was enacted that all such work should be forfeited to the king. The accusation was that "divers persons belonging to the craft of Brouderie make divers works of Brouderie of insufficient stuffe and unduly wroughte with gold and silver of Cyprus, and gold of Lucca, and Spanish laton (or tin); and that they sell these at the fairs of Stereberg, Oxford, and Salisbury, to the great deceit of our Sovereign Lord and all his people." In those days any dishonest work or material was illegal and punishable.[596]

This was, in fact, a protectionist measure in favour of [378]the chartered embroiderers, and gave them a slight taste of the advantages of protection. For a time it was doubtless useful in keeping up the standard of national work. Then followed further measures for the benefit of the established monopolies. First, a statute in 1453 (Henry VI.), forbidding the importation of foreign embroideries for five years. This is re-enacted under Edward IV., Richard III., and Henry VII.; and was partially repealed in the 3rd and 5th George III. While we are on this subject, we may remark that in 1707, the importation of embroidery was forbidden to the East India Company, and we closed our ports to all manufactured Indian goods. The only artistic trade *now* protected is that of the silversmith; no plate from foreign workshops being permitted to enter England—not even do we allow Indian plate to come in, except under certain conditions. This may be the reason that our own plate is so very bad in design and execution, for want of competition and example.

Protection is always more or less fatal to art. The Wars of the Roses had injured our own best schools, and we needed refined imported ideas to raise our standard once again. Perhaps, since embroidery had become a regular industry, our markets were overstocked by home productions which were outrivalled by the works from the Continent, and it was distress that caused the plea for protection.

Pl. 79.
See larger image
Pall of the Vintners' Company (sixteenth century).

It is fair to say that some of the English works of that time, of which we have specimens, are as good as possible. In the Dunstable pall, for instance, the figures of which are perfectly drawn and beautifully executed, the style is excellent and pure English (plate 78). The pall itself is of Florentine crimson velvet and gold brocade, with the little loops of gold drawn through the velvet, showing the loom from whence it came. The white satin border carries the embroidery. It is a more perfect [379]specimen of the later fourteenth century work than the famous pall of the Fishmongers' Company, which shows the impress of the Flemish taste, which was at its perfection in the fifteenth. The style reminds us of that of the fine tapestries from the St. Mary's Hall, Coventry, of which the subject is King Henry VI. and Cardinal Beaufort praying. The Vintners' Company's pall is also very fine (plate 79).

See larger image
Henry VII.'s Cope from Stoneyhurst

Of the time of Henry VII. we have the celebrated cope of Stoneyhurst, woven in Florence, of a gold tissue, the design raised in crimson velvet. It is without seam, and the composition which covers the whole surface is the crown of England lying on the portcullis; and the Tudor rose fills up the space with a magnificent scroll. The design is evidently English, as well as the embroidery, which is, however, much restored[597] (plate 80).

This is one of the "whole suite of vestments and copes of cloth of gold tissue wrought with our badges of red roses and portcullises, the which we of late caused to be made at Florence in Italy ... which our king, Henry VII., in his will bequeathed to God and St. Peter, and to the Abbot and Prior of our Monastery at Westminster,"[598] which were designed for him by Torrigiano.

From the portraits of the fourteenth and fifteenth centuries we can judge of the prevailing taste in dress embroideries of that period, which consisted mostly of delicate patterns of gold or silver on the borders of dresses, and the linen collars and sleeves. Of this style I give a small sampler, from Lord Middleton's collection. We have a good many specimens of the work of these centuries, both ecclesiastical and secular. [380]They had still a Gothic stamp, which totally disappeared in the beginning of the sixteenth century in the new style of the Renaissance.

Fig. 27.
Sampler, from Lord Middleton's collection.
Time, Henry VIII.

The next great change throughout northern Europe affecting all the conditions of life, most especially in England, was caused by the Reformation, which swept away both the art and the artist of the Gothic era. The monasteries which had fostered painting, illumination, and embroidery, and the arts which had been so passionately devoted to the Church, were doomed. George Gifford, writing to Cromwell of the suppression of a religious house at Woolstrope, in Lincolnshire, after praising that establishment says, "There is not one religious person there, but what *can* and *doth* use either embrotheryng, wryting bookes with a fayre hand, making garments, karvynge, &c."[599]

In the general clearance the churches and shrines were swept, though never again garnished, and the survivals have to be painfully sought for, and are so few that a short catalogue will tell them all.

The greater part of the fine embroideries which escaped the "iconoclastic rage" of the Reformation, and the final sweep of the Puritans, are to be seen now in the houses and chapels of the old Roman Catholic families, who [381]have either preserved or collected them; also in the museums of our cathedrals, and spread about the Continent. For instance, at Sens are the vestments of Thomas à Becket, and at Valencia, in Spain, there are yet in the chapter-house a chasuble and two dalmatics, brought from London by two merchants of Valencia, whose names are preserved—Andrew and Pedro de Medina. They purchased them at the sale of the Roman Catholic ornaments of Westminster Abbey in the time of Henry VIII. They are embroidered in gold, and represent scenes from the life of our Lord. The background of one is a representation of the Tower of London.

In 1520 was held the famous tournament of the Field of the Cloth of Gold.[600]Here came all England's chivalry surrounding their splendid young king; followed by squires and men-at-arms, and carrying with them tents, banners, and hangings covered with devices and mottoes. Their own dresses, of rich materials and adorned with embroidery (as well as the housings of their horses), vied in ingenuity and splendour with those of the still more luxurious court and following of Francis I., the French king. The tradesmen and workmen and workwomen in England were driven crazy in their efforts to carry out the ideas and commands of their employers. It is recorded that several committed suicide in their despair. It was worse than the miseries caused by a Court Drawing-Room now. Ingenuity in devices was the order of the day. Francis and his "Partners of Challenge" illustrated one sentimental motto throughout the three days' tourney. The first day they were apparelled in purple satin, "broched" with gold, and covered with black-ravens' [382]feathers, buckled into a circle. The first syllable of "corbyn" (a raven) is *cor*, a "hart" (heart). A feather in French is *pennac*. "And so it stode." The feather in a circle was endless, and "betokened sothe fastnesse." Then was the device "Hart fastened in pain endlesse."

The next day the "Hardy Kings" met armed at all points. The French king and his followers were arrayed in purple satin, broched with gold and purple velvet, embroidered with little rolls of white satin, on which was written "Quando;" all the rest was powdered with the letter L—"Quando Elle" (when she). The third day the motto was laboriously brought to a conclusion. Francis appeared dressed in purple velvet embroidered with little white open books; "Liber" being a book, the motto on it was, "A me." These books were connected with worked blue chains; thus we have the whole motto: "Hart, fastened in pain endlesse, when she delivereth me not of bondes." Could painful ingenuity go further? On the English side we have similar devices. Brandon, Duke of Suffolk, the bridegroom of the Dowager Queen of France, Henry's sister, was clothed on one side in cloth of frise (grey woollen), on which appeared embroidered in gold the motto,—

"Cloth of frise, be not too boldThat thou be match'd with cloth of gold."

This parti-coloured garment was on the other side of gold, with the motto,—

"Cloth of gold, do not despiseThat thou be match'd with cloth of frise."

Besides mottoes, cyphers and monograms were the fashion, embroidered with heraldic devices. These particulars we find in Hall's account of the tournament, with a [383]detailed description of the golden tent in which the monarchs met, and which gave its name ever after to the plain near Guisnes, where the jousts were held. What we read of its construction recalls the Alexandrian erections, of which I have spoken already, as well as their hangings and embroideries.

Pl. 81.

See larger image
English Specimens of Spanish Work. Time of Henry VIII. Lord Middleton's Collection.

Pl. 82.

English Specimen. Spanish Work. Henry VIII. Louisa, Lady Waterford's Collection.

Incrustations of pearls and precious stones gave a dazzling brilliancy to the tent, divided into many rooms, and adapted to the climate of the north. It covered a space of 328 feet. Hall describes the tent, the jousts, and the splendid apparel belonging to this last chapter of the magnificence of chivalry. Brewer remarks that magnificence was, in those days, often supposed to be synonymous with magnanimity (at any rate, it was erected into a royal virtue). "The Mediæval Age," he says, "had gathered up its departing energies for this last display of its favourite pastime, henceforth to be consigned without regret to the mouldering lodges of the past."[601]

We cannot say how much of French taste was imported from this meeting of French and English luxury. The spirit of the Renaissance, fresh from Italy, was reigning in France, but we had also in Italy our own emissaries. John of Padua was probably only one of many Englishmen who travelled to learn and improve themselves in their special crafts.

Catherine of Aragon introduced the Spanish taste in embroidery, which was then white or black silk and gold "lace stitches" on fine linen (plate 81). This went by the name of "Spanish work," and continued to be the fashion down to and through the reign of Mary Tudor, who remained faithful to the traditions of her mother's and her grandmother's work[602] (plate 82). Catherine of Aragon had [384]learned her craft from her mother, Queen Isabella, who always made her husband's shirts. To make and adorn a shirt was then an artistic feat, not unworthy of a queen. Isabella instituted trials of needlework amongst her ladies. In the days of her disgrace and solitude, Catherine turned to her embroidery for solace and occupation. She came forth to meet the Cardinals Wolsey and Campeggio with a skein of red silk round her neck.[603] Taylor, the water poet, says,—

"Virtuously,Although a queen, her days did passIn working with her needle curiously."

At Silbergh Castle, in Westmoreland, was a counterpane and toilet embroidered by Queen Catherine.

Anne of Cleves brought with her the taste for Flemish and German Renaissance designs; and all the cushion stitches were in vogue. The Renaissance borders for dress were mostly worked in gold on coloured silk on the linen collars and cuffs. Holbein's and other contemporary portraits illustrate this peculiarity of the costumes of the time. The women's head-dresses also carried much fine, beautifully designed, and delicate work.

In the reign of Henry VIII. fine hangings were worked and woven in England; the royal inventories give us an idea to what extent. Cardinal Wolsey's walls were covered with splendid embroideries, besides the suites of tapestries still adorning the hall at Hampton Court. One room was hung with embroidered cloth of gold.

[385]Mary Tudor, as I have said, was Spanish in all her tastes, and we have lists of her "smocks" all worked in Spanish stitches, black and gold, or black silk only.[604]This taste, following the political tendencies of the time, entirely disappeared under Elizabeth. It survives, however, in peasant dress in the Low Countries.

Queen Elizabeth spent much of her time in needlework. She herself had received the education of a man, as well as her cousin, Lady Jane Grey; and doubtless many women were taught at that time Greek and Latin, and to study philosophy, mathematics, and the science of music, as a training for serious life. Elizabeth studied and embroidered too; at any rate, she stood godmother to many pieces of embroidery, which are to be seen still in the houses she visited or occupied.

[386]While at Ashridge, and afterwards as a prisoner at Hatfield, she so employed herself; and among the specimens of work of the sixteenth century exhibited at South Kensington in 1873, were her shoes and cap, worked in purl, a semainière in the same stitch, also cushion-covers in divers cushion stitches, and a portmonnaie in exquisitely fine satin-stitch; all of which articles, and many more, were left by her at Ashridge when she was hurried away in the dead of night to Hatfield.[605]

The character of the Renaissance of the sixteenth century, just released from the trammels of Gothic traditions, was somewhat lawless in England, being unchastened by the classical element which entirely controlled the movement in Italy.

The queen's dress soon departed from the severe simplicity which she at first affected, and every part of her costume was covered with flowers, fruit, and symbolical designs; while serpents, crowns, chains, roses, eyes and ears crowded the surfaces of the fine materials of her dresses. These symbolical designs were rich without grace, and ingenious rather than artistic, although their workmanship was perfect. In Louisa, Lady Waterford's collection we find a jacket for a slight girl's figure, of white linen, covered with flowers, fruit, and berries, all carried out in satin and lace stitches. There are butterflies with their wings disengaged from the ground; pods bursting open and showing the round seeds or peas; caterpillars stuffed and raised; all these astonish us by their quaint perfection, and shock us by [387]their naturalistic crudeness of design, and the utter want of beauty or taste in the whole effect. The impression left on the mind is, how dear it must have cost the pocket of the purchaser and the eyes of the workers. There are, however, exceptions to these defective poor designs; and in the same collection is a cushion-cover worked in gold and silver plate, purl and silk, on a red satin ground, which is as good as possible in every respect, and is purely English in style. The stitches and materials are most refined and varied. Purl, which was a newly made material imported from Italy and Germany, was then in much vogue, and we have seen a few fine specimens of it, that have been imitated from the Italian cinque-cento raised and stuffed needlework, which are very curious and almost very beautiful,— only one feels that the same effect could have been produced by simpler means. This work is characteristic of the reigns of Henry VIII., Elizabeth, and James I. We have needlework of another most unhappy queen of this date. Poor Mary, Queen of Scots, tried to soften Elizabeth's heart towards her prisoner by little gifts of her own embroideries.[606]

We have no account of the cause of the incorporation of the Embroiderers' Company by Queen Elizabeth,[607] in [388]the third year of her reign, Oct. 25th, 1561, confirmed by James II., April 12th, 1686, which is still a London guild. It received the lions of England as a special favour. The arms are thus blazoned: "Palée of six argent and azure on a fess gules, between three lions of England pass. gardant or. Three broches in saltire between as many trundles (i.e. quills of gold thread), or. Crest: on a wreath a heart; the holy dove displayed argent, radiated or. Supporters: two lions or (guttée de sang). Motto: 'Omnia Desuper.' Hall, 20, Gutter Lane." There were branches, incorporated and bearing the arms, at Bristol and Chester, in 1780. (See Appendix.)

Fig. 28.
Arms of Embroiderers' Guild.

In the reign of James I. it was the fashion to do portraits in needlework, stitched flat or raised. Some are artistic in design and execution, but they are mostly ridiculously bad.

The East India Company was founded in 1560, under Elizabeth, and obtained the monopoly of the Anglo-Indian trade, under Cromwell, in 1634. This would have been the moment for encouraging a fresh importation of Oriental taste into our degenerate art. Cromwell's own service of plate was scratched over ("graffito") with a childish and weak semi-Indian, semi-Chinese design; and we must accept this as typical of the artistic Oriental knowledge of that day. Grafted on the style of James I., it shows, however, that Indian ideas were creeping in and sought for, if not understood in high places, under the auspices of the East India Company. Needlework alone was excluded from all benefit. From [389]that date, for 150 years, Indian manufactures were imported, *with the exception of embroidery*, which was contraband by the ancient statutes. This accounts for our faint and ignorant imitations of Indian work, and the extreme rarity of the true specimens to be met with in England, unless of a later period.

See larger image
Cushion cover Temp. Queen Elizabeth
XVI. Century

But our Aryan instincts have always led our English tastes towards conventional naturalism. Although we have lost the rules and traditions which converted natural objects into patterns, we are continually, in our style, leaning and groping in their direction, and twining flowers, those of the field by preference, into semi-conventional garlands and posies.

In the seventeenth century, when James I. was king, protection had done its worst. The style of work called "embroidery on the stamp" was then the fashion. This sort of work in Italy continued to be artistic, but the English specimens that have survived from this reign are mostly very ugly. Continental art had ceased to influence us, and bad taste reigned supreme, except in our architecture, which had crystallized into a picturesque style of our own called "James I.," and was the outcome of the last Gothic of Henry VIII. and the Italian style of Edward VI. and Elizabeth. But the carvings of that phase of architecture were semi-barbarous. Nothing could have been poorer than their composition, or coarser than their execution, and the needlework of the day followed suit. Infinite trouble and ingenuity were wasted on looking-glass frames, picture frames, and caskets worked in purl, gold, and silver. The subjects were ambitious Solomon and the Queen of Sheba, and James and Anne of Denmark,[608] and other historical figures were stuffed [390]with cotton or wool, and raised into high relief; and then dressed and "garnished" with pearls; the faces either in painted satin or fine satin stitch; the hair and wigs in purl or complicated knotting. Windsor Castle as a background for King James and King Solomon alike, pointed the clumsy allegory, and the lion of England gambolling in the foreground, amid flowers and coats-of-arms, filled up the composition.

The drawing and design were childish, and show us how high art can in a century or less slip back into no art at all. Any one comparing the Dunstable or the Fishmongers' pall with one of the best caskets of this period would say that the latter should have preceded the former by centuries. In James I.'s time, ignorance of all rules of composition was added to the absence of any sort of style.[609] I give the illustrations of the time of James I. Plate 83 is a cushion from Hatfield House, rich and rather foolish, with tiny men filling in the corners left vacant by large flowers, caterpillars, &c.

Charles I. gave a raised embroidered cope to the Chapter of Durham, of this description of work.[610]

Pl. 84.

See larger image
English embroidered curtain (James I.), at Cockayne Hatley, Beds.

Pl. 85.

See larger image
Embroidered Hangings. Crewels on Linen. Hardwicke Hall.

[391]The other fashionable work of that day had its merits. It was the custom to embroider hangings or linen in crewels. Considering how often in this book and my preceding lectures I have said that this style of work was common (even in the early days of Egypt and Assyria), it may well be said, when was it *not* the fashion? and I must answer, "only since the days of Queen Anne." It seems as if before that time our designs for work were partially influenced by the fine Indian specimens which had surreptitiously crept into England. Some of these are very cleverly executed. Huge conventional trees grow from a green strip of earth carrying every variety of leaf and flower done in many stitches. The individual leaf or flower is often very beautiful. On the bank below, small deer and lions disport themselves, and birds twice their size perch on the branches (plate 84).[611] But even where the work is finest, the incongruities are too annoying. The modern excuse for it, "that it is quaint," does not reconcile us to its extravagant effect. To be quaint in art is, as I have said before, to be funny without intending it; and these curtains are funny by their absence of all intention or perspective, and when hung [392]they make everything in the room look disproportionate to the unnatural size of the foliage. (Plate 85.) Specimens of this work are to be found in most English country houses. It has lasted till now, partly because the crewels first manufactured in the sixteenth century were of an excellent quality, and secondly, because there was no gold to make it worth any one's while to destroy them; so the old hangings went up into the attics in all the disgrace of shabbiness, and have come down again as family relics. Even the moths have been deprived of their prey, by these curtains having served for the beds of the household, so that they have been kept for their nearly 300 years of existence, aired and dusted. Much of this work has been recovered from farmhouses and cottages in tolerable preservation. In many cases the flowers have survived the stout linen grounds on which they were worked. The Royal School of Needlework has often been commissioned to restore and transfer the crewel trees on to a new backing. The hangings and the curtains I have described, prevailed from the end of Elizabeth's reign to that of Queen Anne, and gradually deteriorated. The stitches, of which the variety at first was infinite, had given place to a coarse uniform stem stitch—"gobble stitch." The materials also were of inferior quality, and less durable, so that the latest specimens are in general in the worst condition.

It is remarkable how little the beautiful Continental work influenced our English school. We were enjoying perfect protection, and were clumsily taking advantage of our security from all competition. In the Italian palaces this was the moment of the finest secular embroideries in satin stitches, gold and silver, and "inlaid" and "onlaid" appliqués. Likewise in Spain and Portugal the Oriental work, especially that executed at Goa, filled the palaces and the convents with gorgeous [393]hangings, carpets, table-covers, and bed furniture. We feel it painful to contrast with these our own shortcomings in art, and our faded glories.

The fact is, that, owing to our art-killing protectionist laws, embroidery had the misfortune to be treated at that time as textile manufacture, and not as art at all.

In the reign of William and Mary, Dutch taste had naturally been brought to the front.[612] This included Japanese art, or imitations of it, and also had something of late Spanish. The Georges brought into England, and naturalized a rather heavy work, in gold and silver—the design being decidedly a German "Louis Quatorze"—richly stitched and heavily fringed, and much employed on court dresses and on state furniture. We have seen royal beds and court suits which show very little difference in style. It does not appear that this was worked by ladies. It has, somehow, a professional look.

Fig. 29.
Part of James II.'s Coronation Dress.
From an old Print.

Occasionally, however, we meet with pieces of exceptionally beautiful work of the end of the seventeenth and early part of the eighteenth centuries. The style is the most refined Louis Quatorze, but the work is actually English. The white satin coverlets belonging to the Marquis of Bath and the Duke of Leeds are not to be exceeded in delicacy and splendour. The embroidered dresses of the Duke and Duchess of Buckingham, [394]in Westminster Abbey (early eighteenth century) are of this description.

From Queen Anne to George III., a great deal of furniture was covered with the different cushion stitches, either in geometrical or kaleidoscope patterns, or else displaying groups of flowers or figures, quaint and sometimes pretty. These designs are generally, however, wanting in grace, and their German feeling shows them to be the precursors of the Berlin wool patterns.

When the crewel-work hangings ceased to be the fashion, home work took another direction. All the ladies imitated Indian dimity patterns, on muslin, in coloured silks or thread, with the tambour-frame and needle;[613] but in 1707 the "Broiderers' Company," we presume, found that the Indian manufactures were engrossing the market, and a fresh statute was obtained, forbidding the importation from India of any wrought material. This cruel prohibition carried its own punishment. The Indian trade was ours, and we might have adapted and assimilated the Indian taste for design. We might have brought over men and women great in their most ancient craft, and so produced the most splendid Indo-English School. The Portuguese at least sent out their own silks and satins to be worked at Goa; *we* threw away our chance, and signed the death-warrant of our art.

About the middle of the last century, several ladies, [395]notably Miss Linwood, Miss Moritt, of Rokeby, and Mrs. Delany, copied pictures in worsteds. Some of these are wonderfully clever and even very pretty, but they are rather a painful effort of pictorial art under difficulties, than legitimate embroideries. These pictures would have served the purpose of decoration better as medallions in the centres of arabesque panels, than framed and glazed in imitation of oil paintings. Some of the followers of this school produced works that are shocking to all artistic sense, especially as seen now, when the moths have spoiled them. They can only be classed with such abortive attempts at decoration as glass cases filled with decayed stuffed birds, and vases of faded and broken wax flowers.

I may record with praise the efforts of Mrs. Pawsey,[614] a lady who started a school of needlework at Aylesbury. She was patronized by Queen Charlotte; and for her she worked the beautiful bed at Hampton Court, of purple satin, with wreaths of flowers in crewels touched up with silk, which look as if they might have been copied from the flower-pieces of a Dutch master. The execution is very fine, and reminds one of the best French work of the same period. Mrs. Pawsey taught and helped ladies to embroider in silk and chenille, as well as crewels, and in many country houses we can recognize specimens of her style; usually on screens worked in silk and chenille, with bunches of flowers in vases or baskets, artistically designed.

This was our last attempt at excellence, immediately followed by the total collapse of our decorative needlework, and the advent of the Berlin wool patterns.

[396]

POSTSCRIPT.

A postscript to this chapter will perhaps be acceptable to those who have taken an interest in the "History of English Embroidery," and who will therefore care to know about the revival which has filled so many workshops with what is now called "Art Needlework."

There was a public demand for something better than the worsted patterns in the trade, and the Royal School of Art Needlework rose and tried to respond to that call by stimulating original ideas and designs, and imitating old ones in conformity with modern requirements. The difficulties to be overcome were at first very great. The old stitches had all to be learned and then taught, and the best methods to be selected; the proper materials had to be studied and obtained—sometimes they had to be manufactured. Lastly, beautiful tints had to be dyed; avoiding, as much as possible, the gaudy and the evanescent.

The project of such a school was first conceived in the autumn of 1872.

Lady Welby, herself an accomplished embroideress, had the courage to face all the difficulties of such an undertaking. A small apartment was hired in Sloane Street, and Mrs. Dolby, who was already an authority on ecclesiastical work, gave her help. Twenty young ladies were selected, and several friends joined heartily in fostering the movement.

H.R.H. the Princess Christian of Schleswig-Holstein gave her name as President, and her active co-operation.[615]

[397]The school grew so fast, that for want of space for the work-frames, it had to remove into a larger house, No. 31, Sloane Street, and finally in the year 1875 it found its present home in Exhibition Road, when the Queen became its Patron. In 1878 the Association was incorporated under the Board of Trade, with a Managing and a Finance Committee, and a salaried manager to overlook the whole concern.

From 100 to 150 ladies at a time have there received employment. Their claims were poverty, gentle birth, and sufficient capacity to enable them to support themselves and be educated to teach others.

Branch schools have been started throughout the United Kingdom and in America.[616]

The education of the school has been much assisted by the easy access to the fine collections of ancient embroideries in the Kensington Museum, and by the loan exhibition of old artistic work, which was there organized in 1875, at the suggestion of H.R.H. the President; and since then there have been three very interesting loan exhibitions in the rooms of the Royal School.

It was, indeed, necessary that the acting members should avail themselves of every means of instruction, in order to fit themselves for the task they had undertaken. They were expected at once to be competent to judge all old work, to name its style and date, and even sometimes its market value. They were to be able to repair and add to all old work; to know and teach every stitch, ancient and modern; and produce designs for any [398]period, Gothic, Renaissance, Elizabethan, James I., or Queen Anne; besides contemporary European work,—all different, and each requiring separate study.

Some important works have been produced which will illustrate what has been said:—

1. A suite of window curtains for her Majesty, at Windsor (style, nineteenth century; sunflowers).

2. Curtains for a drawing-room for the Duchess of Buccleuch: crimson velvet and gold appliqué (Louis Quatorze).

3. Curtain for Louisa, Lady Ashburton: coloured silk embroidery on white satin (Venetian, sixteenth century).

4. Curtain, also for Louisa, Lady Ashburton: brown velvet and gold appliqué (*Italian*).

5. Dado for the Hon. Mrs. Percy Wyndham: linen and crewels. Peacocks and vines (*Mediæval*).

6. Furnishings and hangings for state bedroom for Countess Cowper, Panshanger: crimson satin, embroidered and coloured silks (*Chinese*).

7. Curtains for music gallery for Mr. Arthur Balfour: blue silk, appliqué, velvet, and gold (*Italian*).

The earnest attempt to produce an artistic school of embroidery met with recognition and help from the highest authorities. Sir F. Leighton granted permission for appeals to his judgment. Mr. Burne Jones, Mr. Morris, Mr. Walter Crane, and Mr. Wade gave original designs.

We cannot guess whether the taste which has sprung up again so suddenly will last. Perhaps its catholicity may prolong its popularity, and something absolutely new in style may be evolved, which shall revive the credit of the "opus Anglicanum." Of one thing we may be sure—that it is inherent in the nature of Englishwomen to employ their fingers. And the busy as well as the ignorant [399]need a guide to the principles of design, as well as the technical details of the art of embroidery. This should be supplied by the Royal School of

Art Needlework, which by inculcating careful drawing, by reviving old traditions and criticizing fresh ideas, becomes a guarantee for the improvement of domestic decorative design.

FINIS.

FOOTNOTES:

[555]"The people of Babylon, the Accadians, had a written literature and a civilization superior to that of the conquering Assyrians, who borrowed their art of writing, and probably their culture, which may have been the centre and starting-point of the western civilization of Asia, and therefore the origin of our own. Accadian civilization was anterior to that of the Phœnicians and the Greeks, and is now received in these later years as the original form, and become again the heritage of mankind. It has been said that Assyrian art was destitute of originality, and to that of the Accadians, which they adopted, we ourselves owe our first customs and ideas. Four thousand years ago these people possessed a culture which in many of its details resembles that of our country and time."—"Assyrian Life and History," p. 66, by M. Harkness and Stuart Poole.

[556]"The arts of spinning and the manufacture of linen were introduced into Europe and drifted into Britain in the Neolithic Age. They have been preserved with but little variation from that period down to the present day in certain remote parts of Europe, and have only been superseded in modern times by the complicated machinery so familiar to us.... The spindle and distaff are proved by the perforated spindle-whorls, made of stone, pottery, or bone, commonly met with in Neolithic habitations or tombs. The thread is proved, by discoveries in the Swiss lakes, to have been made of flax; and the combs that have been found for pushing the threads of the warp on the weft show that it was woven into linen on some sort of loom."—Boyd Dawkins' "Early Man in Britain," p. 275.

[557]I am aware that the presence of the Phœnicians (or Carthaginians) on our coasts has been disputed; but I think that the evidence of the Etruscan ornaments I have mentioned gives more than probability to the truth of Pliny's account of the expedition of Himilco from Gades, 500B.C. By some he is supposed to have been a contemporary of Hanno, and of the third century B.C. There is some confusion in the imperfect record of the voyage; but it is difficult to interpret it otherwise than that he touched at several points north of Gaul. (See Boyd Dawkins' "Early Man in Britain," pp. 457-461; see also Perrot and Chipiez, "L'Histoire de l'Art dans l'Antiquité," t. iii.; "Phénicie et Cypre," p. 48.) For a contrary opinion, see Elton's "Origins of English History." Elton ascribes the first knowledge of the British islands to the voyage of Pytheas in the fourth century B.C.; he acknowledges that the geography of Britain was well known to the Greeks in the time of Alexander the Great. We owe to Pliny and Strabo the few fragments from Pytheas that have been rescued from oblivion, and to Pliny the notices of Himilco. (See Bouillet's "Dictionnaire d'Histoire et de Géographie.")

[558]See Rock's Introduction to "Textile Fabrics," p. xii.

[559]I give the following amusing tradition, which was probably founded on the celebrity of the English pearl embroidery of the Anglo-Saxon times, of which much went to Rome:—

"Then Cæsar, like a conqueror, with a great number of prisoners sailed into France, and so to Rome, where after his return out of Brytaine, hee consecrated to Venus a surcote of Brytaine pearles, the desire whereof partly moved him to invade this country."—(Stow's "Annales," p. 14, ed. 1634.) Tacitus, in the Agricola 12, says that British pearls are grey and livid.

[560]See Rock's Introduction to "Textile Fabrics," p. xii.

[561]These are the poor results of the Roman invasion and neglect of Britain during their occupation. The second invasion of Britain by the Romans, under Claudius, was caused by the squabbles between the chiefs of the different tribes. Comnenus, the prince of the Atrebates, was at war with the sons of Cunobelinus (Cymbeline). He took his grievances to Rome, and the Roman legions were despatched to settle the matter, and to dazzle the world by the echoes rather than the facts of the triumphant victories in the land of the "wintry pole." Claudius marched with elephants clad in mail, and bearing turrets filled with slingers and bowmen, accompanied by Belgic pikemen and Batavians from the islands in the

Rhine, A.D. 44. The dress of Claudius on his return from Britain was purple, with an ivory sceptre and crown of gold oak leaves. One officer alone was entitled to wear a tunic embroidered with golden palms, in token of a former victory. The Celts, the Gauls, the Gaels, the Picts, the Scots, and the Saxons,—all crowded and settled in Britain when the Romans left it in 410, after nearly four hundred years of misgovernment. (See Elton's "Origins of English History," pp. 306-308.)

|562|Semper, "Der Stil," pp. 133, 134. See Louis Viardot, "Des Origines Traditionnelles de la Peinture en Italie" (Paris, 1840), p. 53, note. Also see "Les Ducs de Bourgogne," part ii. vol. ii. p. 243, No. 4092. Muratori was born in 1672; and he says the Empress Helena's work was in existence in the beginning of the eighteenth century. (See p. 316,*ante*.)

|563|When St. Augustine (546) came to preach to the Anglo-Saxons, he had a banner, fastened to a cross, carried before him, on which was embroidered the image of our Lord. (See Mrs. Lawrence's "Woman in England," pp. 296, 297.) Probably this was Roman work.

|564|Quoted by Mrs. Lawrence, "Woman in England," p. 49, from one of Adhelme's Latin poems. Adhelme, Bishop of Sherborne, died in 709, having been thirty years a bishop. He wrote Latin poems, of which the most important, in praise of virginity, is in the Lambeth Library, No. 200. The MS. contains his portrait. See Strutt's "English Dresses," ed. Planché.

|565|An Anglo-Saxon lady named Aedelswitha, living near Whitby, in the sixth century, collected a number of girls and taught them to produce admirable embroideries for the benefit of the monastery. (See Rock's "Church of our Fathers," p. 273; also his Introduction to "Textiles," p. xxvii.) Bock speaks of Hrothgar's tapestries, embroidered with gold, of the thirteenth century. See Appendix 8. But the earliest English tapestry I have seen is that in York Minster, in which are inwoven the arms of Scrope, 1390. Wright says of the Anglo-Saxon women, "In their chamber, besides spinning and weaving, the ladies were employed in needlework and embroidery, and the Saxon ladies were so skilful in this art, that their works were celebrated on the Continent."—"History of Manners in England during the Middle Ages," by Thomas Wright, p. 52.

|566|See Mrs. Lawrence's "Woman in England," i. p. 296-7.

|567|See Rock's "Church of our Fathers," ii. p. 272, quoting Th. Stubbs. "Acta Pontif. Th. ed. Twysden," 1. ii. p. 1699; also Bock's "Liturgische Gewänder," i. p. 212, and p. 325 *ante*.

|568|Appendix 9.

|569|This could hardly have been intended originally for an ecclesiastical purpose. It sounds as if it were a stray fragment from Græco-Roman art, rather than a survival of the classical legend employed as a pretty motive for decoration. Wiglaf's veil is named by Ingulphus. See Strutt's "English Dresses," pp. 3, 7. See also "Historia Eliensis," l. 2, ed. Stewart, p. 183.

|570|See Rock's "Textile Fabrics," p. xxi.; also for Council of Cloveshoe, see his "Church of Our Fathers," p. 14.

|571|The Benedictines drained the marshes of Lincolnshire and Somersetshire to employ the poor in the eighth century. St. Bennet travelled to France and Italy, and brought back from his seven journeys cunning artificers in *glass* and stone, besides costly books and copies of the Scriptures, in order (as is expressly said by Bede) that the ignorant might learn from them, as others learned from books. See Mrs. Jameson's "Legends of the Monastic Orders," pp. 56, 57.

|572|See Raine's "St. Cuthbert," pp. 50-209. Mr. Raine describes it as being "of woven gold, with spaces left vacant for needlework embroidery." Beautifully drawn majestic figures stand in niches on rainbow-coloured clouds, and the effect is that of an illumination of the ninth century. The style is rather Greek or Byzantine than Anglo-Saxon. For further notices of St. Cuthbert's relics, see chapter on Materials, *ante*; also see Rock's "Introduction," p. cxvii.

|573|Appendix 10.

|574|See "Calendar of the Anglican Church," by J. H. Parker (1851): "St. Dunstan was not only a patron of the useful and fine arts, but also a great proficient in them himself; and his almost contemporary biographers speak of him as a poet, painter, and musician, and

so skilled a worker in metals that he made many of the church vessels in use at Glastonbury."

[575]See Rock's "Church of our Fathers," p. 270.

[576]Strutt's "English Dresses," p. 70, quoted from Ingulphus' "History of Croyland Abbey."

[577]Shot, or iridescent materials, were then and had been some time manufactured at Tinnis in Egypt, a city now effaced. It was called "bouqualemoun," and employed for dresses and hangings for the Khalifs. See Schefer's "Relations du Voyage de Nassiri Khosrau," p. cxi. The original was written in the middle of the eleventh century.

[578]See Duchêsne's "Historiæ Normanorum." Fol. Paris, 1519.

[579]Queen Matilda was not the originator of the idea that a hero's deeds might be recorded by his wife's needle. Penelope wove the deeds of Ulysses on her loom, and it is suggested by Aristarchus that her peplos served as an historical document for Homer's "Iliad." See Rossignol's "Les Artistes Homériques," pp. 72, 73, cited by Louis de Ronchaud in his "La Tapisserie," p. 32. Gudrun, like the Homeric woman, embroidered the history of Siegfried and his ancestors, and Aelfled that of the achievements of her husband, Duke Brithnod. The Saga of Charlemagne is said to have been embroidered on twenty-six ells of linen, and hung in a church in Iceland.

[580]Domesday ed. Record Commission, under head of Roberte de Oilgi, in co. Buckingham. See also another entry under Wilts, where "Leivede" is spoken of as working auriphrigium for King Edward and his Queen.

[581]Canon Jackson, writing of embroidery, says: "That this was cared for in the great monasteries at this early date appears from a MS. register of Glastonbury Abbey in the possession of the Marquis of Bath. It is called the Liber Henrici de Soliaco, and gives an account of the affairs of that abbey in A.D. 1189 (Richard I.)." There was a special official whose business it was to provide the monastery with church ornaments generally, and specially with "aurifrigium," or gold embroidery, on vestments. For this a house and land, with an annual allowance of food, was set apart. Another tenant also held some land, to which was attached the obligation to find a "worker in gold."—Letter from Canon Jackson to the Author.

[582]See Mrs. Lawrence's "Woman in England," vol. i. p. 360. She quotes an entry from Madox, a sum of £80 (equal to £1400 of to-day) for an embroidered robe for the Queen, paid by the Sheriffs of London.

[583]Matthew Paris, "Vit. Abb. St. Albani." p. 46; Rock, "Church of our Fathers," vol ii. p. 278.

[584]See Mrs. Dolby's Introduction to "Church Vestments."

[585]Strutt's "Royal and Ecclesiastical Antiquities of England," ed. mdcclxxiii.

[586]Though the work was domestic, the materials came from the East and the South; and while the woven gold of Sicily and Spain was merely base metal or gilded parchment, our laws were directed to the preservation of pure metals for textile purposes.

[587]Matthew Paris, "Hist. Angl.," p. 473, ed. Paris, 1644. See Hartshorne's "Mediæval Embroideries," pp. 23, 24.

[588]The reproduction by the Arundel Society of this picture will familiarize those who care for English art with what is, perhaps, its finest example, next to the crosses of Queen Eleanor. It has been erroneously attributed to Van Eyk, but it is undoubtedly English. That its art is contemporary with the time of Richard II., is shown by the design and motives of the woven materials and embroidery in which the king and his attendant saints are clothed. They remind us of the piece of silk in the Kensington Museum, into which are woven (probably in Sicilian looms) the cognizance of the King's grandfather, the sun with rays; that of his mother Joan, the white hart; and his own, his dog Math. This is a good example of the value of an individual pattern. It helps us to affix dates to other specimens of similar style.

[589]See Miss Strickland's mention of the Countess of Oxford in her "Life of Queen Elizabeth of York," p. 46.

[590]From the fragments found, it appeared that King John's mantle was of a strong red silk. Till lately, when it was effaced by being completely gilt, the mantle on the

recumbent effigy was of a bright red, bordered with gold and gems. See Greene's "Worcester," p. 3, quoted in the "Report of the Archæological Association of Worcester," p. 53.

[591]"Notice sur les Attaches d'un Sceau," par M. Léopold Delisle (Paris, 1854); and also Rock's Introduction to "Textile Fabrics," p. xxii.

[592]The opus Anglicanum often included borders and orphreys set with jewellers' work (or its imitation, worked in gold thread), gems, and pearls.

[593]Edward III. had from William de Courtenay an embroidered garment, "inwrought with pelicans, images, and tabernacles of gold. The tabernacles were like niches, with pinnacles and roofs."

[594]Bock, "Liturgische Gewänder," i. p. 211, says there is a piece of opus Anglicanum in the treasury of Aix-la-Chapelle, called the Cope of Leo III.

[595]For further notice of the "opus Anglicanum," see chapter (*ante*) on ecclesiastical embroideries.

[596]Appendix 11.

[597]The orphreys are probably not the original work.

[598]"Testamenta Vetusta," ed. Nicholas, t. i. p. 33.

[599]Woolstrope, Lincolnshire. Collier's "Ecclesiastical History of Great Britain," v. p. 3 (ed. Lothbury). This proves that the monks sometimes plied the needle.

[600]See Hall's "Union of the Houses of York and Lancaster," pp. lxxv-lxxxiii.

[601]See Brewer's "Reign of Henry VIII.," vol. i. pp. 347-376.

[602]In the Public Record Office is an inventory of Lord Monteagle's property, 1523 A.D.; amongst other things, is named a piece of Spanish work, "eight partletts garnished with gold and black silk work." This Spanish work is rare, but the description reminds us of a specimen belonging to Louisa, Marchioness of Waterford (Plate 82)—a square of linen, worked with ostriches, turkeys, and eagles in gold and black silk stitches. See Mrs. Palliser's "History of Lace," pp. 6, 12.

[603]Quoted from Cavendish by Miss Strickland, "Queens of England," iv. p. 132.

[604]"The invalid queen, in her moments of convalescence, soothed her cares and miseries at the embroidery frame. Many specimens of her needlework were extant in the reign of James I., and are thus celebrated by Taylor, the poet of the needle:—

"'Mary here the sceptre sway'd;And though she were no queen of mighty power,Her memory will never be decay'd,Nor yet her works forgotten. In the Tower,In Windsor Castle, and in Hampton Court,—In that most pompous room called Paradise,—Whoever pleases thither to resort,May see some works of hers of wondrous price.Her greatness held it no disreputationTo hold the needle in her royal hand,Which was a good example to our nationTo banish idleness throughout the land.And thus this queen in wisdom thought it fit;The needle's work pleased her, and she graced it.'

"According to Taylor, Mary finished the splendid and elaborate tapestry begun by her mother."—Miss Strickland's "Life of Mary Tudor," v. p. 417.

[605]"After the action at D'Arbre de Guise, Elizabeth (of England) sent to Henri IV. a scarf embroidered by her own hand. 'Monsieur mon bon frère,' wrote the queen, 'its value is naught in comparison to the dignity of the personage for whom it is destined; but I supplicate you to hide its defects under the wings of your good charity, and to accept my little present in remembrance of me.'"—"Henri IV.," by Miss Freer, p. 311.

[606]In the year 1683 the Marchese Luca Casimiero degl' Albizzi visited England, and his travels were recorded in manuscript by Dr. A. Forzoni. At Windsor he observed over a chimney-piece a finely wrought piece of embroidery—"un educazione di fanciulli"—by the hands of Mary Queen of Scots.—Loftie's "History of Old London;" also article on "Royal Picture Galleries," by George Scharf, p. 361 (1867).

[607]"The Company of the Embroiderers can make appear by their worthy and famous pieces of art that they have been of ancient use and eminence, as is to be seen in divers places at this day; but in the matter of their incorporation, it hath relation to the fourth year of Queen Elizabeth."—Stow's "Survey of London and Westminster," part ii. p. 216; also see Edmonson's "Heraldry," vol. i. (1780). "The Keepers, Wardens, and Company of the Broiderie of London.... 2 keepers and 40 assistants, and the livery consists of 115

members. They have a small but convenient hall in Gutter Lane."—Maitland's "History of London," book iii. p. 602.

[608]The fashion of this work began much earlier, for we find in the inventory of "St. James's House, nigh Westminster," 1549: "42 Item. A table wherein is a man holding a sword in his one hand and a sceptre in his other hand of needlework, partly garnished with seed pearl" (p. 307).

[609]The merit or blame of this rounded padded work (a caricature of the raised embroidery of the opus Anglicanum) is often erroneously awarded to the "nuns of Little Gidding." The earliest specimens we know of this "embroidery on the stamp" are German. At Coire in the Grisons, at Zurich (see chapter on ecclesiastical art), and in the National Museum at Munich are some very beautiful examples. The Italians also executed elaborate little pictures in this manner; but I cannot praise it however refined in execution or beautiful the design. I have seen no English specimens that are not beneath criticism; they are only funny.

[610]In the Calendar of the State Papers Office (Domestic, Charles I., vol. clxix. p. 12), Mrs. H. Senior sues the Earl of Thomond for £200 per annum, her pay for teaching his daughter needlework. Mrs. Hutchinson, in her Memoir, says she had eight tutors when she was seven years old, and one of them taught her needlework. This shows how highly this accomplishment was still considered in the days of Charles I. and the Commonwealth. Later, Evelyn speaks of the "new bed of Charles II.'s queen, the embroidery of which cost £3000" (Evelyn's Memoirs, January 24, 1687). Evelyn says of his own daughter Susanna, who married William Draper: "She had a peculiar talent in designe, as painting in oil and miniature, and an extraordinary genius for whatever hands can do with a needle." See Evelyn's "Memoirs," April 27, 1693; also see Mrs. Palliser's "History of Lace," pp. 7, 8.

[611]The tree-pattern, already common in the latter days of Elizabeth, reappeared on a dress worn by the Duchess of Queensberry, and described by Mrs. Delany; she says, "A white satin embroidered at the bottom with brown hills, covered with all sorts of weeds, and with a brown stump, broken and worked in chenille, and garlanded nasturtiums, honeysuckles, periwinkles, convolvuluses, and weeds, many of the leaves finished with gold." Mrs. Delany does not appreciate this ancient pattern.

[612]Queen Mary only knotted fringes. Bishop Burnett says: "It was strange to see a queen work so many hours a day." Sir E. Sedley, in his epigram on the "Royal Knotter," says,—

"Who, when she rides in coach abroad,Is always knotting threads."

Probably it was the fashion, as Madame de Maintenon always worked during her drives with the king, which doubtless prevented her dying of *ennui*!

[613]I quote from the *Spectator*, No. 606: "Let no virgin receive her lover, except in a suit of her own embroidery."

[614]Her style was really legitimate to the art. It was flower-painting with the needle. Miss Moritt copied both figures and landscapes, with wonderful taste and knowledge of drawing. Miss Linwood's and Mrs. Delany's productions are justly celebrated as *tours de force*, but they caused the downfall of the art by leading it on the wrong track.

[615]Lord Houghton alludes to H.R.H.'s patronage of the revival of embroidery in his paraphrase of the "Story of Arachne," p. 238, *ante*.

[616]"Opposed to the 'utility stitches' are the art needlework schools that have branched out in many directions from New York.... The impulse that led to their formation was derived from South Kensington (England), and affords a striking instance of the ramifications of an organization."—*Atlantic Monthly* ("Women in Organization"), Sept., 1880.

[400]

APPENDICES.
APPENDIX I., TO PAGE 105.
By Ch. T. Newton.

Though the embroidered and richly decorated textile fabrics of the ancients have perished, all but a few scraps, we may form some idea of the richness and variety of Greek female attire from the evidence of the inventories of dedicated articles of dress which have been preserved for us in Greek inscriptions.

In the Acropolis at Athens have been found a number of fragments of marble on which are inscribed lists of various female garments dedicated, for the most part, in the Temple of Artemis Brauronia, in the Archonship of Lykurgos, B.C. 338-35. These articles were thus carefully registered because they formed part of the treasures dedicated to the gods of the Acropolis, which it was the duty of the state to guard, and to commit to the custody of officers specially selected for that duty. One of these fragments is in the Elgin Collection at the British Museum, and has been published by Mr. Hicks in the "Collection of Ancient Greek Inscriptions in the British Museum," Part 1, No 34; and the entire series has since been given to the world in the "Corpus Inscriptionum Atticarum" of the Academy of Berlin, ii., Part 2., Nos. 751-65.

The material of these garments seems to have been either linen or fine woollen; the colours white, purple, or some shade of red, mostly used as a border or in stripes; or a shade of green, the tint of which is described as "frog colour," saffron, or sea-green.

The borders and patterns noted remind us of those represented on the garments of figures in vase pictures, such as the embattled border, the wave pattern, and certain patterns in rectangular compartments. A group of Dionysos pouring out a libation while a female serves him with wine, and a row of animals, are also noted among the ornaments.

The inscription, "Sacred to Artemis," woven into the fabric of the garment, occurs twice. Gold, as an ornament fixed on the dress, is mentioned in these entries. It is noted that some of these dresses served to deck the statue of the goddess herself. Most of the garments are the *chiton* or tunic, flowing to the feet; the *chitoniskos*, a shorter and more ornamental garment worn over it; and the mantle, *himation*. Pieces of cloth or rags are also mentioned among the entries; these were probably the remnants of cast-off garments dedicated by their wearers. Some of the dresses are described as embroidered with the needle.

In the worship of the Artemis Brauronia, certain Athenian girls between the ages of five and ten were solemnly dedicated to the goddess every five [401]years. In publishing the inventory in the British Museum already referred to, Mr. Hicks remarks, "It may have been the custom sometimes to dedicate to the goddess the garments worn by children at their presentation, just as we know that the garments in which persons had been initiated at the Greater Eleusinia were worn by them until threadbare, and then dedicated to some god. If so, the number of children's clothes mentioned in our inventory is easily explained. Or were these the clothes of children cut off by Artemis in infancy, such as bereaved mothers nowadays often treasure for years, having no temple wherein to dedicate them?" Mr. Hicks further remarks that it was usual for the bride before marriage to dedicate her girdle to Artemis; and at Athens the garments of women who died in childbirth were likewise in like manner so dedicated. It is probably on account of such dedications that Artemis was styled Chitonè—the goddess of the *chiton*.

Another list of vestments is preserved in an inscription found at Samos, and published by Carl Curtius in his "Inschriften u. Studien zur Geschichte von Samos," pp. 17-21. The garments in this list were dedicated to the goddess Herè (Juno) in her celebrated temple at Samos. The entries relate chiefly to articles of female attire, but some few are dedicated to the god Hermes. Some of these articles were doubtless worn by the deities themselves on festive occasions, when their statues were decked out. The toilet, *kosmos*, of goddesses was superintended by a priestess specially chosen for that purpose. She was called *kosmeteira*, or "Mistress of the Robes."

In the Samian list of garments, those which are embroidered or ornamented with gold are specially noted. Some of the tunics are described as Lydian. Curtains or hangings are also mentioned in this list. These must have been used to ornament the interior of the temple, or to screen off the statue of the goddess on the days when she was withdrawn from the gaze of the profane. Such hangings were, probably, a main cause of the conflagrations by which Greek temples were from time to time destroyed in spite of the solidity of their walls.

APPENDIX II., TO PAGE 210.

In the Castle of Moritzburg, built by Augustus the Strong, Elector of Saxony and King of Poland, is a quaint apartment, on the walls of which are hung rugs of feather-work, of which the borders are adorned with set patterns of fruit and flowers, and the colouring is as soft as a Gobelins tapestry. The feathers are woven tightly into the warp, in the same manner as the tufts are set in a velvety carpet; forming a surface as delicate as silk to the touch. There are four high-backed chairs covered with the same work in smaller patterns. But what is especially remarkable is an immense canopy, like that of a state bed, with urn-shaped ornaments of stiff feathers at the corners; and a pretty bell-shaped fringe of scarlet feathers. The same ornament edged a large rug like those on the wall, thrown over what at first appeared to be a bed; but on examination it was found to be a rough wooden platform, said to be the throne of Montezuma. The story is that [402]Augustus the Strong went to Spain incognito at the age of eighteen, in search of adventures, and distinguished himself at a bull-fight. When the king (Charles II.) heard the name of the young hero, he gave him a hospitable reception, and afterwards sent these Mexican treasures to him as a token of friendship.

APPENDIX III., TO PAGE 237.
Story of Arachne, abridged by Earl Cowper from Ovid's Metamorphoses.

Arachne's tale of grief is full:Her father was of low degree;No thought beyond his crimson'd wool,His daughter and his wife had he.

The wife had fill'd an early tomb,The daughter lived—and all the landOf Lydia boasted of her loom,Her needle, and her dexterous hand.

To watch her task the nymphs repairFrom fair Timolus' vine-clad hill;They deem the work divinely fair,The maid when working fairer still.

The softness of the fleecy ball,By skilful fingers taught to flowIn lengthening lines—they watch'd it all—And round and round the spindle go.

Wondering, they view the rich design:Ah, luckless gift! ah, foolish pride!'Twas Pallas taught the art divine,But this the haughty maid denied.

"Me taught," she cried, "by Pallas! MeBy Pallas! Let the goddess firstAccept my challenge. Then, should sheSurpass me, let her do her worst."

Vain, impious words! The goddess cameIn likeness of an ancient crone,With grizzled locks and tottering frame,And spoke with warning in her tone.

"Though matchless in thine art," she cried,"Though first of mortals, tempt not fate.Age makes me wise. Thou hast defiedA goddess. It is not too late."

[403]The unhappy maid, with madness blind,Replied, and scarce restrain'd the blow."'Tis plain, old woman, that your mindIs drivelling to address me so.

"Some daughter or some slave may wantYour counsel. Let her but appear,This mighty Pallas whom you vaunt!"The goddess answer'd, "She is here."

She spoke, and lo! that ancient croneWas young and fair, and tall and proud:—The nymphs fell prostrate. She alone—Arachne—neither shrank nor bow'd.

One blush quick came and pass'd away,Hovering as clouds, when night is done,Grow rosy at the dawn of day,Then whiten with the rising sun.

She did not shrink—she did not pause—But headlong to destruction ran;And thus the strife ordain'd to causeSuch dark calamity began.

Each for the contest takes her stand—The goddess here, the mortal there—And each proceeds with skilful handThe means of victory to prepare.

The beam each loom supports full well,And to the loom the warp is tied;Nor will I now forget to tellThe reed that doth the warp divide.

The woof the shuttle in doth bring,The nimble fingers guide its way;And still from either work-frame ringThe blows inflicted by the slay.

Each to her bosom binds her vest:The arms of each, quick moving, feelNo sense of toil, no need of rest,For weariness is quench'd by zeal.

And all the gorgeous tints of TyreIn varying shades are mingled there;And every hue the sun's bright fireCan kindle in the showery air,—

[404]When the wide rainbow spans the sky;The bow whose colours, in the endSo different, yet so like when nigh,In harmony's own concord blend,—

And precious threads of glittering goldEnrich the growing web. But say!What ancient tale by each was told?What legend of an earlier day?

178

Pallas her well-known triumph drew;The gods assembled in their force,And Neptune with his trident, too,Exulting in the fiery horse,—

Which from the rock he made to bound:But she herself, more deeply wise,A greater blessing from the groundThe olive brought, and gain'd the prize.

The border of this main designWith Rhodope's sad tale was set;And all who dared the gods divineTo rival—and the fate they met.

Meanwhile Arachne wove the wool:The web with many a picture shone.She drew Europa with her bull,And Leda with her snow-white swan.

Deois with her snake display'd,And Danäe with her shower of gold;And many a tale besides the maid,Had fate permitted, would have told.

But the dread goddess now no moreTo check her rising envy strove;The half-completed task she tore,And all the pictured crimes of Jove.

The shuttle thrice the air did rend,Thrice did the heaven-directed blowFull on Arachne's head descend,And made her purple blood to flow.

Arachne's soul was proud and high:She drew a cruel cord aroundHer tender neck—and, driven to die,Was from a beam suspended found.

[405]Her death the unpitying goddess stay'd;"Henceforth, vain fool! for such a crimeFor ever shall thou hang," she said;"A warning to the end of time."

In scorn she spoke, and over allHer rival's face and form she smear'dA deadly drug. The head grew small,And each fair feature disappear'd.

And off the beauteous tresses fell;The tender waist that was so slim,In loathly sort was seen to swell,Shrivell'd and shrank each comely limb.

The spider's fingers still remainTo spin for ever.—We may vieWith fellow mortals, but 'tis vainTo struggle with the gods on high.

January, 1885. COWPER.

APPENDIX IV., TO PAGE 318.
Extract from "History of Christian Art." By Lord Lindsay.
Vol. i. pp. 136-139.

"But perhaps the noblest testimony to the revival under the Comneni is afforded by the designs on the Dalmatic or sacerdotal robe, commonly styled 'Di Papa San Leone,' preserved in the sacristy of St. Peter's—said to have been embroidered at Constantinople for the coronation of Charlemagne as Emperor of the West, but fixed by German criticism as a production of the twelfth, or the early part of the thirteenth century. The Emperors wore it ever after, when serving as deacons at the Pope's altar during their coronation-mass. You will think little of it at first sight, and lay it aside as a piece of darned and faded tapestry, yet I would stake on it, alone, the reputation of Byzantine art. And you must recollect, too, that embroidery is but a poor substitute for the informing hand and the lightning stroke of genius.

It is a large robe of stiff brocade, falling in broad and unbroken folds in front and behind,—broad and deep enough for the Goliath-like stature and the Herculean chest of Charlemagne himself. On the breast, the Saviour is represented in glory, on the back the Transfiguration, and on the two shoulders Christ administering the Eucharist to the Apostles.

The composition on the breast is an amplification of No. V. (as above enumerated) of the Personal traditional compositions.—In the centre of a golden circle of glory, 'Jesus Christ, the Resurrection and the Life,' robed in white, with the youthful and beardless face, his eyes directly looking into [406]yours, sits upon the rainbow, his feet resting on the winged wheels[617] of Ezekiel, his left hand holding an open book, inscribed with the invitation, 'Come, ye blessed of My Father,'—his right raised in benediction. At the four corners of the circular glory, resting on them, half within it, half without, float the emblems of the four Evangelists; the Virgin and the Baptist stand to the right and left of our Saviour, the Baptist without, the Virgin entirely within the glory, the only figure that is so placed; she is sweet in feature and graceful in attitude, in her long white robe.

Above Our Saviour's head, and from the top of the golden circle, rises the Cross, with the crown of thorns suspended upon it, the spear resting on one side, the reed with the sponge on the other, and the sun and moon looking down upon it from the sky.

The heavenly host and the company of the blessed form a circle of adoration around this central glory; angels occupying the upper part, emperors, patriarchs, monks and nuns the lower; at the extremity, on the left side, appears Mary Magdalen, in her penitence—a thin emaciated figure, imperfectly clothed, and with dishevelled hair.

In the corners, below this grand composition, appear, to the right, St. John the Baptist, holding the cross, and pointing upwards to Our Saviour; to the left, Abraham seated, a child on his lap, and resting his hand on another by his side.

The background and scene of the whole composition is of blue, to represent heaven,—studded with stars, shaped like the Greek cross.

The Transfiguration, which corresponds to this subject on the back of the robe, is the traditional composition, only varied by the unusual shape of the vesica piscis which encloses Our Saviour. The two compositions representing the Institution of the Eucharist, on the shoulders, are better executed and more original. In each of them, Our Saviour, a stiff but majestic figure, stands behind the altar, on which are deposited a chalice and a paten or basket containing crossed wafers. He gives, in the one case, the cup to St. Paul, in the other the bread to St. Peter,—they do not kneel, but bend reverently to receive it; five other disciples await their turn in each instance,—all are standing.

I do not apprehend your being disappointed with the 'Dalmatica di San Leone,' or your dissenting from my conclusion, that a master, a Michael Angelo I might almost say, then flourished at Byzantium.

It was in this Dalmatic—then *semée* all over with pearls and glittering in freshness—that Cola di Rienzi robed himself over his armour in the sacristy of St. Peter's, and thence ascended to the Palace of the Popes, after the manner of the Cæsars, with sounding trumpets and his horsemen following him—his truncheon in his hand and his crown on his head—'terribile e fantastico,' as his biographer describes him—to wait upon the legate.[618]"

FOOTNOTES:

[617] In the 'Manual of Dionysius,' recently published by M. Didron (p. 71, &c.), these winged wheels are interpreted as signifying the order of angels commonly distinguished as Thrones. Their interpretation as the Covenants of the Law and Gospel, sanctioned by St. Gregory the Great in his Homilies, is certainly more sublime and instructive.

[618] Cited from the original life, printed in Muratori's 'Antiquit. Ital. Medii Ævi,' tom. viii., by M. Sulpice Boisserée, in his essay, 'Ueber die Kaiser-Dalmatica,' &c.

[407]

APPENDIX V., TO PAGE 320.

The Hon. and Rev. Ignatius Clifford has permitted me to make extracts from his "Memoranda of some remarkable Specimens of Ancient Church Embroidery." First on his list is the Cope now in the possession of Colonel Butler Bowden, of Pleasington, near Blackburn, Lancashire. I give his account of the mutilated condition, from which he has made his beautifully drawn restoration. "Formerly," he says, "portions of this cope, some made up into chasuble, stole, maniple, and some scraps detached, were at Mount St. Mary's College, Spink Hill, near Chesterfield, Derbyshire."

The well-known architect, the late Augustus Welby Pugin, having seen them (or at least the chasuble), wrote on the 20th April, 1849, to the Rector of the College, "I found it to be of English work of the time of Edward I., and have no hesitation in pronouncing it to be the most interesting and beautiful specimen of church embroidery I have ever seen."

Other portions of the cope had been made up into an altar-frontal, and were in the possession of Henry Bowden, Esq., of Southgate House, Derbyshire, some four or five miles from the college.

The ground is crimson velvet. The designs are wrought in gold, silver, silk, and seed pearls. The silks are worked in chain, or rather in split stitch. It contains between seventy and eighty figures.

Only two small fragments remain of the quasi-hood.

In the orphrey are kings, queens, archbishops, and bishops. In the body of the cope are the Annunciation—Adoration of the Magi—Our Lady enthroned at the right of her Divine Son. *Lowest row* of single figures—St. Simon, St. Jude, St. James, St. Thomas, St. Andrew, St. Peter, St. Paul, St. Barnabas, St. Matthew, St. Philip, St. James, St.

Bartholomew. *Middle row*—St. Edward the Confessor—a Bishop—St. Margaret, St. John the Evangelist, St. John the Baptist, St. Catherine, an Archbishop, St. Edmund king and martyr. *Top row*—St. Lawrence, St. Mary Magdalene, St. Martha (or St. Helen?), St. Stephen. In the intervals, angels seated on faldstool thrones, and bearing stars; also two popinjays.

Mr. Clifford describes the Steeple Aston Cope. The ground is of a richly ribbed faded silk. The design worked in gold and silks is enclosed in quatrefoils of oak and ivy. The Syon Cope he refers to Rock's "Textile Fabrics." See Appendix.

The Dalmatic from Anagni, exhibited at Rome in 1870, he thinks is probably English.

The Pluvial in the Basilica of St. John Lateran at Rome, he speaks of as "having much the appearance of the celebrated Opus Anglicanum."

He describes the subjects embroidered on it thus: "No border round the curved edge. The orphrey is divided into tabernacles containing an archbishop, two bishops, and three kings and queens. Between the tabernacles are four angels, each accompanied by one of the evangelistic symbols. The body of the cope is cut into a most elaborate system of tabernacles, with a centre compartment of a different form for the group of the Crucifixion. The subjects are chiefly from the life of our Lord and the Blessed Virgin. [408]The small quasi-hood is embroidered with two wyverns or griffin-like creatures. The pelican and the phœnix are introduced over the top central group of the enthronement of our Lady."

Mr. Clifford gives the history of the Cope of Pius II. (Bartolomeo Piccolomini, "Æneas Silvius") fifteenth century. It is a masterpiece of Italian embroidery of the early Renaissance. The material was gold brocade, covered with wonderful designs carried out in needlework, representing saints and angels, trees and birds, and arabesques. The whole was adorned with pearls and precious stones valued at £80,000. At his death the pope bequeathed this vestment to the cathedral of his native town. The cope was stolen in March, 1884, from the treasury at Pienza; and shortly afterwards discovered in the shop of a dealer in antiquities at Florence, but completely stripped of its precious stones and of some of its more valuable embroidery. After magisterial investigation, the cope was restored to Pienza.

The cope at Bologna is thus described: "Subjects from the New Testament contained in two rows of tabernacle compartments, twelve in lower, seven in upper row. Spandrils occupied by angels playing on various musical instruments. After each row, a border containing medallions with heads (of angels, prophets, &c.), twenty-three in lower, nine in upper row. No orphrey; no border or outside curve; quasi-hood very small."

APPENDIX VI., TO PAGE 326.
From Rock's "Textiles," p. 275.

"The Syon Monastery Cope; ground green, with crimson interlacing barbed quatrefoils, enclosing figure of our Lord, the Blessed Virgin Mary, the Apostles, with winged cherubim standing on wheels in the intervening spaces, and the orphreys, morse, and hem wrought with armorial bearings; the whole done in gold, silver, and various coloured silks. English needlework, thirteenth century; 9 feet 7 inches by 4 feet 8 inches.

"This handsome cope, so very remarkable on account of its comparatively perfect preservation, is one of the most beautiful among the several liturgical vestments of the olden period anywhere to be now found in Christendom. If by all lovers of mediæval antiquity it will be looked upon as so valuable a specimen of art of its kind and time, for every Englishman it ought to have a double interest, showing, as it does, such a splendid and instructive example of the opus 'Anglicum,' or English work, which won itself so wide a fame, and was so eagerly sought after throughout the whole of Europe during the Middle Ages."

Dr. Rock gives a list of the subjects. St. Michael overcoming Satan (from Rev. xii. 7, 9). The next quatrefoil above this is filled with the Crucifixion. Here the Blessed Virgin is arrayed in a green tunic, and a golden mantle lined with vair; her head is kerchiefed, and her uplifted hands sorrowfully clasped. St. John—whose dress is all of gold—is on the left, at the foot of the cross, upon which the Saviour, wrought all in silver—a most unusual [409]thing—with a cloth of gold wrapped about His loins, is fastened by three (not four) nails.... In the highest quatrefoil is figured the Redeemer in glory, crowned as a king, and seated on a cushioned throne. Resting upon His knee and steadied by His hand is the Mund, or ball representing the earth.... This is divided into three parts, of which the largest, an upper horizontal hemicycle, is coloured crimson (now faded to a brownish tint), but the lower hemicycle is divided vertically in two, of which one portion is coloured green, and the other white or silvered....

The next two subjects to be described are—one on the right hand, the death of the Blessed Virgin Mary; the other, on the left, her burial....

Below the burial we have our Lord in the garden, signified by two trees; still wearing the crown of thorns; our Lord in His left hand holds the banner of the Resurrection, and with His right bestows His benediction on the kneeling Magdalene, who is wimpled, and wears a mantle of green, shot yellow, over a light purple tunic.

Below, but outside the quatrefoil, is a layman clad in gold, upon his knees, and holding a long, narrow scroll bearing words which cannot now be satisfactorily read.

Lowermost of all we see the Apostle St. Philip, with a book in one hand, in the other the flaying knife.

A little above him St. Peter, with his two keys, one gold, the other silver; and somewhat under him is St. Andrew with his cross. On the other side of St. Michael and the Dragon is St. James the Greater—sometimes called of Compostella, because he lies buried in that Spanish city—with a book in one hand and in the other a staff, and slung from his wrist a wallet, both emblems of pilgrimage to his shrine in Galicia.... In the next quatrefoil above is St. Paul with his sword, and over to the right St. Thomas; still further to the right St. James the Less. Just above is our Saviour, clad in a golden tunic, and carrying a staff, overcoming the unbelief of St. Thomas. Upon his knees that Apostle feels, with his right hand held by the Redeemer, the spear wound in His side.

As at the left side, so here, quite outside the sacred history on the cope, we have the figure of an individual probably living at the time the vestment was wrought. The dress of the other shows him to be a layman; by the shaven crown of his head, this person must have been a cleric of some sort; but we cannot tell ... for the canvas is worn quite bare, so that we see nothing now but the lines drawn in black to guide the embroiderer.... This Churchman holds up another scroll bearing words which can no longer be read.

"When this cope was new, it showed, written in tall gold letters more than an inch high, an inscription now cut up and lost ... the word *ne*, and a V on some of the shreds are all that remains of it.

"In its original state it could give us the whole of the twelve Apostles. Portions can still be seen.... The lower part of the vestment has been sadly cut away, and reshaped with the fragments; perhaps at that time were added the present heraldic orphrey, morse, and border, probably fifty years later than the other portions of this matchless specimen of the far-famed [410]'Opus Anglicum.'" "Of angels," the "nine choirs," and the three great hierarchies, Cherubim, Seraphim, and Thrones, are figured here. Led a good way by Ezekiel, but not following that prophet step by step, our mediæval draughtsmen found out for themselves a certain angel form. To this they gave a human shape, that of a comely youth; clothing him with six wings, with human feet; instead of the body being full of eyes, the wings are often composed of the bright-eyed feathers of the peacock. On this cope the eight angels standing upon wheels are so placed that they are everywhere nearest to those quatrefoils wherein our Lord's Person comes, and may therefore be taken as representing the upper hierarchy of the angelic host. The other angels, not upon wheels, no doubt belong to the second hierarchy; while those that have but one pair of wings (not three) represent the lowest hierarchy. "All, like our Lord, are barefoot. All of them have their hands lifted in prayer.... For every lover of English heraldry this cope, so plentifully blazoned with armorial bearings, will have a special value, equal to that belonging to many an ancient roll of arms." The orphrey, morse and hem contain the arms of Warwick, Castile and Leon, Ferrars, Geneville Everard, the badge of the Knights Templars, Clifford, Spencer, Lemisi or Lindsey, Le Botiler, Sheldon, Monteney of Essex, Champernoun, England, Tyddeswall, Grandeson, FitzAlan, Hampden, Percy, Chambowe, Ribbesford, Bygod, Roger de Mortimer, Golbare or Grove, De Bassingburn, with many others not recognized, and frequent repetitions....
"Besides their heraldry, squares at each corner are wrought with swans and peacocks of curious interest for every lover of mediæval symbolism...." These coats of arms, being mostly blazoned on lozenge-shaped shields, suggest that possibly they record those of the noble

ladies who worked the border; while those on circles may be the arms of religious houses or donors.

"A word or two upon the needlework; how it was done; and the now unused mechanical appliance to it after it was wrought, so observable on this vestment, lending its figures more effect."

"We find that for the human face, all over this cope, the first stitches were begun in the centre of the cheek, and worked in circular lines, into which, after the first start, they fell, and were so carried on through the rest of the flesh tints.

"Then with a little iron rod, ending in a small bulb slightly heated, were pressed down those parts of the faces worked in circles, as well as the wide dimple in the throat. By the hollows thus sunk a play of light and shadow is brought out that lends to the parts so treated a look of being done in low relief. Upon the lightly clothed figure of our Lord the same process is followed, and shows a noteworthy example of the mediæval knowledge of external anatomy.

"We must not, however, hide from ourselves that the unequal surfaces, given by such a use of the hot iron to parts of the work, expose it to the danger of being worn by friction more than other parts, and soon betray the damage by their threadbare, dingy look, as is the case in the example just cited. The method for grounding the quatrefoils is remarkable for being done in a long zigzag diaper pattern (laid stitch)....

[411]"The stitching on the armorial bearings is the same as that now followed in many trifling things worked in wool (cross stitch).

"The canvas (or linen) for every part of this cope is of the finest sort, but its crimson canvas lining is thick and coarse....

"A word or two about the history of this fine cope...."

Dr. Rock now enters into the history of the guilds, which included noble laymen and women, and members of the clergy; and tells us that the rolls of these associations sometimes grew to be exceedingly wealthy. He says that each of these guilds had usually in its parish church a chapel or altar of its own, splendidly provided for, to which offerings were spontaneously given by individuals, or by members clubbing together that their joint gift might be the more worthy.

Perhaps the cleric and the layman worked on the cope may have been the donors. Dr. Rock suggests that possibly Coventry may have been the place of its origin, "where the famous Corpus Christi plays" (which this cope so well illustrates) "drew crowds every year to see them, as is testified by the Paston letters. Taking this old city as a centre, with a radius of no great length, we may draw a circle on the map enclosing Tamworth, tower and town, Chartley castle, Warwick, Charlcote, and Althorp. The lords of these broad lands would, in accordance with the religious feelings of those times, become brothers of the famous Guild of Coventry, and on account of their high rank find their arms embroidered on the vestments belonging to their fraternity. That such a pious queen as the gentle Eleanor, wife of Edward the First, who died 1290, should have in her lifetime become a sister is very likely, so that we may easily account for the shield—Castile and Leon."

The other noble shields may possibly record munificent benefactions. "The whole must have taken very long in the working, and the probability is that it was embroidered by the nuns of some convent which stood in or near Coventry....

"Upon the banks of the Thames at Isleworth, near London, Henry V. built and munificently endowed a monastery, to be called 'Syon,' for the nuns of St. Bridget's order. Among the earliest friends of this new house was a Master Thomas Graunt, an official in one of the Ecclesiastical Courts of the kingdom. In the Syon Nun's Martyrologium—a valuable MS. lately bought by the British Museum—this Churchman is gratefully recorded as the giver to their convent of several precious ornaments, of which this very cope seemingly is one. It was the custom for a guild or religious body to bestow some rich church vestment upon an ecclesiastical advocate who had befriended it by his pleadings before the tribunal, and thus to convey their thanks to him with his fee. After such a fashion this cope might easily have found its way, through Dr. Graunt, from Warwickshire to Middlesex.

"At the beginning of Elizabeth's reign it went with the nuns, as they wandered in an unbroken body through Flanders, France, and Portugal, where they halted. About sixty years ago it came back again from Lisbon to England, and has found a home in the South Kensington Museum."

For want of space I have been obliged to omit a great deal of Dr. Rock's interesting account of the Syon Cope. The reader is referred for further [412]details, especially regarding the heraldry and the subjects in the quatrefoils, to Rock's "Textile Fabrics," pp. 275-291, in the South Kensington Museum (No. 9182).

APPENDIX VII., TO PAGE 350.

The Assyrians were great in fringes. Of this we can judge from their sculptures, in which the rich deep and broad fringe forms the ornament and accentuates the shaping of the garments of kings and priests and nobles. Loftus, in his "Babylon and Susiana," tells of the only actually existing remnant of their textile art of which I can find any record. Some terra-cotta coffins were opened at Warka (the ancient Erech), and in one of them was a cushion, on which the head, gone to dust, had reposed. It was covered with linen—fringed. Nothing else had survived the ages except a huge wig of false hair. Such fragmentary echoes from a life, a civilization, and an art dead for thousands of years, are curiously pathetic, and touch and startle the thinking mind.

APPENDIX VIII., TO PAGE 369.

The following poem from the Anglo-Saxon poem of Beowulf shows that the hospitable hall of the Saxon earl was hung with tapestry embroidered with gold.

Fœla þœra wasMuch people wereWera and Wifa þe þat win ruedMen and women who that wine houseGest sele gyredon gold fag scinonThat guest-hall garnished. Cloths embroidered with goldWeb-after wagum. Wundersiòna feldThose along the walls many wonderful sightsSioga gustryleum para pe on swyle stara ♀To every person of those that gaze on such.

Translation by Thomas Arnold.

The poem of Beowulf is supposed to have been written in the early part of the twelfth century.

The lines which follow are from a poem, recomposed from earlier sagas, in the beginning of the twelfth century. It serves to show that arras was used in bedrooms thus early in Germany.

From the "Niebelungen Lied," übersetzt von Karl Simrock, p. 294.

Manche schmucke Decke von Arras da lagAus lichthellem Zeuge und manches UeberdachAus arabischer Seides so gut sie mochte sein,Darüber lagen leisten du gaben herrlicher Schein.

[413]I owe these notices to the kindness of the Rev. A. O. Winnington Ingram.

APPENDIX IX., TO PAGE 362.
Abridged from Trans. by Sir G. Dasent.
(*From the Ezrbyggja Saga.*)

In that summer in which Christianity was established by law in Iceland (A.D.1000), there came a ship from off the sea out to Snowfellsness, in Iceland. It was a Dublin ship, and on board it were Irishmen and men from Sodor and the Hebrides, but few Norsemen.... On board the ship was a woman from the Hebrides, whose name was Thorgunna. Her shipmates said that they were sure she had such treasures with her as would be hard to get in Iceland.

Thurida, the housewife at Frida, was envious and covetous of these precious goods, and received Thorgunna into her home in hopes, by some means, to possess herself of them, especially the embroidered hangings of a bed; but Thorgunna refused to part with them. "I will not lie in the straw for thee, though thou art a fine lady, and thinkest great things of thyself." Thorgunna made her own terms with Thurida and Master Harold, and set up her bed at the inner end of their hall. Her richly worked bed-clothes, her English sheets and silken quilt, and her bed-hangings and canopy were such "that men thought nothing at all like them had ever been seen." An air of truth is given to the whole story by the details. Thorgunna is described as "tall and strong and very stout. She was swarthy brown, with eyes set close together; her hair was brown and very thick. She was well-behaved in daily life, and went to church every morning before she went to her work." Then comes an account of a storm, and a rain of blood; and how Thorgunna sickened and died, and at her own desire was carried to be buried to Skilholt, which she prophesied would one day be considered holy, and that priests might there sing dirges over her.

There is a curious and picturesque account of the two days' journey to Skilholt, and the adventures that befell the funeral cortége; including the incident of the corpse cooking the supper of the convoy at an inhospitable farmhouse where they had sought refuge and received no entertainment.

On Harold's return home after the funeral, he proceeded to carry out the wishes of Thorgunna, who had warned him that the ownership of her embroidered hangings would cause trouble, and therefore she had desired they should be burned. Thurida, however, could not bear to lose them, and persuaded Harold to spare them. "After this followed many signs and portents, and deaths of men and women, and apparitions of ghosts, until Kjartan (Thurida's son) brought out all Thorgunna's bed-hangings and furniture, and burned them in the fire."

[414]

APPENDIX X., TO PAGE 365.

Aelfled or Athelfleda was the founder of a race of embroiderers. Their pedigree is as follows:—

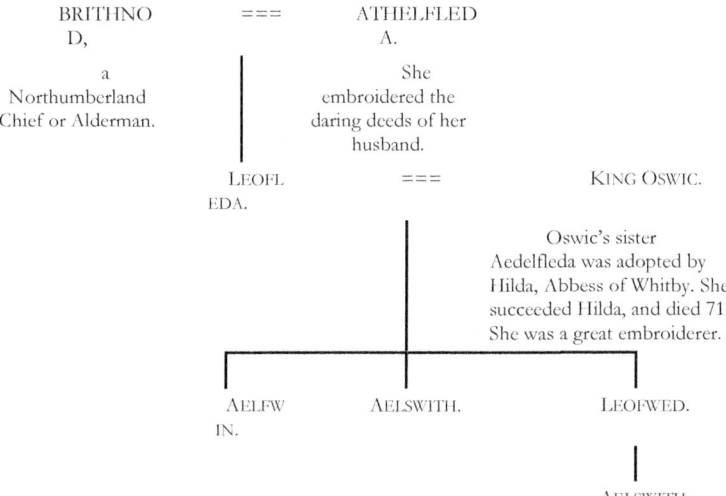

Leofwed made her will in the time of King Cnut; dividing her revenue between her daughter Aelswith and the Abbey of Ely. Aelswith accepted the residence of Coveney, a small property belonging to the convent, and there she embroidered with her maidens. See Liber Eliensis, ed. D. J. Stewart, "Anglia Christiana," vol. i., 1848.

APPENDIX XI., TO PAGE 377.

In the Statutes at Large there is the following in vol. i. p. 526 (in old French):—
2 Henry VI.

A penalty on deceitful workers of gold and silver embroidery.

Item. pur ceo que diverses defautes sont trovez en loveraigne de diverses persons occupiantz le mestier de brouderie. Ordonnez est & assentiez, que tout loveraigne & stuff de brouderie d'or ou d'argent de Cipre ou d'or de Luke melle avec laton de Spayne & mys a vent en deceit des lieges du Roi sont forfait au Roi ou as Seigneurs et autres accenz franchises d'autielx forfaitures ein quy franchise autiel overaigne soit trouvée et durera c'est ordinance longue parlement prochainement avenir.

33 Henry VI.

That if any Lombard or any other person, Stranger or Denizen, bring or cause to be brought by way of merchandize any wrought silk thrown, Ribbands, Laces, Corses of Silk, or any other thing wrought, touching or concerning the mystery of Silk women, the corses which come from Genoa only excepted, into any part or place of the Realm from beyond the Sea, that the same ... be forfeit.

3 Edward IV.

Whereby the importation of any wrought silk thrown, Ribbands, Laces, Corses of Silk, or other things wrought, concerning the craft of Silk women is prohibited or restrained.

22 Edward IV.

That no Marchant, Stranger, nor other person shall bring into the Realm to be sold, any Corses, Girdles, Ribbands, Laces, Coll. Silk or Colein Silk, thrown or wrought, upon pain of forfeiture of the same.

Also Richard III. "An Act touching the bringing in of Silk Laces, Ribbands, &c."

Also 19 Henry VII. "An Act for Silk Women."

These acts appear to have been partially repealed, 3 and 5 George III.

Printed in Dunstable, United Kingdom